Women Leaders at Work

Elizabeth Ghaffari

Apress®

Women Leaders at Work

ISBN-13 (pbk): 978-1-4302-3729-7

ISBN-13 (electronic): 978-1-4302-3730-3

President and Publisher: Paul Manning
Lead Editor: Jeff Olson
Editorial Board: Steve Anglin, Mark Beckner, Ewan Buckingham, Gary Cornell, Morgan Ertel, Jonathan Gennick, Jonathan Hassell, Robert Hutchinson, Michelle Lowman, James Markham, Matthew Moodie, Jeff Olson, Jeffrey Pepper, Douglas Pundick, Ben Renow-Clarke, Dominic Shakeshaft, Gwenan Spearing, Matt Wade, Tom Welsh
Coordinating Editor: Jessica Belanger
Copy Editor: Kimberly Burton
Compositor: Mary Sudul
Indexer: BIM Indexing & Proofreading Services
Cover Designer: Anna Ishchenko

Distributed to the book trade worldwide by Springer Science+Business Media New York, 233 Spring Street, 6th Floor, New York, NY 10013. Phone 1-800-SPRINGER, fax (201) 348-4505, e-mail orders-ny@springer-sbm.com, or visit www.springeronline.com.

For information on translations, please e-mail rights@apress.com, or visit www.apress.com.

Apress and friends of ED books may be purchased in bulk for academic, corporate, or promotional use. eBook versions and licenses are also available for most titles. For more information, reference our Special Bulk Sales–eBook Licensing web page at www.apress.com/bulk-sales.

For Fereydoon

Contents

About the Author

Elizabeth Ghaffari is President and CEO of Technology Place Inc. a California corporation she founded in 1989 to deliver strategic technology advisory services to U.S. and international business clients. Previously, she was a manager of IT at major financial institutions in California and a consulting economist to major development firms here and abroad.

Since 2009, she's been a director of Pacific Coast Regional-SBDC, certified by the US Treasury as a Community Development Finance Institution. Ms. Ghaffari is the author of *Outstanding in their Field: How Women Corporate Directors Succeed* (Praeger: 2009).

Ms. Ghaffari received her MS, Management from the University of California, Los Angeles (Anderson School of Management) and her BS, Political Science from The American University, Washington, DC.

Acknowledgments

This book exists because eighteen women professionals chose to share their insight, experience, and wisdom in order to build bridges to new opportunities for the next generation of women who will become leaders. I can't thank them enough for their time and their inspiration. It was a delight to listen and to learn from them, personally and professionally.

This book also was made possible by their "gatekeepers" whom I've come to admire, respect, and appreciate. Assistants, associates, secretaries, public relations personnel—among their many titles—are the people to whom successful leaders delegate their schedules as well as their best interests. They challenged me to prove that this project would be worthy, so I am grateful to them for making me work to earn their confidence.

I would like to acknowledge just a few of today's women in media—leaders themselves—who have made it their business to highlight and advance the word about women of achievement and women in leadership. These would include Alice Krause, who hosts and writes the blog www.NewsOnWomen.com; Sheila Ronning, President & CEO of Sharp UpSwing and founder of Women In The Boardroom; Joann Lublin of the *Wall Street Journal* and Moira Forbes of *ForbesWoman*, both of whom regularly write respectfully about women leaders. There are more, but these women especially spoke up and wrote positively about accomplished women at a time when it was way too easy simply to write about the challenges.

I am grateful for friends and advisors like Dr. Susan Murphy, co-author with Dr. Pat Heim of *In the Company of Women*, who taught me to look for women who inspire me and make me stretch—and that the decision to do so was a choice that I could make.

I am sincerely grateful to Jeff Olson, who brought the idea for this book forward and who spent so much time teaching me what I need to know to improve my craft. Thank you.

Kristen Ng gave me back hundreds of hours of writing time by her wonderful work transcribing the recorded interviews. And Kimberly Burton took the fine-tooth comb through the copyedit process. Thank you to these and to all the other production staff, without whom this book would not have happened.

Jessica Belanger, from start to finish, advised, edited, trained, coached, and cajoled me in so very many facets of the writing process. Thank you.

There are a host of unnamed but very appreciated friends, family members, and colleagues who kept asking me "How's the new book progressing?" Their interest in the subject enflamed my own ardor. Their expectations pushed me toward my goal. When the women in my life—whether it was my dental hygienist, my dry cleaner, my doctor—kept asking me whom I'd interviewed lately, I knew the subject of women in leadership had hit that chord that now echoes resoundingly.

Thank you also to the very many men from my work and my life who suggested names of women in leadership whom they considered worthy of inclusion. It gives me great personal satisfaction to know that I have such open-minded and enthusiastic advisors.

Thank you to Hans and Cynthia Ghaffari for all their help during challenging days and weeks over the past year while this project has been underway.

Finally, thank you to my friend, partner, mentor, coach, muse and husband, Fereydoon—who probably is the only person who truly understands what it took to complete this book—because he has been there from the beginning.

Elizabeth Ghaffari
Los Angeles, California
November 2011

Introduction

I was seven years old when my mother showed me her most treasured jewels. Taking my hand in hers, she walked me through the giant oak doors of our town library where she showed me the Orange Books, biographies of historical men *and women* of achievement. Certainly, there were far fewer books of women than men, but there they were—women of achievement on the library shelves, books of the same size, same covers, different stories. My mother's most treasured gift for me was the library card that allowed these stories to be mine—stories which I continue to hold in my memory to this day—Amelia Earhart, Clara Barton, Marie Curie and Jane Addams, to name just a few.

I've been fortunate to have learned from a host of women leaders: teachers, primarily, but also advisors, colleagues, peers, caretakers, authors, friends, and relatives. A few women have inspired me even though I have never met them or have only "met" them through e-mail.

As an adult, I was directed by a friend to the powerful stories of twenty-five women of achievement in *Written By Herself: Autobiographies of American Women: An Anthology* by Jill Ker Conway. I still recall the story of the woman who told her brother, a medical school student, to return home each night and teach her everything he learned each day because women were neither accepted in medical school nor certified as doctors.

A woman corporate director pointed me to the stories in another book, *The Door in the Dream: Conversations with Eminent Women in Science* by Dr. Elga Wasserman, consisting of interviews with eighty-six women who had been elected to the National Academy of Sciences (five percent of the total membership by 2000).

The common thread, guiding my own career and experience, is that there are many women leaders who inspire us, many women of achievement whom we might follow, many women into whose "tall heels" we might step.

This book was motivated by the question, "Are we hearing about the women who are in leadership, today?" By our tunnel-vision focus on a few media headliners, we miss the thousands of talented, competent, and outstanding women of achievement in myriad other public and private companies, in science, medicine, law, venture and investment entities, government and politics, academia and education, and in major philanthropic endeavors.

Our challenge is to expand the writing, reporting, and interviews with these very interesting women. That's what this book is about—telling stories, learning lessons, experiencing the wonder, once again, as I did once before when my mother, walking through the great doors of our town library, shared with me the joy of intellectual curiosity. Enjoy with me, once more, the wonderful true tales of women leaders at work, succeeding in their own very special way at whatever they choose to accomplish.

What are the lessons that these women provide? First, they are everywhere. It was easy to locate talented women in leadership and to research their backgrounds and careers.

In the example of aerospace engineer, Celeste Volz Ford, CEO/chair of Stellar Solutions, I found enthusiasm for her career and the contagion of her personal choices. Women like her often wanted to talk less about themselves as leaders or their success and more about their companies or organizations as the vehicles for their leadership and proof of their success. I had heard her speak about the innovations of her company's benefit program before I knew much about her multi-company creations—Stellar Ventures, Stellar UK, and Stellar Foundation.

The women didn't always follow a straight line to their current position. They tended instead to find the niche of opportunity, the best route available, the unfettered path to success. They followed "their gut" and believed in their own intuition. Laura Roden, founder and managing Director of VC Privé, LLC, for example, began in corporate marketing, then finance, traversed the nonprofit and trade association world that related to venture investment before founding her own investment boutique bank.

Women in leadership weren't discouraged by their exceptional status. They didn't let being among a small headcount translate into being a small thinker. That was true of many of the women, but especially Deanell Reece Tacha, newly named dean of the School of Law at Pepperdine University and formerly judge of the 10th Circuit Court of Appeals in an era when women in law were more scarce than rare.

Consistently, the women demonstrated "possibility thinking." It was something more than open mindedness. It was the capacity to think outside of the silos of professional, academic, or scientific limitations. They showed an ability to understand complementary disciplines and what those other perspectives might add to their own development or career. They were intrigued by the different ways their profession might grow and benefit through contact with other similar or dissimilar professional interests. That describes Dr. Sandra Witelson—professor, Psychiatry and Behavioral Neurosciences, Inaugural Albert Einstein/Irving Zucker Chair in Neuroscience at the DeGroote School of Medicine, McMaster University (Hamilton, Ontario)—who developed "The Brain Bank" for comparative analysis of the brain's structure. It also describes Dr. Jennifer Tour Chayes, distinguished scientist, mathematician, co-founder, and managing director of Microsoft's NERD Center (New England Research & Development).

Those among them who chose to have children are extremely proud of their families and their individuality. Achieving the chimera of "work-family balance" was accomplished through the help of, and active delegation to, a valued support team. Not all first choices made the cut to a long-term relationship, because spouses are seen as equal partners who both deserve an appropriate amount of support and from whom an equal measure of support is essential for a successful career—personally and professionally.

Many women leaders at work include very creative professionals who have designed careers and fields of endeavor that did not exist before they came this way. Variations on traditional entrepreneurship, executive compensation, investment, corporate responsibility, and a host of other modern fields of endeavor happened because these women designed new products and services inside and outside of traditional professional parameters of their careers. Examples include Dr. Kellie A. McElhaney, Alexander Faculty Fellow in Corporate Responsibility, who essentially created the Center for Corporate Responsibility at the Haas School of Business, University of California at Berkeley in the face of "doubting Thomases" from faculty and business. This also describes Robin A. Ferracone, founder and executive chair of the executive compensation advisory firm Farient Advisors LLC, and chief executive officer of RAF Capital LLC, which invests in new products and services to support corporate human resource functions.

These are women of courage, plain and simple. Some saw rights that needed to be asserted, while others saw that appropriate protections ought to be put into place. These would include Anita L. DeFrantz, who challenged a president in our courts, advocating on behalf of athlete rights, and then became president of the LA84 Foundation and president and director of Kids in Sports, advocating on behalf of young athletes after the 1984 Olympic Games in Los Angeles, California. It would include Debra Bowen, currently secretary of state of California, who demanded that electronic voting systems provide the protections that a democratic electorate required.

Many took on significant challenges that might have cowered others, including Lise Luttgens, chief executive officer of the Girl Scouts of Greater Los Angeles, who took over the helm just as it consolidated six separate legacy councils on the eve of the organization's one-hundredth anniversary. It would also include Amy Millman, president of Springboard Enterprises, whose organization educates, sources, coaches, showcases, and supports high-growth, women-led entrepreneurial companies as they pursue equity capital for expansion. Not only did Julia Gouw, president and chief operating officer of East West Bank, lead that company to financial heights, but she also led peer executive women to invest in pilot programs benefitting women's health programs at a major university medical center.

All of these women are inspirations to other women who would become leaders. Two in particular have pushed the envelope in the advancement of women in academia by educating and facilitating the progress of young women faculty, women entrepreneurs, and women from business returning to re-career. They are Dr. Jacqueline K. Barton, Arthur & Marian Hanisch Memorial Professor and Chair, Division of Chemistry & Chemical Engineering at the California Institute of Technology; and Dr. Myra M. Hart, professor (retired) of entrepreneurship at the Harvard Business School at Harvard University. Dr. Barton has mentored young women in science who are now taking on top faculty positions in chemistry and chemical engineering at our major universities. Dr. Hart has trained and educated countless women in business through the vehicle of business-case development and her creation of MBA, executive education, and extension courses directly advising women in how to handle the challenges of re-careering.

In today's economy, it is a challenge to find individuals who marched up the corporate ladder, acquiring ever-increasing levels of responsibility all the way to the top. Certainly they mentioned mentors and coaches along the

them to test their wings and discover themselves. Not every step of advancement came with ease—sometimes they had to take more than one time at bat and at other times they had to step out of their comfort zone in order to stretch, grow, and reach their ambition.

The fascinating career of Jeanette Horan, CIO of IBM, highlights all of the major twists and turns of the technology industry over the past few dec-

counting in Canada and later helped to define the corporate governance area of emphasis in the US. Barbara J. Beck, CEO of Learning Care Group, provides interesting perspectives on the prerequisites for advancement—especially in this new global economy. Dr. Karen Guice, Principal Assistant

Secretary of Defense for Health Affairs, US Department of Defense, tells of her circuitous journey through medicine, to academia, and on to public policy positions, yet weaves a clear consistency throughout.

All of the women interviewed candidly shared their advice and insights for the next generation of women who might aspire to leadership. They truly wish those women success. Their enthusiasm and optimism was contagious, even as they recognize the challenges of today's more difficult economy. Some of these women have been through times that were far more adverse than today.

There are women in leadership who ran the gauntlet of being "The Only Woman" to take on a job, an education, or a career choice. Been there–done that. Most young women do not have to face those extremes today because the bridges have been built, thank heaven. What is required now is different from what had to be accomplished back then. Now, we can celebrate, and learn from, the achievements of talented women in just about every field of endeavor. That is why this book was written.

Celeste Volz Ford

President and CEO, Stellar Solutions, Inc.

Born 1956 in Washington, DC.

Celeste Volz Ford *is president and CEO of Stellar Solutions, Inc., located in Palo Alto, California. Stellar Solutions is a professional systems engineering company that Ms. Ford established in 1995 to provide engineering products and services for critical government and commercial aerospace-related programs.*

As "the Mom who is a rocket scientist," Ms. Ford traveled unchartered territory by establishing an aerospace company to serve national and international clients through operations in California, Colorado, Washington, DC, and more recently overseas through Stellar Solutions Aerospace Ltd., the company's UK-based international arm.

Ms. Ford's corporate benefits strategy is an award-winning program that combines employee-choice with charitable donations on behalf of employees through the Stellar Solutions Foundation. Stellar Ventures, an investment incubator for employees' entrepreneurial ideas, rounds out the Stellar family of enterprises, all contributing to a "dream job" for the firm, its founder, and its employees.

Celeste Ford and Stellar Solutions together exemplify the concept that women can build different companies to achieve different goals.

Elizabeth Ghaffari: Why did you choose the education that you did?

Celeste Volz Ford: I went to a high school, Cherry Creek, in the suburbs of Denver, Colorado, which was known for being very good in math and science. Anyone who went to that high school excelled in those subjects. I embraced it, because the expectation in those days was that girls were not inclined to have an interest in math or science. I remember being told that if I was good at math and science, I should be an engineer. I'd never been exposed to engineering. Both my parents had law degrees, and my father was an FBI agent. The more I asked engineers about what they did, the less I understood.

Then I began looking at college brochures, and aerospace engineering caught my eye. I thought, this is perfect—something new and different. I wanted to pursue something I hadn't learned before—something fun and interesting. I didn't want to take the same old classes in college that I'd taken in high school. Aerospace engineering sounded perfect. My choice was much more practical than inspirational.

I went to Notre Dame because it was a great undergraduate institution—in engineering, the undergraduate courses were taught by full professors, not just grad-student instructors.

Ghaffari: What was your first job after graduation?

Ford: My graduating class in aerospace engineering had seven students—six men and me. Throughout the 1970s, companies had been laying off engineers. By the end of the decade, they hadn't hired at a pace to offset retirements. I interviewed with everyone who came to campus. All seven of us were wined and dined, coast-to-coast, because there was a critical need for engineers at that point in time.

My first job was with Communications Satellite Corporation [COMSAT] in Palo Alto, California, where they were monitoring an international telecommunications satellite built by Ford Aerospace. Usually, you would need a senior person in this position because it's a systems engineering job which draws on a lot of experience. But a company vice-president back East had seen my résumé and told the people on the West Coast to give me a try. It was a bit of an experiment on their part, but it worked out great for all of us.

COMSAT was hired by INTELSAT to ensure that the satellite, INTELSAT 5, would work as designed. My area was guidance and control. I followed the satellite all around the globe. Testing was done in Germany, integration in California, launch in Florida, and mission control in Washington, DC. Hardware was built and assembled at the home base in Palo Alto. The satellite was either being tested, launched, or flown in other locations, so you followed the box as it moved along in the process. There were a lot of business trips.

Ghaffari: Did you need to get advanced training or education?

Ford: After building and launching a couple of INTELSAT satellites, I decided I wanted to see what else was out there. Defense sounded like it would be the next logical step in my career. What drew me to the defense sector and Aerospace Corporation was that it was high tech. The new, cutting-edge technologies were being developed in the defense sector behind the black curtain. Aerospace Corporation supported the Air Force in its satellite programs. I worked in the field office in Northern California—the Onizuka Air Force Satellite Test Center, the operations center, known as the Blue Cube.

While I was with COMSAT, I earned my master's degree at Stanford. In some of my interviews, especially at Aerospace Corporation, a master's degree was a pre-requisite for employment. I had always really wanted to go to Stanford and had always been interested in Stanford as a place for a master's degree.

Ghaffari: This sounds like a great way to start a career.

Ford: I was very lucky to have a great first job. Comparing notes with colleagues, I realize that most engineers have a terrible first job. As a result, we lose a great deal of potential engineering talent. I had the good fortune of an engaging first job, where I got to see a satellite program from beginning to end, from design to build to launch. I was a part of the entire life cycle in a brief two-year time frame. It was a crash course. Very exciting and very fun work.

Ghaffari: Did you ever think of leaving aerospace?

Ford: No, I had great, fun jobs. In the satellite business, you can see the fruits of your labor, like fireworks on launch day. All the projects were fun, interesting, and different. That's why I stayed in the industry.

Ghaffari: Did you take anything away from those experiences that shape how you run your own company?

Ford: I had seen some things at my earlier companies that really worked well, like getting people together and doing strategic planning—planning your future together—those were the good things that I copied. We just held our sixteenth annual business planning meeting at Stellar Solutions, which is our strategic planning session. It's a great way of planning your future together.

There also were other things in engineering companies that just didn't work, and the bigger the company, the worse it was. There was a lot of bureaucracy. Some things just didn't make sense to me. Money was spent on things people didn't care about. Reports just sat on shelves. Some people did the same thing over and over again. Or there was the syndrome where

20 percent of the people did 80 percent of the work. I just wanted none of that. That was another reason I started my own company.

Ghaffari: How did your first jobs frame the work you did later?

Ford: My early aerospace jobs provided me with the building blocks to understand what it takes to get a satellite launched. And it gave me exposure to all of the sectors where this happens: commercial, international, defense, and intelligence. The defense and intelligence work, at that time, also entailed working on the space shuttle, so I was very involved with NASA. Between those first two jobs, I was exposed to all the critical sectors associated with aerospace, in addition to all of the nuts and bolts of how to build and launch a satellite.

Ghaffari: How did you start your business? And how did it evolve and grow?

Ford: I was just thirty-nine years old, with three young kids, when I started Stellar Solutions. In the back of my mind, I always knew that I wanted to start my own business some day. After working at COMSAT and Aerospace Corporation, that desire became more focused. I was introduced to the founder of Scitor Corporation, Roger Meade, by an Air Force Colonel, Jim Church, who was a mentor of mine and my Air Force boss while I was working at the Aerospace Corporation. Jim was the client counterpart to my work and was in charge of the Northern California satellite operations. I told Jim that someday I wanted to start my own business, and he said, "Let me introduce you to someone who just started a business." He introduced me to Roger.

Roger invited me to join Scitor by saying, "You could start your own business within my company." I didn't really know anything about business—just engineering. Scitor was more of a computer aerospace company, and they asked me to start a division that did launches, operations, and the building of satellites. I basically got to start a business within a business. At Scitor, I learned about contracts, how to close, how to sell—all of things I needed to learn about the non-engineering side of the business.

When Roger Meade and Gene Priestman started Scitor in 1979, they envisioned "a place where exceptional people could make a difference." Scitor ended up being the third stepping stone for me and my career. All three jobs were important foundations for me to eventually start my own firm. I didn't know it at the time. It just turned out that they were each very important stepping stones in my career.

Ghaffari: What did you think you could do differently on your own?

Ford: The main thing I wanted to do, because of my career experience, was to be operating in each of the different aerospace sectors. With that in mind, we chose the name Stellar Solutions to reflect the five points of the star: commercial, international, civil—NASA, defense—Air Force, Army, etc., and intelligence—NRO, NSA, etc. Our value proposition was that we could cross the boundaries. If you're in the commercial world, like INTEL-SAT, you have no clue what's going on in the Air Force. If you're in the Air Force, you have no idea what's happening inside NASA. We wanted to be the people who could bring something extra to the project because we crossed those boundaries. The same thing happened with the international work as well—we got big enough to do the same thing on a global scale.

Ghaffari: So you saw some unmet needs you could step in and fill?

Ford: I started with a clean slate. I knew the aerospace industry, so I went around and met with people who had critical needs that I thought I could solve. Our first contract was for three months. My first client was a company that was doing commercial imaging from space, up until then strictly a government operation. Because I'd been in the space business, I knew what it took to get the satellites out the door. That was identifying the customer's critical need. That's what we still do every year when we do our strategic planning and every day as we work.

That initial contract was followed by the next contract and the next one, slowly building the business around people with whom I had had mutual positive personal experiences. When we added more people, we made sure their skills were tailored to the programs and needs of the customers that were coming on board.

Ghaffari: Did you know from the start that Stellar would be a success?

Ford: I laugh because I started the company thinking, failure is not an option—I've been in this business, I know what's needed, I know how to do it. It just never occurred to me that I would not be successful.

Years later, I went to a mini-MBA course at Stanford where I saw statistics about the high failure rate of new businesses, and I thought, it's a good thing I didn't know that before I started—I might not have done it.

I really felt I knew what was important. Some of the people who start businesses don't understand the concept of knowing what your customer wants, and how essential that is to the core of your business. I hosted a group of MBA students from Stanford who wanted to meet an entrepreneur. They asked, "What did you do about the medical plan or the marketing plan? What was the most important thing in your success?"

I told them, "There's only one thing: a customer. Does someone want what you have? If the answer is yes, then you have a successful business." The minute I found someone who said they would hire me to do X, I had a business. It had nothing to do with the medical plan or the infrastructure or the technology I would use. Once you have identified your first customer, you have accomplished the most critical step in starting a business.

Ghaffari: What were some early key decisions?

Ford: I think a key part of our success came right at the beginning when we came up with the concept that our strategic plan, which ends up being our tactical plan, actually flows down to each and every individual's bonus plan. Everyone at Stellar Solutions is aligned around the importance of satisfying the customer's critical needs and, at the same time, working at their dream job.

We get everybody together for the strategic planning session every year. Every single employee is in charge of his/her own future and their customer's future, doing the right thing and giving input into that. Your bonus plan is paid around the goals. Those goals are aligned to your customer's critical needs. We survey our customers, we survey our employees. We ask if you are serving customer critical needs. We ask if you are in your dream job or working towards it. It gets reinforced in everything we do. We believe we all are focused on the important stuff.

Another key factor was that I never wanted to lose the small-company feel, even as we got bigger. There are one hundred thirty-three total employees working full time for the company, plus another sixty "Stellar Advisors" who work part-time for the company. They may be retired or parents who want or need to work part-time. It's pretty much evenly split among California, Colorado, and the DC area. We grow only if it makes sense based on our strategic planning process, which addresses the right size and right scope of our support to current customers and innovation—new projects, new people.

Positive results lead to growth and a larger company. We have monthly "touches" with employees and customers—we always maintain that small-company feel with face-to-face meetings between our leaders and employees and customers every month, at a minimum.

Ghaffari: I understand Stellar's benefit strategy is considered one of the most innovative in the business.

Ford: I am always talking about our benefits package. Medical plan costs have gone through the roof. Having flexible benefit plans is very important to be responsive to the unique needs of each employee's family and to support all of our employees in the best possible way. Every employee has medical, disability, life insurance, maternity/paternity leave, tuition reimbursement, and retirement contributions. Employees are able to utilize up to a total of six weeks of vacation, holiday, sick, or personal days off as they choose, consistent with customer needs and requirements. They also are encouraged to spend a week each year to attend training or conferences.

Stellar's total compensation program is best-in-class—it's flexible. We maximize compensation and minimize taxes. When job candidates bring our offers to their financial planning consultants, we receive positive feedback, such as, "This is unique and flexible" and "Where can I get a job like this?" Stellar puts 25 percent of base salary into a tax-deferred benefits package. Employees can use it for things like medical cost reimbursements on a pre-tax basis, or for other items on a taxable basis. The key is that they get to choose—our benefits are flexible and not "one size fits all." The way we do benefits at Stellar is stellar.

Another key element is the Stellar Solutions Foundation, which we established in 1998. As soon as we were cash flow positive, I knew I wanted to create a foundation. Even though I'd like to believe that our employees get up every day and think about nothing but Stellar Solutions and our customers, I knew that people have a lot of other things on their minds. I wanted to support that.

We funded the Foundation from the beginning by donating 10 percent of the profits of Stellar Solutions. We've adjusted it every year in order to provide a charitable donation of at least $1,000 per employee, but we also make additional discretionary donations in response to special needs, like a hurricane or a walk for the spouse with cancer. Special donations are made on a case-by-case basis.

Ghaffari: Do you think these help you retain good employees?

Ford: Yes. Employees are free to donate to any qualified charitable organization. There is one person who administers the Foundation, writing the checks, making sure the employee gets the credit for their contribution, and our CFO approves the donation to be sure the charity is IRS-qualified. The Foundation was established early on so that we could give back to the community and support other aspects of our employees' lives and interests. I wanted to be a part of the communities in which we worked, and be a good corporate citizen wherever we worked. When I did this in 1998, it was unusual, but today we're seeing more companies do the same thing.

Ghaffari: What was your motivation in creating Stellar Ventures?

Ford: Stellar Ventures was launched in 2000 as a venture investment enterprise and incubator to foster early-stage technology development and market applications. David Wensley was CEO and Kevin E. Ford was CFO. We founded Stellar Ventures during the big dot-com boom. Our company had stellar engineers that competitor start-ups wanted to hire, with stock options and promises of becoming rich and famous.

Again, because we wanted to stay small, stock options were not in our model. We didn't want to borrow a lot of money and get big. We decided to do something so our employees could have that equity-sharing experience, but not have to leave our company to get it. We co-invested in some ventures and funded others, so our engineers could feel they were involved in emerging businesses through this fund of funds. Of course, the bust came after the boom. It wasn't like everyone got rich and retired. But Stellar Ventures is something that differentiated Stellar—you see what needs to be done, so you do the right thing.

That's also how we founded QuakeFinder—our humanitarian R&D division involved in research for early warning of earthquakes. QuakeFinder is headed by Tom Bleier, one of our Stellar Solutions engineers who was working on an intelligence sector project at the time, but told us that his "dream job" was this earthquake research. He developed a sensor and demonstrated it at his children's high school. As time went on, it looked more promising. Tom became the lead and took over the project. Early on, we built up a quake signaling network throughout California, and now we have sensors deployed in Peru, Taiwan, Chile, Greece, and Turkey.

Finally, Stellar Solutions Aerospace Ltd. [SSAL], founded in 2004, is our sister company in London that serves non-US customers with non-US employees and consultants. Our two companies sub-contract to each other, as needed, across the boundaries. SSAL has about a dozen engineers that come and go on projects as needed.

Ghaffari: Does SSAL conduct business mostly in Europe?

Ford: The work of SSAL includes any non-US location: Latin America, Asia, pretty much the world over. Our first big contract was a NASA/DOE project, working for the people who were providing the sensors used to discover the origins of dark matter in the universe. They were all located in Pisa, Italy, where Galileo studied. They know a thing or two about astrophysics. It required us to have people on site in Italy to help get that project out the door.

In the early days, we did the international work from within our domestic commercial group. Then, after getting on airplanes, talking to customers in Europe and other locations, we realized that it's not the same—we were not seeing customers frequently enough. After a while, we realized that we did not understand their critical needs. The clients wanted what we had to offer, but they also wanted local talent and local responsiveness. The vice president of our commercial group, Melissa Farrell, went overseas, full time, to head the international company. She spent five years building SSAL and just recently came back to run our commercial group again. We found a UK citizen to succeed her as head of our London office. Rainer Koll is CEO of SSAL and is based in the UK. He's a perfect fit for that position—he also brings contacts and interesting work in the aircraft field, in addition to the aerospace field.

Ghaffari: Do you ever want to quit and do something else? What keeps you going?

Ford: Having high impact, stellar customers, and stellar employees keeps me going. I have never wanted to quit. The only thing that keeps me up at night revolves around doing a better job for our customers and our employees.

Ghaffari: Have you ever thought about pursuing external investment or taking the company public?

Ford: We self-funded Stellar Solutions from the beginning. That was hard. You do it in stair-steps, so it's not quite as difficult as a product-based company where you have to buy a lot of equipment on the front end. But, it's still difficult because there's always a time lag between paying people and getting paid by the client. But, we grew in a logical fashion—a contract here, a person there.

Today, our business is more government than commercial. Our defense and intelligence work represents more than half of the company just because there are more dollars for those projects. The company has grown 10 percent annually—a rate that continues today. Some years are higher. It's been slow, steady growth over time. The two visions—solving critical needs and crossing boundaries—have worked very well in hard times.

When commercial and telecom work gets cut, we turn to the defense sector. When defense gets cut, we turn to commercial work. There's a built-in diversity. Since we are, by definition, focused on critical needs, the work we do is important. It's not as if our work can easily be cut in the first place. We don't just write documents that nobody reads—that just sit on shelves or could easily be cut from contracts. We leave that work for others. That might be revenue, but it's revenue we don't want.

Ghaffari: Is there anything else uniquely different about your business that contributes to your impressive annual growth?

Ford: We do not have any dedicated marketing or sales function in the company. I never wanted to be that way. I never wanted to grow that way. We want to grow around critical needs identified by our technical engineers working closely with our customers.

Ghaffari: How do you accomplish that?

Ford: Our engineers in the field are constantly on the lookout to identify new critical needs. We have an inclusive strategic planning process—every year, each and every employee identifies his/her client's critical needs, as well as the cool, neat new programs that they think we should be working on. Those identified critical needs and new projects are discussed and included as sector goals and targets on an annual basis. There's a leader for each sector, and they basically facilitate the strategic conversation, as well as tactical goals to lead the team in a collaborative direction toward the desired results. The leads are responsible for the business development of their sector. They also directly work on contracts on a part-time basis. They are both good leaders and good engineers.

Ghaffari: How did you work through or around the inevitable challenges you faced?

Ford: We get through every challenge by removing the obstacles one step at a time and never losing track of the finish line and where we want to be when we are done. For me, I think that's the most important role a leader can perform. Never give up on anything that is truly important. Be persistent and passionate in solving problems. Act with a sense of urgency.

Ghaffari: What job/boss had the biggest impact on you, and what did the experience teach you?

Ford: All three of my bosses had very important impacts on different aspects of my career. Each one was a mentor in his own way. To my mind, a mentor is anyone who is a role model of the behaviors that you think are important. Each one taught me something different.

At my first company, COMSAT, my very first boss was Kurt Eriksson, who was a technical expert in controls and testing of satellites. He was a great mentor who taught me to be a good engineer. In the second job, Aerospace Corporation, my mentor was Air Force Colonel Jim Church, the client representative who taught me how to remove obstacles and get things done. My third mentor, at Scitor, was the founder, Roger Meade, who taught me how to create a good company, what are the business skills to run a company, and why a special focus on employees is key. My early career was great. The job content was great. And each of my bosses and co-workers were mentors, in one way or another.

Ghaffari: How do you define your own position as a "leader?"

Ford: As my kids were growing up, I spoke at more schools than I can count. The word gets out and everyone wants to hear "the Mom who's a rocket scientist" come talk at their school. I probably do less of that now that my kids have grown. But, I certainly did a lot of that in the early days. I encourage our employees to do that. In fact, a part of the bonus plan for employees is to do outreach like that. I speak at industry events, on panels, and at conferences. I think it's important to participate in these activities because there are so few women entrepreneurs and engineers that are in a CEO-type role. I think getting out there, being seen and participating in these activities, is important. I still do a lot of that and try to be a good role model for the next generation of women.

Ghaffari: How would you describe your decision-making style?

Ford: I am very inclusive in gathering input. But, when it's time to make decisions with our leadership team, I am decisive—"benevolent dictator" leaps to mind. I make decisions. I don't let things swirl and swirl. The decisions that we make are in the best interests of our employees and our customers. We have our strategic planning process and our situational awareness visits with customers and employees. We are always trying to be responsible and responsive. We work to get people what they need, when they need it—both customers and employees. That takes a lot of skill in removing obstacles.

Ghaffari: What were some of the key initial strategy decisions you made?

Ford: The initial strategic decisions I made have stood the test of time—to have a company that satisfies its customers' critical needs and aligns that with the dream jobs of the employees, to have high impact and cross boundaries to facilitate innovative solutions. Looking back on it, I think the decision to be self-funded was an initial important decision as well. At the time I made that decision, I'm not sure I really considered anything else or even knew all the options available.

Ghaffari: Tell me about your long-term view of Stellar Solutions' future.

Ford: It's very important to us that Stellar Solutions is a sustainable business. In five to ten years, we want it to look and feel as it does now. Every employee will know about customer critical needs aligning with their dream job, and that is what is important. Every customer will continue to feel we are the one to call when they need someone to do the important work to satisfy critical needs for mission success.

We definitely are a "built-to-last" company, not a "built-to-flip" company. I mention this because so many companies are not that way. All they are focused on is how quickly they can flip the company and how much they can make, whether to sell out to another company or to an investment bank. We really want to leave a lasting legacy. We want this company to be here for our kids and their grandkids because it's a great place to work and it's personally and professionally rewarding. We want every employee to get up every morning and feel that they are doing something important—that they love what they do. And that they know they are making a difference in the world. We think our mission and vision will survive the test of time.

Ghaffari: Have you placed any special emphasis on hiring and developing women?

Ford: We have received a number of awards as top entrepreneurial company, best company to work for, and for excellence in a number of categories. We have not experienced a "leaky pipeline" at Stellar—where women leave a company just below leadership levels. Two of our sectors are run by women. The defense sector is run by Betsy Pimentel. The commercial sector is run by Melissa Farrell. The other sectors are run by men.

We role-model well—we're pretty diverse in our leadership group. Our leaders are role models who prove that we have opportunities for all of our people. We have a mix of genders. I don't have the specific number off the top of my head, but we have a higher percent of women compared to other companies in the aerospace and defense field. Maybe it's because I am a woman leader. It's still lopsided. We have maybe 25 percent [women team members], but that is probably higher than other engineering firms.

The "leaky pipeline" definitely is a factor elsewhere. It probably influenced me, because at every company where I worked or that I was associated with, I never saw a woman in a senior leadership position. So, I concluded it would be easier to head up my own business if I wanted to be the leader than it would be to overcome all the obstacles to reach that position in these other firms.

It's not just a diversity problem. It's also the "Bubba factor"—a leader is comfortable with the people that he/she has worked with before. That is more important than gender in determining who is chosen for a senior leadership position.

Traditionally, our industry has been dominated by white males, so leaders were selected from a homogeneous pool of candidates. The differentiator is about relationships—I choose people with whom I have had a positive working relationship. I have followed that axiom with our company. I will hire someone with whom I worked on a launch at two o'clock in the morning and who has proven themselves to be dependable and reliable—someone who really pulled through and that I could count on. That takes the diversity where it takes it.

In my day, there weren't a lot of women majoring in engineering in college—and not enough women engineers in the workforce. But that's changing, and it will eventually open doors for more women at the senior management level as well.

Ghaffari: What is your succession planning strategy?

Ford: For me personally, succession planning is very important. In the early years, I was the chief cook and bottle washer. I got the work and I did the work. Over time, we've built a strong leadership team in every sector. I think that's important because I don't want to be the kind of founder where the company goes away if the founder gets hit by a car. There are a lot of people who depend on this company now.

Mike Lencioni, our president and COO, really runs the tactical, day-to-day things that need to be done and has been with us since the end of our first year in business. He's an example of how we build succession from the inside. He came on board to do engineering work, then took on project leadership, and eventually moved into a senior leadership role within the company.

For me personally, I've been able to transition from the tactical to the strategic. I am now providing more of a board-type role at Stellar. And I have taken on more board responsibilities at other companies and more of a senior government advisory role on panels and commissions. I do see myself doing more of those kinds of things.

Ghaffari: How do you manage senior managers and key partners?

Ford: We provide our senior leaders and employees a framework to manage our company with our inclusive strategic-planning process, and then we let them go out and make things happen.

I believe in letting people discover their own greatness. We don't micromanage, but we do hire self-starters. As Wayne Gretzky is supposed to have said, "You miss 100 percent of the shots you don't take."

Ghaffari: What are your biggest achievements?

Ford: When you talk about leaving a lasting legacy, I think my biggest achievements are Stellar Solutions and my three kids. I could talk about my kids all day. My family has been the center of my universe, as much, if not more so, than Stellar Solutions.

My youngest, Hillary, is a junior at Princeton, a volleyball player, majoring in engineering with a business emphasis. My son, Nathan, earned an engineering degree and played football and baseball at Cornell University, and played professional baseball for one season with the Malvern Braves in Australia. He returned to the US and is working for the National Reconnaissance Office, which designs and builds the nation's spy satellites. Miranda, my oldest, graduated in 2006 with a business degree concentration in finance from the University of Notre Dame. She was a soccer player on their national championship team and currently lives in Washington, DC. When they were here at home, we juggled sports and work. Now that they've graduated, we're juggling getting on airplanes, so that we can see them in their new endeavors.

Ghaffari: How do you manage family expectations or commitments?

Ford: My three children were all born before I founded Stellar Solutions. They were born in 1984, 1987, and 1990. I was hired by Scitor when I was eight months pregnant with my first child. That was a pretty big risk on their part. If Roger Meade had been a traditionalist who thought that women would have babies and not come back to work, I might not have been given that opportunity. But Roger never brought it up, and I never did either. It wasn't a problem. I was the first employee to have a baby that they had to deal with and vice versa. But it worked out fine.

Ghaffari: To what extent have you involved the family in your business?

Ford: My family has been intimately involved with the business from the beginning, either directly or indirectly, and are very supportive. My husband, who is an accountant, thought that it was *not* a good idea at the beginning to start a new business because we had just moved to a new house and had a big new mortgage. I was making a pretty good salary at Scitor. He thought that it was just not a good time, financially. Initially it was just a question of how we would make ends meet. Since then, he definitely has been an important part of the team. He feels good about Stellar, where we've been and where we're going.

But, other than that, my family has all been tremendously supportive all the way. They all believe in the goals, share the vision, they all love the company and the people in it, and have been a big part of it throughout the years. It's been very positive.

Ghaffari: Inevitably, women ask about how to "balance work and family commitments." How do you see this issue and how would you describe your approach?

Ford: The issue of work-family challenges in a high-stress/high-travel environment might have played a part in my starting Stellar Solutions. For a person like me, if you get up and go to work in the morning, you want it to be for something really important and high impact. I think the more your career evolves, the more you understand where you can have that high impact. So, it was a natural thing for me to start Stellar Solutions around the theory that I wanted to surround myself with like-minded people who, when they get up in the morning, want to be doing something really important, satisfying a critical client need, but also be in their dream job. That has been the vision of Stellar Solutions from the beginning.

In a sense, that may be driven by your family. You don't want to feel regret that you're not spending time with them. If you have a job where you're away all the time, or you don't even like your job, or you don't feel like you're con-tributing—all that makes the work-family arrangement a non-starter on the home front as well as at work.

When I started my own business, I wanted a laser-sharp focus on the things that I thought were important. I wanted to put into place the kind of infra-structure for employees to have the benefit support that they needed, and most importantly, for our customers, to really solve the truly hard problems.

You could ask any of the over one hundred thirty employees that just gath-ered together for our sixteenth annual meeting last weekend, and they would all say the same thing—that our vision is the alignment between satis-fying their dream job and solving our customers' critical needs. That's been true all along.

Ghaffari: How did you address negative reactions to your efforts, if any?

Ford: I didn't really encounter a lot of negatives. I could always think back on those events that you wish hadn't happened, but they did. I think you just move through them with integrity and simply get on with life. You are meas-ured by your accomplishments and by the people you really care about. You just can't bother with the naysayers. And you find that other people don't care about the naysayers either.

Some of the negatives came about because I was entering a field with a lot of older men who had not worked with women before. It wasn't things that were said or done so much as awkwardness. There was never any intent to be deliberately cruel. There is much less of that awkwardness today. And there is a greater awareness today of things that are appropriate to say or not say.

Ghaffari: What key advice would you give to other women?

Ford: Follow your passion. If you enjoy doing something, follow that passion. Remove all the obstacles and never give up. Persistence really does pay off.

Every year there are a whole new set of challenges. If you're still pursuing those cool and interesting projects that you have a passion around, you have to just remove the obstacles that get in the way.

Ghaffari: What advice, especially, do you have for young women?

Ford: Engineering typically is not considered by women as a fun career option or thought of as a fun career. You don't see any TV shows about "The Young Engineers." There is a fun side to engineering—you just have to be diligent in finding a good fit with your skills and interests. Find out for yourself.

Ghaffari: Would you give any different advice to men?

Ford: Do what you love. Find your dream job. Do the important work. Persistence. One step at a time. That's the same advice you'd give anyone. Not just women.

Ghaffari: What do you see as the area of greatest opportunity for young women professionals?

Ford: Today, opportunities for women are better than they were when I started out and certainly better than my mom's generation. Where are there great opportunities for women? I can't say it enough: engineering, engineering, engineering! Here is a field where there are lots of jobs, lots of important things to be done. It really is a family-friendly field. It is the type of field where you can have a family and work and make the two work together. At least for me in my career, people were very supportive of others attending parent-teacher conferences, not just for women, but for guys, too. If there was something that needed to be done on the home front, people expected you to take care of it.

Now, that also means that, when there was a launch or something important at work, they expected you to take care of that first. There was a very balanced approach that I found very different from my classmates who became accountants or lawyers, with billable-hours targets. For them, it was all about more hours and that was all. It was not a family-friendly environment if you really wanted to get ahead.

Ghaffari: Would you do anything differently if you were starting out today?

Ford: The only thing I would have done differently is to start Stellar Solutions sooner.

Ghaffari: Where do you see yourself in the next five to ten years? Any political or governmental or other leadership role for yourself in the future?

Ford: I'm enjoying doing the board work. It's a chance to give back to other companies, but also get ideas from other companies, too. My boards are all very different, as you can see—a bank, a high-tech company, a nonprofit theater. They're all unique. Each entity tries, in its own way, to have entrepreneurial spirit and success within the framework that it exists, whether entrepreneurial, regulatory, or nonprofit fundraising. I'm impressed by how similar all businesses really are at the end of day. You want to have happy employees who are doing really good work and moving the mission forward, and you want to be delighting the customer no matter what business you're in.

Another example of something I'm involved with outside the company is the California Space Authority, which is an industry association that I think is doing a good job trying to cross the boundaries among disparate aerospace industry people who never interface with each other. We have universities, government—NASA, JPL, Edwards, Boeing, Lockheed—all these stovepipes of aerospace spread all around California that never talk to each other and if they did, you'd see how many dollars that represents, probably an amount that is greater than the GDP of many countries in the world. The Authority has a good mission, I think. I have participated on congressional commissions and panels in both the aerospace and emerging business arenas. I hope to be doing more of that in the future.

Anita L. DeFrantz

President, LA84 Foundation, Kids in Sports

Born October 4, 1952, in Philadelphia, Pennsylvania.

Anita Lucette DeFrantz *is president and a director of the LA84 Foundation (formerly the Amateur Athletic Foundation of Los Angeles), a private foundation seeded by the $93 million surplus of the 1984 Los Angeles Olympic Games. LA84 provides grants for Southern California youth sports organizations and maintains the largest sports library in North America. She is also president and director of Kids in Sports, Los Angeles, a non-profit public charity created in 1994 to foster youth in sports and to educate the volunteers and coaches that serve them.*

Anita DeFrantz brings passion to all of her avocations: youth in sports, sports research and media, rowing, the International Olympic Committee, the US Olympic organizations, and the law. The mission of the LA84 Foundation is "to serve youth through sport and to increase knowledge of sport and its impact on people's lives." The mission of Kids in Sports LA is "Building communities, one team at a time." These are also the personal missions of Anita DeFrantz.

A national- and world-class champion rower, Ms. DeFrantz was one of hundreds of Olympians denied the opportunity to "go for the gold" in the 1980 Moscow Olympic Games because of the boycott by President Jimmy Carter. Tapping her strong sense of fairness and justice as a lawyer, Ms. DeFrantz publicly defied the President's boycott, filed suit against the US Olympic Committee (USOC)—of which she was a member—arguing that the USOC could vote to send American teams to compete in Moscow in spite of the administration's boycott. She said that the Amateur Sports Act of 1978 barred anyone from denying an athlete's right to compete in the Olympic Games, that athletes alone had the right, the authority, and the power to determine if they would participate in the games or not.

In April 1980, Ms. DeFrantz made an impassioned speech before the USOC, but it voted to support the boycott. She next filed suit against the USOC to force them to allow the athletes to compete, but the case was dismissed. (DeFrantz v. United States Olympic Comm., 492 F. Supp. 1181 [D.D.C. 1980]). While she did not win in the courts, she won the respect of the International Olympic Committee (IOC) and was honored in July 1980 with the Bronze Medal of the Olympic Order in recognition of her leadership role in challenging the boycott.

In 1986, she was elected as a member of the IOC, making Ms. DeFrantz not only the first African-American but also the first American woman to serve on the committee. Ms. DeFrantz remains a voting member until she is eighty. She was named a member of the IOC Executive Board [1992–2001]. In 1997 she became the organization's first female vice president, a position she held until 2001. From 1989 to 1994 she served on the IOC's Summer Program Commission, which determines what sports will be included in Olympic competition. In 1995, she became chair of the IOC's Women and Sports Commission. She is credited with getting women's softball and soccer added to the Olympic ticket. She serves on the Juridical Commission of the IOC, which is made up of lawyers, and on the Finance Commission, which reviews the investments and spending plans.

In addition to her extensive nonprofit contributions, since 1998 Ms. DeFrantz has been a director of Western Asset, an investment fund in Pasadena, California. She has been a director at OBN Holdings, a film, media, and television holding company based in Los Angeles, since 2003.

Elizabeth Ghaffari: You are both an Olympian and a lawyer. How did you come to follow these two paths?

Anita DeFrantz: I was offered an academic scholarship by Connecticut College, in New London, Connecticut, where I graduated in 1974 [BA in political philosophy, with honors].

A chance meeting with rowing coach Bart Gulong in my sophomore year at Connecticut began my life-long interest in rowing. I was on the Connecticut rowing team, the US women's rowing team [1975–1980], and was team captain and a member of the bronze-medal-winning women's rowing team at the 1976 Montreal Olympic Games.

I chose law because I wanted to speak the language of power. In the mid seventies, there was no question that those who spoke law spoke the language of power. One needed only to think back to what was happening in the mid-1970s with the Watergate trials and the decisions that people in power were making. Many of those people had law backgrounds. That's why

I thought it would be wise to learn this special language—one that has served me well throughout my career. Sometimes I forget that I'm an attorney, and other people sometimes forget, too. When I need to bring out that credential, it's quite helpful.

Ghaffari: What was your first job after graduation, and how important were your first jobs?

DeFrantz: My first job after law school was as staff attorney at the Juvenile Law Center of Philadelphia [1977–1979], which was only in its second year when I joined it. Working on behalf of children is something that I longed to do. I have always believed that the way we treat children is a reflection of how we treat ourselves. And, too often, the picture is not pretty.

Anyway, I saw a listing for the job on a bulletin board and just bicycled over there wearing my running shoes. I thought nothing of it—I didn't have any other shoes to wear. Evidently, they were quite taken with the fact that I appeared at the interview with running shoes. I guess I was a good enough match because I was hired and began work that summer.

The Juvenile Law Center is a wonderful institution that does remarkable things—from institutional litigation to, most recently, joining in the Supreme Court case that recognized that you cannot put a child in jail for life. That decision also recognized that peoples' brains do not finish development until they're in their early twenties, so deciding that a child of fifteen could be responsible as an adult is not quite correct.

Ghaffari: How did you come to challenge President Carter about the 1980 boycott of the Olympic Games?

DeFrantz: After the Montreal Games, before my third year of law school, I asked my coach if he thought I could be an Olympic gold medalist. I already had the wonderful experience of being a bronze medalist. The only reason to compete again would be to try for the elusive gold medal. He said, yes, he thought I had it in me to do that. I decided to commit four more years to training and competition. Whatever happened in 1980 would be the end of my rowing career—after that, I would move forward into whatever my legal career might offer.

In order to have no regrets for 1980, I decided in the fall of 1979 to take a leave of absence and train at Princeton University with the coach of the women's Olympic rowing team. In January 1980, President Jimmy Carter announced that, in response to the December 1979 Soviet invasion of Afghanistan, the United States would boycott the 1980 Moscow Olympic Games.

I was at a friend's birthday party in a bar that evening, and noticed that the President of the United States was about to make an announcement. So, I went over and listened. He said, "If they [the Soviets] don't leave [Afghanistan], we won't send our spectators and athletes." I realized that there was a lack of understanding about how the Olympic movement worked if he thought there was some kind of central sending-office for spectators and athletes. It worried me deeply.

Ghaffari: How did this change your life?

DeFrantz: At the time, I was pretty naïve. After all, who was I? I was just the seventh seat in a bronze-medal-winning, eight-woman rowing team. Just one person among 260 million people. But, I believed that his decision was wrong. I believed that only an athlete who had earned the right to be an Olympian for the 1980 team was the only person who could decide to compete or not. We were private citizens. Not one penny of federal money supported us. To me, the notion that we were suddenly to be commanded by the President of the United States was just rubbish. We were individual citizens pursuing our own goals. And somehow, we were metamorphosed into being the only solution to [object to the] sixty thousand troops on a border that the Soviet Union shared with Afghanistan. That, to me, made no sense.

The boycott was, in one way, masterful politics. There were barely five hundred of us Olympians, plus our families and coaches—a tiny number of people directly affected by this decision. But, our lives forever would be changed by this decision. The lives of those athletes who never competed in the Olympic Games were especially impacted—they were never actually Olympians. They could always say they were members of the US 1980 Olympic team. But they don't exist in the list of Olympians that the IOC maintains. That's a terrible thing to do to them.

Ghaffari: When did you begin to reject conventional career wisdom and why?

DeFrantz: Do you mean—do I think I've been right? Am I willing to take the case to those people I think are wrong? Well, there we have it, don't we? Even as a child, I was troubled by injustice and things that just didn't seem right.

I probably got that growing up in the wonderful family I had. My parents had been involved in the civil rights movement at Indiana University [Bloomington]. My mother, Anita Page DeFrantz, had been one of five women who integrated the student housing. My father, Robert David DeFrantz, was president of the campus chapter of the NAACP. His father, Faburn E. DeFrantz,

Sr., had been the executive director of the Senate Avenue YMCA,[1] which was an important gathering place for the African-American community.

They had an annual speaker series called the Monster Meetings, which under his leadership became one of the nation's most highly-respected public forums, hosting the leaders of the African-American community at that time, who would come and speak. He met W. E. B. DuBois, George Washington Carver, and Langston Hughes—those [men] and other leaders in art, science, and industry who gave presentations at the Monster Meetings of the Senate Avenue YMCA.

My grandfather also had been active in helping Indiana University let an African American play on their NCAA basketball team following Jackie Robinson's breakthrough in baseball in 1947. He helped the president of Indiana University, Herman Wells, and the basketball coach, Branch McCracken, understand how important it was to let this talent play. After an earlier unsuccessful attempt, they finally succeeded in getting Bill Garrett to play as the first African-American basketball player in the Big Ten athletic conference following his graduation from high school [the year Garrett's team won the Indiana State Basketball Championship].

Before that era, my great-grandfather, Alonzo DeFrantz, was part of the Exodusters,[2] which made it possible for emancipated black people to migrate to Kansas after Reconstruction. Alonzo DeFrantz reportedly helped over two hundred Tennessee transplants relocate to Dunlap Colony, Kansas, in the 1880s, and made it possible for them to select and put down payments on small farms. At one time, he was secretary/treasurer and later president of the Pap Singleton organization.

So I have a long tradition in my family of fighting for what we believe to be the right thing to do.

Ghaffari: Which explains your work on behalf of the Amateur Sports Act and your challenge of Jimmy Carter over the 1980 Olympic Games.

DeFrantz: I had testified before Congress in support of the Amateur Sports Act of 1978, which established the US Olympic Committee, the national governing bodies for each Olympic sport, and important legal protections for individual athletes. This Act resolved a territorial battle that had gone on for years between the two amateur athletic organizations. The

---

[1] Founded in 1913 in Indianapolis.

[2] A group that was part of a movement led by Benjamin "Pap" Singleton (1809–1892), who was known as the "Father of the Negro Exodus."

Amateur Athletic Union had represented the U.S in international competition matters and, generally, regulated amateur sports. The National Collegiate Athletic Association [NCAA] was a semi-voluntary association of institutions, conferences, organizations, and individuals that had organized US college- and university-level athletic programs.

Later, I guess I caught the attention of the media in 1980 when a journalist called me and asked for a comment on the President's statement that "We will not be going to Moscow for the Olympic Games." My response was, "What does he mean 'we'? Where were we when I was freezing a part of my anatomy off in training? What does he mean, 'We will not be going?'" I guess I was the first athlete to suggest that it was not a decision of someone else—that it should be my decision, once I made the team. That's what brought me to the attention of the public. That really had its bad times too, because I received a lot of hate mail and many, really mean things were said.

Ghaffari: When did you become part of the Olympic organization?

DeFrantz: In 1976, I was selected to the US Olympic rowing team. Shortly thereafter, I was chosen as captain of the women's rowing team. Then, I was elected a member of the USOC's Athletes' Advisory Council [AAC]. I was elected to the USOC board of directors in the same year. Then in January 1977, I became one of two athletes named to the USOC executive board. The Los Angeles Olympic Organizing Committee [LAOOC] was created in 1978 to plan and prepare for the 1984 Summer Games. The USOC had a certain number of members to represent them on the LAOOC board. By then, I was vice chair of the AAC. Since my term on the USOC executive board could continue through the LA Olympic Games, I became one of the nominees proposed by the USOC to the LAOOC board.

Ghaffari: What was your role on the USOC board? On the LAOOC board?

DeFrantz: As a member of the LAOOC Board, I was representing the USOC and looking after the needs of the athletes as the 1984 Olympic Games were being organized.

The USOC Board was huge [120 persons]. The women's 1976 Olympic rowing team had elected me to serve on the Athletes Advisory Committee, which in turn elected me to serve on the USOC Board of Directors. I am not sure how I was elected to the Executive Committee of the USOC. I was at a US rowing committee meeting when one of the people there, after taking a phone call, announced that I had been elected to the Executive Committee of the Board.

I hope I was helpful on the USOC board. I hope I asked good questions about decisions that were made to be sure they made really good sense. I know I helped and was a part of the decision-making to sell the house in New York and move to Colorado Springs.

Ghaffari: What was that about?

DeFrantz: In 1977, the USOC relocated its headquarters from New York City in order to establish Olympic-caliber training facilities and a new national headquarters in Colorado Springs. The USOC built a new Olympic Training Center (OTC) on thirty-five acres of the former Ent Air Force Base. It became the USOC administrative headquarters in July 1978. We sold "the old Olympic House" for $5 million. They called it "the tidy, patrician, Ivy League-dominated Olympic House" located at 57 Park Avenue at East 37th Street in the Murray Hill section of New York. It was built in 1909 for a New York socialite, Adelaide Townsend Douglas, reportedly the mistress of the building's financier, J. Pierpoint Morgan.

I joined the staff of the LAOOC as an assistant vice president in 1981 and was responsible for planning the three Olympic Villages, where the athletes live during the Olympic Games. In 1984, I became a vice president and was made the chief administrator for the Village on the campus of the University of Southern California [USC].

I've been a member of the USOC since 1976 except for an eighteen-month hiatus. At one point, I thought I'd finished my time on the USOC in February 1985. Then in 1986, I was elected to the IOC and then re-joined the USOC as required by the IOC.

Ghaffari: How did you get the LA84 Foundation job?

DeFrantz: I was already working at the Foundation when the current president, Dr. Stanton Wheeler, decided to return to Yale. The Board members knew me from my work for the LAOOC and recognized that I had a passion for the work at hand.

The USOC had a special relationship in that it was the financial guarantor of the 1984 Olympic Games. The City of Los Angeles was not. A deal was made in 1979 between the LAOOC and the USOC whereby the USOC pledged to cover the LAOOC deficits, if any. Any surplus was to be allocated 60 percent to the USOC.[3] The remaining 40 percent would stay in Southern California. The 1984 games produced a $225 million surplus.

---

[3] Forty percent for the USOC itself and 20 percent to the national governing bodies of sports within the United States.

Southern California was to receive $93 million for youth sports. That initially seeded the Amateur Athletic Foundation [AAF], a private foundation, in 1985, which became the LA84 Foundation in 2006.

The first head of the foundation, Dr. Wheeler, had been on the faculty of Yale Law School. He was one of the few professors at a law school who did not have a law degree. He was a sociologist. His was fascinated with issues like juvenile delinquency. In 1985, he took a two-year leave of absence to serve as president of the Amateur Athletic Foundation of Los Angeles. But, he missed the academic community, and he's also a jazz musician, if the truth be known. So, he returned to New York and the position came open.

Ghaffari: Were you trying to solve a problem? Address an unmet need? Do something "good"? Fix something "broken"?

DeFrantz: I wanted to lead this institution. I believe that sport is a powerful force for good. I was senior vice president of the foundation and applied for the head position. We all had to do that because this was a job that a lot of people wanted. I got it. For me I could not have dreamed the job would fit so perfectly with my beliefs and goals that I would like to accomplish in life.

It is exactly what I believe in. Our mission is to serve youth through sport by enhancing the knowledge of sport's role in society. I've long believed, ever since living in the Olympic Village, that there is a tremendous power that sport has. Living there taught me that the world could live in peace together. That experience, along with my childhood interest in fairness and justice, all came together. While the work at the Juvenile Law Center was remarkable, I wanted to be able to reach a lot more kids with something good and positive in their lives than we could through the litigation process. The foundation was the perfect place for me.

In June 2006, the foundation adopted the name LA84 Foundation to establish a unique identity and honor the spirit of the 1984 Olympic Games, which created the foundation's endowment.

Ghaffari: What are the most satisfying parts of your work with the LA84 Foundation?

DeFrantz: Seeing other people become successful. Whether it's a child who's learned a skill on the field of play or someone who's discovered that she can be part of a team and her teammates don't have to be her very best friends to be able to work together, which is so important for girls today. That is one of the very important reasons for girls to take part in team sports. This is an opportunity, every day, to mentor young women and men as they look for their role in the larger world.

Ghaffari: Do participants go on to become major athletes?

DeFrantz: Not so much, but sport enriches their lives. We see some studies that say that people are better citizens when they are part of a team. We haven't actually subsidized those studies ourselves, but we know of them. We have chosen not to spend our money that way. It costs a lot to do those studies. You have to do longitudinal studies. But we know, and believe, and have found that people are better citizens when they've had a chance to be a part of a team. A lot of these kids will come back and support the next generation. They come back and volunteer to coach and undertake other tasks. Having a chance to be a part of something larger than yourself is really important. And sports provide that.

Ghaffari: What was the most satisfying opportunity you encountered in your career?

DeFrantz: I once had the opportunity to present a gold medal to a young woman at the Olympic Games who had started her career in sports in a program that the LA84 Foundation had created. It was extraordinary—both knowing how she had gotten her start and that she had done the remarkable work to become an Olympian. I felt very special to be able to present her gold medal to her and tell her that she would forever be "First and Olympic Champion."

I think that sport is not well understood. We don't pay enough attention to that. It is a great, unexplored part of what we are and how we live in this world. Sport needs a great deal more investigation. To me, sport is the mind directing the body through the dimensions of time and space. We humans enjoy doing sport, talking about sport, watching sport. We are the only species who would set up hurdles and then race across them to see who can get there first. I've seen ants use twigs to get across a puddle, but I've never seen them line them up to race across.

We speak of being in the zone of excellence in sport. How do we get there? If we understood it in sport, could we get there in other parts of our daily lives? Then of course, there are the other parts of sports—the ethical questions that arise. Are sports based on situational ethics? Are there certain ground rules of ethics for sports to exist? Do we have to agree to abide by a set of rules or sports won't work? Why are we willing to do that to play a game? Does that mean we should be able to do that to play life? There is so much to the world of sport, and we do so little with it. So, for me, there's a whole world yet to be explored in relation to sport.

Ghaffari: What is your strategy for identifying and capturing opportunities at either organization?

DeFrantz: I used The LA84 Foundation to create the idea of opening sports clubs in 1989 to provide community-led, after-school sports programs for kids in underserved areas of LA County. In 1994, it became Kids in Sports, Los Angeles, a nonprofit seeded initially with funds from the foundation. On an annual basis, though, we have to fundraise to bring in about $1 million to operate their programs. So we're looking for ways to endear ourselves to the people who will write checks. We do that by finding ways for the kids to tell their stories about what sports mean to them so that more people will support them and the remarkable work our volunteers and coaches do for young people in sport. Their motto is "Serving communities one team at a time."

At the LA84 Foundation, we believe in "the TLC of sport"—teaching, learning, and competition. For us, the coaching is really the teaching part of the program. Our coaching programs are called the Art of Coaching. We have a lot of our workshops and workbooks on our web site. Our web site[4] is very extensive. We're very proud of that—we were one of the first web sites to go up around the world.

For Kids in Sports LA, the donation button on the web site has worked okay, but we have to promote it on a regular basis. For the foundation, we don't want to miss any opportunity for people to make gifts to us. Having the donation button there is important.

We finally have a feature where you can make a gift with a credit card. It costs a lot to set up such a program. We try not to create a cost line unless we're really going to benefit from it. We didn't want to spend the money on credit card fees where we would have to explain to the donors that, if you gave a gift, only a certain percentage of their donated dollar would go to the foundation and the rest went to service the credit card feature.

Ghaffari: What is the greatest challenge in your work?

DeFrantz: Media coverage of women's sports is a critical area. There's the sports page, which I consider primarily for betting. Sad, but true, I think. Why on earth isn't there more and better coverage of women's sports? Why is this long-term discrimination allowed to continue?

My responsibility in the Olympic movement has been to solve the problem of women in sport, and I'm proud to say that we have managed to make sure that every sport on the program of the Olympic Games is available to both

---

[4] www.la84foundation.org

men and to women. That just happened with the London Olympic Games. Women's participation percentages are exemplary in both winter and summer Olympic Games. That was all accomplished very quietly and not at all painfully. If we can have gender equity in the two weeks of the Olympic Games, we can do it any time.

The foundation did studies of newspaper and television coverage of women in sports in the 1990s and in the 2000s. Early on, that research provided some unique lessons about televised coverage of women in sports. Women were infantilized in the finals of US Tennis Open. The women were given little girl names—Chrissy and Martina. For the men, it was Agassi and Sampras. Chrissy could never "own" anything. Sampras could be a manager, an owner, all sorts of thing—he was a fully formed human being.

Our research also looked at coverage of the Final Four basketball tournament. At the opening collage for men, trumpets were blaring and the athletes looked like giants with camera shots taken from the floor upward. For the women, literally it was a lullaby—pictures were of little girls on swings. These were just normal girls, and then they decided to play basketball. For the men's games, there were five to seven cameras, but only three cameras for the women. The number of statistics put up for the women were a fraction of those for the men. For the men's game, it always was *The* National Championship. For the women, it was the *Women's* National Championship. The diminutive was always used for the women. Ticket prices were always lower for the women's game compared to the men's game. It drives me nuts, among other things.

Ghaffari: How are you handling this challenge?

DeFrantz: All we can do is present the facts and demonstrate how to think critically about these issues. Representatives of the media are making these conscious choices. The first time we did a study on televised media, we looked at local television and newspapers, and the results were fractions of coverage for women. The media executives always said that people don't ask for it. But how can people ask for something they don't know about? It's illogical.

Ghaffari: What did you learn from these experiences?

DeFrantz: When we did our first research, I met with the presidents of the sports networks. We had some wild discussions. To their credit, each of them asked for one hundred copies of our first report. For a while, it was better listening to the coverage. It made a difference that you could hear. They used our information. But now, it's returned to the old way it was.

They say they cannot discriminate. It just gets imbedded. Until someone tells them that it is not to be allowed, it just continues.

We did follow-up studies three times, and then a lot of other organizations began doing similar research—taking a similar approach. We haven't been able to afford to continue doing them, but we are pleased that more research like this is being done around the world. Our own studies remain available on our web site.

Certainly, the thing that delights me today is that girls believe they have access to sports, and they should. In my day, we had to struggle for it. We were always accepting some second-class position for no reason other than that we accepted it.

Now, I'm grateful for Title IX. I want today's women and men to understand the history of women in sport so that we will never have to repeat it. Yet, almost every month there are cases lodged against Title IX trying to break it. I mean, really—equal educational opportunity. What is hard to understand about that? I mean really? Why wouldn't you want that for all your children?

Ghaffari: What job/boss had the biggest impact on you, and what did the experience teach you?

DeFrantz: Working for Peter Ueberroth at the LAOOC had an enormous impact on my life. He made us recognize that we had to be perfect for the athletes of the world. The challenges that that knowledge presented helped me understand my potential for leadership.

The LAOOC was faced with giving the games back if we didn't find a solution that the IOC would accept. A lot of people worked hard to come up with the idea that the USOC would be the financial guarantor—almost a ludicrous idea—because the USOC only had about $5 million in assets itself. The USOC and the LAOOC invested in an insurance contract worth another $50 million. But that wasn't near enough to guarantee the games—the LA 1984 Olympic Games were going to be a project of over $750 million, on a good day. Fortunately, Los Angeles had many facilities already in existence.

We had a great leader, a tremendous leader, in Peter Ueberroth. And Harry Usher was his Number Two man—he was just brilliant. Peter had the vision, and Harry knew where everything was. He was just amazing. They hired a lot of people who were willing to work really hard to create a surplus to support sport in the US. With the right leaders, it just worked.

Ghaffari: Who were the mentors who directly influenced your work?

DeFrantz: Jewel Plumber Cobb, whom I first met as dean of Connecticut College and researcher in melanoma, certainly was a mentor. She came up to me one day asking if I was related to Bobbie and Fay DeFrantz, Jr., my father and uncle. They had met as teenagers. She took an interest in me, always asking how my studies were going. Later she moved to Douglass College [a women's college at Rutgers University], was dean and professor of biological sciences there when I was training at Princeton. Before I moved out to Los Angeles, she became president of California State University at Fullerton. I always knew that she was there, sort of expecting me to reach my full potential.

Then, of course, there was my mother, Anita Page DeFrantz, who was just a remarkable woman. She went from being born into poverty to having her doctorate degree and teaching at the graduate level at the University of San Francisco. She earned her bachelor of arts and master of arts from Indiana University and a doctorate in communications from the University of Pittsburgh in 1975. She became one of the first African-American speech pathologists working with aphasia patients at the Indiana University Medical Center, and later joined the faculty of the University of San Francisco Graduate School of Education, where she began its program in International Multicultural Education and was a professor emeritus of the university. She just passed away in 2008.

My dad passed away just before the games in 1984. It was very strange. I must have known. I had worked until almost midnight that night, getting everything ready. We had a philosophy that you should be ready for someone else to take over at any time because you only get one shot at the Games. So, you can't pretend that someone couldn't just come over and come in and take over your work. I'd had a staff meeting the next day, so I was prepared for that. Little did I know that I would be gone for a few days.

Ghaffari: What are some of the key strategy decisions you made that are working out for you?

DeFrantz: I work on crafting consensus around an idea. That way people can feel that they are a part of the decision-making process and are more likely to be involved with creating a successful implementation of an idea. People ask me if I fight for an idea, and I respond that—rather than fight—I work to convince others that the idea is valuable.

We've learned a lot from our interesting research projects. We'll teach pretty much anyone who comes in the door how to be a good coach. If you can get ten people together, we can provide a coaching clinic. If you're in track and field, we have higher levels of clinics with specialties. We do specialty clinics in long-distance running in track and field, soccer, and volleyball.

We've found that there are so many so-called experts in basketball. We had one project where we had enough kids to establish a league, then divided the coaches and kids into two groups. Half of the coaches received feedback from the kids about their experiences being coached. The other half did not get feedback about their coaching—they were more dictatorial. The idea was to find out what would happen—which kids would do well? To my great delight, although it was a small sample, the kids that gave coaches feedback did as well if not better than the kids in the dictatorial coaching situation.

We are doing another study where the coaches are asked to have only certain amounts of feedback. What are the different kinds of things they can say to their athletes? And we'll find out what works. That's one of the wonderful things that we can do. We can undertake studies to look at how coaching is done, for example.

We're also doing a project on a new way to prevent the head injuries that are endemic in football. We're working on a different way of tackling as a different way to solve the problem of head injuries among youth. The helmet only works to keep all the parts in place once you have the problem. It doesn't solve the issue of preventing concussions or spinal injuries. It was never designed to deal with any of that. We're looking for ways to avoid the injuries that typical, head tackling produces.

Ghaffari: How do you decide what to study?

DeFrantz: Our Education Services department is headed by Wayne Wilson. He has his doctorate, but he doesn't like to use that. But, I like to. He pretty much comes up with most of the research projects, although it's a collaborative process. Wayne, and Patrick Escobar, who is our vice president for grants and programs and an attorney, were giving me a presentation earlier today on a project to get more Latinas in the world of sport. It's a wonderful place to work, if I do say so myself. Here you can propose new ideas to work on, share it, and build on it interdepartmentally.

Ghaffari: What is your strategic plan? Do you expect the LA84 Foundation to become a larger entity?

DeFrantz: It would be wonderful if the foundation could have a larger endowment, but that's hard to do. It's difficult to keep the endowment growing, because we are a private foundation. If we were a public charity, we could do fundraisers and ask people to support us. As a private foundation, there are some limits through the IRS. Contributions have a less beneficial tax effect for the individual donors when they're giving to a private foundation as opposed to a public charity.

We have received most [98 percent] of our income from our investments. Since the late 1990s, the financial markets have not been as predictable as before. There was the dot-com bust in 2000 and then the financial meltdown beginning in 2008. Bonds used to go in the opposite direction of the stocks, but there is no guarantee of that anymore.

The size of our endowment struggles when the financial worlds shift like that. So we work our way back as best we can, and we continue to serve. It's just about having a good, solid investment plan that serves your needs so that you can have the funds available when you need them.

Ghaffari: Do you work with partners to reach your goals?

DeFrantz: We have been making partnerships with others—both public and private entities. We partner with civic pools for our summer swim programs. We partner with four or five municipalities to provide the summer swim program and then produce a culminating event in swimming, synchronized swimming, and diving or water polo. So the kids learn to swim and they get to take part in a competition.

In some cases, we partner with corporations. For the past three years, we've been working with Nike to renovate and create new play sites. They've been great partners with us in that. We're always looking to partner with other corporations if there's a project or a program that makes sense for us. We'll work with them to help them understand it and understand how it will benefit them.

Ghaffari: What are some of your major internal problems or competitive challenges?

DeFrantz: Our biggest challenge is that we're a regional foundation and our reach is Southern California—the same counties that hosted the LA Olympic Games. So, our expenditure of funds is limited to just this area. Most corporations want to give to an entity with a national reach. That's been the greatest challenge for us actually in getting them to support our programs. Although so many of our programs could be replicated throughout the country. My hope is that we could do more of that work because we have built excellent structures that could easily be put into place practically anywhere in the country.

An example of a national effort might be the opportunity to associate with Michelle Obama's "Keep Moving" program. We would hope so. Her program is far more general and accepts almost anything. Our research tells us that, while it is important for anyone to want to move, kids are more purpose-driven. They are more interested in the fact that movement means something. So, that, while it's great to be able to do sit-ups and pushups, it's better to say that "If you do this many sit-ups or push-ups, then you'll be better at volleyball or some other sport." At least that's what we've found over the years.

Part of the way that we teach people how to coach is for them to recognize that, even more than the competitive spirit, kids appreciate having fun. If you *don't* make it fun, you will *not* have athletes to coach. We've learned that many people who coach have just been given a clipboard and a whistle and told, "Now, you're a coach." Then they delve back into their own experiences, which may not have been happy, and they make the same mistakes that were made in their lives.

That's why we started teaching people how to coach in January 1986 with our own coaching program. We knew that it was very important. I'm really proud of how many people we've reached—around 68,000 in total. In the last three years, we've reached 8,000 people a year. At some point, we might tap out because there are just so many coaches needed each year. But, as people age or their children age out, there is a constant need.

Ghaffari: What is your succession planning strategy?

DeFrantz: I've been thinking about that. In ten years, I will definitely not be here, but it's up to the board, any day between now and ten years, to make that decision. I don't know. I still believe that we have a lot to do in the area of education on what sports is and what it provides, and I'd like to focus more on that. I would like for us to find ways for the endowment to grow. Maybe we can do that with gifts from people who are leaving this mortal coil. And to have more people understand the great value of sports.

Ghaffari: How do you manage senior managers and key partners in the organization?

DeFrantz: I believe that everyone has a great deal to offer. My management style is based on respecting each person and letting them know what I expect from them.

In terms of headcount, we have seventeen full-time employees at the foundation and Kids in Sports has seven full-time people. We have a huge volunteer base. We have a lot of consultants who work with us to help train people to coach. At any point in time, we would have four hundred people working on projects. Volunteers would be the largest percentage.

The number and size of Kids in Sports' clubs fluctuates. Today, we have thirteen clubs reaching about seven thousand children and about two thousand adults help that process. Sports clubs have a lot of volunteers. Sometimes a club will close up shop, but then the kids can go to another club.

Ghaffari: How do you define success?

DeFrantz: Success is hard to define. If anything, I guess I define my success as other people being successful—people that I've maybe helped or haven't hindered. I remember in coaching, one of the main things is to *not* get in their way. I'm about helping others—I think that's why we're here on the face of this earth, that's why there's more than one person here. We're supposed to help one another. If people have a great idea that I can help with, that's fine. I hope I have some great ideas that other people would like to help with too. To move forward in ways that benefit everyone.

Ghaffari: How do you manage family expectations or commitments?

DeFrantz: I'm not married. I have three million children in Southern California that I take care of.

Ghaffari: What key advice would you give to other women—especially young women?

DeFrantz: I urge them to ask for help. We forget about that too often. We're forced to forget about it. We are admonished to be strong and to be able to do it all, all by yourself. But you need to ask for help. And you need to ask more than one person so you can select among the advice that you do get.

Even more important, I tell them you have to think critically. If something doesn't sound quite right, it probably *is not* right. Too often we just listen to things and accept them without challenge. All the ads that constantly assail us are not true. We have to stop just taking in what's being given to us and begin to be more critical about what we hear.

Ghaffari: Would you give any different advice to men?

DeFrantz: Absolutely I'd give the same advice, but I know it's harder for women because there are so many more messages being given to women only that suggest you'd better not ask because you'll get what you deserve. There are all sorts of horrible messages being given to women from the media.

The sports pages—the national editions—are the most irritating ones. Often when I'm speaking in another country, I look at their national sports page and too often there—nada—no coverage of women in sports. Not a word. I know there are women taking part in sports, because they are doing that every day, but there is no media coverage of them.

Ghaffari: Would you do anything differently if you were starting out today?

DeFrantz: How can one answer that question? Life's been good. I've had some great challenges and great opportunities. I've been able to share a lot. I've taken it as it's come. I would have loved to have my Mom or my Dad with me today, but those things are beyond my ability.

Would I do anything differently? The one regret I have about 1980 was that I couldn't sit with President Carter to explain to him that there were better ways to deal with that issue. Just as I predicted, the Soviets and Eastern European competitors said we were just ashamed that we would be defeated on Soviet grounds. If you're not there, you cannot be heard. Why would we do that?

Ghaffari: Tell me about your election as a director of the investment fund Western Asset. It's a private board of directors, right?

DeFrantz: One member of that board thought that I could be helpful in what they were doing. I met the principals there, and they agreed to nominate me. Then, I was elected by the shareholders starting in 1998. So far, I've been re-elected by the shareholders every year.

It has been a positive experience. I've learned a lot, and I think I've been able to add the common person's touch to the decision-making there, which is important. That's why you have a board of directors—you want to hear from them. It's five to seven members, all of them inside. So many things are changing there.

Ghaffari: And what about OBN Holdings, where you are also on the board?

DeFrantz: OBN Holdings is a film, TV, and media holding company that has gone through tough times getting the funds they've needed to carry out the projects they wanted to do. What's interesting is that they have bought several companies, one in Mexico and a couple in China.

They diversified again in product lines. I wanted them to do more in the entertainment area. Among one of their projects was getting the "oldies but goodies," helping them re-launch [artists'] singles. They did one project with The Four Tops, where they helped produce a show that became a video show and relaunched [The Four Tops'] music very successfully. That's a good thing to do now that Baby Boomers want to hear the old vocalists they heard as youths. Just as they were trying to get that going, the market's investments in IPOs just dried up. Timing is so important.

Ghaffari: Where do you see yourself in the next five to ten years?

DeFrantz: In five to ten years, the LA84 Foundation will be viewed as the premier center of thought for youth sport and for sport in general. We have created this institution, and I know that I will move away leaving it as a strong independent organization serving the Southern California community and the world.

I will find another place to use my skills and my passion for making certain that children have a fair chance for success in the world.

I have received so many wonderful experiences in life. I want to continue to share what I have learned. Perhaps I will become a professor, following in my mother's footsteps. I am certain that I will have many years to give back to the world the many gifts I have received.

Robin Ferracone

Founder and Executive Chair,
Farient Advisors LLC

Born 1953 in Englewood, New Jersey.

Robin Ferracone *is founder and executive chair of Farient Advisors LLC, an independent executive compensation consulting firm that she founded in October 2007. The firm is based in Los Angeles, California, and New York.*

Ms. Ferracone is also CEO of RAF Capital LLC, a private, portfolio-management firm that she founded in April 2007 to make strategic investments in companies within the human resources software, information, and consulting fields.

She was instrumental in commercializing four highly successful companies, one of which was the forerunner to FreeCreditReport.com, and three others that were sold to publicly traded companies.

Given today's battle over excessive executive compensation, it is a challenge to run an executive compensation advisory firm, yet Ms. Ferracone has taken the high road and, through such innovations as her proprietary Pay Alignment Model, shows top-tier corporate boards how to construct fair and reasonable relationships between executive pay and performance for CEOs and the other named executive officers. Her data-driven model tracks almost 50,000 data points over three-year periods back to 1995 for the entire S&P 1500, including by company size, industry, and performance.

Ms. Ferracone is the author of Fair Pay, Fair Play: Aligning Executive Performance and Pay *(Jossey-Bass, 2010). She also is an accomplished speaker and* contributor to top-tier governance journals, and was named in 2011 to the Directorship 100, marking her as one of the most influential people in the boardroom today.

Elizabeth Ghaffari: Why did you choose the education that you did?

Robin Ferracone: I'd done pretty well in high school, was valedictorian of my class and had always been very quantitatively oriented. The northeastern colleges—Harvard, Radcliffe, Smith—were impressive, but they seemed a little too radical for me—as a girl from Indiana. I wanted a top education, but was tired of the Indiana winters. I visited the Duke University campus and found it to be absolutely stunning. I said, "This is the place for me."

Ghaffari: How did you get started in your current field? Did you need to get advanced training or education?

Ferracone: I started in science because I loved the quantitative aspect of it, but the labs were solitary activities that required a lot of patience. I'm short on patience, and I like social interaction. Business gave me the interaction I sought, while an economics major fit best with my quantitative interests. A dual undergraduate major in management science and economics made perfect sense.

I decided to go to business school, applied to Harvard, and was admitted with a two-year deferral. Since there was no other place I wanted to go, I decided to spend a couple of years working beforehand.

Ghaffari: What was your first job after graduation, and how important was your first job?

Ferracone: I had a boyfriend at the time who was graduating from Duke Medical School with a residency at the University of Colorado. I thought "Why not just try to find a job in Denver?" That was in 1975, in the middle of one of the worst economic recessions we'd ever seen. The Denver economy was heavily dependent on energy and was in a deep recession. Undaunted by facts, I traveled to Denver on my spring break of my senior year of college in search of a job—all by myself, knowing no one, staying in some cheap motel, trying to scrounge around for whatever work I could find. It was probably one of the loneliest weeks of my life.

Because I had worked the summer before my senior year as a marketing research analyst at Colgate-Palmolive in New York, I was fortunate enough to get a job in marketing research at Samsonite Corporation in Denver. Their head of marketing looked at my background and said, "This person is perfect for a market research role." I started work right after Memorial Day.

Ghaffari: Did anything change in your life that led you to your current career path?

Ferracone: I've tended to do things more opportunistically than linearly. I started out in marketing, but saw that the consulting firms recruiting heavily at Harvard. They hired the smartest people and offered the plum jobs that paid well. I thought, "Consulting is great. You work with smart people, get paid a fair wage, and work on a variety of assignments."

I got a summer internship with Booz Allen in their New York office between my first and second years of business school. I liked it very much and ended up working full-time with Booz Allen after graduation. But, I still wanted to live in a warmer climate, and didn't want to work in New York City at the time. I asked Booz Allen for a job in their San Francisco office, and they gave it to me. I worked for Booz Allen there for the next five years.

Ghaffari: Would you say you purposefully planned your career or reacted to events?

Ferracone: I'm very planful—not serendipitous. I'm purposeful. I actually have a plan. I have a ton of motivations and I'm a self-starter. But, when new facts present themselves, I'll change. I'll shift. That's been the history of my career. I'll plan to do one thing, but I'll end up doing another if and when some opportunity presents itself. Then I go for it.

Ghaffari: How did you start your business?

Ferracone: I co-founded SCA [Strategic Compensation Associates] with Gary Hourihan, one of the Booz Allen partners who really deserves the lion's share of the credit for starting the firm. I had worked with him at Booz Allen and liked him very much. He was leaving Booz Allen to start a company focused on executive compensation.

Gary invited me to come and be his number two and help start the business. We were financed by Peter Mullin in Los Angeles, probably one of the best business development people I know. We moved to LA and started SCA at the beginning of 1985.

Ghaffari: What made you decide to leave the corporate world and take on this venture?

Ferracone: When I first talked about this with Gary, I was concerned about the narrow focus of the new firm on compensation. At the beginning, the subject matter of executive compensation was a negative for me because I was a strategy consultant with more of a big-picture orientation. But I decided that this was an opportunity to start a new business, to get in on the ground floor and to have an ownership stake. All those things trumped the subject matter.

Ghaffari: Were you trying to solve a problem, address an unmet need, or fix something broken?

Ferracone: First, we thought we could differentiate our approach to executive compensation from our competitors. Our competitors looked only at the pay side of the equation. Our thought was to add a strategic and performance orientation to the pay side—"pay for performance," which constituted a new approach to compensation design. Pay for performance considerations are talked about a lot, today, but were unheard of back then.

Second, we thought we could drive this idea forward in an entrepreneurial environment. We really were upping the game as to how executive-pay programs were designed. We wanted to make it a strategic board and top management activity, as opposed to a technical exercise that lived in the corporate compensation department. We changed the nature of how our field works. We literally "changed the frame" through which companies view executive compensation.

Ghaffari: What were the biggest challenges you faced as an entrepreneur?

Ferracone: We were blessed with a booming economy when we started. Peter Mullin, our financier, had multiple contacts, which generated a lot of business. The biggest challenge was to get people to join a small start-up company, starting from scratch—getting people to come in and learn our craft at the level that we wanted to deliver our work. The people side of the business was the biggest challenge. The business side, getting the business in the door, wasn't as big a challenge back then. But, just getting the work out the door—that took a lot of time and effort.

Today, it's different. The economy has turned pretty significantly, so today we face the opposite challenge. Getting business in the door is tough today.

Ghaffari: What were some key turning points?

Ferracone: Key turning points probably were our expansion to five offices. SCA's growth began with the LA office opening in 1985. The next year, we started the New York office by bringing on a Booz Allen partner as principal. In 1991, we brought in someone else we knew from Booz Allen to head up the Chicago office. Before he showed up, I went to Chicago with another associate, lived there for a month, and started that office.

Gary, and Simon Patterson, another Booz Allen person we knew, set up the London office in the mid-1990s. Dallas, our fifth office, was totally opportunistic. The wife of one of our New York partners needed to move to Dallas for professional reasons, so he decided to start our Dallas office for us.

Ghaffari: What kept you up at night? What kept you going?

Ferracone: In 1989, we'd sold half of our firm to Korn/Ferry. Later, we saw we were not getting the synergies that we all wanted and so decided to buy back the other half of our firm. That was a burden on the partnership because it meant that we had to take the money that we were earning, and instead of putting it into our pockets, we had to put it into buying back our shares from Korn/Ferry.

Four of our partners wanted to reinvest in our business for growth and four wanted to harvest our business. While we all agreed we wanted to buy ourselves back from Korn/Ferry, some partners thought that it was too painful and wanted the cash. They had a "take the money and run" attitude—to just pocket as much cash as possible rather than reinvesting for growth. So, there were some issues and disagreements. It was kind of a tough time, because we were disagreeing about our priorities.

Ghaffari: Ultimately, you did decide to sell. How did that come about?

Ferracone: The sale of SCA to Mercer was an interesting learning process for me. In 1998, Gary decided he wanted to leave SCA to build a leadership solutions practice at Korn/Ferry. Our Chicago partner wanted a value-realizing event—he wanted to sell the company. We looked at a lot of firms that were potential buyers. Mercer presented the best opportunity. We all decided to sell.

I had arguments going on in the partnership. For me, the sale to Mercer was an optimization. The final solution had something for everybody. Anybody who wanted money in their pockets would get money in their pockets. Those who wanted to grow and experience new challenges could do that as well. But the sale was born out of disagreements rather than a decision that we purposefully pursued. After the sale to Mercer, I was determined to try something different at a much larger firm and see how that worked out.

Ghaffari: You went to work for Mercer. How did that work out?

Ferracone: I was at Mercer for six years. They pitched their acquisition of us as a "reverse takeover." We would be allowed to run certain aspects of the business within Mercer, while they would benefit from our strategic approach and high-level relationships. They said that there would be synergies and that we could help shape the business. One plus one would be equal to three.

I really wanted to play a positive role at Mercer. They wanted to combine the efforts of their strategy group, Mercer Management, with their HR unit, Mercer Human Resources, so I was put into the role of chairing Mercer's Linkage Committee, which was a committee charged with extracting more synergies out of the strategy and HR business units.

I also was a senior client person, where I was responsible for continuing to grow the executive compensation business. I did all of that, but I really missed having line responsibilities and running a business unit like SCA. In big corporations, it's very hard to make room for people to play line roles, particularly at the higher levels.

Ghaffari: Were you ultimately successful in dealing with that challenge?

Ferracone: On numerous occasions, I approached Mercer leadership about my interests but did not find any enthusiasm until 2004 when I encountered a person who finally saw my talents, Mathis Cabiallavetta. I really liked him a lot. He said, "Why don't you do global development in the western US as vice chair of Marsh & McLennan—MMC, the parent company—play a linkage role there, to extract the synergies between all the MMC companies, including Mercer. Why don't you do that for two years, and after that, we'll find you a line role."

Ghaffari: What did you learn from these experiences? Any surprises?

Ferracone: By this time, I'd learned how to do linkage—to deploy what I learned. I was having a very good time in that job. I liked the people, my boss, the impact we were having, meeting new people, and doing new things. I thought at the end of my two years, I would go back to the line.

Things never follow a straight line. Nine months later, Eliot Spitzer—then attorney general of New York—accused Marsh, the insurance brokerage unit of Marsh & McLennan, of bid-rigging and engaging in anti-competitive behavior. It was a very serious accusation. In response to the investigation, the company broke up the corporate center. They decided that all of the units had to act independently to avoid any appearance of untoward practices. The global development department went away. Jeff Greenberg, then the CEO of Marsh & McLennan, was replaced by Michael Cherkasky.

That was a very defining moment. I thought my job was going away, and I was ready to take a severance package. MMC said I could go back to Mercer. I said I didn't want to go back unless I could have a line job. They brought in a new person to run Mercer named Brian Storms. My last day at work at MMC was supposed to be January 31, 2005. I had accepted my severance package, given up my parking space, turned in my keys. And, literally, at the eleventh hour, fifty-ninth minute, I got a phone call from Brian in New York who said, "You can stay. I want you to run Mercer's human capital business. Let's work it out."

I went into the human capital business as its president and really enjoyed that job. I enjoyed working for Brian. I had a lot of fun. We were growing and inventing new things. It was a line job. It was a global post. I liked the global scope. We spent the next two months working to organize my group and determine how the business would operate and grow.

Ghaffari: Did you make any mistakes? And how did you get past them?

Ferracone: Not so much mistakes as the challenge of organizational upheaval. From 2005 through 2007, I went through multiple bosses. Brian left to go run Marsh. Michael Caulfield was brought in to run Mercer. Then Cherkasky and Caulfield had a falling out, and Cherkasky put Michele Burns in charge of Mercer. Michele added a layer of management between her and me. All these changes in direction were difficult.

At the end of 2006, executive compensation firms were facing major new independence requirements from the government and investors. In order to be considered "independent," executive compensation companies reporting to boards had to avoid doing other business for management. I wanted to address that conflict of interest issue by spinning off Mercer's executive compensation business. They finally did exactly that in 2009. But, I was making that recommendation in 2006 with no action in sight.

By early 2007, I realized that things were not adding up for me at Mercer. Changes were not carefully thought through from a succession standpoint. Mercer was in the business of succession planning, but we weren't practicing good succession planning ourselves. I was not having an impact. I was not being heard. So I decided to "ease on down the road" and leave the company.

Ghaffari: What did you do then?

Ferracone: After Mercer, my plan was to form RAF Capital and become more involved with private equity firms, to help them find good deals in the human capital space, to go in and run one of those ventures, and to create value for investors. Here again, the best-laid plans just don't work out. Private equity deals were slow in coming. It was a lot of work, but deals were hard to find. The reality is that, for the most part, if someone is looking for money, he or she just wants the money—he or she does not want to step down from running the company. Somebody who wants to come in to run the company on behalf of the private equity firm isn't very popular.

In the meantime, I started Farient Advisors as an executive compensation and performance consultancy. It's sort of a next-generation SCA. I began to get calls from clients and referrals from people wanting me to do consulting assignments. Then, the recession hit in the beginning of 2008, and it was unlike anything I'd ever seen before.

Ghaffari: Have you decided not to pursue external investments? Might you do so in the future?

Ferracone: The recession was extremely difficult, but we managed to get through all of that. Here I am, financing the company, we were down to our last dollar, and I decided to invest anyway in the business. I invested in developing intellectual capital around performance and pay alignment, and wrote a book, *Fair Pay, Fair Play: Aligning Executive Performance and Pay* as a result of this research.

During this time, we also opened our New York office. I think we did extremely well. We hired some pretty key people. But, growing the client base and revenues has been slower than I would have liked. It was slower than I was used to at SCA. Doing all of that in the face of a recession, as a new business, was not easy. But, we've done it, and I think we're over the hump—I know we're over the hump.

Today, I'm now running Farient. We now have about twenty people in offices in Los Angeles and New York, and we have an affiliation with my former partner from SCA, Simon Patterson, in London. We have a good and enjoyable client base.

So far, we haven't taken external capital because we haven't needed it.

Ghaffari: What methods do you use to uncover opportunities?

Ferracone: I'm now down the road in terms of start-ups and doing very entrepreneurial things. I'm a lot more at ease doing that now. I think I developed nerves of steel while weathering that last recession.

On the private equity side—RAF Capital—the deals really weren't happening. So I changed the format. The market has started to pick up a bit with the economy turning around. Today, on the private equity side, I'm starting to capitalize on all those early calls and meetings. I just changed it up—rather than go in and be the CEO, now my format is to make an investment and have an impact usually through a board seat. I can only do a couple of those at any given time. That's a way for me to have influence with a lighter time commitment because most of my time is given to Farient and its clients. That's kind of where it is now. It's been very interesting.

I saw opportunities along the way. In the 1990s, when the capital markets were good, there were entrepreneurial opportunities—I made an investment and took a board seat in two companies of note. One is ConsumerInfo.com, which is now FreeCreditReport.com, which most people know. That was a company I started. The second was A Breed Apart Veterinary Centers, which we sold to Veterinary Centers of America. In the 2000s, I made an investment in and took a board seat on Worldwide Compensation, a company we sold to Taleo last year. These have all been rewarding and gratifying ventures for me.

All these were separate businesses. I was not the lead on ConsumerInfo.com. A good friend and client from my days at Booz Allen had stayed in touch with me, and he brought the idea to me. He asked if I could help him. I helped him with the strategy, went on his board and helped him get financing. It was totally separate from SCA.

ConsumerInfo.com was a real home run, probably my best investment to date—we sold it for ten times my investment. A Breed Apart and Worldwide Compensation were sold for five times my invested capital. Now, I'm invested in, and on the board of, a company called PayScale. The prospects for this company are bright, but it remains to be seen what will happen there.

I've also had my failures—they tend to be those businesses that I wasn't really involved in. I lost more money in the shortest period of time in the dot-com boom in ventures where I wasn't fully engaged. You go into these things and make mistakes.

Ghaffari: What job/boss had the biggest impact on you, and what did the experience teach you?

Ferracone: Gary Hourihan certainly was one of my mentors. We worked well together. Gary is very sharp and has an expertise in organizational design and compensation. He has a Princeton undergraduate degree, a Chicago graduate degree, and a second graduate degree from the University of Louvain, Belgium.

Between my strategy expertise and Harvard MBA, and his expertise, we were able to combine that in a pretty powerful way in the marketplace. It was a lot of fun to work with, and to learn from, Gary. It was the two of us combined that really made it work. I felt as if it was always, "Go for it! Grab it!" Gary says that hiring me was one of the smartest things that he ever did.

Peter Mullin is another mentor, probably one of the best business development people I know. He's also is good at thinking about business models and reinventing businesses. He was our financier for SCA and an incredibly gifted mentor.

Ghaffari: Who or what else taught you important lessons?

Ferracone: There are other people I've learned from along the way. I had one client, Kate DCamp, who was always on the client side while I was always on the consulting side. We kind of grew up together. We'd learn from each other as we went along. I feel as if there are people out there with whom you resonate and from whom you learn. Even if an experience is painful, you need to think about, "What are the lessons to learn from this experience?" If you don't learn the lessons, you're not going to grow.

Ghaffari: Could you have made it to where you are without mentors/coaches?

Ferracone: Absolutely not. I'm still learning. We all can learn from people. I learned a lot from Gary Hourihan. He was one of the people who told me things I didn't want to hear. My biggest blind spot is with people. I'm a pretty tough and demanding manager. I tend to put a premium on getting the task done and done well. But, I've learned over the years that that is really only part of the equation. Real leadership is inspiring people to co-create, buy into, and help execute a vision.

We need relationships and ways to motivate and inspire people. Gary does that pretty well. He's been able to tell me when I've been too hard on people or when I need to try a different way of working. He's been extremely instrumental in my success, plus he's good at what he does and I've learned from that. I've learned to be a good consultant working with him. He's definitely a mentor who is pretty significant.

Recently, I hired Gary into Farient as an SVP. I also hired Gary's son, Ryan. So, we're growing our own here, so to speak.

Another group of mentors are the people in my Young Presidents' Organization Forum. They are all terrific. We've been a forum for twelve years now, and I'm still learning from them. They will hit me between the eyes when I need it, and then pick me up and dust me off afterwards to make sure I'm better for the wear. I've probably learned more from them than anyone since they deal with both the business and the personal side of things, which are inextricably linked.

Ghaffari: What other areas interested you besides business?

Ferracone: Educational and philanthropy. There's a friend in business, Jaynie Studenmund, with whom I worked at Booz Allen. We kept in touch all of these years. She went on the board at Harvey Mudd College [HMC]. She knew they were looking for women who could bring a valuable perspective to the board, but who also were able to make gifts to the college. She sug-

She suggested my involvement. I thought it was a good way to be associated with a college with a scientific orientation.

HMC is a very prestigious science and engineering liberal arts college. I liked its mission and the fact that it put a high premium on teaching rather than just research. It just seemed like a really good fit for me. I think I made my mark there since I was on the search committee that brought in the new president, Maria Klawe, former dean of Princeton University's School of Engineering and Applied Sciences, chosen in January 2006. She's been terrific. I felt like I had a hand in that. I also headed the personnel and compensation committee while I was there. I think we professionalized the activities of the committee and moved the college in a good direction in that regard.

I'd been on the Harvey Mudd board for ten years and felt it was the time to move off the board in 2009. I'm a believer that it's good to have new blood on a board. It was a good time to step aside at Harvey Mudd and let someone else add value while I joined the Duke University board.

Ghaffari: How did you get the Duke University board position?

Ferracone: I had been on the undergraduate board—the Trinity College board of visitors. I'd go twice a year to the meetings. I missed very few meetings. It's basically a development board. I had been giving to Duke over the years, so I'm sure the head of development at Duke suggested me. Nan Keohane, then the president of Duke, came to see me in Los Angeles and asked if I would consider going on the board of trustees at Duke.

So far, the Duke board has been a great experience. I feel that I am making my mark there. For example, they needed to conduct a governance study. I raised my hand and said, "I know something about governance" and volunteered to chair the ad hoc committee on governance.

My view is that you get out of things whatever you put into them. Now, I chair the human resources committee and am a member of the executive committee, as well. Duke has been a fabulous experience and is just a great board. I'm loving my time on it and hope I'm having a positive impact there.

That's something I think about more today. When I start something, the issue, for me, is: "How can I make an impact? What do I want to say happened?" It doesn't always turn out—what actually happens is different from what you might expect in the beginning. But to have some kind of intent is really powerful.

Now, what I'm trying to do is to give back. I really like mentoring young adults. Dennis Rohan, head of the Entrepreneurial School at Stanford Business School, has me in his contacts He'll just call me if any of his project teams at the Stanford Business School ever need help in the field of HR. I'm here for them if they need me.

Ghaffari: How would you describe your decision-making style?

Ferracone: I'm fairly decisive. I feel like I sort through things. At the end of the day, a lot of decisions end up being more emotional than analytical. I am a very good analyst, and I certainly look at the facts, but at the end of the day, career and investment decisions have an emotional component as well.

As I've gotten older, I've decided I'm only going to work with people I like, trust, and respect because life is too short to spend time on the ones you don't. A lot of deals can get into trouble and are painful. So, you want to be in the boat with good people. I've put a much bigger premium on that in my later years than I probably did in my earlier years.

During the recession, I knew I couldn't always control the "outputs," but I knew I could control the "inputs." As long as I was behaving well vis-à-vis the market, my people, and myself, like keeping myself healthy, I knew I would figure it out.

Getting through the recession is one of the hardest things I've ever done, but also one of the things of which I'm proudest. I look at what came of it. We continued to build our firm, opened our New York office, developed a significant body of research, and wrote a book.

Ghaffari: What were some of the key initial strategy decisions you made?

Ferracone: The name of the company, Farient, is a made-up word that combines f-a-r, which is my initials backwards, together with "ient," which sounded sort of scientific and intelligent. We liked the feel of it. It was unique enough so that we could get the domain name. We went through many names before we came up with that one.

I decided to start a business that wasn't about me. It was Farient, not my name. A lot of people in this field name the business after themselves, not a generic name. I chose a different name on purpose because I wanted the business to be more than me. The problem is that most of the business comes back to me and through me as the point person. While I wanted to be out of the limelight, I'm sort of back in it. That's why I hired a senior cadre of people to take up the charge. I also decided to create a clear mission and focus in our business and our marketplace. Our mission has guided us throughout.

Ghaffari: How do you design longer-term strategies?

Ferracone: I design long-term strategies with my partners, but I retain veto power. I founded Farient. I'm the sole owner and financier. I've brought in partners and given then "phantom ownership," but the control is with me. I chose that because of the SCA situation and because I really wanted to control the quality and integrity of what we're doing in the governance marketplace, which is delicate to navigate.

Will I always need to retain control of the business? I don't know. I've learned too much to know that you can't plan everything. So you do the best you can with the information you have and where you are at that point in time. It doesn't mean it can't change.

Ghaffari: What is your succession planning strategy?

Ferracone: When I started Farient, I was not going to run it. I was going to just sponsor it like Peter Mullin sponsored SCA. That didn't work out because I couldn't find anyone willing to take the risk. I ended up just running it myself. I would love to find a successor at some point. I have a cadre of four good senior partners and a CFO, some of whom might be candidates to run this some day. I don't know. I'll decide on my exit when the time comes.

I'm deeply steeped in this. I have a format that works right now. I know I'll invent it when I need to. I think I'll figure it out when the time comes because to try to plan for it too much probably is not worth it. I'm not planning an exit at this juncture.

Ghaffari: How do you manage senior managers and key partners?

Ferracone: I've decided on a highly developmental approach—I have a coach who works with me and all of my people—that takes people wherever they want to go. One person might want to emphasize building skills in business development. Another might want to build technical skills. And yet another might want to build writing skills. People get assignments and resources that help them realize their potential. We'll see where it goes.

Ghaffari: Do you find it easy to work with, or influence, key stakeholders?

Ferracone: Can other people do more of the business? Can I get leverage for the business? It's happening to various degrees—but it's not as complete as I would like. I want this business to outlast me. I don't want the business to fold up when I leave. A lot of founder-led places do that. I really want Farient to have a life of its own, where it goes on beyond me. And I want to leave a legacy of what this business is all about—that it stands for good governance, best-in-class consulting, great intellectual capital, and multiple revenue streams. We want to have some recurring revenue around both consulting services and products. That's what I would like to happen. That is very different from what it looked like at SCA.

Ghaffari: How do you define success?

Ferracone: I'm a pretty tough critic. I look at whether the business is highly profitable and growing, and whether it has a good reputation. To me, that's success in this business. If we're making money, then we can attract the best people, and pay them well.

But, I also want to feel good about the business, the clients, the work we're doing, the delivery system. Ultimate success is going to be me feeling good about how everyone else—the clients and our people—are doing in this business.

Ghaffari: What do you think are secrets to becoming a successful entrepreneurial business leader as a woman?

Ferracone: Women in my era were not on sports teams. There was no Title IX when I was growing up. I was more of an individual contributor and didn't cultivate a team mentality. Men have had that for a very long time. They call it "the old boys' club." You have men supporting men, talking in the locker room or going out for drinks or golf. Women do more of that now, in this environment.

My advice to women is to pay attention to forming relationships and mentorship. It's not just about getting the task done. It's about doing the work through and with people. It's important to put as much energy into that as it is to just get the job done. I did not do that as much in my career. It was something of a barrier for me. But I'm learning.

Ghaffari: What are your biggest achievements?

Ferracone: We grew SCA by having a better capability around the performance side of the executive compensation equation. I've continued that at Farient, but I've also invented new things here. I want people to think about innovation and pay for performance when they hear the name "Farient Advisors." That's what *Fair Pay* is about—the emphasis is on performance. I put performance ahead of pay in the title on purpose. The book is very practical—trying to differentiate ourselves in a very crowded market. It's a very fragmented business and very competitive. It's tough to break through all the noise. I think we are succeeding.

Ghaffari: How do you define your position as a "leader?"

Ferracone: As a leader, one has to have vision, courage, follow-through and compassion. I have vision as a thought leader in our industry and in seeing the possibilities of what our firm can be and the role it can play. Sometimes that takes courage because it requires me to be unconventional—to think unconventionally. In addition, I need to make investment decisions for the future in order to back that vision and execute against it. That also takes courage. Finally, I think a good leader, at least one in consulting who hires knowledge workers, operates a sort of upside-down pyramid. I need to be there to support others—give them the tools, processes, and environment they need to realize their potential on behalf of our clients. It also requires me to have compassion so that I can be attuned to their needs.

Ghaffari: Has your family been behind you? How do you manage family expectations or commitments?

Ferracone: My parents have been extremely supportive of me. My dad was his own tough taskmaster. I got a great deal of drive and competitive verve from him. My mother was extremely supportive and always told me I could do anything I set my mind to. Those were the people who continued to give me strength throughout my early background and career.

I have a wonderful husband, four great step-children, and two "feline" children. My step-kids range in ages from twenty-two to thirty-two years old. My husband, Stewart Smith, manages investments—the family office—for his family. He is very involved in philanthropy and gives generously of his time, skill, and money.

Ghaffari: Do you find it easy to balance work and the rest of your life?

Ferracone: I don't see it as work-life balance. I see it as successfully blending work-life priorities. I work extremely hard and a lot of hours. The entrepreneurial thing kind of lends itself to this. It has no boundaries. There is always more that can be done. My husband has been very good at helping to set priorities and does it in a way that preserves our relationship without destroying my entrepreneurial verve. He knows when to let me loose and just let it roll, and when to reign me in, saying, "Hey this is getting dysfunctional." He's very supportive.

For example, when I wrote the book, I knew I would go through some very tough, manic phases. Toward the end, I warned him, "You're not going to see me for six weeks. I'm going to be writing my book as my priority." He just said, "Okay." It was just a deal we made. He's been very good at that. It hasn't been easy, but he's been terrific. Sometimes he feels as though I am not paying enough attention to him or giving him what he needs. I am more mindful of that now than I used to be.

The step-kid route has been terrific for me. I'm not their primary caregiver as their mother is, but I can be the career coach, provide another role model for them, and be their friend without having it conflict with what their mother wants. I'm very appreciative of my step-kids—they're really nice, and I like them all.

Ghaffari: Have you experienced any negative reactions? How did you deal with them?

Ferracone: In my first marriage, I experienced some similar themes. But, Stewart and I have been married now for fourteen years. He is great—a real keeper. Some of the same issues emerge, and I have to watch myself. You have to learn to watch out for the pitfalls and pay attention.

Ghaffari: What key advice would you give to other women?

Ferracone: My advice is to have self-awareness about what gives you energy, then do some homework around exploring pathways to follow in that regard. Sometimes I see women who are afraid to give up security to follow their dreams. But, to me, not taking risks means not growing. I encourage people to take some risks, to grow, and not be afraid of failure. Because when you do fail, you learn a lot. The question is, "Can you learn from that and take it forward?" Most things—successful and unsuccessful—have value to them. To frame it in those terms—as opposed to more traditional, linear terms—that's what I tell people to think about.

Ghaffari: What advice, especially, do you have for young women?

Ferracone: I just advised a young woman the other day about her career and opportunities. I listened to where she gets her energy. I think it's good if people have an awareness of where they get energy and what drains their energy. That's how they can follow their passions.

One young person I advised is in the financial services arena, but loves food and wants to shift to being in the restaurant business. She has a lot of good insight and self-awareness around that. She's doing research right now, and I'm helping her make contacts. How fast this happens and when it happens is open. But if she's purposeful about it and explores various career opportunities, she will find her next place that brings her joy, happiness, and energy.

Ghaffari: Would you give any different advice to men?

Ferracone: There's no advice that I would give to women that I wouldn't give to men.

Ghaffari: What do you see as the area of greatest opportunity for young women professionals?

Ferracone: There are many opportunities into which money will flow. Financial services is much more open to women than ever before. Traditionally, it's been a testosterone-laden industry, and still is to some extent, but the acceptance and prominence of women in the industry are much better than when I came out of business school. That's always a good business.

People are clamoring for women in the sciences areas. Harvey Mudd College really wants women students. All the science and engineering schools do. And organizations want women with a scientific bent. So, if you're at all interested in the sciences, following that passion is great. That path can take all kinds of twists and turns, from healthcare to environmental studies to business.

If you look at the economy, healthcare is growing because baby boomers are getting older and spending all of their remaining wealth on healthcare. And there are government mandates to do that. Clean energy is an alternative because we're ruining the planet.

Having a global perspective is extremely important, today. I have always traveled extensively. And the global brief or "portfolio" was a terrific asset for the Mercer job. I enjoyed it, and it was a great part of my arsenal. I understand global opportunities much more than having simply a local or US-centric perspective. It gets you out of your own backyard, both in terms of responsibilities and reach. Extensive travel is an important piece of this.

Ghaffari: Would you do anything differently if you were starting out today?

Ferracone: I sometimes wonder what may have happened had I not sold SCA. I may have reinvested in and grown the business. Other times, I wonder whether I should have gotten a degree in engineering, rather than management science and economics. There are more "what ifs" rather than deep regrets.

Ghaffari: Where do you see yourself in the next five to ten years? Any political or governmental or other leadership role for yourself in the future? Why? Or why not?

Ferracone: I went to the White House last year because Duke won the NCAA tournament. Obama wanted to congratulate the team, and the trustees were invited. I said, "This is the only time I've ever been invited to the White House. It may be the only time I ever will be invited to the White House." I'm not that politically correct. I speak my mind. I have a feeling that politics is not in my future.

Nevertheless, one of the people I've gotten to know better is Meg Whitman. She was my client when she ran eBay. I got to know her better and saw her in action during her campaign for governor of the State of California. There are women like her from whom I can learn. As a role model, I think she is outstanding.

Jaynie Studenmund has been another great role model and inspiration. She took a different path. She decided to become a mom and makes conscious compromises while working her way up the corporate ladder. She adapted her career to what she wanted out of her personal life and did it very successfully. I think this paradoxically put her on top. She now sits on a number of boards.

There's another woman named Georgia Nelson, who has a really interesting story. She was a secretary at Edison International. She was offered a challenge that nobody else would take on—to run a very difficult plant and turn it around. She successfully managed to accomplish that and eventually became one of the top executives at Edison. She ended up running a power generation division. Now she serves on a lot of boards. There are many women like that who are more than role models—they're inspirations.

Lise L. Luttgens

CEO, Girl Scouts of Greater Los Angeles

Born in 1953 in San Francisco, California.

Lise L. Luttgens *was appointed the first chief executive officer of the Girl Scouts of Greater Los Angeles (GSGLA) in December 2008. The GSGLA is the result of an historic merger of six legacy Los Angeles-area councils into a new organization, one of the largest in the nation, with an initial enrollment of over 41,000 girls and 24,000 adult members in a wide range of settings and programs.*

She founded and operated her own professional training and coaching consultancy, Luttgens & Associates, from 2005 to 2008. During that time, she also served as interim CEO of the Ronald McDonald House Charities of Southern California, helping to unify six entities into a single organization.

As the COO of Fulfillment Fund (a nonprofit college access organization) from 2003 to 2005, she established business systems and processes, and realigned operations and the financial structure to serve students in the LA Unified School District.

In her almost 30 years as a hospital administrator, Ms. Luttgens served as senior vice president and chief operating officer at Children's Hospital Los Angeles (CHLA); CEO of the Doheny Eye Hospital and COO of the Doheny Eye Institute at the University of Southern California (USC) Keck School of Medicine; and associate director of the University of California at Los Angeles (UCLA) Medical Center.

Ms. Luttgens received a bachelor's degree in psychology from Beloit College, a master's degree in public health (with an emphasis in hospital administration) from Yale University's School of Medicine, and an advanced fellowship in academic medical center administration from the University of Michigan. She completed the

Executive Management Program from the UCLA Anderson School of Management and received certification from the College of Executive Coaching.

A Girl Scout while growing up in San Francisco, Ms. Luttgens brings to all of her leadership positions an enthusiasm that draws upon her deep reservoir of opportunities seen and experienced during Girl Scouts. She brings a true business compass to all of her roles in the nonprofit world. Her inclusive leadership style persuades, with grace, medical titans to work through the challenges of administering healthcare facilities in service to men, women, and children.

Elizabeth Ghaffari: You've had quite an extensive education—Beloit, public health at Yale School of Medicine, advanced fellowship at University of Michigan, UCLA certificate in management, and then a certification in coaching. Tell me about the choices behind your education. Why did you go all the way to Wisconsin?

Lise Luttgens: I was slightly impatient in my youth. I graduated from high school as a junior—a year earlier than expected. I was accepted at Pitzer College in Claremont, California, and actually only stayed there for two years before moving to the Banff School of Fine Arts in Canada for one summer, thinking I might want to pursue an acting career.

I knew I needed a liberal arts degree, so I next chose Beloit College in Wisconsin, in large part, because I had never been out of the West. I wanted some experience outside of California—felt that some diversity would be good. My family is now a fourth-generation California family. Not everyone in the world does things the way they're done in San Francisco.

I think I was just restless. By the time I landed somewhere, I was looking ahead and asking myself, "Where am I going to go next?" But I've since learned to sit still—I stayed in one job for twelve years. Back in those days, I was young, ambitious, and had a lot of pent-up energy. To their credit, my parents allowed me to pursue my dreams in my way. They were very supportive and allowed me to find my own set point—my own "true north"— even though they could imagine some of the mistakes I could make along the way. I'm really grateful for that support.

I did make some mistakes along the way. Transferring to multiple schools as an undergraduate is not a recommended way of putting down roots, learning a routine, establishing yourself and making lifelong friends. Although I managed to have a few of those—my roommate from Pitzer and a classmate from my senior year abroad at Beloit both are still very dear friends. I see them regularly, now almost forty years later. I have a good network because

I like to stay in touch with people who have made a difference in my life. I've learned how to be resilient, adaptable, and flexible. Then again, when my own daughter was ready to go to college, I made it extremely clear that I felt it was important that she choose a school and stay with it for four years, regardless of whether she was happy or not in the first semester.

My education really is the reason I've been able to have such a strong career trajectory. I was fortunate to enter into a career at a time where people, women especially, could move up very quickly.

I knew, early on, that I wanted to work in hospital administration. After I graduated from college, I did some pretty extensive interviewing of leaders—community leaders, both men and women—because I wanted to get my arms around where I could fit well, where I could be of service, where I could be happy, productive, and sustain a lifelong career. I was trying to decide between a position in a university setting or in a hospital setting—I felt that both options were very attractive as microcosms of the way the world works.

Ghaffari: It seems like you have this pattern of interviewing people. How did you figure that out?

Luttgens: When I came back to San Francisco—after my undergraduate work at Beloit and working in London for seven months—I found myself in the same situation as most young people back then. I had a liberal arts education and a bachelor's in psychology. I'd done some work in communications—engineering and operations at a public broadcasting television station. But, I had no clue what I wanted to do. I had just turned twenty-one years old. It was important to me to take some time after graduating from college.

I was fortunate in that my mother, Leslie Luttgens, was an active community leader and board leader in many organizations in the Bay Area. She encouraged me to think deeply about where I could find a space for myself in the world. She opened doors for me by putting me in touch with some of her colleagues and contacts. I was fortunate to be able to interview key leaders in San Francisco who had an association with her through her community and board work. I asked questions about how they got to their positions, gathered information about what inspired them, and listened to their advice. That experience is a model that I use to this day—to seek input, ask for counsel, and be open and receptive to whatever people have to offer about their opinions or passions.

Ghaffari: Tell me a little about your family.

Luttgens: I am an only child. My father was a physician—a hematologist—in private practice in San Francisco. He died in 1982 after a long bout with Parkinson's disease.

The whole time that my father was in private practice, my mother was working as well as parenting. She was always very involved in the community. I'm aware that she played roles of being a great mother and being active outside our home, which in those days was different from many of my friends. I had no idea what she did. And it really wasn't until I became an executive that I developed an appreciation for how extraordinary it was to have that kind of role model. She was one of the first women invited to serve on public company boards in addition to her extensive charity and community work.[1]

Ghaffari: Tell me about your first job and how important it was.

Luttgens: My first real job after college was working at Presbyterian Hospital at the Pacific Medical Center [PMC] in San Francisco. I was the assistant to the director of the Department of Education and Ancillary Services, basically a staff role supporting the director. It was a clerical, secretarial, and administrative role. I worked for a very enlightened woman, Dr. Sandra Hellman. She shared her responsibilities as director with me and allowed me to stretch in my function as her assistant. She was well ahead of her time, treating me more than just an hourly employee.

I did a lot of hard work and moved quickly into all of the realms in which she worked, learning as much as I could about how a hospital functions. We provided education for house staff, interns, and residents—continuing medical education, nursing, in-service, and management training. As she moved up in the organization, so did I. She was a role model as a respected woman in leadership with an advanced degree in public health. She was tough, but fair. She worked very hard and expected me to do so as well.

Ghaffari: She was one of your first mentors?

Luttgens: Ironically, once I was on that job, my first real mentor was the chief operating officer, Frederick C. Meyer. He took an interest in many of the front-line staff and really went out of his way to encourage me, talking with me from time to time about my career interests.

---

[1] Leslie Luttgens, "Organizational Aspects of Philanthropy: San Francisco Bay Area, 1948–1988 in the History of Bay Area Philanthropy Project, Oral History Transcripts of Interviews Conducted by Gabrielle Morris," http://www.archive.org/stream/organizphilanthr00luttrich/organizphilanthr00luttrich_djvu.txt

He nudged me to go back to graduate school, probably a little bit before I felt ready. I credit him with encouraging me to think big, to be ambitious, and to look for the strongest graduate program possible, and then excel in it.

Fred said, "It's time for you to go back to graduate school, and I don't think it will serve you well to go into a part-time public health program and keep working here." I had planned go to UC Berkeley while continuing to work full-time at PMC. He said, "No. I think you should go back to a full-time graduate program, immerse yourself as a student, and really take a deep dive in. And I think you can go anywhere you set your mind to." Together, we sent away—in those days everything was snail mail—for university catalogs, looking at everything that was being offered in hospital administration.

I interviewed with admissions officers and professors at Washington, Columbia, Harvard, Yale, University of Michigan, UC Berkeley, North Carolina, and Duke. I was very pleased to be accepted at Yale. Based on Fred's advice, I moved to New Haven, Connecticut, and was wildly happy for two years. In between my two academic years at Yale, I served as Fred's administrative resident at PMC, which was one of the highlights of my career.

Ghaffari: What was the Yale experience like?

Luttgens: There were twelve students in the hospital administration program. We all did well, but several of my classmates have become giants in the field. One in particular is Marna Parke Borgstrom. She and I studied together all the way through our two-year curriculum. She became the administrative resident at Yale New Haven Hospital right after graduate school, and today she is the CEO of Yale New Haven Medical Center. That is an example of the caliber of people that Yale was turning out during my era. We had the pick of positions and were able to rise rapidly.

I was fortunate to be allowed to do a joint curriculum with the School of Public Health and the School of Organization and Management—the then new business school at Yale. While I didn't get a formal degree from the latter, my master's thesis was jointly read by one faculty member from the School of Organization and Management and another from the Department of Epidemiology and Public Health, Yale School of Medicine. That was the first time that two readers from two different schools within Yale shared the responsibility for thesis-reading.

Ghaffari: Your thesis was on the role of HMOs in health education, and yet this was before federal HMO legislation had even been passed, is that right?

Luttgens: The National Health Planning and Resources Development Act of 1974 had recently been passed, and HMOs were just beginning to be created. There were two hundred prepaid group health plans in the country at that time. A friend from PMC had given my name to the Department of Education at Metropolitan Life Insurance Company because they wanted a student to find a way to create greater visibility for MetLife in the prepaid group health plan arena. Most prepaid group health plans—other than Kaiser-Permanente and Ross-Loos Medical Group in California—were brand new and just finding their way.

The hypothesis for my thesis drew upon my work in education at PMC— that the numbers and types of health education offerings provided in an HMO might be a predictor of size and future success. As it turns out, after doing t-tests and chi-squares for a year, I learned that there are no predictor variables—no regression analysis that aligns those characteristics.

But, in the process of gathering data, I talked to every single executive director or CEO of every prepaid group health plan—all two hundred of them. I really parlayed that into something. I got MetLife to agree to publish the findings and give me credit as the author. They let me hire some first-year graduate students to compile and analyze the interview data under my supervision. We put together this great publication, which MetLife then published and distributed widely.

Unfortunately, just several weeks before graduation from Yale, I was contacted by my primary thesis reader who expressed concern that my work was being published by MetLife. Unbeknownst to me, there was an academic requirement that any thesis material belonged to the department, not the individual student.

Ghaffari: What did you do?

Luttgens: Fortunately, my second thesis reader was from a department in another school at Yale—Organization and Management. I was able to have that professor petition on my behalf. At the last minute, my thesis was approved, and I was able to graduate.

I seem to live on the edge all the time. I've been a risk-taker from the beginning, and this situation was just another example. The thesis itself—learning research methods—wasn't as important as the two more practical lessons learned. First, the interview process exposed me to a wide spectrum of "real world" thought on an important and contemporary subject. Second, I learned how to negotiate within a traditional system that had "always done it this way," and get a solution that kept our focus on doing the right thing.

Ghaffari: Would you say that this taught you how to get yourself out of such quagmires?

Luttgens: Yes, you're going to hear me say this over and over again. Be inclusive. As a servant leader, always share power, information, and build a platform with your stakeholders so that everyone can see and understand the same points of view. I believe the role of leadership is to get everyone in the same boat. Once they're all in the boat, my role is to get everyone rowing in the same direction.

It's a major theme that keeps coming up throughout my career. Another important theme that you've already touched on is that I've always bucked the system a bit. For some reason, I always find myself in these situations where change is required to move forward. I don't think I've ever been in a real leadership job that has *not* required pretty intense change management.

When I was associate director of UCLA Medical Center, where I worked for almost twelve years, one of the executives paid tribute to me at my going-away party by saying, "You know, Lise always took the assignments that we didn't want to take on. She oversaw departments that needed oversight and turnaround, and she enjoyed helping make them better."

I never really set out to be that way. It's just what resonates with me—when you are dropped into the whitewater, you just figure out how to navigate down the rapids. My résumé says, "Special expertise in leading organizations in transition. Key accomplishments in turnarounds, restructuring, team building, and in inspiring stretch goals and results." I really just like to do that.

Ghaffari: Tell me about your transition through the fellowship at Michigan.

Luttgens: The University of Michigan, Ann Arbor, fellowship in the academic medical center administration was very highly sought-after. There just weren't a lot of fellowships in hospital administration back in the seventies, and this particular fellowship was the only one in the country that specialized in academic medical centers—organizations that were teaching hospitals in a medical school setting.

It was a working fellowship where I spent the first year reporting to the hospital CEO and the second year working for the dean of the School of Medicine. I got to see the same issues from two very different perspectives. Deans and hospital CEOs seldom see eye to eye—and Michigan, at the time, was no exception.

By working in the hospital the first year on projects and staffing committees, I was able to build a trusted relationship with the hospital and executive staff. The second year, I had to sever all my ties to the hospital staff and move into the School of Medicine. Being a non-MD in a school of medicine administration was very unusual. It was a unique and remarkable experience—truly one of the highlights of my career. I'm still in touch with three of the executives from there.

Ghaffari: Why do you think that you have this ability to jump in and morph? Where does that come from?

Luttgens: I believe I'm seen as trustworthy. I try to act in a responsible and accountable manner. I see the good in people until they give me a reason not to. That's served me well in every job I've had because people tend not to be guarded with me. They know I will hold those confidences, be discreet, and use their input for the good of the organization rather than for my own personal benefit. I try to be mindful and intentional about putting the organization's best interests first, always.

Ghaffari: What brought you to UCLA in Southern California?

Luttgens: When my father was diagnosed with Parkinson's disease, I wanted to be back on the West Coast, where I could be involved with his care. As an only child, I felt the responsibility of helping my mother with this, so I looked at opportunities in every academic medical center in California.

I was offered a staff job in strategic planning at Stanford Medical Center, but about a week after having accepted that job, I met Dr. Raymond Schultze, the newly appointed CEO of the UCLA Medical Center, a physician and associate dean of the School of Medicine. Dr. Schultze was looking to build an executive team that could understand the integration between the School of Medicine and the hospital. I'd just completed my fellowship in academic medical center administration in Ann Arbor. He convinced me to take a step back from the job I was going to accept at Stanford, which proved to be the right decision for me.

Ghaffari: How do you think he heard about you?

Luttgens: All the hospital CEOs of the UC system met monthly and talked. I'd sent out my résumé to all of them. My name came up when they were comparing notes about their staffing decisions. Dr. Schultze called me, saying, "I'd like to take you to lunch."

Literally, by the end of the lunch, I agreed to go work for him. I started as Dr. Schultze's staff assistant, where he gave me great latitude, just as Dr. Hellman had at PMC. I then moved into line roles, first as an assistant director and associate director, picking up more responsibility as I went. I played a staff role for two years, then—in 1983—decided that the action in hospitals was on the line, and I wanted to move there.

Ghaffari: Has your family been supportive of your moves?

Luttgens: My family in San Francisco was very supportive, even though I was in Southern California. Remember, my father was a physician and had a faculty appointment at UCSF, so he understood my passion for this work. In 1984, I married a pediatric cardiologist who was practicing in Philadelphia. He moved across the country so my career could continue to progress at UCLA, which is about as supportive as it gets!

Ghaffari: What have been some of the key work challenges that you faced?

Luttgens: Dr. Schultze knew that I was looking back East, and he came to me and said, "What could I do to keep you?" I told him, "You can give me a line role," and he did. They gave me more and more responsibility. Later on, I learned that I was given the departments that other members of the team felt were challenging. Some of the really tough departments were headed by physician leaders in the School of Medicine. Most physician leaders don't see hospital administrators as their equal, so we had to work that out.

Ghaffari: How did you do that?

Luttgens: By doing what I always do. By showing up, telling the truth, being trustworthy, giving people the benefit of the doubt and aligning with them until they gave me reason not to. Trying to do the best for them. My whole academic and personal upbringing was working with physicians. So I don't view physicians as the enemy. It just doesn't make good business sense.

Ghaffari: How many departments did you end up having under you?

Luttgens: I had a total of ten professional services departments. Most of them were physician-led or physician-supported.

Ghaffari: What was your performance metric that you did for them?

Luttgens: Back in those days, the early eighties, we didn't have quality management or outcomes as we do today. You needed to control expenses, enhance revenue, increase patient volume, and get along.

I was well-known around the medical center for getting substantial capital funding for items in my capital budgets each year. Most of my departments were very capital-intensive. The radiology department needed MRIs and CTs. Radiation oncology needed linear accelerators and stereotactic brain irradiation devices. The anesthesia department needed several different machines each year. We're talking about multiple, multiple millions of dollars. I became very good at capital budgeting.

Sometimes as a leader, you can't really pinpoint how you are doing—you might have a feeling, but you just don't know for sure. So, you have to have systems and processes in place to take some of the subjectivity out of the equation. There was one instance where I knew something in the department wasn't right, but I just couldn't pinpoint it. Eventually there was an internal audit, and the problem was uncovered, but it had reached a pretty significant point.

Ghaffari: Can you give some insight as to the key turning points or critical challenges you faced as a leader?

Luttgens: One key turning point was leaving my comfort zone at UCLA in 1991 after almost twelve years of being something of a "golden girl." I'd been around for a while, had earned the respect of the faculty and of the staff, and had benefitted from getting some protection from the CEO. I was getting impatient to move up, but the two people above me in the organization weren't going anywhere any time soon.

One of the smartest things that I did in the first fifteen years of my career was move up quickly, early. It was the time, in the seventies and eighties, when there were a lot of opportunities, particularly for women. You were rewarded if you were smart, accountable, worked hard, were trustworthy, and got the job done. I think that today, young people don't have the same opportunity to do that—there just aren't the wide-open career paths that we had available to us.

I never felt I was treated or compensated differently as a woman. I wasn't—I don't have that experience or point of view. Maybe that was other people's realities, but not mine.

Most of my mentors were male. I've talked about Fred Meyer and Ray Schultze. I had a marvelous mentor at the University of Michigan, Dr. Jeptha Dalston, who taught me a lot about integrity and how to reach solutions with key stakeholders. He had worked in politics in Oklahoma, and led turnarounds in many healthcare organizations that had complicated politics.

Jep gave me a speech on my first day of my fellowship. He said, "You work for this organization and don't ever put yourself in a position where your integrity is called into question. Never take office supplies home. Don't make long-distance phone calls from your office phone. Don't make personal copies on the duplication equipment. At some time, someone will see you do that and make assumptions about your character."

I've never forgotten this advice, and it's served me well thirty-five years later.

Ghaffari: What made you decide to go to the business administration executive education program?

Luttgens: I didn't have enough finance in any of the education that I'd had. I intentionally avoided anything quantitative for most of my educational career other than biostatistics in epidemiology. I knew I wasn't going to be able to get ahead if I didn't have more finance, so Dr. Schultze sent me back to the UCLA Anderson School of Management. It was a great time.

My daughter was a one-year-old at the time, and we had my two stepsons living with us while we were both working more than full-time. I'm not sure how I made it through that business program. I met some really interesting people in that class, and got a number of new skills, including enough finance to get by, although it is still not my strongest suit.

Wherever I've gone, I've always made a point to hiring a very strong CFO who understands what I'm good at and what she needs to help me with. I'm a fantastic budgeter and love thinking about ways of using resources more wisely. But I'm not technical, as any of my CFO partners would be quick to tell you. I know two CFOs, one who is still at Children's Hospital, the other one worked with me at the Fulfillment Fund. I might send them an e-mail saying, "Could you please help us out with this?" They'd always get extra Girl Scout cookies—they love Girl Scouts cookies.

Ghaffari: How did you get the job at Doheny?

Luttgens: After more than eleven years at UCLA, I was contacted by an executive recruiter, Jack Schlosser, whom I trust and respect, to look at a job on the USC Health Science Campus. My first reaction was, "Why would I want to leave a job I'm doing well with to go to a smaller place across town?"

He said, "Lise, think of Doheny as off-Broadway. You're going to have a big role in an organization that's growing." The CEO of the Doheny Eye Institute was Dr. Steven J. Ryan, who was also the dean of the School of Medicine. He was a very high-powered, impressive, and inspirational leader who taught me a lot.

As the COO of the Institute, I was responsible for the day-to-day operations of a medical group, a research institute, a department of ophthalmology and a small teaching hospital. Once again, I had chosen a role that built on my background in academic medical center administration, tapping an understanding of how these component parts work together.

Those were rough times. I had to close the hospital because it really didn't have a sufficient patient base with an average daily census of just 1.2 patients. We collectively decided that there was no way to provide a twenty-five bed accredited hospital with the support it needed, and we knew we'd have operating losses draining our financial stability. We re-leased the space to the USC Health Sciences campus and entered into a long-term, ten-year lease with Tenet Healthcare to take over the hospital and the operating rooms. Dismantling that structure was challenging.

Ghaffari: Did any of these activities keep you up at night?

Luttgens: Well, at the time I was at Doheny, I was getting a divorce, and it was very, very difficult for me. It felt like a large tidal wave to balance the responsibilities of closing a hospital, laying off staff, negotiating legal agreements with other entities at the same time I was dismantling my marriage and family. It gave me a lot to think about, all the time, and I learned a lot about personal and professional fortitude. I can't think of any other time that required such difficult decisions.

Shortly after we closed the Doheny Eye Hospital, I was approached by the new CEO of Children's Hospital Los Angeles. I was chairing a consortium of all the hospital CEOs associated with Keck. There were five at the time— Norris, the USC Tenet hospital, Doheny, CHLA, and the big LAC+USC county hospital. I chaired this group of hospital CEOs, all male, mostly older, and pretty "command and control" oriented. Totally unbeknownst to me, these gentlemen recommended that Walter "Bill" Noce, the new CEO of CHLA, get to know me to see if I'd fit on his team.

I had invited him to lunch to welcome him to the new group. By the end of lunch, he said, "So, I'd like you to come work for me as my new COO." It was déjà vu from my lunch with Dr. Schultze fifteen years earlier. That move turned out to be six of the most wonderful and fulfilling years of my life.

Ghaffari: What were some of the principal challenges you faced during the time at Children's Hospital?

Luttgens: Building trust between the administration and the medical staff. Bill was new at that time to academic medical centers. He recruited me to "warm the place up." We were a really good team, and the overall leadership team was outstanding during Bill's tenure.

I forged strong relationships with the medical staff and helped create a collaborative culture. I recruited some strong leaders, including someone to tackle the ambulatory care issue and someone to lead the Cancer Center of Excellence. There were several physicians who historically had not trusted the administration, but who respected me. One was the medical director of the cancer center. After I left Children's Hospital, he got me on the board of the LA Ronald McDonald House and later hired me as the interim CEO of Ronald McDonald House Charities of Southern California, where he was the chairman of the board.

Ghaffari: Do you see yourself as bouncing from CEO to CEO in a way?

Luttgens: Not at all. I view it that I've been very blessed. Right about the time that I'm at the end of something, before even I know that I'm at the end of it, the universe just sort of shows up and says, "Well, we've got this need over here."

The Girl Scouts of Greater Los Angeles had to merge six small councils, some of them with multi-million-dollar budgets. Together, we now have a $15 million operating budget. There were also six different cultures we had to merge, which is exactly what I did at Ronald McDonald House Charities. I took six different houses and put them together under one umbrella 501(c)(3).

Ghaffari: Do you consider yourself a merger and acquisition specialist?

Luttgens: No, I'm a generalist, but I've taken organizations, moved them around, put in systems, processes, and quality management. There were no mergers at UCLA, Doheny, CHLA, or the Fulfillment Fund. Doheny was the opposite of a merger—an unbundling. So I don't really see myself as a mergers and acquisitions specialist. I do think I'm a change management leader and someone who can influence organizations in transition.

Ghaffari: Would you describe your network as people you've seen prove themselves?

Luttgens: Sure. These are people who have expertise and who are respected in their field. And they also are people with whom I have a personal relationship. There are a lot of people who are respected in the field, but they're not approachable or accessible, or there's no reciprocity. In general, I try to give as much as I take and be responsive to those who ask for my help.

Ghaffari: As you look at your network, would you say there is a greater percentage of men or women?

Luttgens: My personal network happens to include a lot of women, in large part because I've grown up in a professional environment where I've always been fortunate to have really smart, ambitious, courageous, competent—beyond competent—women around. I don't really think I consider gender in my network. Here at the Girl Scouts, my executive team is all women, but we have some very capable men on our senior management team as well.

Ghaffari: Do you think if you had been in the business world, you could do the same kind of thing?

Luttgens: I do consider myself in the business world—the nonprofit business world. Anyone who is running a nonprofit in this day and age, who isn't running it as a business, isn't going to have a nonprofit a few years from now. I think that everybody has some blind sides where they need to tap outside advice.

Ghaffari: Why did you transition into forming your own company?

Luttgens: Bill Noce—the CEO at CHLA—was one of the people who in-fluenced me the most. He was looking for his own successor, but that wasn't going to be me. It wasn't what I wanted, and I wasn't a good fit to take over his role. Bill started succession planning in 2001, although he didn't intend to leave until 2007 when the replacement hospital project was completed. That meant six more years of being groomed during a time when I had family re-sponsibilities for a pre-teen daughter.

I was, by then, a single parent. You sometimes ask yourself, "What was your moment of truth?" My moment of truth was in 2001. I looked at my twelve-year-old daughter and said to myself, "I can spend the next six years climb-ing this ladder and furthering my career—then Kate will go to college, and I won't really know her. I will have no foundation of influence. I will have to look back and say, 'I could have, I should have, and I didn't.'"

That was the hardest—and the easiest—decision I've ever had to make. The hardest was preparing and wrestling with the decision. Once I knew I had to leave, I was phenomenally relieved. And Bill worked with me on a transition that allowed me to move forward. I announced I was leaving in June of 2001.

CHLA had had a long history of administrative instability. When Bill as-sumed his CEO role and recruited me, that six-year run was one of the lon-gest periods of stability Children's Hospital had experienced in years. The staff finally was enjoying that stability. The physicians were enjoying a good relationship with our administration. It was truly a marvelous time in the life of the hospital. We celebrated the one hundredth anniversary, so people were feeling very bullish about their future. When I announced I was leaving, they were concerned that it might mean the end of an era.

Bill put a lot of energy and trust into supporting me as a leader, and here I was walking away without really knowing what I was going to do next—other than to be a mom. So, there were a couple of months of disappoint-ment and anger. My going-away party was scheduled for October 11, 2001. And then 9/11 happened.

In that brief period of time, between September 11 and October 11, every-body in the hospital had a chance to process the idea that, if this was your last day on Earth, what would you do? Everybody began to understand the meaning of "carpe diem"—to seize the moment and the balance between family and profession. Many people have told me personal stories since then, how their point of view changed dramatically after 9/11. My own deci-sion was made before 9/11, but people in the organization began to realize how that event changed everything, dramatically.

I made a decision to take my daughter out of school on October 11 for my going-away party on the front lawn of Children's Hospital. There were hundreds of people there. My twelve-year-old daughter (unbeknownst to me) had contacted the mistress of ceremonies and asked if she could say a few words. She got up and stood behind the podium and said, "You have had my mommy for the last six years. It's time for me to have some time with her. It's time for you to give her back to me."

There really wasn't a dry eye in the house. So many people contacted me later and said, "Now we get it." It was a combination of things—an "aha!" epiphany after 9/11, and people seeing a twelve-year-old in action saying, "I really need my mom." And let's face it—it *is* a children's hospital. The people that work there really understand the importance of family.

Ghaffari: Was there anything that you could have put in place for the organization to make that transition easier?

Luttgens: I did an extensive formal transition plan for Bill, saying, "I have an amazing executive team. This person can take on more responsibility. This person should report to that person. These are the issues in each department that will need to be addressed in this manner."

I've never left a job without preparing a written transition plan. I did that for UCLA, Doheny, CHLA, and the Fulfillment Fund. I've always had a person in place to step in if the CEO wanted it. I have never left an organization unprepared for their future.

Ghaffari: Forming your own company let you manage your life on your terms?

Luttgens: I formed Luttgens & Associates as an LLC—a limited liability corporation. It was a great opportunity to be on my own, to be my own boss, and to have a lot of flexibility in terms of my time. It came at a great time in my family's life, too—right when my daughter and I were traveling all over the country looking at colleges. I don't know how many frequent-flier miles we racked up that year.

We wound up visiting thirty-two potential schools—probably a record for any parent and college-bound student! But, we did that because I didn't want to make the same mistake with Kate that I did with myself, bouncing around as I did. I was very clear about it. Kate was accepted as an early-decision candidate. She has just graduated with distinction from Colorado College in Colorado Springs, which was the thirty-first college campus we visited. She's as happy as a clam. All that research and input proved to be a good return on investment.

Ghaffari: How does Kate view this attention to detail in her life?

Luttgens: She shares the same view—we both have lot of attention to detail and like to be prepared. All three generations of women in my family are pretty assiduous at options analysis.

Ghaffari: How did the Ronald McDonald job fit in with your Luttgens & Associates role?

Luttgens: I was a paid consultant and interim CEO to Ronald McDonald House Charities of Southern California. It quickly turned into a long-term, full-time assignment. I always wanted the opportunity to run my own business, to choose my own clients, to be able to say and do what I wanted to say and do. Up to then, I had been a COO, always responsible to a CEO. I wanted to be the CEO. The timing was just never right. So, running my own business and being the principal really gave me the opportunity and confidence to lead differently. Luttgens & Associates served me well in preparing me to take on the CEO role at Girl Scouts of Greater LA.

When I took the job at the Girl Scouts, one area of mutual agreement was that I would sideline my consulting business. This was an easy decision, given the effort it took to get the new council off the ground. It is still a pretty big job.

Ghaffari: Was your assignment at the Fulfillment Fund similar to your Ronald McDonald consulting role?

Luttgens: No, they were very different. The Fulfillment Fund is a nonprofit youth development organization, and I was brought on as their first COO. I was recruited to establish some business systems and processes. Once I did the job that needed to be done—I was there for two years—there wasn't anything more for me there.

Ghaffari: How significant was the Girl Scout's merger of six area councils, and how do you view the consolidation?

Luttgens: Girl Scouts of the USA—GSUSA—began realignment at a national level several years before LA actually merged as part of a national core business strategy. There had been almost four hundred Girl Scout councils around the country, and the goal was to create fewer, stronger, and more "high performance" councils. Now, we have a total of one hundred and twelve councils nationally.

The Girl Scouts of yesteryear are nothing like the Girl Scouts of today or tomorrow. My elevator speech is, "Girl Scouts is so much more than cookies, camping, and crafts. We build opportunities for leadership development, life skills, and community service." The compelling reason to take this job was the challenge of merging six different cultures into one unified council, creating one unified board, one leadership team, and one set of business practices. Taken together, these challenges hit all of my hot buttons. And it really has turned out to be the perfect job in a wonderful organization with strong, mission-driven goals.

Ghaffari: Initially, you resisted the offer for some time, right?

Luttgens: Yes, I was very happy running my own company. I told the search committee, "Why would I want to put on Spanx every day, drive through rush-hour traffic, and report to a board when I could be sitting at home wearing my headset in my pajamas, coaching a client?"

I worked hard and had inspiring coaching clients and wonderful coaching engagements. I lived a pretty flexible life and called the shots. If I didn't want to take a client, I didn't.

Then in April 2008, a very prescient friend of mine, Susan Leary, had just left the Fulfillment Fund as their CFO. She's now chief administrative officer of First Congregational Church in Los Angeles. We went out to breakfast at Shutters Restaurant where, she said, "I really think you should look at this job. I don't think there's anyone else who could do it as well as you can. You have the chops for some of the difficult challenges we will face. Furthermore, are you aware that there's probably going to be a recession? Coaching and consulting probably will be one of the first things that corporations lop off their budget. And, add up how much time you're spending volunteering with Ronald McDonald House and your church." And I realized she was right. It was about thirty-two hours a week.

I'd been contacted four times, and responded each time saying, "I'm not interested. I'm happy where I am." After breakfast with Susan, I called the search firm back. I asked if the position had been filled yet. They said they were sending candidates to their client. I asked if they would still be interested in me. They said they really would.

Ghaffari: For the Girl Scouts of Greater Los Angeles, are you following a script you've been given or are you searching out opportunities on your own initiative?

Luttgens: That's a big question. Before the merger, there was a concern nationally that membership was declining. That was one of the motivating factors behind the national realignment initiative and the national CEO's focus on creating a contemporary core business strategy that focused centrally on girls as leaders. We had lots of smaller councils around the country that didn't have the resources or market position necessary to lead a large high-performance, high-capacity organization. They were competing for the same fundraising dollars, and the public support was not as strong as it needed to be. There has historically been an over-reliance on revenue from our cookie program.

After we merged, we created a critical mass. We now serve more than forty-one thousand girls in partnership with more than twenty-four thousand adult members who are the conduit for delivering service to these girls. We have almost three thousand troops in our jurisdiction. Our current operating budget is now $15 million. We now have one hundred and fifty FTEs[2] and are growing.

We have identified five focus areas for our programs: environment/outdoor adventure, arts and culture, wellness and healthy living, STEM—science, technology, engineering and math—and business smarts. Doing this work in our first six months after the merger allowed us to consolidate and create some three hundred council-led activities while assuring the countless activities continue at the troop-level.

Ghaffari: What's the smartest thing you ever did?

Luttgens: Certainly, taking this job. It has built upon every strength—and mistake—I've ever experienced in my career. There was no playbook or script for this job, and I've loved being able just to use my instincts about people, programs, and culture to get to this place. Of course, it's not just about me. I have an incredible team and board of directors, and our volunteers are the most dedicated I've ever experienced.

Ghaffari: Has it been an easy process?

Luttgens: It was very fluid at the start. I moved every key executive from a legacy council [those that were being merged] who wanted to stay with the Girl Scouts, into a role on my new executive team with an understanding that they'd have eighteen months to prove themselves. There were six key executives—some were CEOs, others were COOs, one was a director of development, plus one executive whom I recruited from outside the merged councils.

I locked everyone in a room at the City Club for two days. We built our organizational structure from scratch. We had flipcharts, we had yellow sticky-tabs. We created the framework for what this new council might look like based on the experiences and vision of these six key people.

---

[2] Full-time equivalents.

We tried to figure out how many FTEs we needed to have without overstaffing, since we knew there was some redundancy. We had six CFOs, but no human resources director. We knew we needed to integrate all the service delivery functions—membership recruitment and retention, volunteer liaisons, and program staff—across the vast regions of our new council even though the communities were very different. There really was no model for us to follow because our catchment area—the Los Angeles market—is the most diverse girl market in the country. It is also challenging because we have three hundred and fifty different cultures and languages of girls and their families to work with. There is no one-size-fits-all approach because it's such a diverse area.

What we have learned through this realignment process is that we are not your mother's Girl Scouts—we are building the Girl Scouts of the future while honoring the strong history and tradition this organization represents. The predominant ethnic representation in Los Angeles is Hispanic. We have to develop Girl Scout programming that is sensitive and uniquely appealing to Latinas who do not have the Girl Scout tradition as part of their family experience or background. We are fortunate to have a new CEO at the national level, Anna Maria Chávez, who is a Latina.

Currently 25 percent of our girls receive some financial assistance to participate in Girl Scouting. That number will only grow as we broaden our membership to more girls in more underserved communities in LA. Girl Scouts is already the largest girl-serving organization nationally. Here in Greater Los Angeles, there are still too many girls who need us and will benefit by being part of the Girl Scout Movement.

Ghaffari: Do you see competition coming from special diversity sub-groups that market to girls based on their unique ethnic or cultural origins?

Luttgens: I don't view it as competition. I think that the Girl Scouts is the best-kept secret in town. Our challenge is to get the word out. We compete effectively when people understand what we do, how we do it, what is our promise and our winning proposition—how we help girls reach their full potential to become leaders and active citizens. For some girls, that might mean reaching their full capacity within their family, or in their neighborhood. For others, they will lead in their larger community, go to college, or become president of the United States.

If you look around at the women business leaders in Greater Los Angeles, I think you would be surprised at how many of them were Brownies or Girl Scouts. I am really excited to be able to use our one hundredth anniversary in 2012 to highlight some of these women and how their successes tie back to their Girl Scout experience. We will have our first GSGLA "Women of Distinction" event to gather these women together and connect them to one another.

The fact that so many of our Girl Scout alumnae are accomplished leaders in their fields is something to be really proud of. Every single female astronaut was a Girl Scout, and a large majority of women members of Congress were Girl Scouts. One of the key messages I want to get out is that if you *were* a Girl Scout, you *are* still a Girl Scout. Those lessons and experiences don't leave you. I've witnessed women saying this to me over and over again.

Our one hundredth anniversary is all year long in 2012. We kick it off on October 29, 2011 with the largest girl expo in the history of the country called "Girltopia." We will open that up to both Girl Scouts and non–Girl Scouts at the LA Convention Center to highlight our upcoming "Year of the Girl." It's patterned after Maria Shriver's Women's Conference in Long Beach.

Ghaffari: Was your mother's Girl Scouts competition to the "new" Girl Scouts?

Luttgens: When I first took this job with the Girl Scouts, the two questions people asked me most often were, "How do I get cookies?" and "Do you have to wear a uniform?" I always sort of goodheartedly lean into that and then talk about what we are doing to help girls become leaders. What I say is, "Let's talk about cookies—the mission of the cookies. Let's talk about the entrepreneurship that girls learn in selling this product and setting goals, making connections, following up with their customers, and finally deciding how to use that money for troop activities."

Another key enhancement moving the Girl Scout brand forward is the creation of the "Girl Scout Leadership Experience," which is a model where girls discover themselves, connect with others, and take action to make the world a better place. "Discover, Connect, and Take Action." Nationally, GSUSA has identified fifteen outcomes for this leadership model and each outcome has specific definitions for the girl, depending upon her age and development level.

It's both a branding challenge and also one of the reasons that we realigned as a Movement, so that we could create a voice. We're not doing Girltopia—the girl expo I mentioned earlier—just to open up something fabulous to girls. We're expecting a wide-scale collateral impact and influence all over Los Angeles, where people will say, "Oh, the Girl Scouts. I haven't thought about them as an option." And as they learn about us, they will see why we provide meaningful and relevant experiences for today's girl or young woman.

If you search YouTube, you'll see a marvelous clip about today's Girl Scouts entitled, "What Did You Do Today?," which illustrates the choices girls of today have in determining how they use their time. They can sit in front of a computer screen, go to the mall and text their friends, or they can be out in the world having unique experiences—kayaking, going to space camp, rock climbing, traveling to venues outside their community, volunteering in a wide variety of settings.

Girls today are so community-minded. Every year I become more and more impressed with the level of Bronze, Silver and Gold Award projects our girls undertake. They also are focused on how they're going to get to college and what they're going to bring to college.

I think the competition we face in attracting and retaining girls is the extraordinary pressure girls receive in our society, and the disassociation and disconnectedness that girls feel growing up. And if you look at the statistics, girls in Los Angeles face stunningly difficult social challenges to stay on course. Our job is to give them a safe environment with qualified leaders so they have alternatives to these challenges.

Ghaffari: Were there any major surprises that you encountered in your career?

Luttgens: The biggest surprise has been putting thirty years into a career in hospital administration and winding up as a nonprofit executive. I mean, some people can see the bridge between those two fields pretty easily, but I certainly didn't know this was where I was going to end up. While unanticipated, it was a delightful surprise.

I think probably the lesson that I learned is that when you trust the universe, trust the process, do a good job and keep your good reputation, then you can trust that you will wind up right where you need to be. You don't really need to worry. I'm fifty-eight and the older I get, the more I realize that when I worry about something in the future or I try to write the script and control too much, chances are that I get disappointed. Instead, when I am able to lean into some of the uncertainty or dive into the whitewater that comes up, things have a way of working out better than I'd planned.

Ghaffari: Do you feel that this has been an experience like whitewater rafting?

Luttgens: The work that I do feels a little like whitewater rafting sometimes. I've frequently been involved in turnarounds where you take a job without knowing what exactly you will encounter. You get into the boat and launch on a journey where there is no turning back once you commit. There are other people in the boat, and hopefully these are people you can trust and will work together as a team. But out on a river you don't know what's coming up or exactly what technique you will use to stay upright. Sometimes the rapids come at you so fast that you have to work to keep from getting thrown out of the boat.

Ghaffari: Who are your primary, the most important, mentors in your life?

Luttgens: I'm so blessed to have had so many mentors. First and foremost, my mother has been my consummate mentor and continues to be. I was just up in San Francisco for Mother's Day, and we were chatting about my current role. She's still active, providing advice to people in her community and being a source of wisdom and experience.

In the sixth grade, I went to an all-girls' school where there was a lot of cliquishness. I would come home and tell my mother, "So and so doesn't like me." My mother would just say, "Be nice to everyone." Her advice has served me well. I'm a big believer that you never burn a bridge. I've tried to pass that advice on to my daughter, Kate.

I've gotten to know a lot of my mother's friends. I've been fortunate that she has shared her network with me, and I've been able to develop relationships with them myself. Toni Rembe is an attorney friend from San Francisco. We have the same birthday, so we're birthday buddies. We walk her dogs through the Presidio whenever I'm in San Francisco, and she has given me some invaluable perspectives on my career choices.

Ironically, most of my mentors have been men. The mentors that stand out for me are the people who have told me the unvarnished truth and have been my mirror. The most difficult conversations have been the ones where I needed to change something. I've always been a high performer, but I wouldn't be where I am if I hadn't received direct feedback about how to improve myself. Those have been some of the conversations I've carried with me and played back in my head long after the person has gone. I've also had mentors who really celebrated me. The one person that has been outstanding since the very beginning of my career is Fred Meyer, then the chief operating officer of Pacific Medical Center, who now has his own consulting company. I've known Fred since I was a sixteen-year-old candy striper in the sixties at Pacific Medical Center.

Ghaffari: Why did a rebel like you listen to these mentors?

Luttgens: They were smarter than I am. They know more than I do. They were more experienced, more successful.

It wasn't that I was an unfocused rebel who had to fight City Hall because I had a chip on my shoulder. I was raised to know that there was a path for me, but that it might not be the well-trod path. I think that was why I had all those changes in college. I kept landing in places that I had chosen that I thought were right for me. Once I got there, it didn't feel quite right. In retrospect, that was just my youth and inexperience trying to determine where I fit.

Ghaffari: How would you describe your decision-making style?

Luttgens: Definitely inclusive. I have a really strong executive team of four C-suite people, any one of whom could step into my role if I were hit by a truck tomorrow. And that answers your question about succession among the ranks.

Ghaffari: Do you always hire people who are smarter than you?

Luttgens: Yes, absolutely, and people who work as hard as I do, or even harder. I have a hard-working team, very dedicated and loyal. Loyal to each other, loyal to me and loyal to the Girl Scouts. I really try to build an esprit through sharing information and the decision-making process, even if it doesn't directly involve everybody on the team. I think it's really important that when a team makes a decision, it's a team decision. One of my mantras is that the whole really is greater than the sum of the parts, especially when people are well-informed and have the right intent.

Ghaffari: What's your process of developing the organization's long-term strategy?

Luttgens: There definitely is a national strategy—a core business strategy around increasing membership, providing a unified leadership curriculum for girls, and positioning the brand. The national strategy provides a framework, and then we as the council translate that to the individual characteristics of our area and our population's unique requirements and needs. That's the "take the best and leave the rest" approach. We are fortunate to have a national framework while maintaining our regional flexibility.

Ghaffari: How would you say two of the things that you've developed, the STEM program and the Business Smarts, offer opportunities to increase the visibility of women in leadership?

Luttgens: Actually, all five of our program areas do that. But since you asked about Business Smarts and STEM, we can talk about the number of opportunities in these fields and the disproportionately low number of women filling these positions. When Girl Scouts have the opportunity to try new things and become confident of their achievements in these more traditionally male fields, the ripple effect is remarkable. Add to the mix positive female role models who have been successful in these fields, and we have a perfect alignment of relationships and experiences for leadership.

Ghaffari: How do you define a leader? How do you define leadership?

Luttgens: I think leadership is recognized when an individual can influence the thinking and the progress of others. When I look at the women and men I consider leaders, they are not all from one profile. A common characteristic is that they are people others pay attention to and follow because they are believable and inspire confidence.

Some leaders I've known are quiet but effective, while others are charismatic and larger than life. I've been fortunate to be a member of the Organization of Women Executives, which has members who are leaders from all industries and with many different approaches and perspectives on leadership. Being part of this group has been greatly enriching and has helped my understanding of how leadership can be shared—how leaders support as well as lead.

Ghaffari: The Gold Award is the highest, most prestigious award a girl can earn in the Girl Scouts. How is that acknowledged outside the Girl Scouts?

Luttgens: Well, first of all you've touched on a point of sensitivity for us as a Movement. The girls who earn this award are extraordinary young women doing amazing things with their lives and serving their communities locally and globally. Each year, we honor about two hundred Gold Award Girl Scouts here in Greater LA, and I have the opportunity to see their projects and congratulate them. It is the most joyous day of my Girl Scout year.

We've heard anecdotally from college admissions officers or human resources interviewers that—when a girl submits her application and states that she's a Gold Awardee—she automatically goes into the next level of the process. Unfortunately, I often have to explain what this award represents by comparing it to boys who are Eagle Scouts. I look forward to the day when I don't have to qualify the Gold Award in this way.

Ghaffari: Why is the Girl Scout's Gold Award not as well known?

Luttgens: The first reason is that the Eagle Scout has been the Boy Scouts' award for almost all of their one hundred years. Over that same century, the Girl Scouts of the USA has renamed this prestigious award several times. It has been called the "Curved Bar," the "Golden Eaglet," the "First Class," and most recently the "Gold Award." Four different names over one hundred years. It's really hard to have a brand identity, but I believe the Gold Award is here to stay.

Secondly, I'm not at all a feminist, but I do think that, historically, men have been better self-promoters and networkers than women. It follows that the critical mass of Boy Scouts has done a great job promoting the notion of the Eagle Scout.

Ghaffari: Is there any hesitance on the part of the girls themselves or the volunteers to flaunt their Gold?

Luttgens: No, not at all. I wish you could witness the pride at our annual Gold Award ceremony. They, their families, their fellow troop members and leaders, and our staff are incredibly proud! Our alumnae can attest to how their Gold Award, or its earlier equivalent, has shaped them as outstanding individuals.

It is a secret that has been too well kept. As with breaking up some of the stereotypes and myths about the Girl Scouts overall, and cookies in particular, having conversations about the Gold Award is very important to help the general public understand what they are supporting.

Ghaffari: Can you tell me the best responses you've had to your career aspirations and the worst responses you've had and how you've dealt with them?

Luttgens: It's a hard question because everyone has been supportive, but obviously my mother is the standout. She's been the most knowledgeable and present for me over time. I would also say my family—my daughter and my former husband—have been extremely supportive of my career. There was never any question that I would not only continue my work after marrying and having a family, but that I would continue to dedicate myself and advance in my career. My daughter has been incredible in working around my professional advancement and knows how important she is. She comes first, even when it doesn't feel like it.

I haven't really had any worst responses. I've been very blessed in that I've been surrounded by supportive people. We're not a big family, but there's strength here. I've worked after school ever since I was fourteen. There was never a question that you worked, that you paid your own way. That's just the way I was programmed, and it's continued in the way I've raised my daughter. I was fortunate that my parents funded my undergraduate education. My father used to tell me it was the best gift they could give me.

Ghaffari: What advice would you give to young women today as they think about a career?

Luttgens: Join the Girl Scouts! Not to be glib, but I do think it provides a network, a safe environment with other females where you can be yourself, where you don't have distractions, where you're not competing with boys, where you really are able to find your self-esteem—your true north—in your own way, where you have supportive female mentors. All of this just happens to be the model for the Girl Scouts. I didn't know that at the time that I took this job. But, I do think it's important to surround yourself with people who expect you to reach your full potential and who show you how to do it.

That's certainly true for me, even today. Our board expects nothing less than that this new council reaches its full potential, quickly and without detours. They expect me to lead GSGLA expertly, and I expect nothing less of my senior management team. I expect nothing less of my daughter. I expect nothing less from the people with whom I volunteer at church. I think it's a mindset—no one else is going to change the world for you. If you want to change something, it's up to you to take responsibility for it.

That's why, when I said, "My advice is to tell the girls to join the Girl Scouts," I really do think that girls today are faced with such serious—and traumatic—challenges, that it's up to all of us to be a safe harbor for them.

Ghaffari: In any of the advice that you've given me, would you say anything differently for men?

Luttgens: I really wouldn't have. I don't differentiate much between men and women. I'm pretty gender-blind—which is interesting working in an all-women's organization.

Ghaffari: The Girl Scouts as an organizational role model looks a lot like a political government—the delegation, the representation. Do you see yourself moving into the political or government arena?

Luttgens: No, I see myself staying right here, until the universe finds something different for me.

Debra Bowen

Secretary of State, California

Born October 27, 1955, in Rockford, Illinois.

Debra Bowen's early experience challenging the status quo began in Rockford, Illinois, where she orchestrated a junior-high school protest over a school policy that barred girls from wearing pants to class (resulting in her being thrown out of her geometry class). Also, she resisted faculty censorship of the student-run newspaper.

After receiving a BA in communications from Michigan State University (1976) and a JD from the University of Virginia School of Law (1979), she volunteered and practiced law in California.

Ms. Bowen served six years in the California State Assembly (1992–1998) and eight years in the California State Senate (1998–2006). As a legislator, she authored a pioneering law (1993) that put California legislative information online, giving the public access to information about bills, committee analyses, state legislators' voting records, and much more.

She was the first California lawmaker to voluntarily put her own campaign finance reports online in 1995, several years before all candidates for state office were required to do so. She authored landmark consumer protection laws, providing safeguards such as banning businesses and government agencies from using Social Security numbers as public identifiers; requiring credit card numbers to be removed from receipts kept by merchants; giving people the right to freeze access to their credit reports; and giving people the tools to fight back against unsolicited e-mail and fax advertising.

While a legislator, she chaired the Senate Elections, Reapportionment and Consti-tutional Amendments Committee; the Senate Energy, Utilities and Communications Committee; and the Assembly Natural Resources Committee.

At the national level, she chaired the National Conference of State Legislatures (NCSL) E-Communications Steering Committee, served on their executive board, and was California's appointee to the NCSL Task Force on State and Local Taxa-tion of Telecommunications and Electronic Commerce.

She was elected California Secretary of State in 2006 and re-elected in November 2010. She will hold office through 2014. On August 3, 2007, Secretary Bowen, as the chief elections officer for the largest state in the nation, withdrew approval of electronic voting systems made by Diebold Election Systems, Hart InterCivic, and Sequoia Voting Systems electronic voting systems after commissioning a top-to-bottom review (conducted by an independent team of experts) that revealed the equipment and software were highly vulnerable to security breaches. She simulta-neously re-approved all three, subject to stricter security conditions and auditing requirements and rescinded approval of a fourth system by Election Systems & Software, which did not submit its system in time for review.

For her efforts, Secretary Bowen was recognized with the 2008 John F. Kennedy Profile in Courage Award, the nation's most prestigious honor for elected public servants who choose principles over partisanship.

Elizabeth Ghaffari: Were you an elected officer in your early school days in Rockford, Illinois?

Debra Bowen: No, I was definitely a nerd, but we didn't call it that back then. My family was pretty tolerant of my challenging the system.

My father has a degree in mechanical engineering and later got an MBA. He did the marketing work for assembly lines used in building Boeing wing struts and automobiles. My mother was a prolific volunteer—Junior League, Easter Seals, United Way.

I have an adopted younger brother who's five years younger, and my family hosted an exchange student from Japan in my junior year of high school. She returned ten years later and married a young man through the American Field Services orientations. That's how I happen to have a Japanese family now in California.

Ghaffari: Why did you go to Michigan State for your undergrad degree?

Bowen: I wanted to go to the veterinary school, but the only way to get in as an out-of-state student was to attend Michigan State as an undergrad. I started on a heavy science track because I was very interested in doing genetic research. Then I learned that to be a researcher, you spent a lot of time alone. I didn't want to do that.

At that time, nobody was encouraging women to be large-animal veterinarians. And I didn't want to work on small animals. I was in the honors program at Michigan State and had a great academic advisor who re-directed me to a communications class that just blew my socks off. It was so interesting.

Ghaffari: What interested you in particular?

Bowen: It was the very beginning of the communications field, looking at the impact of television and media. They taught us to look at organizational communication, intercultural and international issues, and interpersonal communication. Michigan State was one of the very few places in the country where there was any real research being done in communications.

I took a heavy class load and surprised myself by graduating early—in three years. University of Virginia School of Law was a definite first choice for me. I actually turned down an opportunity to go to Harvard Law. I liked the atmosphere at UVA better. It was a lot less expensive, and I was concerned about how much debt I was going to have to pay off when I got out.

Ghaffari: What attracted you to the law?

Bowen: My career path, in many ways, has been very sort of accidental. I always want to encourage young people to follow their instincts. I took a business law class and was fascinated by contract law because it's an amazing system that provides structure to business transactions and reduces the costs of transactions—the time cost—because it guides people's understanding of normal business dealings. It's just really beautiful. This may sound "geeky," but I think it's incredible how business law, contract law, and the Uniform Commercial Code all reflect the understanding that people have about commerce. They provide the legal structure so that people know what to expect when they enter into a contract or what the results will be from a dispute. I was just captivated by it.

Ghaffari: How important to your career were your first jobs?

Bowen: I clerked between my second and third years at Hughes, Hubbard & Reed—two months on Wall Street and a month in the Los Angeles office. I then got a job through the normal recruiting process right out of law school with Winston & Strawn in Chicago.

But, I always thought that I would like to live in California. I loved the month that I spent working there in 1978. I lived in the Oakwood [corporate apartments] and went everywhere in Southern California—from the Sawdust Festival to driving up Pacific Coast Highway to visit San Francisco.

I loved the people and the sense of personal freedom that we have in California. Coming, as I did, from a fairly socially conservative place in Illinois, that was just not part of the framework.

After I moved to California, I joined the LA office of Hughes, Hubbard & Reed for a couple of years. Then, as was common at the time for satellite offices, they went through some growing pains, and the partner who had all the business clients took his portfolio to another place, leaving a whole bunch of corporate and tax associates with not much to do.

In that job, I faced my first experience with an ethical dilemma about the work. At the time, Continental Airlines was in financial difficulty and terminated their pension plan. This is now a widely reported case study over pension plan issues.

Before they terminated the plan, though, they amended it to create a very large actuarial surplus by modifying the minimum required benefits that would allow tax qualification. Then they terminated the plan and took the surplus. They got sued by their employees and eventually had to put all the money back.

I was one of the young lawyers who worked on the pension plan modifications—amending and terminating the plan. As a young person starting your career, you begin to define your ethics and boundaries. For me, that was an ethical boundary.

Ghaffari: Is that what persuaded you to leave and start your own law firm?

Bowen: When I left, I wanted to do something different. I worked briefly with some people on starting up a toy company that ultimately didn't go anywhere. That experience gave me a good insight into what it's like to work for a start-up business, so it was very valuable even though it didn't succeed. Then, when I went back to practicing law, it was on my terms. I got to choose what work I did. I vowed to myself that I would never work on something that wasn't in line with my ethical standards.

Ghaffari: After you started your business in '84, how long did you keep the firm going, and what kind of clients did you have?

Bowen: There were a lot of small business start-ups, some tax and securities work—the kinds of things I had been doing before. I was based in Marina del Rey. Then I spent about a year back in DC working at Winston & Strawn at the time they were talking about opening an LA office. But the timing was wrong. Today, they have an LA and a San Francisco office.

I've stayed very close friends with the now-managing partner, Tom Fitzgerald, who's in the Chicago office. He and I were two of the three tax associates who started on the same day in 1978. I took some of my clients with me, but ultimately it didn't work out. I came back to LA to pursue my own work.

Ghaffari: You were involved with the Neighborhood Watch and "Heal the Bay." Was that as a lawyer or as a volunteer?

Bowen: My pathway into politics was through the Neighborhood Watch and a local group called the Venice Town Council. The council was not an elected governmental organization—it was something of a precursor to the current neighborhood council movement. Development issues were hot at the time.

I worked a lot with Ruth Galanter [a Los Angeles councilwoman] on the various community groups such as the Venice Town Council, a group called COAST, and other organizations. I was doing a lot of legal work on a volunteer basis for those groups and then for Heal the Bay. Then people started calling me, asking me to do similar kinds of legal work as a paid attorney. I didn't solicit legal work deliberately—it happened because people who needed legal advice were aware that I did that kind of work.

I did environmental work, urban planning, and administrative law. A lot of the work I did related to permitting and development issues concerning the city charter, the regulations, or California law. I helped people understand the required procedure for approving an environmental impact report. A great deal of environmental law work actually concerns itself with administrative law because that's how it's carried out.

I had moved my offices around to various places—from Century City to Venice Boulevard, then Carthay Circle for a while. Later on, I had an office that was just me, but earlier I worked on an "of-counsel basis," associating with other small firms because it was critical to have shared resources like a copy machine and a law library. The law library was really critical. If you didn't have access to a law library, you'd spend a lot of time driving to downtown LA or going to the UCLA law library. At that time, nothing was online.

Ghaffari: When did you become politically active in LA?

Bowen: Around 1989, I became aware of an organization called the Coro Foundation [a leadership training program]. I'm not sure how I first heard about it, but I did a three-month program called Community Invest that was intended for people who were working in the community to broaden their skills and to be more effective. That experience was really formational. Without that training, I don't think I would have run for office.

Then, too, I was involved with a group of people from the City of Los Angeles who put together a coalition of homeowner and residents' associations from around the city—called PlanLA—because at the time there was really no way for somebody who was working on an issue in Tujunga to know what was going on in Venice or San Pedro or South Central. All of us, the community groups, were working on very similar issues, yet we were very isolated. And as a result, the groups did not have much power.

That effort was the precursor to what ultimately became the neighborhood councils. I met a lot of people through that effort. Bill Christopher[1] was one of the people who was involved. I met Emily Gabriel Luddy, who was on the planning commission in LA at the time. I met George Millston doing legal work for the Venice Town Council. I've become really close to a lot of these people in politics from back in '89.

Ghaffari: How did you happen to campaign for your first assembly office?

Bowen: As a part of the PlanLA group, I was involved in redistricting in 1990 after the '90 census. I was just one of the people working as a volunteer on those issues. We worked primarily on the county district lines. We had one person with a computer and enough information to be able to re-work the files. We were successful, actually, in some of the proposals that we made to change the original district boundaries. In the final analysis, though, the court ended up drawing the redistricting maps that took effect in 1992.

There was one assembly district, the fifty-third, that previously had been an east-west slot, extending from El Segundo to Inglewood. The court redrew the line so that it became a coastal district, north-south. Being a new district, there was no incumbent. I talked about it with many of the people in the community with whom I had worked. I was so naïve that I didn't know that because the margin in the district was so tight—42 percent Democratic and 41 percent Republican—it was considered a "safe" or highly probable Republican district.

At the beginning of the campaign, there were four Democrats who were looking at running. By the time the filing was done, there was just me and Roger Donaldson, the Green Party candidate.

I was very worried about the spoiler effect because, at that time, the Green Party rules provided that if "none of the above" was a choice in a primary, then "none of the above" potentially could win the most votes—resulting in

---

[1] Past president of the Los Angeles Board of Neighborhood Commissioners.

no one going to the general election ballot. The Green candidate actually sent out a letter to all Green party members, asking them to vote for "none of the above."

The three moderate, pro-choice Republican candidates beat each other up in the Republican primary, leaving the most conservative Republican candidate to stand in the general election. Nobody paid any attention to it until about three weeks before Election Day, when the *LA Times* wrote a story about the fact that all the money contributed to the Republican candidate was coming from the religious, right-wing side of the Republican constituency. At that time, there were no campaign contribution limits.

That was quite a campaign for a first-timer. There was one mailer that called me a "Nazi." I have it still. Being called a Nazi in one hundred and forty thousand people's mailboxes was a pretty big deal to me. I was pretty upset. In the end, the mailers backfired badly, and I won by a huge margin.

Life is interesting. Roger Donaldson continued his work as a computer programmer in the open-source movement. He showed up in my life again as part of a group of people who were very concerned about voting system issues many years later. He was interested in seeing what open source could bring to that table.

Ghaffari: Your three terms in the California Assembly established the beginning of your reputation as a computer geek. How did that happen?

Bowen: Earlier, I had volunteered with the state bar's public law section as the legislative liaison. I would get these envelopes from the state bar's lobbyist with copies of paper [legislative] bills, and I'd have to go through them all, one by one—manually—trying to figure out what we might want to follow or not.

Later, when I became a legislator, I discovered that much of that information was on my computer, but no one could have access to it unless they were willing to pay one of two private providers. I think one service was about $200 a month. The other was an annual subscription for a couple of thousand of dollars—well beyond the means of most people.

When you're doing volunteer work—trying to get as many people as you can to work on the same thing, how else could you get stuff back and forth? We were struggling with some of the very early versions of the internet. We had CompuServe, Prodigy, and AOL—and none of them "talked" to each other at the beginning. You had the problem of configuring your modem—we were using an old 300/1200/2400-baud version. And then there was the serial port. Ugh!

So, I introduced a bill that would require all of the legislative information be put on a dial-up bulletin board. At the time, that was the only mechanism I was aware of. My bill was based on what the City of Santa Monica had done with their planning board agendas and materials. After I introduced that bill, two guys from Silicon Valley showed up in my office saying, "There's a better way to do this." Jim Warren was the main guy—somebody with a major interest in, and a long history working on, First Amendment issues. The other was Ray Kidde, a programmer from Apple. We worked on that bill together and got huge editorial support, as you can imagine, from all the newspapers.

I am proud of that law. It was the first in the world and has served as a model for other US states and countries. It gives the public access to information about California bills, committee analyses, and voting records.

I had a lot of very interesting experiences around that bill. I discovered that the Legislative Counsel (basically, the lawyer for the assembly and senate) was meeting with the two businesses, StateTech and LegiTech, who were opposed to the bill, without telling me. The idea that my lawyer would be meeting with someone who is opposed to my bill without telling me was so shocking.

Ghaffari: What did you do?

Bowen: I was a new member. What do you do? I went to my friend, John Vasconcellos, one of the longest-serving members of the assembly, and asked him, "What should I do?" And he said, "You should just invite yourself to the meetings."

And that's what I did. I basically just knocked on the door and said, "Hi, I'm here for the meeting between so-and-so and so-and-so." Of course, they let me in because they had to.

I had a lot of support for the legislation. I discovered that local governments and groups were paying enormous sums of money for subscriptions to track bills. The League of Conservation of Voters was tracking legislation using paper bills, a very cumbersome task. Committee analysis was simply not available at all, nor were voting records. Newspapers had to send somebody to the capitol to record a vote, and then run back to their offices with the final tally.

Ghaffari: Was that your most outstanding piece of legislation?

Bowen: In many ways, yes, because it was the start of my legislative work in that area. After that, I put my own campaign contributions online. And I helped then-Secretary of State Bill Jones get the funding to get campaign contribution information online.

Ghaffari: Now, you don't accept gifts in office. Has that been a problem at all?

Bowen: No, it's not been a problem. It just means if I want to go do something, I pay for it myself.

Another influential player for me was appellate court justice George Nicholson, who was one of the very early players in looking at what the needs of the courts would be in the coming digital age. Around 1994, he persuaded then-chief justice Malcolm Lucas to put together a group to look at what the needs of the courts would be in an IT era. And I got a lot of more formal training in "geekery" through that experience.

I attended a program about IT projects and managing IT at the Kennedy School at Harvard. I also did some work with MIT, looking at various computer systems—what had worked and what hadn't. That gave me the real nuts and bolts education that I needed through the court system.

I had come to Justice Nicholson's attention because of the bill that put the legislature online. The court project lasted about a year, and then it was followed by a governing committee that served as a steering committee for the courts to help them wind their way through the challenging change process. Ultimately, we produced our recommendations in a report informally called the "20/20 Report."

Before 1998, California had two different classes of trial courts: the superior and the municipal courts. Before they were merged into fifty-eight county superior courts, there were three hundred-some courts, each with its own computer system—if they had anything. Nobody could move any information digitally. Anything that was needed from Corrections or the Department of Motor Vehicles came to the courts on paper. It was a disaster.

There are major issues involved with trying to put together an integrated system that depends on that many government agencies. It's a big challenge, and they've had their struggles.

Ghaffari: You really developed a solid foundation to do in-depth assessments required to implement technology projects in the public sector.

Bowen: I do think that having an in-depth perspective was important because there were not many people who could do that at that point. At the state level, almost any agency with an IT proposal would come forward, but nobody on the Budget Committee knew much about technology, while the Legislative Analyst's Office was just beginning to develop the capacity to analyze IT projects.

Early on, I challenged a proposal to automate the state welfare system. I persuaded the Legislative Analyst to write a report that, ultimately, resulted in that project having the plug pulled. The Analyst's report concluded, "This is just not workable. This is just not scalable to California." It would have been a billion-dollar boondoggle had it gone forward. California is still struggling with IT. Our procurement system is still not up to the task.

Ghaffari: Why did you decide to move on to the California Senate position in 1998? Was it because of term limits?

Bowen: It is interesting that the one thing that I didn't do—but could have, and actually got a lot of pressure to do—was to run for the 36th Congressional District in 1998, the year Jane Harman didn't run for that office because she ran, unsuccessfully, for the office of California governor.

I was getting calls from many people in Washington, asking me to run for Congress. At that time, I had developed a relationship with Maya, a young woman—I call her my foster daughter because there's not a better word—who had been through so much at a very young age. She had been living with me and was pregnant with my first grandchild, Avida, who is now twelve years old. I just didn't want to be going back and forth to DC with my first grandchild on the way. Her second daughter is Amiela.

It just seemed a natural thing to run for the state senate. I loved what I was doing. In the assembly, I had the opportunity to chair the Natural Resources Committee. I helped with the first-ever hearing on the role of fire in the ecosystem and what we were doing with fire suppression and what that meant for ecosystem health.

It was a lot of learning the nuts and bolts of how to be an effective legislator, while also pursuing not just the geek issues, but some of the newer environmental issues. I never served on the Assembly Energy Committee, but there was an opportunity to do a lot of things that have a huge environmental impact, so I jumped at the chance to chair the Senate Energy Committee when I was elected to the senate in 1998. Then, California wound up in the middle of the energy crisis.

Ghaffari: How did you get to be chair?

Bowen: The decisions about who chairs what committee are made by the speaker in the assembly and the president pro tem in the senate. There's always a discussion with new members: "What do you want to do and what's available?" Some of the slots are already filled. Before term limits, people in the senate would chair a committee forever and ever. For example, Senator Hersh Rosenthal chaired the Energy Committee for a very long time. After him was Steve Peace, and then he moved on to chair the Senate Budget Committee, so that left a vacancy in the Senate Energy Committee chair.

I was fortunate because I was able to move from the assembly to the senate. I really have never planned my career. I have done what is of the greatest interest to me and followed my passions. Opportunities have then presented themselves. I've just been fortunate to be able to take advantage of those.

Ghaffari: Has your family been a supportive part of your career?

Bowen: My mother died in a car accident when I was twenty-five, and that's been a huge, huge motivator for me because you just don't know what is going to happen. To me, it means whatever you want to do, do it, because you never know what might happen.

And then, on the other side of that, I've frequently found myself with Maya and, now, with groups of young people realizing that it's my way of giving back.

My first husband, though, was not at all supportive. He didn't like me being gone. It wasn't the politics—just the travel. So that marriage didn't survive my first term in office, not even the first year. It ended in 1993.

Ghaffari: Is your husband, Mark Nechodom, supportive?

Bowen: Yes, very supportive. We met in '97 and were married in 2003. He had run a training program—first at California State University, Sacramento State, and then at the University of California, Davis—for resource managers in the political process. A lot of scientists and technical people tend to think that, if you do good work, the policy will, somehow, take care of itself. And, of course, it doesn't. So, the Natural Resources Committee, which I chaired in the assembly, was one of the labs for him for that class. You could say that I was a part of his classroom. He would bring his students over to watch the Natural Resources Committee.

He knew who I was and had been following me professionally. We met at the Freeport Bakery, in line for coffee, and—we joke it wasn't a pickup line —but it was, "I really like that work you've been doing on GIS [geographic information systems]."

I have to look at his business card because his job keeps changing depending on the politics of how the United States government is going to deal with climate change, if at all. He started out as the assistant director of the Office of Environmental Services and Markets, which was created in a section of the Farm Bill at the end of the Bush Administration. There have been a number of reorganizations of the functionality since then.

Ghaffari: How did you deal with the challenges of managing a family and two political careers?

Bowen: Haphazardly. Truly! As much as you try to figure out how to do it, I think everybody kind of makes it up as they go along. Maya and Ben moved out to start their own family at the end of '97 as I was getting ready to run for the senate in early '98. Now, today, they've returned—they're living with me again because, when you have young people whose careers are in the arts and the economy is tough, that's what happens. You adjust. You deal with it. We pretty much made it up as we went.

I did have some helpful advice from other members about trying to balance time and to make sure that you make some time for your family and your marriage. But it is a challenge.

Ghaffari: Tell me a little bit about some of the major people in your life whom you consider mentors and advice givers.

Bowen: Oh dear, there are so many. And many are not in the political world. Certainly, in the political world, Richard Katz and John Vasconcellos were mentors. John was one of the people I would go to when I was trying to figure out how to handle a situation. He served in the legislature for thirty-eight years. He has remained a close friend for all these years even though he's been out of the legislature since 2004.

Richard Katz was actually the person who was assigned to my campaign by the Democratic Caucus in 1992. I sat with him on the assembly floor during my first term. Then—here's some more "geeky" stuff that I'd forgotten—through Richard, I met Deborah Estrin,[2] who has been very involved with advanced technology at UCLA.

Deborah is an incredible woman and the leader of the Center for Embedded Network Sensing [CENS].[3] It is a multi-school effort that looked, very early on, at the role of computers and issues like privacy and security. The same issues that I had looked at in the court context and in the legislature came up again in CENS. They're now focusing on concerns about voting and online voter registration. Later, I became a member of their external advisory board.

---

[2] Professor of computer science with a joint appointment in electrical engineering at UCLA. Dr. Estrin holds the Jon Postel Chair in computer networks.

[3] The CENS web site is research.cens.ucla.edu.

It was through that network that I started to learn about the institutions that are focused on women leaders in technology, such as Grace Hopper[4]—and the many things women have done that are centered around technology issues, which I find to be just fascinating. In fact, I was just watching something I had recorded on the subject of cyber security.

Ghaffari: What was your reason for going after the secretary of state of California position?

Bowen: It was specifically to address the mess surrounding our electronic voting systems. Without that issue, I very likely would not have run for this office. I was coming up on the end of my legislative term. I wasn't really sure what I was going to do. Not running for any elected office was one of the options. I didn't feel like I needed to run. Then, another dear friend, a techie, sent me a link to some of the work that had been done by Black Box Voting.[5]

For the next few days, I read all of it and was horrified! I realized that, with something of this scale, it was the kind of thing that somebody needed to get in there, do the homework, do the research, sort it all out and solve the problem because elections are the foundation of democracy. If we start having people doubt the outcome of elections, we're really in trouble as a democracy.

If I hadn't had a background with the courts, the online legislative system and CENS, it would have been much more difficult to do the top-down review of the electronic voting systems that I conducted in 2007. All of that work both motivated me to seek the office and then gave me enough confidence in the direction that I chose to make a tough decision to impose stricter security and use conditions on all vendors' systems and stick to it.

Ghaffari: You received the Profile in Courage Award for making that tough decision. What did you think when you heard that you received it?

Bowen: It had to be the single biggest shock of my career. I was just so surprised. In the life of a kid who grew up in Rockford, Illinois, and started out pre-vet—Caroline Kennedy doesn't call you.

Ghaffari: Now that all of the top-to-bottom review has essentially been done, what are your priorities as secretary of state, now?

Bowen: Well, I have an ongoing technology project—a new and improved statewide voter registration database, which I am required to do by federal law.

---

[4] American computer scientist and US Navy officer who conceptualized COBOL.

[5] An election watchdog organization based in Renton, WA. See: www.blackboxvoting.org/.

I'm working to bring the secretary of state's web site up-to-date to be a much more functional site. We need much more work to be done on our business systems automation, which also requires a completely new computer system at some point.

My enduring goal is to make democracy work better. For me, that means making government more transparent, accessible, and accountable. Budget cuts haven't always helped me get there, so I look for the most cost-effective ways to do everything.

I am working on enhancing the online public database that helps people monitor political campaign contributions and lobbying activities. The database already provides twenty-four-hour access to this important information, but I want it to be easier to use.

I am working on more ways to make registering to vote as easy as possible. For example, I created an easy-to-fill-in voter registration form online, so all people have to do is type in their information, print the form, sign it, and mail it. The new statewide voter registration database will allow us to make online voter registration possible.

I am also expanding the high school mock election. The year before I took office, there were 383 California schools participating. In 2010, the number was 433. It's hard to reach the scattered, unregistered voters throughout the state, but if you can get young people registered and involved in voting right away, then in the long term you have much more participatory democracy.

Ghaffari: You're going to be termed out in 2014. Do you have a master plan?

Bowen: No, I have no idea, but that's really a long time in the future. I didn't expect [Jane Harman's] congressional seat to open up in 2010. That election didn't turn out the way I had hoped it would, but that can happen in an election.[6]

Ghaffari: Was it hard to manage a Southern California Congressional campaign from the middle of the state, in Sacramento?

Bowen: The nature of how we work has changed a lot in the last five or ten years, because with a phone, a laptop and an internet connection, you can be in two or more places at once.

That may not be as true in the legislature, where you have committee hearings, because the hearings process is much more of an interactive thing.

---

[6] Bowen missed out on the runoff by 709 votes.

One of the things that I've always tried to do is surround myself with really good, smart people and then let them work. For the Congressional campaign, I had a small, core group. Then we brought in various field organizers on an as-needed basis. This was a very different campaign compared to what I had experienced running either for the assembly or the senate. It was even different from the statewide secretary of state campaign. This time I had over eleven hundred volunteers and eighty interns.

Recently, I was invited to speak to the [UCLA] Bruins Democratic Club. Now, the test for me is to see whether I can take what I've been doing, which is working to inspire young people and get them engaged, and see if I can do the same thing in a partisan political campaign. And the answer is definitely yes. It was just amazing. On Election Day, there were so many volunteers that people were sitting on the sidewalk with their laptops because there wasn't room in the office. It was extraordinary.

Even though I lost, I have a number of things now that I will work on that I wouldn't have considered. Now, I will use those learning experiences. I'm just starting the process of sorting things out. "What things do I want? What things do I take from this?"

One of the most obvious lessons for me relates to all the time I've worked on voter registration and teaching people about democracy and how it works. Registering to vote is one thing, but as a new voter, how and where do you go to educate yourself about the issues? My office publishes a voter information guide for each statewide election that contains summaries, fiscal analyses, as well as arguments for and against every proposition that voters are asked to weigh in on. But I'm always looking for new ways to expand on this.

Ghaffari: Would that be inside the secretary of state's office?

Bowen: State budget cuts have meant that we're basically doing civic engagement on a shoestring, so I try to do a lot of things by working in partnerships with schools, chambers of commerce, or nonprofits. We're trying to set things up that will endure. That's an experience that I had in my first year of law school at UVA—where I started an admissions and orientation program. I was sort of lost as an out-of-state student, so I set up a program of small-section advisers from the class ahead, and that still exists to this day.

I don't have the whole picture in my mind—just this recognition that there's a piece missing in our efforts to educate for democracy. There's another piece missing because it's not enough to just get everybody registered. You still have the ongoing issue of low turnouts, especially in special elections.

Ghaffari: Do legislators or procurement departments come to you for IT expertise?

Bowen: No. You know, there's an established process controlled by the [California] Department of Finance and the Department of General Services. I think there has to be some different way, for the good of the state, because the amount of time that it takes us to procure is just incredible. And part of it is because we're so big and doing some things that smaller states, like Iowa or Vermont, would never experience. There's a lot more room for things to be imperfect when you have to scale to suit thirty-seven million people.

Ghaffari: Do you plan on staying in politics or have you thought of leaving?

Bowen: I have no idea, actually, what I'll do next. I have until 2014 to build on the things done in the secretary of state's office that are important and to try to institutionalize some of the things I've established so that they survive.

Ghaffari: How would you describe your own decision-making style?

Bowen: I put a whole bunch of information into the hopper and then work through it all. It's just the way I was built. I grew up in a house full of engineers. I think if I had been a boy, I very well might have been directed into an engineering kind of profession.

Ghaffari: How do you define success?

Bowen: I think I define success in untraditional ways. If I define success as, say, the number of bills signed or something like that, I will miss an important part of what I've been about—which is to identify issues that need to be addressed and begin to or actually establish the competency in government to address those issues.

And that's why I've often been ahead of the curve—sometimes just too early in the sense that the time wasn't quite right for legislation or government action. We're still at the point where there's just starting to be an understanding that something is an important issue. I think that cyber-security is at that point right now. It's just not something that people are thinking about enough.

Ghaffari: What advice do you have for women who are considering careers in law, politics, or technology?

Bowen: Get involved with a group of people who can support you, because it's still harder for women than it is for men. That's changing, but it's still true. I will never forget going to an energy conference—something Enron sponsored, actually—and I did a count of the one hundred and fifteen people in the room of whom one hundred and twelve were white men.

And so having that support and having a group of people to whom you can talk, who can help you figure out what to do, that is important. There's some very interesting research out at Rutgers, for example, about why women still are not running for political office in the kinds of numbers that one might expect.

Women tend to be harder on themselves and spend a lot of time evaluating, "Oh, am I really qualified to do this job?" By the time they finish that evaluation, the man in the contest has already raised $200,000.

There are a lot of great groups. For me as a pro-choice Democrat, it's been the National Women's Political Caucus, EMILY's List, and California Women Lead.

And, too, I think the most important thing is for people to do what they're really passionate about, because if you're going to work at a high level, either in politics or in the corporate structure, you put up with a lot, so you have to be doing something you really care about and want to do. Otherwise, the tradeoffs just aren't worth it.

Ghaffari: How do you deal with the negatives, especially in a political environment?

Bowen: I think you have to keep your core sense intact—who you are and what you are about. Also, keep the perspective that everything that happens becomes fuel for a greater understanding and for some future work that will change things for those who come next. Like getting kicked out of geometry class for wearing pants. You know, this is not a new theme for me.

Ghaffari: Do you think your advice would probably fit for men political candidates as much as for women?

Bowen: It does. The other thing is to keep your own counsel. Particularly when you're beginning, you get a lot of different political advice. Much of it's good. Some of it's not. And you have to develop a strong core, have a sense of your own values because they will be pushed. It's the nature of politics.

The other day I was looking at some notes about women in politics and on the corporate side. I don't know who might have said it, but what I wrote down was, "Corporate America gets better one retirement at a time." And I thought that really is part of what happens when we're undergoing the kind of change happening with regard to the role of women.

The same is true with civil rights for LGBT[7] people. I mean, some of the things that are happening now used to be inconceivable. As one generation moves away, there's room for something different to happen. Not that we object to the men who are there. The men who are in their seventies and eighties, most of them—and there are some huge exceptions to this—have done things in a particular way and, when they're gone, there's just more room for something different to happen.

It's not an insult, but it just struck me as being an interesting perspective.

Ghaffari: Is your family in Sacramento with you or in Southern California?

Bowen: Maya, Vida, Ami, and Ben are all in Los Angeles. Nora is starting college this fall. And Mark is in Washington, LA, Sacramento, and many other points in between. And it's an open question where the cats will live—'cause for me, home is where the cats are.

---

[7] Lesbian, gay, bisexual, transgender

Julia Gouw

President and Chief Operating Officer, East West Bank

Born 1959 in Surabaya, Indonesia.

*In 1978, **Julia S. Gouw** was the first of her family to emigrate from Indonesia to the United States to earn a college degree at the University of Illinois at Urbana-Champaign. She initially wanted to pursue a degree in chemistry, but switched to accounting and finance. After graduating, she became a certified public accountant and eventually worked for KPMG LLP, an international accounting firm, as a senior audit manager (1983–1989).*

Ms. Gouw joined Pasadena, California-based East West Bank in 1989 as vice president and controller, rising quickly in the company to become executive vice president and chief financial officer by 1994. She was instrumental in the $238 million management-led buyout of East West in June 1998. She was in charge of East West Bank's acquisition of Pacific Coast Federal Savings Bank of San Francisco from the Resolution Trust Corporation in 1991 during the savings and loan crisis, as well as eight other bank acquisitions that took place from 1999 to 2010, including the FDIC-assisted acquisition of United Commercial Bank (UCB) in 2009.

Gouw served as the chief risk officer for East West Bank and vice chairman of both the bank and the holding company in 2008. She has served as president and chief operating officer of both entities since November 30, 2009. She has been on the board of directors of both the bank and its holding company, East West Bancorp Inc., since 1997. In January 2011, she joined the boards of Pacific Mutual Holding Company and Pacific LifeCorp.

Highly recognized by the financial community for her work and contributions, Gouw has been named in the following rankings: "25 Most Powerful Women in Banking" by U.S. Banker magazine (2003, 2005, 2006, and 2007); "Top 10 CFOs in Banking" by U.S. Banker magazine (2006); and "Best CFOs in America" by Institutional Investor magazine (2006 and 2007).

Even more important to Ms. Gouw is her ability and opportunity to serve women and her community through involvement in several medical boards and charitable roles. She is one of the original members of the United Way of Greater Los Angeles Women Leaders (2002); founder of the Executive Advisory Board of the Iris Cantor Women's Health Center at the David Geffen School of Medicine at UCLA (since 2005); a member of the Board of Visitors of the David Geffen School of Medicine at UCLA (since 1997); a member of the board of directors of The UCLA Foundation (since 2006); a trustee of Saint John's Health Center (since 2003); and a board member of the John Wayne Cancer Institute at Saint John's Health Center (since 2007).

Ms. Gouw has been recognized as a leader in philanthropy as much as a leader in the banking community. Her notable achievements include being named the Philanthropist of the Year by the National Association of Women Business Owners— Los Angeles in 2003, and Philanthropist of the Year by the Los Angeles Business Journal at both their 2003 and 2008 annual Women Making a Difference events.

Elizabeth Ghaffari: Where were you born and raised? What was your family like?

Julia Gouw: I was born in 1959 in Surabaya, which is the second-largest city in Indonesia—the coastal port from which the *Venture* expedition set sail in the movie *King Kong*.[1] I have an older sister, then there's me, my brother, and my younger sister.

My dad had a big influence on me because he always encouraged me to have a career and be financially independent. He never wanted me to be dependent on a husband to support me. He was a pessimist who told me, "I cannot take care of you. I cannot leave you an inheritance, but the one thing I can do is to pay for your education." I requested to be sent to college in the United States. He agreed saying, "If you have a college degree, then you can take care of yourself." That was an encouragement.

None of my mom's generation had any career outside home. The nice thing about my mom is that she was very, very proud, and she felt my

---

[1] The 1976 film version.

achievements vicariously. When I started my first job, I was making just $14,000 at Texaco, but my mom thought that was a huge salary because she never had any opportunity to make any money herself.

Some mothers are "tiger moms"—very demanding. There are pluses and minuses to that. Sometimes their kids may feel as if they can never do enough. I didn't have a tiger mom. The good thing is that I learned to be demanding for myself—not for my parents.

But then I turned out to be a tiger mom, myself, because that's how I took care of my brother and my sister. I came to the United States in 1978 to go to college at the University of Illinois, and helped my brother and sister who came here later. My brother came here to go to college in Illinois, and my sister came here at a much younger age—she went to boarding school in eighth grade, also in Illinois. My parents were still in Indonesia, so in a way, I became a substitute parent. They would tell people that I'm a "tiger mom" or their "tiger big sister."

Ghaffari: What was it like in your early years, coming to the US from Indonesia?

Gouw: It's interesting to me that, in Indonesia, I never heard or experienced any prejudices about women not being good in math or sciences. I was a very good student and very good at math—better than the boys in my class. Academically, whether it was math, science, or whatever, I was always at the top of the class. The first time that I heard that women are not as good as men in math was when I was in college. I was sitting in the front—I always like it in the front of the class. It was accounting or finance, and the professor said something like, "Women are not as good as men in math." So I made a face at him, and then he said, "Well, in general."

But, I noticed the difference. Women who grew up in Asia never heard such biases, so we didn't fear math or science. Girls and women brought up in the US hear it much more often. My husband and I don't have kids, but I've sensed that, among my friends' kids, Asian girls who are born here and go to school here are more afraid of math and science. Ever since my favorite niece—my brother's daughter—was very young, I've told her, "You are good at math. I'm going to teach you math." Today, she excels at math. I just want to encourage her to make sure that she doesn't feel inferior. I do believe that a lot of the girls and women growing up in America are sensitized to think that way because they get a lot of negative feedback. That thinking limits girls' view and discourages them from going after fields that require math and science.

Ghaffari: Why did you switch to accounting and finance?

Gouw: When I was growing up, actually I thought I'd become a spy because I read books about detectives and spies. Then, I realized I didn't like the idea of being tortured.

When I was growing up in Indonesia, the most important thing was just, "Oh, you have to go to college." Over there, you become a doctor, a scientist or an engineer, so I just choose chemistry without really knowing what I would do with it after I graduated.

After that, people told me, "If you study chemistry, then you'll work in the lab to do research." But, I decided that wasn't for me, so I changed my major to business. At first, I selected finance, then later took accounting classes and really liked it. I was good at both accounting and finance. I graduated from Illinois with an accounting degree in 1981.

Ghaffari: How did you happen to come to Los Angeles?

Gouw: Some friends introduced me to my future husband. I was going to school while he worked in San Jose. We had a long-distance relationship for two years. Then he moved to Los Angeles. I didn't want to stay in Illinois because it was too cold—especially for someone like me who came from the Indonesian tropical islands. He owned an aircraft spare parts business with my brother and some partners. He sold the business twelve years ago and retired.

Ghaffari: What was your first job?

Gouw: My first job was as an accountant at Texaco in Los Angeles. I didn't know anything. I just got a job because I needed a job. I had a great mentor in my first boss, Paul Archer, at Texaco—a wonderful man. Later on, he actually was the one who helped me to get a job at KPMG because he told me that working for a public accounting firm would accelerate my ability to move up. His wife, Jean Archer, was the assistant to the managing partner at KPMG, so he asked her to give my résumé to her boss and help me get an interview there.

Ghaffari: Did you have other mentors?

Gouw: I've had two wonderful mentors—one is a man and the other is a woman. The other mentor was a partner at KPMG. Her name is Norma Lawrence. I think it was very interesting that Jean Archer told her husband, Paul, "When Julia gets here to KPMG, she's not going to have you to protect you." Paul told her, "She'll find somebody."

I didn't feel that I needed protection, but I appreciate the way KPMG did business. The great thing about KPMG is that they gave you a variety of assignments—new things to do. They pushed you very hard, and you always felt that you didn't know what you were doing at first, because they moved people up and around. In the beginning, before I met Norma Lawrence, I was just doing my best. It was very different working for her. She told me, "You're very good—very analytical." I think she made me realize my strengths.

She had a similar background—a math major, but with an MBA from UCLA. She was very analytical, and she valued that in others. When you're young, you just don't know what you're good at or not good at. Getting feedback and encouragement makes you realize where your talents lie.

Ghaffari: How do you define a mentor?

Gouw: It's really interesting that, back in 1981, Paul Archer told me, "Julia—you're smart and have a great personality. Had you been a male Caucasian, you would go very far in corporate America."

It's something that has stayed in my mind for over thirty years—it was a very difficult time because I was a woman and I was an immigrant. He said that as a friend. When he said that, he was being honest and well-meaning.

Norma Lawrence was a really good mentor because she also told me honestly that she ranked me very high for analytical skills or productivity, but then she also said, "You need to improve your writing skills," because it was not my strong suit.

When she went to get her MBA at UCLA, she said they trained her to write better because her undergraduate degree in math also did not require a lot of writing. She put me in a writing training class reserved for managers and higher. I wasn't yet a manager, but she recommended me for that course, "… because it will help you improve your writing."

So, to answer your question, I believe it's important to have people who will be honest with you—tell you what you're good at, what you're not good at. I think that sometimes today people are overly concerned about saying things that are politically incorrect. They don't tell you the truth you need to hear.

The other thing that I learned was that she really cared about the people who worked for her.

She made sure to attend all the KPMG management meetings to support the people under her. In accounting firms, you work for many different partners or managers. If they are not in on the management meetings, you're just a name on a piece of paper. They don't know who you are when it comes time for promotions or raises. With her support, I became a manager very quickly—in three and a half years. I was so scared when I was promoted. I said, "Oh my God, most people have at least five years of experience before they got promoted. I probably don't know what I'm doing." And then she told me, "Ahh, don't worry. You're a better manager than all those people."

She had confidence. And she had more confidence in me than I did myself at the time, but then—if I had a problem or I couldn't resolve something—I could count on her to always be there.

Ghaffari: How did you come to work for East West Bank?

Gouw: I did audits at financial institutions, real estate, and construction companies for five years at KPMG—1983 to 1989. In public accounting engagements, you have a partner, a manager and a "senior in-charge," which is a staff-level person. I rose to the level of senior audit manager.

I used to audit East West Bank. At the time, the bank was looking for a controller, so the CFO asked me if I would join East West because I was familiar with everything there. Back in 1989, East West Bank had $400 million in assets and, today, we now have $21 billion. We used to make over $1 million a year, while last year we made $163 million. This year, we should make over $200 million.

Ghaffari: How did you progress at East West Bank?

Gouw: I began as vice president and controller. In 1994, I got promoted to executive vice president and CFO. In 1997, I was elected to the board of directors of the bank and the holding company. They have identical boards. The bank holding company structure allows us to do things that a bank is not permitted to do. For example, we have an insurance agency under the bank holding company or subsidiaries which issue trust-preferred instruments or other kinds of capital.

Ghaffari: What were your responsibilities as CFO?

Gouw: I was in charge of the finance department, overseeing probably fifteen to twenty people. Finance includes accounting, investment, the treasury function, and budgeting. When the bank went public, it added investor relations.

Ghaffari: How involved were you in the management-led buyout of East West Bank?

Gouw: Sometimes opportunities just come about. East West was owned by a single shareholder from Indonesia—a family had bought it in 1991. The financial crisis hit Asia in 1998, and the owners wanted to sell the bank very, very quickly to a Singaporean bank, but the Federal Reserve said regulatory approval would take years. We realized we could do a private placement with accredited investors—mostly institutional investors where no single investor would own more than 9.9 percent. A private placement did not require regulatory approval and could be done in about a month.

The former owner told us that we had one month to do the deal. If we couldn't meet that deadline, they would have to find another buyer. Dominic Ng, the East West CEO, and I went to Wall Street and we raised $238 million in two weeks and closed the deal in one month. That was June of 1998, and the timing turned out to be so great, because by August or September, the market shut down because of the failure of the Long-Term Capital Management hedge fund following the Russian financial crisis. Had we missed that window of opportunity, we would not have been able to raise any capital.

Ghaffari: How did the company fare after the IPO?

Gouw: Most of our growth came after we went public. We've had compounded growth of assets, loans, and capital increasing by 18 to 20 percent annually since then. It's been a combination of internal growth and good acquisitions. Internal growth has all come from domestic US sources. We do a lot of real-estate lending, as well as business lending. Our customers are importers, exporters, and companies located here in California.

Ghaffari: What did you do differently from the local California banks that failed during the latest financial crisis?

Gouw: We learned a great deal from the nineties when Southern California real estate got hit hard. A lot of banks chose not to address their problems. I still remember July 2007, after the Bear Stearns hedge fund blew up, we went to our board and said, "Real estate may have a problem." Early in 2008, we started to curtail our construction lending and at the same time began selling some of these loans. I engaged KPMG to review 100 percent of our portfolio of construction loans. We took the necessary charge-offs and raised capital. Our timing was extremely fortunate. We raised $200 million in preferred stock in April of 2008. Had we waited just a few months, the market would have shut down.

We wanted to make sure that we were protected against the downside, rather than simply focusing on the cost of raising capital. As it turned out, we can now look back and say that raising capital early, when it was available, was the best thing that we ever did.

Ghaffari: How did it happen that you retired from the bank, but then came back?

Gouw: My original plan was to stay until the end of 2008 and retire officially December 31, 2008. We were already looking for my successor in early

2008. I was still on the board, and I kept this office, coming in to work once a week. I was gone for the entire month of August 2009, traveling. When I come back in September, Dominic asked me, "Are you well rested?" And I said, "Why?" [He then asked,] "Can you help with this United Commercial Bank acquisition?"

I had done eight bank acquisitions for the bank after we went public in early 1999. Earlier, in 1991, East West Bank had acquired Pacific Coast Federal Savings Bank in San Francisco from the Resolution Trust Corporation during the savings and loan crisis. But, the UCB transaction in November 2009 was much more complex—involving almost $10 billion in assets and negotiations with the Federal Deposit Insurance Corporation. It was a transformational event for us—an opportunity to acquire a major competitor. We had to merge all those bank branches in and trim the duplication.

Ghaffari: You just recently went on a Fortune 500 company board. How did that come about?

Gouw: In January of this year, I went onto the boards of directors of Pacific Mutual Holding Company and Pacific LifeCorp. They're a holding company and an insurance company. I was approached by Caroline Nahas of Korn Ferry, the search firm engaged by Pacific Life. Caroline is a good friend and is very involved with UCLA Anderson School. I've known her for many years through United Way.

Ghaffari: You're involved in quite a few community activities. Tell me why you chose to be associated with some of them?

Gouw: The bank has been partners with United Way for the last fifteen years, so I'm involved in that role. When they wanted to establish a women leaders group within United Way, I was one of the original members.

I really enjoy my association with UCLA. It started with my contributions to the medical school, and then they asked me to join the Board of Visitors of the David Geffen School of Medicine at UCLA.

I have a family member who was diagnosed and treated for mood disorders at UCLA in 1997. I learned that UCLA has one of the best medical treatment and research facilities in the field. Dr. Lori Altshuler, Director of Mood Disorders Research at UCLA, is a world renowned expert and has become a dear friend. In addition, she has a keen interest in improving the treatments especially for women.

I set up the Julia Gouw Endowed Chair for Mood Disorders Research in 2003, and Dr. Lori Altshuler is the chair holder. Since then, I learned that there are about one hundred endowed chairs at the David Geffen Medical

School at UCLA, but only 7 percent of the endowed chair holders are women. Dr. Janet Pregler, director of the Iris Cantor–UCLA Women's Health Center, told me that without my endowed chair for Lori, only 6 percent of the endowed chairs would be held by women. This is one measure of how few women doctors/scientists there are who made it to the top at academic centers.

I got to know Dr. Pregler when the Iris Cantor–UCLA Women's Health Center invited me to a breakfast meeting about seven years ago, where Dr. Pregler talked about gender-based health bias. She said that when she went to medical school in the eighties, they didn't even teach women's health, but simply assumed that, since women weighed 70 percent of what men weighed, all the treatments and the dosages for women should be 70 percent of whatever men receive.

Doctors didn't even know that the symptoms and treatments for a heart attack were significantly different for women. For men, the typical warning sign for a heart attack is chest pains, but for women it's more likely to be nausea or fatigue. Many women were misdiagnosed and died of a heart attack for that reason.

The only thing they studied directly with women was the reproductive area, for obvious reasons. For everything else, the study is based upon men. Much later, they began to have medical courses about how women's bodies are different and, therefore, the research has to be different, too. She said that the funding for women's health is much less than that for men.

So, I told her and the director of development, "If you want to expand the funding for women's health, why don't I put together an executive advisory board for women's health?" I got a group of women, mostly my women executive friends, and told them, "Let's each contribute $10,000 a year for a three-year commitment and authorize the Center to use the money for research on women's health, as well as for community outreach."

The response from my women executive friends was amazing. They also brought their friends to join. In less than six months, we had nine board members. We have about twenty-six board members at this time.

Dr. Pregler divided the money fifty-fifty for research and community outreach, with the research funds used only for pilot studies. We've funded sixteen pilot studies to date. An investment of $600,000 in pilot studies has returned $6 million in government and foundation grants. Later, Dr. Pregler opened the application process to many scientists throughout UCLA.

I feel that we are the venture capitalists for women's health. We do seed funding for pilot studies. The much bigger project funding comes from National Institues of Health [NIH], but those grants wouldn't have come if the scientists hadn't developed the data in the pilot study. Sometimes, their needs are very simple. Maybe it's just a case of holding onto samples that can be used as input into other studies. Since we started, we probably have raised over $1.5 million from these women.

Our executive advisory board meets about two or three times a year. At one event, Dr. Pregler organized lunch with the scientists to tell us about some of these studies they are doing.

I'm also on the board of directors of The UCLA Foundation, the fundraising arm of the UCLA campus—undergraduate and graduate. The foundation manages the funds and also serves as an advocate for the UCLA campus in general.

Because of my involvement with UCLA, I met one of the persons from UCLA who went to St. John's Hospital, and they introduced me to the John Wayne Cancer Center, which is the affiliate of St. John's in the cancer research area. It's just been a wonderful association.

Ghaffari: You are involved in a number of women-in-leadership efforts. Are you seeing progress in this area—more women taking on leadership roles?

Gouw: I do enjoy that a lot, helping other women. I do think more and more women are taking on leadership roles. It's just not enough yet, given the percentage of the population represented by women.

We have a number of women in leadership at East West Bank. Irene Oh is our executive vice president and chief financial officer. She is a very smart, qualified person, so when the opportunity [came] for me to promote her, I think she was ready.

Our board includes Iris Chan—formerly from Wells Fargo's National Commercial Banking Group—who just came on board after Peggy Cherng decided to spend more time on her own business, Panda Express. I've been involved in recommending we bring these new women onto the board.

Ghaffari: What have been some of the most satisfying things that have happened to you in your career?

Gouw: I do think that an outstanding aspect is ensuring that the bank is doing well, that we continue to sustain the financial performance. That really is a must. If you don't do well, there's no way that you can take care of your employees, your customers, and your investors. To me, those are the three most important things. They're all equally important because we don't exist without all three of them. We have to balance the needs of all three constituents. At the end of the day, we are not going to be around if we don't deliver a strong financial performance.

I'm very proud of the fact that, because of our financial performance, we were ranked as the second-best bank in the whole country by *Forbes* magazine and *Fortune* magazine picked us as one of the ten best stocks in 2011. We are the only bank in that listing of top stock picks.

Ghaffari: Is there anything different about the way you approach investments that explains this?

Gouw: I think that we always try to be prepared for the worst case and we're willing to raise capital even when it was dilutive. I think the problem with a lot of banks is they don't want to unload the problem loans because they don't want to recognize the losses. But, we always think that safety is priority number one, so if it means that we have to dilute the common shareholders to raise capital, we are better off doing that. We always want to make sure that we have a buffer, in case something bad happens. Risk management is important.

We want to be in the business where we have the value proposition our customers want. We don't simply price everything the cheapest, because eventually, if you have to be the cheapest in town, your profitability will suffer or you have to take huge risks to make up for that discounting. But, if you offer a certain value proposition that is a win-win for the customers, then you make money and the customer also wins. I think we try to build a business based on long-term relationship banking, which is in the best interests of both the customer and the bank. That is how we can sustain our financial performance.

Ghaffari: Are most of your customers very long-term?

Gouw: Yes, although some may not be as long-term as the others. Overall, we do have high customer loyalty. When East West got started in Los Angeles in 1973, it was very difficult for the Chinese immigrant to get mortgages. We were a savings and loan thrift institute, and mortgage loans were our initial financial offering.

Over time, with the economic growth and the increase in Chinese population in Southern California, we were able to branch out and grow beyond that business. In 1995, we converted from a savings and loan to a commercial bank because many of our Chinese customers owned businesses, but we could not give them business loans as a thrift. Now, many of our customers are in the import-export business, so today we can provide them a full range of trade, finance, and commercial loans.

Ghaffari: If you converted to a commercial bank in 1995, that means you were one of the few that actually weathered the Resolution Trust era as an S&L. Is that true?

Gouw: Yes. Actually, we did not have any loss years in the nineties, despite the fact that we were 100 percent in real estate. We had eleven years of consecutive record earnings from 1997 to 2007. Unfortunately, that got interrupted in 2008 and 2009, but we resumed our record earnings in 2010. And there is a very high likelihood that 2011 will be another record year.

Ghaffari: You said there was some dilution of your shares when you went after more capital. What was the response of your shareholders? What is your relationship with your shareholders?

Gouw: Very good. Actually, some of the shareholders bought into the new issuance. We have a large presence of institutional rather than retail investors. The top twenty investors are almost all institutional investors. I think that they spend more time getting to know us. They are long-term investors that believe in our business model, as well as our ability to ride out these business cycles.

Ghaffari: How would you describe your own decision-making style?

Gouw: I use my analytical skills to make a decision. I believe in making a decision quickly, provided it's fact-based. Gather all the facts possible, but also realize you'll never have all the information that you need. Sometimes people are paralyzed and cannot make a decision because they are stuck waiting for more information. To me, the most important thing is that if you have enough information, and it's fact-based, make a decision.

At the same time, I always try to assess what is the worst case. What if things don't go well? Is the downside going to kill you or not?

I know I can always make changes. I don't believe that whatever I decide is always correct. I try to keep an open mind—I could have made a wrong decision. If I keep my options open—that I can change directions before things get worse—I can adjust. Sometimes people want to prove that they are always right. They're so adamant about proving that they are right, they are blind to the possibility they could have made a better decision. Or that they could change and eventually end up with a better outcome.

When I was an outside auditor at KPMG, we would return each year to an engagement that we audited the year before. Every time I finished an audit, no matter how well things went, I always thought we could improve on our efforts. So I developed this habit that has served me very well. I'd leave a note for myself that said, "What would I do to improve for next year?"

Even now, at the bank, I always say to myself, "If I had it to do all over again, what could I do to improve on it?" Because, no matter what, you can always improve on something you've done. You can always look back and say, "I could have done better," or you can look forward and say, "This is what I will do next time."

Ghaffari: Do you consider yourself a leader?

Gouw: In the past, I was just doing what I thought I should do. As it turned out, a lot of young people look up to me. I do hear from young women that think I am a role model in the sense that they say, "I want to be like you some day." In order to be a leader, you have to have followers, people that want to follow in your path. You have to be accountable to them.

Not long ago, the wife of the UCLA chancellor had a gathering of women faculty and invited me to make a presentation on what I believe it means "to lead by guiding principles."

To me, what is important is that everything we do in our organization has to be legal, ethical, respectful, and equitable. We build wealth through equity— we are probably one of the few banks that support junior staff through equity to ensure their interests are aligned with those of all shareholders. That's been possible every year since we went public, except 2008. Equity is in addition to affordable medical benefits and long-term disability. This is how we, as a business, create our value proposition—otherwise we would not have a real competitive advantage.

We see East West Bank as the bridge between East and West. Our mission is to help cross-border businesses—Chinese companies that invested here, immigrants that come to the US from China, as well as American companies that want to establish business in Asia.

Ghaffari: What is your advice to young women starting their careers today?

Gouw: I tell people, "If you love your job, you don't have to work a day in your life." I read it somewhere, and I thought it was pretty good.

I am very focused on the goal of building a deep alignment and commitment across the organization. I believe that everyone needs to know, and buy into, the ultimate goals of the organization because many times people just go through the process mindlessly—just do the busy work to stay active.

We're focused on building a strong team of people—diverse, talented, flexible, confident, collaborative—people who share the same values throughout the organization. Flexibility is important to me because too often people might say, "This is the only way to do things." But time and circumstances change, so you have to be willing to adapt. We also do strategic alliances with outside companies in those cases where we might not have a particular expertise, our own internal resources, or investment bankers. We always try to improve because nothing lasts forever.

This is something I learned at KPMG where we had to develop expertise in many different industries. Instead of researching everything myself, I learned that people who are experts in a field love to share their knowledge with you. I take advantage of that because I don't want to have to learn every- thing myself from scratch. I like to ask people what they know and then from there, I can move on to see what other things that I can research in order to make my final decision.

Ghaffari: Is there anything that you would advise differently if you were talking to men?

Gouw: I think this applies pretty much for both men and women. It's just a style that works for me. I happen to be a woman, but I'm pretty sure there are so many different leadership styles that it's applicable to men or women.

Ghaffari: How would you describe the support from your family?

Gouw: My husband has been very supportive. I think that helps a lot, too. We've been married for thirty years, now. He never complains if I have to travel. If I come home late, he makes sure that there's food. He's very, very supportive.

Ghaffari: When you were young, you heard some negative things about women. How have you dealt with the negative things that might have come your way later in your career?

Gouw: With criticism or people doubting me, I'm not overly sensitive. It is what it is. But, I do tell young people that if you build your confidence, that will help you to be not as sensitive to criticism. You just take everything in as ideas or feedback, and then you make a decision based upon what you think is best.

I just want to make sure that I bring value to the company, to my boss, to my team members, to the shareholders. The nice thing about our share- holders is that we know what they want—it's a lot easier and quantifiable. They just want you to deliver the investment value to them.

Ghaffari: How do you define success?

Gouw: If you achieve what you dream and are content with yourself and your accomplishments, that's how I define success.

Jacqueline K. Barton

Professor and Chair, Chemistry and Chemical Engineering, California Institute of Technology

Born May 7, 1952 in New York, New York.

Dr. Jacqueline K. Barton is the Arthur and Marian Hanisch Memorial Professor of Chemistry and Chair of the Division of Chemistry and Chemical Engineering at the California Institute of Technology (Caltech). She also oversees The Barton Research Group at Caltech.

Dr. Barton's work focuses on the chemical and physical properties of DNA and the biological implications of those properties. Her research has developed DNA-based electrochemical sensors and probes that provide the foundation for the design and development of innovative diagnostic tools and therapeutics.

The White House named Dr. Barton one of seven recipients of the 2011 National Medal of Science, the highest honor bestowed by the United States government on scientists.

Dr. Barton's list of honors is very extensive and includes the National Science Foundation's Alan T. Waterman Award (1985), which recognizes the talent, creativity, and influence of a singular young researcher; Phi Lambda Upsilon's National Fresenius Award (1986), presented annually to an outstanding young scientist who has attained national recognition in research, teaching, and/or administration; the

Mayor's Award for Excellence in Science and Technology (1988), presented annually to recognize important members of the science and engineering communities in New York City; the Havinga Medal (1995), awarded biennially by the University of Leiden (the Netherlands) to an outstanding chemist; and the Paul Karrer Gold Medal (1996), given to an outstanding researcher in the field of chemistry in conjunction with an invitation to present a scientific lecture at the University of Zurich.

Dr. Barton is the third woman to receive the Weizmann Women & Science Award (1998) from the American Committee for the Weizmann Institute of Science. It is a biennial award established to honor an outstanding woman scientist in the United States who has made significant contributions to the scientific community. The objective of the award, which includes a $25,000 research grant, is to advance women in science and to provide strong role models to motivate and encourage the next generation of young women scientists.

The American Chemical Society has presented Dr. Barton with ten awards, each affording her an opportunity to present a paper in her area of expertise. Most recently, she received the Linus Pauling Medal (2007), recognizing outstanding accomplishments in chemistry in the spirit of and in honor of Linus Pauling, a two-time Nobel Prize winner (Chemistry and Peace).

An Alfred P. Sloan Foundation Research Fellow (1984), a Dreyfus Teacher-Scholar (1986), and a recipient of the MacArthur Foundation Fellowship (1991), Dr. Barton was also given a Presidential Young Investigator Award by the National Science Foundation.

She received the Barnard College University Medal (1990) and the University Medal for Excellence from Columbia University (1992) along with nine honorary doctorates of science, as follows: Knox College (1991), Williams College (1992), New Jersey Institute of Technology (1993), Kenyon College (1994), Lawrence University (1994), Skidmore College (1997), Hamilton College (2005), Yale University (2005), and Columbia University (2010).

Dr. Barton has been elected to the American Academy of Arts and Sciences (1991), the American Philosophical Society (2000), and the National Academy of Sciences (2002).

She has served on the board of Dow Chemical Company since 1993. She also served on the boards of Gilead Sciences Inc. (1989–2008) and GeneOhm Sciences Inc. (2001–2005), a biotechnology company co-founded by Dr. Barton. Based upon her industrial board service, she was named an Outstanding Director (2006) by Outstanding Directors Exchange.

Clearly one of the most highly recognized and honored scientists in her field, Dr. Barton is now proud to watch her own postdoctoral students receive similar awards and recognitions.

Elizabeth Ghaffari: Can you give me some background about why you became interested in science, in the early years?

Dr. Jacqueline Barton: There really was no science in my family whatsoever. My father was a lawyer and a judge. When I was a kid, I just loved math. I went to Riverdale Country School for Girls, an all-girls prep school in Riverdale, New York. The girls' school was down by the river, while up on the hill was the boys' school, Riverdale Country School for Boys.

I took a lot of math and loved it—and did really well in it. My high school teacher, Mrs. Rosenberg, suggested to the headmistress that I take calculus, which required that I attend class at the boys' school. There was a little red station wagon that would take me from the girls' school to the boys' school for my calculus class. It was a big deal—my parents had to come in and approve it.

Anyway, I liked math and was always doing math problems for fun. When I went to college, I saw that chemistry was an opportunity to do mathematics and apply it in the real-world setting. And I loved it.

I went to Barnard College, which is an all-women's college. Barnard is a part of Columbia University, this wonderful research university right across the street. I had the advantages of a small college setting in the context of a major research university community. I had my first chemistry courses just with women there. And it was fantastic. I didn't think there was anything funny about a woman doing science. That's where I fell in love with doing science. I graduated in 1974 [summa cum laude].

Barnard is still an all-women's college.[1]

Ghaffari: So, next you went across the street for your doctorate at Columbia?

Barton: I was a New Yorker, born and bred, so I didn't venture very far. I first went to graduate school at Columbia, studying metals and DNA, the beginnings of the work I do now. At first, I wasn't sure I wanted to have a high-powered research professorship. I thought maybe I wanted to go into

---

[1] Columbia College, the oldest undergraduate college at Columbia University, first admitted women in the fall of 1983.

industry. I received my doctorate in inorganic chemistry [1978] from Columbia, working in the laboratory of Steven J. Lippard.

Ghaffari: You studied with both Stephen J. Lippard, a specialist in bioinorganic chemistry, and Robert G. Shulman, an authority on molecular biophysics and biochemistry. Did you select them or did they select you?

Barton: I selected them—that's pretty much the way it works. Typically, you tune your research to match the interests of the professors with whom you want to carry out your research. Steve Lippard was my mentor in graduate school. That's how I got interested in working on DNA.

After that, I was given a postdoctoral fellowship at Bell Laboratories in New Jersey. Bob Shulman was head of the laboratory there until 1979. Then he moved to Yale, and I went to New Haven and spent about six months working with their instruments. At the time, I did a post-doc at Bell Labs, which was the crème de la crème of research within industry. It wasn't pure industry, but it was close enough. Then I decided I really wanted to teach as well as do research.

I took a job as an assistant professor of chemistry and biochemistry at Hunter College, City University of New York City, from 1980 to 1982. It was while at Hunter that I realized how important it was to me to have a position in a state-of-the-art research laboratory. I started my independent research group, The Barton Research Group, while at Hunter.

Ghaffari: Was your experience with Bob Shulman also a case of you selecting him?

Barton: With Shulman, it was more that I wanted to go work in industry, but on a biologically-related problem. At that time, it was the very beginnings of magnetic resonance imaging—MRI. We were looking at the metabolism of cells and cell yeast using nuclear magnetic resonance [NMR] methods. Those were really cool, interesting things to be learning about while I worked with Bob.

In 1983, I returned to Columbia, becoming an associate professor of chemistry and biological sciences in 1985 and a full professor in 1986.

Ghaffari: Were Mrs. Rosenberg, Steve Lippard, and Bob Shulman your primary mentors?

Barton: Yes, and Bernice Segal. Bernice taught me chemistry at Barnard College. And there's no question that Bernice was one tough, tough lady. That's where I learned about high expectations. When you wrote a lab notebook, you'd write ten pages, but she'd write ten pages back. She was a really, really tough, outstanding teacher and mentor—so Bernice gets a lot of credit.

Ghaffari: When did you start publishing?

Barton: You start publishing in graduate school. I've published over three hundred articles by now. My first article was in 1977. I published with Lippard in the mid-eighties and then with Shulman for a couple of papers. Now that I have my own lab, I'm listed as the last author on much of our work. That's the culture of chemistry. Now, I do more research, but I'm teaching my group of students all the time. I have a group of sixteen to eighteen graduate students and post-docs, and they carry out research in my lab.

Ghaffari: What brought you to Caltech?

Barton: I came to Caltech in the fall of 1989 for two reasons. The primary reason is because I fell in love with my now-husband, Peter Dervan, who was on the faculty at Caltech. And the other reason is that Caltech is the best chemistry department, arguably, in the world. They were interested in trying to woo me here. What they didn't know is how easy a task that was.

Ghaffari: You have never co-authored with him, right?

Barton: No, we have not collaborated. That is sort of a rule we've developed. We've talked a little bit about collaborating, but we've decided that that was not necessary for either of us. We're in a very different situation than most. Both of us have had students who were a couple, both with their PhDs, and we've seen how difficult it is for a couple to get two good positions at one university. It's really quite a challenge. In our case, I had already become a professor and had my own independent career when Peter and I fell in love. I was married to Don Barton when I was in my last year of college at Barnard. That's why my publishing name is Barton. We divorced when I was at Columbia. When I met Peter, we were already independent scientific entities, so collaboration didn't seem like a good thing to do.

We've collaborated incredibly successfully with our daughter, Elizabeth, though. And with Peter's own son, Andrew. Elizabeth's at Yale—she'll be twenty-one this fall. Andrew went to Yale, and we just went to his graduation from Harvard Medical School.

Ghaffari: Did you have any challenges raising kids in an intense academic laboratory environment?

Barton: Well, you know, I've got a wonderful husband. We live three minutes away from the lab. I've always been really good at delegating to other people those things I shouldn't have to spend time on. I've had the same nanny, now housekeeper, for twenty-one years. I've had the same assistant in my office, Maureen, for twenty years. She's also fabulous. I've got a wonderful support system, and I sort of make sure my priorities are what I want them to be. And that's my family and my research.

Ghaffari: You've received an incredible number of awards. Did you initiate these, or did they kind of come to you?

Barton: Your colleagues nominate you. I've been pretty lucky. I've had wonderful colleagues, and I've got an outstanding research group that does great science.

Ghaffari: You've received nine honorary degrees. Are there any in particular that have been very satisfying to you?

Barton: Well, I received one from Yale, which was lovely. That was extra special because Yale ended up being a place that was important to my family. That was wonderful, and they're wonderful people. Then, a year ago, I received another one from Columbia—the second recognition. Earlier I had received a medal from them. I now have a lot of degrees from Columbia. I love the university—it's such an outstanding institution.

Ghaffari: How do you look at your corporate board roles—Dow Chemical and Gilead Sciences?

Barton: Earlier, I was on the Scientific Advisory Board of Gilead. I've been on the board of directors of Dow Chemical for almost twenty years. Dow is an extraordinary company. It's important to me as a chemist to be able to contribute to that board. It's an outstanding group of people, who all bring different perspectives to the board. I'm the only scientist—the sole chemist on the board. That provides a unique perspective.

I tend to be one who's always pushing for innovative science and technology. I guess that's what I bring to the company, the board, and the shareholders. Now, we're moving whole hog in that direction, which is really terrific.

The recent webinar broadcast, "The Future We Create," sponsored by Dow, is one example. This [2011] is the international year of chemistry, and Dow is the world leader in chemistry, so it makes sense that they would be supportive of that effort.

Ghaffari: How did you get on the Science Advisory Board at Gilead Sciences?

Barton: It was primarily because of my involvement in nucleic acid chemistry. It also turns out that Peter is the scientific founder of Gilead. I was very involved with that board until I became chair of chemistry and chemical engineering here at Caltech. I had to cut back on some of my outside commitments.

Ghaffari: How did you get that job?

Barton: There was a search committee set up by the provost of the faculty of chemistry and chemical engineering. I was gratified that my colleagues thought I'd be a good person to do this.

Ghaffari: You've done a lot of work with the American Chemical Society. How do you balance the academic with the business side?

Barton: The wonderful thing about chemistry is my involvement in research. Finding the next great idea about how the world works and the technology transfer—how the science actually gets transferred into things that affect our community—is very important. That's something that really distinguishes chemistry and chemical engineering—it is so closely tied to industry in terms of pharmaceuticals, making materials, and to all sorts of practical perspectives. So it makes sense for someone who's involved in chemical research to work with the Society and be involved in technology transfer. That's true of many of my colleagues.

Most of my colleagues aren't on boards. But many of my colleagues are involved in small companies, consulting for large companies, or starting companies. Those roles are something that many of us take on as both a responsibility and an opportunity.

Ghaffari: Tell me about your involvement with GeneOhm Sciences.

Barton: I founded GeneOhm Sciences as a company and was on the board. We started it in San Diego because I wanted it to be separate and distinct from my lab, although it was a spinout of technology developed originally in my lab. We take electrons and shoot them through DNA. That's why it was called GeneOhm. We started this as a diagnostic company with funding by Domain Ventures. We sold it several years later to BD Diagnostics for $230 million.

That's the only spinoff company that I've done, but I loved it. It was a great effort and opportunity. The moment was right to create the business, but our timing was lousy in terms of starting up just when the economy was tanking [in 2001].

When there was an offer to buy us out, it was the right thing to do, but it slightly broke my heart because I thought this was going to be a completely new kind of diagnostics company. I was interested in going forward and seeing if we could do an IPO or something, but the timing was right to sell.

Chapter 7 | Jacqueline K. Barton: Professor and Chair, Chemistry and Chemical Engineering, California Institute of Technology

Ghaffari: Do you see yourself doing more of that technology-transfer/ entrepreneurial thing again in the future?

Barton: I don't know. Maybe. I'm not clear about that now. It was very gratifying. And interesting. For the first time, I was involved in a small company with a lean-and-mean kind of focus. I learned a lot. It was a whole different perspective from being associated with Dow Chemical, an incredibly large, global company. But, now that I'm doing this chair work, that's taking up a lot of my extra time.

Ghaffari: Do you see yourself adding more boards to your roster?

Barton: No. I've been pretty clear about not doing more than one board at this stage of my life. A board is a very large commitment of time. Importantly, I still love to do research. My group is doing some really neat science, so I have to save some time for that.

Ghaffari: The Barton Research Group is impressive in that consistently it's had such a high number of women. How do you account for the fact that something like fourteen out of twenty-three of your current students are young women?

Barton: The one thing that I find most gratifying about my career—more than the awards, more even than some of the things we've discovered—is the fact that twenty-five women whom I have trained are now, themselves, university or college professors.

Ghaffari: Why do you think that's the case? What are you doing right?

Barton: Well, I do have my own theories about this, although it's completely anecdotal. I'm not a sociologist, I'm a woman scientist. People always ask me about women and science. I do know that I'm as tough on my women as I am on the men in my group. I have very, very high expectations for the women in my group. I know that they can do it. So, I look them in the eye and say, "You know, you can do this if that's what you want." Then I'm tough on them. I ask them to raise the bar, and they do it. They're terrific.

Also, I think they see that you can have a life and also be a woman scientist. I've always cared about my daughter and son. If I ever had to get up and leave the lab because I had to do something with Elizabeth, I would do it. I'd say to them, "Everybody, sorry. I'll be back." So they all knew that, in some respects, you can do both. I think that's a good thing for them all to see.

Ghaffari: Do you treat the women differently from the way you treat the men?

Barton: I treat everybody differently. I treat them all as people. I don't treat them differently because they are men or women. But I can generalize that the women often come in with less confidence. I try to push them and give them that confidence.

I tell everyone a story that describes how I think about all this. When you're in graduate school, life is tough. Going through graduate school takes about five years. Along about your third year, everyone starts to hit the wall. Life is tough. Experiments aren't working. You're not getting the data you need to write the papers you want. It's tough—plain and simple. I wonder if, when a young woman scientist starts hitting that wall, she calls her mom or maybe her dad. They tell her, "You know, sweetheart, it's okay. You don't have to do this. It's all right." Or perhaps she talks to her mentor in her research group, and the mentor says, "Why are you killing yourself over this?" So, maybe she doesn't stick with it.

But nobody ever says that to a guy. Not mom or dad. They will almost always say to the male scientist, "You get in there and get the job done." Because it's socially unacceptable for a guy to fail, whereas for a woman—"It's okay, sweetheart. You can do something else."

That's my own personal view of it all. So, when the young women scientists come to me and say, "You know, I don't know if I can do it," I say, "Damn it, yes, you can! Get back in there. You can do it!"

I raise the activation barrier as high for the women in my group as for the guys. And that's sort of my view of the world. I think one of the people with whom I trained, Steve Lippard, also is known for having trained a lot of outstanding women. I guess including me. That's just the way he was. Some of my colleagues are that way as well, and they've been very successful in training women. In the end, it's a matter of high expectations and having confidence in people. Then people meet those expectations.

Ghaffari: You've mentioned your colleagues a number of times. Do you think they treat you differently from other women professors in the field?

Barton: I think I've been very lucky. They've all treated me well and with respect. When I first moved to Caltech, after I married Peter, there were some concerns because Peter was so well established at Caltech. I did have concerns about, "Are they going to treat me like Peter's wife, instead of *me?*"

But that's long passed. Part of the reason it was so gratifying that they made me chair is that there has never been a woman chair in our division ever. That made me feel very good.

Sometimes my students will have concerns like that. I always tell them, "Look, nobody's interested. We're all busy. Don't walk around with a chip on your shoulder. Nobody cares. Just treat people with respect and expect them to treat you with respect. Don't worry about whether you're a woman or you're six-feet-eleven-inches tall. You're you, and they are who they are. That's what's important."

Ghaffari: How would you describe your personal decision-making style?

Barton: I go with my gut. It's the same way I do research. I go with my gut, but you've got to make sure you do all the homework and that you've put the right controls into place. It's strategy. Do I want to go in this direction? Do I want to waste my time? Do I understand the risks and rewards? I'm always interested in learning new things about the world, so that's what directs me. That's what gets me excited.

Ghaffari: What would you say is your biggest, most satisfying personal achievement?

Barton: My daughter—if you saw her, you'd know that she's the most wonderful thing in the whole wide world. Having a child and watching her grow up is incredible. It's not that she's my achievement from an intellectual standpoint. It's that my husband and I had this wonderful kid, and together we have this amazing family that's absolutely important to both of us.

The other side is the women and men that I have trained in my laboratory—my scientific children. That's the flip side.

Ghaffari: Is there anything you would say to advise young women about their interest in science or math?

Barton: Do what you love. Follow your passion. And, if you love doing science, you can do it. There's no reason why you can't. So, do what you love, because whatever you love doing, you'll be good at it.

Amy Millman

President, Springboard Enterprises

Born June 1954 in Brooklyn, New York.

*For more than a decade, **Amy Millman** has been president and principal advocate of Springboard Enterprises—the premier venture-catalyst platform for building women-led businesses. Springboard Enterprises educates, sources, coaches, showcases, and supports high-growth, women-owned firms seeking equity capital for expansion. Under Ms. Millman's leadership, Springboard has helped more than 400 women-led companies raise more than $5 billion in equity financing, including eight IPOs, and legions of high-value mergers and acquisitions. More than 80 percent of Springboard companies are still in business, generating $4 billion in revenues and creating tens of thousands new jobs.*

In 2000, Ms. Millman became one of the founders of the Springboard Venture Forum program which defined the organization's strategic direction. At the organization's venture forums, 20 to 25 women-led, high-growth enterprises showcase their business opportunities to venture investors. Springboard holds educational programs in cities throughout the US, introducing women entrepreneurs to equity capital and strategies that enable them to build high-growth businesses. Backed by Ms. Millman's relationship-building expertise, these two components have expanded the organization's strategic direction.

Prior to Springboard, Amy Millman spent seven years as the executive director of the National Women's Business Council, the federal commission on women's business ownership. The Council was instrumental in some of the earliest women-led business initiatives including passage of the 1995 legislation that established a federal contracting goal for women-owned businesses and access to capital initiatives to increase the flow of both debt and equity to women entrepreneurs.

Ms. Millman began her career as a researcher for Congressional Quarterly Inc. and worked as legislative analyst for the Occupational Safety and Health Administration (OSHA). She was also a lobbyist for both Philip Morris and the American Trucking Associations.

Ms. Millman earned a bachelor's degree in history and law from Carnegie Mellon University in 1976 and a master's degree in public administration from The George Washington University School of Business and Public Administration in 1979.

Elizabeth Ghaffari: Were there entrepreneurs in your family?

Amy Millman: I suppose you could point to my grandparents who came from Europe in the 1880s. They were pushcart peddlers in Manhattan, so I guess you could call them entrepreneurial, although it wasn't their choice—it was the only option to make money to live on.

The view back then was, "Get a good education, a job where hopefully you could stay for thirty years, have a nice family, and live the American dream." My father was a printing supplies salesman. After I was old enough, my mother went back to work for Nassau County New York Social Services as a records management supervisor. It was just a way to help pay the bills. Her real passion was to run a boutique clothing store—something she had done after graduating from high school. Much later, after she retired, she moved down to Washington to be with me, and we got her a job working with a friend who opened a clothing store. It was pretty exciting for her. She really loved it.

Ghaffari: What attracted you to Carnegie Mellon University?

Millman: There was no way that I would have picked that school, myself. My father decided that that was where he wanted me to go. My father worshipped his older brother. So when my uncle's granddaughter, my cousin, went there, my father decided that that's where he wanted me to go.

I wanted to go somewhere other than New York, so I thought, "Why not? This seems like an exotic and interesting change of pace." It was a pretty prestigious school, and I got in. Little did I know that going there would result in a complete change in my whole focus and perception of my career and beliefs.

If I had chosen, for myself, I would have pursued a political science major or something similar because that was my orientation. But Carnegie Mellon had no major like that—everything was very quantitative.

In Pittsburgh, at Carnegie Mellon University, I learned all about profit motives and business and thinking differently from what I'd been brought up to believe. That's were I learned that there could be an entrepreneurial option in my career.

Ghaffari: How did you come to Washington, DC?

Millman: I had done an internship on Capitol Hill during my junior year. Right then, I realized, "This is where I want to be." It was such an information cornucopia. I just loved the city. As soon as I graduated, I hopped on a train and came to Washington.

The first day I landed in town, I got a job through a placement agency working for a super law firm that needed a very, very junior admin person. I thought, "How perfect. I'll take this job and go to law school in the fall. Maybe, I can even get them to pay for my law school."

Unfortunately, it was the worst job experience. In law firms, if you're not an associate, there is little chance that you'll work on cases. I was a first-year assistant paralegal, not even a paralegal, and didn't understand my position in the firm. I thought they'd actually assign me to a case after the first month or so. That was a little delusional, even for a twenty-two-year-old.

After the first month, I went to my supervisor and said, "Okay, I'm ready to be assigned to a case." They laughed and gave me one in which I spent a month copying tens of thousands of Japanese language documents at another law firm involved with the case because we had to make sure that both firms had the same documents. After the month was over and the copying was finished, I came back, handed them my key and left.

Ghaffari: What did you learn from that experience?

Millman: I realized they weren't going make me a lawyer or an associate just because I wanted to be one. Another important thing that really hit me was the fact that there were two hundred lawyers in the firm and one woman partner. She practically slept in her office. I didn't really understand the issue of workaholism at the time. Today, I embrace it. I'm fine with it. But back then I just didn't get it. She had been there seven years already. I realize now that that woman worked 24/7 because in those days—the 1970s—she still had a lot to prove. It probably seemed like pushing a rock up a mountain— one woman partner in a law firm of two hundred. I couldn't relate to her struggle, so I decided to seek my fortune elsewhere.

In those days, I was more into finding myself and learning about life, meeting people, going out, and doing interesting things. So I sent out around five hundred résumés and got about four hundred and ninety-nine rejections until I got the job at a news service, Congressional Quarterly—using my quantitative-based education from CMU to provide our reporters with info on the voting behavior of members of Congress.

We called CQ "graduate school" because the reporters at CQ essentially wrote term papers for a living. My job was to prepare the charts for the daily votes of the members of Congress. I think I was hired because I knew how to operate the computer punch card machine, which I learned at CMU. Nobody else knew how to do it, so I got the job.

CMU was all about the numbers, quantifying and thinking about how to apply that knowledge. In the seventies, the whole world of computers in business was just starting up, and that orientation gave me an edge in the job market.

The job was in a wonderful location close to George Washington University, where I could live, work, and go to school at night. Rather than go to law school, I switched my major to a master's in public administration because I was determined that my career path was government-related. So I went to school at night and worked during the day at Congressional Quarterly.

Ghaffari: What attracted you most about Washington?

Millman: There's a difference between what I call Washington, DC, and "the rest of the world." DC businesses are advocacy-related or focused on providing a service for the government. How you start and run a business in DC is very different from how the rest of the world thinks about businesses.

I'm comfortable as an advocate, so DC was a great place for me to plant. And my master's degree gave me the credentials I needed to get my next job, working at the Department of Labor. I never would have gotten that job without a master's degree. I worked in the legislative office of the Occupational Safety and Health Administration for about a year and a half.

It was the last year of the Carter administration which was interesting because the last year of any presidential administration is stressful, not knowing what the election results will be. Typically, political employees are in a race to make their mark on policy, and career employees are not really predisposed to do much that would have an impact because they assume it's all going to get overturned when the new administration takes over.

The transition was even more disruptive because the leadership changed from Democrat to Republican, which meant a very different attitude about labor interests and occupational safety policy. That experience gave me insight into how government worked from the inside, the human frailties of managing an agency in transition, and a better awareness of why government isn't as efficient as we'd like. It's difficult to get anything done when our system dictates that we reinvent the wheel every four or eight years.

Ghaffari: What would you consider your noteworthy accomplishments while you were at OSHA?

Millman: A couple of things. I learned how to play squash. There was a squash court, and a bunch of people at the department got together regularly to play squash after work. You may not think that's important except for the fact that, in Washington, the most important thing is how many people you know. Playing squash was another way of building relationships with people you needed to do business with.

The second thing I learned is how to write testimony—another really important skill to know in Washington. There's a formula for that, as I learned from my OSHA bosses, who had been on Capitol Hill until their member of Congress retired. They were so knowledgeable about the process and taught me a lot.

I believe that you should look at every experience both as a participant and as an observer—figure out what skill or lesson you can learn from it to apply to the next situation. Every single person that I worked for has taught me a big lesson either positive or negative—things to emulate or to avoid. I also can point to a lesson or skill that I learned from each of the positions I held. I just wish I had been purposeful about this when I was younger.

Ghaffari: How did you get the lobbyist job at Philip Morris?

Millman: When it was clear that Carter had lost the election, my boss at OSHA said, "We're all short-termers here, now. Here's a list of head hunters—start sending your résumé around." I did and soon got a call back, telling me, "I'm doing a search for a major corporation, and they'd like you to come for an interview." The company was Philip Morris.

The company was based in New York City, which was great for me because I was born there and my mother still lived on Long Island. Ironically, I was a complete anti-smoker, but fascinated by the company which was being run by marketing and advertising guys. So I took the job.

Ghaffari: You helped guide Philip Morris's contributions to women's organizations and interests. Is that accurate?

Millman: Actually, it wasn't so much that Philip Morris was interested in women or that the company decided to enter the women's market and get them all to smoke. Rather, it was because many of the guys running the company had really powerful wives who were very interested in politics and sports and were very active in the women's movement in New York. That's probably how the company became involved with women's tennis and sponsored the Virginia Slims tennis tournament. They were heavily involved with women's political groups way before I came to work there.

As I was the only woman professional in the Philip Morris Washington office, I was the logical choice to work with the groups we sponsored. I was interested in the women's political world and the pro-choice movement, so I grabbed the opportunity to get involved. We never marketed our products to these organizations or required them to promote the products—never. The company was a great corporate citizen.

Some of the organizations were reluctant to accept our money. It was difficult for them because it was "tobacco money." They liked me personally because I would be really honest with them. I'd say, "Do not take this contribution if you feel that you will have difficulty with other donors or constituents because of it."

Ghaffari: Did you meet a lot of interesting people in that experience?

Millman: It was a fabulous, ten-year experience. It was a great job. First, because they had all the resources in the world so you could do all kinds of amazing things. And, second, and the most important thing about the whole experience for me, my big takeaway, was learning that everything in life was really about building strong relationships. I learned that if you operate with high integrity and honesty, if people can trust you, if you genuinely help them and understand what they need to be successful—then you'll be successful.

Ghaffari: Why did you decide to leave?

Millman: I'd been there ten years, and new leadership was coming in. I didn't feel that it was the place for me anymore. It was time to see what I'd learned there and apply it elsewhere. A couple of my mentors reaffirmed that, saying, "It's really time for you to move on. And here are some job options for you."

Also, I had two children who were under the age of five then. It was getting a little difficult explaining that I worked for a tobacco company. The anti-smoking movement was picking up intensity in the schools at the time.

Personally, I never had any qualms about working for Philip Morris even though our products were alcohol, tobacco, and snack food. I had no problems with any of that. I never said anything that I didn't believe or that wouldn't pass the "sniff test." I was always open and honest about what I was selling. But it was time to move on, so I took the lobbyist job at the American Trucking Association.

Ghaffari: Can you tell me more about the mentors in your career?

Millman: During my time at Philip Morris, I had two mentors—both prominent Republicans, interestingly enough.

Both were very gracious about trying to mentor me all those years. We'd get together on occasion. One day, they said, "Listen, there's a job opening at the Trucking Association, and we think you are the right person for it. You should take it." They stood to gain nothing from that. They probably realized that Philip Morris was no longer a good situation for me.

There is a very tight-knit group of people in Washington who are the heart and soul of the city. They make things run. And they look out for you and watch your back. Again, the whole town is about relationships.

Ghaffari: What was most memorable about your experience at the Trucking Association?

Millman: It was a great opportunity for me to spread my wings a little. I got to apply what I'd learned at Philip Morris and to try out some new things.

It's like when you leave your family for the first time. Leaving your comfort zone, but feeling the excitement of a new adventure. I could say to myself, "Wait. I don't have to think and do things the way I've always done them. I can think bigger, think more independently." In doing that, you take on more risks. You learn more about what you're good at and what you're not good at. I gained a greater confidence in who I was and what my skills were.

Ghaffari: Was your position as a lobbyist high on the pecking order?

Millman: No, while there are hierarchies, most people in Washington operate on the same plane. Everybody is an advocate. You are differentiated by how bold and connected you are. You're known by how many people you know and your success in making connections. This was a lateral move for me, but any job that I took would have been a lateral, unless I was running an office for somebody.

Ghaffari: How did you get appointed to the National Women's Business Council?

Millman: This was another time of political transition. President Clinton had just won the election and at the time I was on the board of the Women's Campaign Fund—a bipartisan, pro-choice, advocacy organization. Some of the board members who were also helping the "transition effort" approached me about a position in the new Administration running the National Women's Business Council as executive director.

This was a big turning point in my career. I had never really run anything before, including a business. My strong suit was advocating policy positions. I didn't know anything about running a business, and this position involved working with small businesses owned by women. I also didn't know any women business owners at the time. But my recruiters were very interested in learning more about these women and their demographics, political affiliations, and what they needed for their businesses. They wanted to know more about women business owners and how to involve them in the women's political world.

This was perfect for me because I was big into constituency-building. I interviewed and got the job. Then I discover that Congress hadn't funded the Council in the budget and that soon it would "sunset"—be closed. I had just six months to turn this around. You would have thought that, as a seasoned lobbyist, I would have checked all that out before taking the job— but I didn't.

Ghaffari: What did you do?

Millman: At the time, I had two young children, my husband had his own business, but I was the primary breadwinner of the family. My first reaction was to crawl into bed and pull the covers over my head.

But then I thought about it and realized that, "Hey, this is a turnaround situation. I can do this." That was sheer optimism talking. Next, I started talking to people about the Council. I soon realized that Congress had appointed all these women business owners from their districts to serve on this commission, but they were not a homogeneous group by any means. They weren't working well together, and many of them had gone up to Capitol Hill to complain. Well, one thing I learned as a lobbyist is that men hate it when women complain because it then becomes a public problem for them. Their idea of dealing with problems is to get rid of it, not solve it. That is why the Council's charter was scheduled to expire.

I appealed to a lot of people I'd known over the years, saying, "Listen—give me a little more time, and I will make this into a shining star." First, we needed to draft new legislation to allow for a more diverse membership and, to give it more prominence, we asked the president to appoint the chairman. Next, we recruited women's business organizations, in addition to individuals, to serve on the Council. Finally, with the support of the many women's business organizations, we convinced Congress to reauthorize the Council, giving it a new lease on life. If I had learned anything over twelve years as a lobbyist, I knew how to build support for a legislative initiative and get it passed.

With the passage of the legislation and corresponding appropriation, we appointed a whole new group of members: five individuals and five organizations. The council has been reauthorized several times over the years and continues to do great work.

One of the major initiatives during my tenure was to establish a brain trust of about fifty women's organizations who met to develop the policy agenda to support women's business enterprise in the country. Every member organization and individual participated in creating the agenda and then interpreted that agenda for their membership. The collaboration of many organizations and having a presidential appointee on the Council added cachet and importance to our work.

We worked closely with the White House Women's Office led by Betsy Myers, which enabled us to make women's business ownership a topic for policy discussion at the White House. In addition to the research we funded and the initiatives we launched, we also created a "best practices" manual, which we were able to share with policy makers at the 2000 OECD[1] world meeting in Paris.

Ghaffari: What's the most long-lasting performance indicator of this group—what made you the proudest?

Millman: There are so many achievements. People talk about the Council's achievements to this day because they were an important part of the process. If you talk to anybody involved with the Council at that time, Republican or Democrat, they'll say, "That was a moment when the stars aligned." A lot of people were responsible for the success of the programs, initiatives, and policies. It was truly collaborative.

In particular, the research we conducted really put women entrepreneurs on the political map. We used census data supported by case studies. We brought successful women into the public eye. We talked about contracting and passed some of the first legislation that set goals for contracting opportunities for women-owned businesses. We focused on education programs for women business owners. We supported expansion of the women business centers around the country to serve the interests and needs of their communities and support local women in enterprise development, whether in impoverished rural towns or in big cities.

Today there are over one hundred and ten women business centers. There were only three or four when we started. The result—people finally began to believe that "women can run businesses."

We served as advisors to the White House, Congress, and the Small Business Administration, and some of the recommendations and programs we launched were adopted by the SBA. However, many others were intended

---

[1] Organisation for Economic Co-operation and Development.

to be adopted by the private sector. For instance, we served as a catalyst for a women's certification program, the Women's Enterprise Business National Council, and for the Women's Business Center program, which is supported by local clients, corporations, and state government within their communities. We were trying to create an infrastructure that wasn't government-focused, but rather was private-sector driven. Springboard was also one of those initiatives.

Ghaffari: How did Springboard Enterprises come about?

Millman: President Clinton chose Lillian Vernon, a very successful direct-marketing entrepreneur, to be the chair of the National Women's Business Council. When her term was up, she suggested Kay Koplovitz as her replacement. Kay was named by Clinton and her catchphrase was, "We're all about big businesses starting small."

Kay was the founder and CEO of USA Network, a cable television network. She built it from the ground floor to become a $5 billion enterprise before it was sold to NBC.

Kay was very connected and, among her many roles, served on the board of Oracle Corporation. She was very interested in what was going on in Silicon Valley at the end of the nineties and wanted us to learn more about women's involvement in the business scene there. We were co-hosting workshops in California with the Federal Reserve on access to capital and invited some women technology-entrepreneurs to join us.

The women said, "You know, the funding source you are talking about is bank lending, and that's irrelevant to us. We'll never get bank lending. We need equity capital." The statistics were stark—less than 2 percent of venture capital was going to women-led businesses. So, we set out to educate ourselves about what we could do to increase women's access to equity capital. And that's where the whole idea of holding a venture forum featuring women-led businesses came into play.

Ghaffari: How did you start?

Millman: Once we decided we wanted to host a venture forum, we approached a few people who were knowledgeable about those programs—the investor community and the women's entrepreneurial community—and together we formed a team that would produce the forum. We used the Oracle Conference Center as the venue and put the word out that we were looking for women-led technology businesses. We received more than three hundred and fifty applications for only twenty-five presentation spaces.

That first event was January 19, 2000, and five hundred people attended. Many of the investors attending weren't supportive of a women-only event and told us, "We don't invest in women. We invest in companies." However, we thought it was important for someone to shine a spotlight on talented women entrepreneurs. Every company, but one, that we showcased that day received funding.

The success of that day convinced us that we should continue the program, and many people called to offer their help and suggest places to hold the forum. We decided to put groups together in other locations to host similar events.

Ghaffari: What explains why you've been able to do this successfully for now eleven years?

Millman: In the beginning, it was good timing and the financial support of the Kauffman Foundation. As the program evolved, the focus on facilitated coaching of the companies became critical to its success. And as I learned early on in my career, building relationships early is the "secret sauce."

Ghaffari: Did you ask for a direct grant from Kauffman?

Millman: The Kauffman Foundations was the only entity that was interested in funding entrepreneurial programs. I had built a relationship with them when I was running the Council. They weren't necessarily interested in women entrepreneurs, but, in 2000, they released a study called the *Global Entrepreneurship Monitor*, about economic and entrepreneurial activity in many countries, focusing on what are the determining factors of success or impact. The results indicated that the number of women engaged in entrepreneurship in each country was a determining factor of the health of that country's economy. You might say that Kauffman was our angel investor.

Ghaffari: How did the venture forums grow?

Millman: After Silicon Valley, we traveled to Washington, DC, and partnered with AOL to produce a forum and from there to Boston and Harvard. All these venues were places in which we had connections and a team of people who were committed to helping to produce a forum in their region.

The end of 2000 was another election year, and I found myself out of a job with the loss of Al Gore to George Bush. I guess I drew the short straw and became the one to run the organization. I pulled the nonprofit together—filed all the necessary documents. And that's how Springboard Enterprises happened.

I didn't leave the government right away—remember, it took them a while to decide that election. I had an assistant who left earlier, when the grant funds and nonprofit status came through. She managed the whole thing before I left the government. After I joined her, we established policies and procedures, pulled a staff together, convened a board, and started business.

Ghaffari: How did you build your first board?

Millman: For the founding board, we tapped people we knew, as well as those who were involved in producing the first three programs. The board was small and highly engaged. Also, we had a separate group of advisors who had been supporters during the first year of programming.

Ghaffari: How does Springboard differentiate itself from venture capitalists?

Millman: We don't invest money. We are organized as a nonprofit, not a broker/dealer. Neither do we invest cash nor take equity in the companies, but we have invested considerable time, resources, and connections—which sometimes is as valuable as funding.

Ghaffari: What are some of the major differences among the communities you've served?

Millman: Clearly, there are some hubs of venture activity. Silicon Valley has a huge network that's attuned to the types of business and transactions that are interesting to investors. The same is true in Boston. Then there are smaller markets like Austin and Raleigh-Durham. In some areas, say the Midwest, Chicago acts as a center of activity, but Minneapolis has an entrepreneurial market especially for medical devices as does the Madison area. Washington, DC, also has an active venture community. And New York is more active these days than in the past several years. There's a concentration of life sciences companies in San Diego and entertainment companies in LA. You can find companies anywhere, but at some point the companies end up making the rounds in Silicon Valley.

Ghaffari: Is Springboard moving into the international market?

Millman: Gingerly. The only country we've reached out to is Israel because there is a critical mass of both investors and technology companies. Our first Israeli forum was in 2007, and we found some impressive women entrepreneurs there.

We have companies in Canada, China, India, a few African countries, and throughout Europe. Until recently, they sourced capital and customers in the USA, but lately we find they have been successful in raising funds in their own countries.

One of these companies from our portfolio is 51Job.com, founded by Kathleen Chien, a Chinese woman who spent many years in the States, where she saw that she could start a corporate recruiting firm in China based on the success of such ventures in the US. She used that business model to go back home and start a company to meet a new need in the Chinese market. Today she finds people to work for US companies that relocated to China.

Ghaffari: How do you decide to enter a market? What is your decision-making process?

Millman: Actually, I'm more of an intrapreneur than an entrepreneur. I take advice and suggestions from our staff, board, and advisors and create programs that address needs in the marketplace. That said, all the stars have to be aligned to make a program successful, and it takes a lot of involvement from a lot of people to ensure that success. We believe in collaboration with other organizations and institutions who are interested in creating opportunities for women entrepreneurs in their community, region, or country.

Ghaffari: How do you see Springboard growing over the next five years? What's it going to look like?

Millman: I don't have a crystal ball, but the way I anticipate growing is through our community of entrepreneurs who represent a unique expert network. We've spent a dozen years building a network of unbelievably talented women, who have, as my friend Sam Horn says, "been there, run that." They know everything about their industries and launching and building businesses. There's not anybody in our Springboard community who doesn't have an expertise—from rocket science to marketing healthy food or building social media networks to simplifying commerce, and everything in between. So, the idea is to mine that network for the benefit of all women entrepreneurs.

We keep hearing the same questions, again and again—the same questions for the last thirty years. Why isn't anybody paying attention to these talented women? How come women aren't asked to be experts on conference panels? Why is it that every time I go to a conference, there are no women on stage? Where are the women? Are there any women who are qualified for XYZ? We set out to find the women and promote them as experts, and now we have a critical mass of experts in their fields and in new-venture creations who happen to be women. We are in the right place at the right time, with the right people.

Ghaffari: Why didn't you start Springboard as a for-profit entity?

Millman: As I said, I'm not an entrepreneur. I'm an intrapreneur and thought an organization that produced educational programs like a university would be the best model. This model has worked miracles for the first ten years, and I'm anxious to see how we can innovate to make our programs and our network as successful for the next ten years.

Ghaffari: Do your boards and advisors provide you with any special advice about how to conduct business?

Millman: They are invaluable because they all have expertise that I don't have. They fill in the blanks and are committed to helping us help our companies succeed. They are also bringing us their contacts. Our staff is also a major reason for our success. I make it a habit to hire people who are much smarter than I am and have important skills and talents to bring to the organization. I search for people and advisors who are problem solvers—creative, curious, problem solvers. I wish there were a DNA test for this because they are one in a hundred.

Ghaffari: Tell me about your family. How do they view your enterprise?

Millman: I feel pretty lucky. I have great kids—a daughter and a son who are out in the world doing what they love. My daughter works for a filmmaker. And my son is an artist, currently at the Chicago Art Institute. My husband runs his own construction–remodeling–design–build business. I guess all of us have the entrepreneurial gene.

Ghaffari: How would you describe your own decision-making style or method?

Millman: I always said that, in a void, I will make a decision, right or wrong, just to move the process along. I don't read a lot. I'm not somebody who is an intellectual, but I absorb information from many sources. I learn a lot from other people, and my feeling is that sometimes you just have to stop talking and do something. It doesn't have to be perfect. You just have to make a decision and act on it. Everyone has a role to play, and we expect that each person will strive to exceed her own expectations.

Everybody here has to come in with a goal and an idea of what they want to learn and what they want to contribute to the organization. It's not acceptable if you're not adding any value, if you're just here to get a paycheck.

Ghaffari: What kind of advice do you have for women today, especially young women?

Millman: I'm not sure I'm the best person to give advice to young women because what works for me may not work for others. It's like when people ask me about what I think about balancing work and family. I don't think about balance. It's such a personal thing. I don't believe that anybody can achieve balance all the time. I think you just do what you need to do to manage your life. Somehow, you make it work. You figure it out. Your life takes a certain path, and you deal with it as best you can. Sometimes it works, but sometimes it doesn't. So, in that case, you just need to be flexible enough to try something else. I guess I would say that life is about being a problem solver and being able to find the right resources to help you.

What I look for in people is that sense of curiosity, that sense of needing to figure things out. But, I've learned that not everybody is like that. I used to feel really badly when people wouldn't make connections for me. I knew they could, but it seemed as if they wouldn't. Then I read Malcolm Gladwell's book, *The Tipping Point*,[2] and realized that not everybody is a "connector"—the people who link us up with the world. That changed the way I thought about everything.

There are a few things I say whenever I speak to groups. First, "It's not about you." You learn that, when you have a child, you are no longer the most important person in the world. To be a successful mother, you have to recognize this and focus on what the child needs. The minute you understand that—then you can relax, get on the floor, play with your child, listen better, stop worrying about the cell phone or whatever you think you're supposed to be doing. If you take that same approach in your business life, you'll spend your time listening to what your customers need rather than pitching them products they may not need.

The second thing that I tell them is never do anything in life, ever, without a personal advisory board. Many women don't have an external source of feedback. They end up with their back against the wall, with no support network, and no resources to help them re-orient. Always identify a group of people who can offer counsel and who will watch your back.

Ghaffari: Your organization is primarily oriented to women-owned business, but would you say your recommendations would be any different for men?

Millman: I think the experience in launching and building businesses is probably the same, but women have other interests and expectations that come into play. We understood what support women want and recognized that we could help them get access to the resources they need. At the same time, our goal was to build a great network of talented women entrepreneurs, and that's our niche market.

Ghaffari: Do you think things have changed dramatically in the last ten years? Has your market moved on you?

---

[2] Malcolm Gladwell, *The Tipping Point* (Little, Brown and Company, 2000).

Millman: It's a lot easier for companies to enter a market than it was ten years ago. The cost of building a web site for example is infinitely cheaper and, with more people on the internet and accessing info via mobile phone, it's easier to enter a market faster. On the other hand, it's not as easy to access capital to build your company quickly, but then you may not need as much capital. Today, there are a lot more women entrepreneurs—especially those women who have a special expertise based on their years of working for corporations or getting their PhDs or MBAs. There's a huge pipeline full of women interested in running their own business or in forming teams with people they've worked with before.

I was talking with a woman this morning who had twelve years working at Hewlett-Packard, who ran a division there and knows how to build a technology platform and a winning team. She has a passion for fashion, so she decided to start a company that married her skills and her passion. That's our target demographic—women in their thirties to fifties who have been in the corporate world, have run departments, or have expertise in a given area. There are a lot of women out there with the ability and interest to run billion-dollar companies.

Ghaffari: Do you see, among your clientele, that women follow the pink-collar kind of work, staying within the same businesses that women have been in for centuries? Or do you see them branching out of that?

Millman: I don't see those stereotypes these days, but I'm sure there are many women who pursue those careers. I see the engineers, the scientists, the medical doctors, the finance and marketing gurus. Now, I won't tell you that they don't have an interest in fashion, health, well-being, and education. They do. Many of them have the skills to develop solutions to make housework, child care, and family-related products better, faster, cheaper, and more effective. For instance, Helen Greiner developed the Roomba to help her manage cleaning her carpets and floors while she worked to build robots for the Navy.

Ghaffari: Is there anything that you think you might do differently if you were starting out today?

Millman: No, but it would have been an easier life if I'd stayed in the corporate world. I'd be retired by now.

Ghaffari: What's your personal plan for the next five to ten years?

Millman: No crystal ball. This is it for me.

Ghaffari: If women are succeeding in business, are they becoming a source of venture capital themselves?

Millman: Ahh, that's the exciting part. People say that women are Johnny-come-latelies or Joanie-come-latelies to investing. We made it into the corporate C-suite, and then we wanted to be on corporate boards the minute they started putting more stringent regulations on board engagements. It's almost as if the minute we get involved with something, the fun is over. But it's been a journey from housewife to corporate executive to entrepreneur and now to investor.

This was a dream of ours ten years ago—that, once women were successful in starting and growing businesses, women would want to invest in what they knew. And sure enough, that is exactly what is happening right now. Several of our Springboard alumnae are now active investors and find that Springboard companies are a great source of lucrative investment opportunities.

Sandra F. Witelson

Professor, Department of Psychiatry, McMaster University

Born in Montreal, Quebec, Canada.

Dr. Sandra Freedman Witelson *is a professor in the Department of Psychiatry and Behavioural Neurosciences at McMaster University in Hamilton, Ontario, Canada. She is the inaugural recipient of the Albert Einstein/Irving Zucker Chair in Neuroscience at the university's Michael G. DeGroote School of Medicine.*

Her current research is focused on the relationship between brain structure and function using postmortem neuroanatomical study of the brains banked in her brain collection at McMaster University—currently an international public resource for neuroscience, neuroimaging, and molecular biology.

She earned a bachelor's of science, a master's of science, and a PhD in psychology from McGill University in Montreal. She won a postdoctoral fellowship from the National Institute of Mental Health, working at the New York University Medical Center's departments of psychiatry and neurology.

At McMaster University, Dr. Witelson began research into the neural substrate of children with early learning difficulties, exploring functional lateralization of the brain, leading to publication in the journal Science in 1976 and 1977.[1] Early research in brain anatomy led to a joint publication with Dr. W. Pallie in the September 1973 issue of Oxford's Brain: A Journal of Neurology, *followed by a*

---

[1] "Sex and the Single Hemisphere" and "Developmental Dyslexia: Two Right Hemispheres and None Left."

major research grant from the National Institutes of Health to study the relationship between the structure and the language function in the human brain.

For the next 25 years, Dr. Witelson concentrated on expanding the brain bank at McMaster University, as well as her research in cognitive neuroanatomy to understand the relationship between the structure of the brain and the behavior of human beings.

In 1995, Dr. Witelson's discovery of significant differences between men's and women's brains, specifically in the density of brain cells in the language region, was reported extensively in the media. She was then invited to study the brain of the late Dr. Albert Einstein, and with her associates, published the research findings in the June 1999 issue of Lancet, a prominent British medical journal.

Dr. Witelson has been honored with numerous awards, including the Morton Prince Award of the American Psychopathological Association (1976); the John Dewan Prize, awarded by the Ontario Mental Health Foundation (1978), recognizing an outstanding researcher for contribution to significant new knowledge or concepts bearing upon mental health; and the Clarke Institute of Psychiatry Research Fund Award (1978), awarded for outstanding research in the field of mental health conducted in Canada.

Dr. Witelson has been elected a fellow at several, highly regarded professional and scientific associations and societies, including the Canadian Psychological Association (1980), the American Psychological Association (1987), the American Association for the Advancement of Science (1987), and the Royal Society of Canada, Academy of Science (1996).

She was elected as one of the only 250 worldwide members of The Dana Alliance for Brain Initiatives (1998) and inducted into the City of Hamilton (Ontario) Gallery of Distinction (2007).

Since the 1970s, the media worldwide has considered Dr. Witelson as the "go-to authority" on topics of childhood brain development, sex differences in brain structure, biological basis of sexual orientation, Einstein's brain and genius, and a host of other neuroscience topics.

Elizabeth Ghaffari: I read that in high school, you were in French, music, and debating clubs, which are three linguistic foundations. Was your early primary interest in languages?

Dr. Sandra Witelson: My forte was never in writing skills. Oral language, yes, but not written language—as in creative, literary language. I was not very good in French. My interest was always in math and sciences. I don't remember that there was even any biology available when I went to high school, but I was always interested in math and the sciences.

I do remember that when I was in elementary school, six or seven years old, I liked to give speeches. When we all had to do a presentation, the other students recited poems or songs. I knew I couldn't carry a tune at all, so I gave a speech instead.

When I was in university, I chose to be in a debating club because that's what I liked to do—to debate and to speak. I still do. I enjoy giving lectures—the one-to-one or the one-to-a-group. I truly enjoy communicating information or ideas orally.

Ghaffari: Would you tell me a little about your family—your father, your mother, your siblings? Your father was an accountant, but he wanted to be a physicist. Where did that interest come from?

Witelson: My father was the youngest of five children. There was not that much money in the family, but he was the first in his family to go to university in Montreal. He was a scholar who wanted to be a physicist. He just loved reading and absorbing information. But, to become a physicist would have meant many more costly years in the university, so he ended up going into accounting. He never really enjoyed it, though—he was not passionate about his work.

My mother was a very bright, energetic woman who never worked outside of the home. She would have been a wonderful businesswoman, but my mother acquiesced to my father, who was quite conservative. He said that he didn't want my mother to work because it would reflect poorly on him—suggesting that he couldn't make a sufficient financial living.

I knew that my mother wanted to work outside the home. There was a typical little cigar, newspaper, and candy shop at a major intersection in the Snowdon area of Montreal. She wanted to buy that and to run it. It was a brilliant business idea, and she would have been fantastic at it. She wanted to do that, but she listened to my father. Those were the times, but also that was her choice.

In reflecting on this as an adult, it had no effect on me, either positively or negatively. I think I did what I did because my temperament was different from hers in some ways.

I had a brother who was five years younger than I, and we were very close throughout our whole life. He ended up coming to live near us in Hamilton. Tragically, he just died this past January.

My father died when I was about thirty, so I didn't have a chance to really get to know him when I was an adult.

Ghaffari: Why did you attend McGill University in Montreal, Quebec—just because it was close to home?

Witelson: My mother started me in school a year early, because she convinced the school I was bright enough. In Montreal, at the time, there were only eleven years of elementary to high school, so I graduated high school when I was sixteen. In contrast to what I see my students doing nowadays, I went to McGill because it was there. I remember having absolutely no desire to go anywhere else. I wasn't interested in traveling to Europe or other distant places. My adventures were in my head. I had no desire to leave the city. I even lived at home during my university years until I was married because it was so easy.

Ghaffari: You went in quick succession from a bachelor's to a master's and to a doctorate at McGill. Were they all in psychology?

Witelson: In those days, some bachelor's degrees were "honors programs"—that just meant it was a focused specialization. I specialized in psychology.

When I started at McGill, I thought I was going to be a mathematician—an actuarian, only because it had something to do with numbers. I thought I'd be very good at that because I was good in math and liked numbers. It soon became clear to me that the few other students who were taking advanced math with me had a conception of, and passion for, math that I just didn't have.

So, I reconsidered and found psychology and never turned back. McGill University, in the sixties, had one of the best psychology departments in North America at the time. Psychology was in the science faculty, not in the arts faculty, as was the case at many other universities. They had prominent physiological psychologists like Professors Donald Hebb and Peter Milner. McGill definitely was on the forefront of biological psychology where anatomy, chemistry, and the workings of the brain were considered in the understanding of behavior and thinking.

When I was growing up, my father had shelves of hardcover books throughout the house—paperbacks were not yet available. I gravitated to the ones on biology, the structure of the body and how structure is important to the function. That's what intrigued me. Once, when I was about eight years old, I got into trouble with a friend's mother because I read to my friend, over the phone, the anatomy of male and female human genitalia. I'd found it in my father's books and thought nothing of it, but when my friend's mother heard my "lecture," she forbade her daughter from speaking with me.

So, biology was something that intrigued me very much—one might say, like a chemical attraction. That's why I found psychology and behavior, as it's related to the brain, right up my alley. I never left. I ended up being in one of the best programs I could have selected.

Ghaffari: Was Donald Hebb your mentor?

Witelson: No, I wouldn't say he was my mentor. I had many teachers, but I really didn't have any mentors. Don Hebb was the role model that I tried to pattern myself after. He was my hero, although he probably never knew it. We all thought he was one of the most brilliant men. He was a theorist as well as an experimentalist. When he died, a CBC radio host requested that I comment on Dr. Hebb's contributions. I declined, feeling I was inadequate to the task and not senior enough to do this. In retrospect, I think this was a very "female" act. I do not think this way now.

One of the traits that I developed as a scientist is to be quite theoretical following the data. Some scientists stick very close to their data in developing theoretical considerations. I think I go a little further, which is what Hebb did.

Ghaffari: You went right on to get your doctorate in psychology at McGill?

Witelson: There were about fifteen of us who graduated at the same time from the same honors psychology program. We'd taken many psychology courses because it was such a specialized program. We all thought we really knew *everything* about psychology. I decided to go into a two-year master's program in clinical psychology so that I would learn something new before I went on to get my PhD in physiological psychology. I never intended to be a clinician or a clinical psychologist.

My doctorate also was in "physiological psychology," what today would be called "cognitive neuroscience." I was studying the effects on learning resulting from brain damage in children, sustained at different points in their development. In other words, if a child had brain damage at age two years as opposed to age twelve, were the consequences the same or not? The whole hypothesis that there would be differences, and that the differences would be in specific types of learning, came from a long, theoretical paper that Don Hebb had written and which I borrowed from his library numerous times. These were the days before photocopying.

When I finished my doctorate, I learned that McGill didn't like to take their undergraduates into graduate school because they believed that students should have experience with different departments and different approaches. I didn't know this. I had gone ahead and did what I wanted to do. I applied to the master's program, and then I applied to the PhD program. Somehow, along the way, the administrators allowed me to get into the doctoral program, not realizing that I already had two McGill degrees.

Ghaffari: Did you encounter any negative feedback as a woman in science?

Witelson: I was married right after completing my bachelor's degree. My husband was a medical student at the time. Our daughter was born a year and a half later. I was already in the master's program when I applied for my doctorate. At the interview, the chairman of the department asked me, "What would happen if you get pregnant and have another child?" I suspect that many women today would consider that an inappropriate question. I did not. I remember very clearly that I thought it was most appropriate because I would be receiving a graduate stipend, and the department would be putting a lot of resources into giving me a slot in the doctoral program. He was trying to assure himself that I would complete my studies. I told him, "I don't intend to have another child while in graduate school as it would interfere with my studies." And that was the end of that discussion.

Ghaffari: Was your family supportive of your academic and professional work?

Witelson: I was in the middle of my PhD when my husband graduated from medical school. He chose ophthalmology and was accepted into a residency program in New York City, where there were some of the best ophthalmology programs in the United States. I had about a year and a half left to finish my PhD program and was working at the Montreal Neurological Institute, which is one of the best places for brain research as well as clinical work.

So, he went to New York, and I stayed behind to finish my PhD. It just never dawned on me that anybody would think this was unusual. It never occurred to me, or even to him, as far as I know, that I should leave my PhD studies to join him right away in New York, even though we were already parents. Subsequently, I learned that his family thought that we might be separating but didn't want to tell anybody. Anyway, I didn't have another child when I was in graduate school. We weren't separated or getting a divorce. And I graduated and received my PhD.

Ghaffari: How did you manage child care while you were working and studying?

Witelson: My daughter, Tamar, stayed with me in Montreal. She was in a wonderful pre-nursery program. I had a wonderful Hungarian babysitter,

Zezi, who became a very close friend—she would come every day to look after Tamar and take her to ballet classes, art classes, and pre-nursery classes. Eventually, after two years, Tamar and I moved to join my husband in New York City.

Ghaffari: What was your first "real job" in New York?

Witelson: By this time, I knew that I was going to have a career. I wanted to do something with all the psychology that I enjoyed so much. I applied for, and won, a National Institute of Mental Health postdoctoral fellowship working at New York University Medical Center, located on First Avenue near Thirtieth Street, right in Bellevue Hospital, which is part of the center.

In fact, in the movie *Midnight Cowboy*, Dustin Hoffman goes into the door of Bellevue, which was the exact same door I used to go in and out of several times a day.

The work was very exciting, and there were some very extraordinary scientists who were working in the department of psychiatry and neurology, which is where my postdoc position was. One of them subsequently won a Nobel Prize in Medicine and Physiology for his work in neuroscience.

Ghaffari: Were there any people that you'd consider mentors from that era?

Witelson: Just faculty, fellow students, and people from whom I learned a great deal. Certainly, there would be useful discussions, but I never had a mentor of any kind on a continuing basis—someone who might have guided me in any way.

I was already a married woman and a mother who would go home right at the end of the day. My life in those days was not all wrapped up with my colleagues, fellow students, or the faculty. Also, I always seemed to be generating ideas and hypotheses that I thought were worth doing, and then I would just go do them within the context of where I was in the program. I never seemed to be part of a little group where everyone was doing something together.

Ghaffari: How did you come to write your first seminal work on the study of the anatomical asymmetry in newborns, published in 1973?

Witelson: That was a key paper, both in terms of neuroscience but also for me professionally. After I finished my postdoc, my husband and I decided to go back to Canada and chose Hamilton, Ontario, where I joined McMaster University. I was hired to work on brain function in children with learning disabilities following my master's and PhD work on that topic.

At McMaster, I focused on brain lateralization—why the two hemispheres of the human brain are involved with different aspects of cognition—the left side is more important for language functions, while the right side for visual perception. In my research on children, I was finding that lateralization seemed to be present early on, before the development of speech might have caused the different localization of functions to emerge. Functional lateralization was present before behavior developed.

I read a paper written in 1968 by the prominent neurologist, Norman Geschwind, who observed an anatomical difference between the left and the right hemisphere in the normal adult brain. He read German fluently and had found reports of this in the German literature. He was able to get one hundred brains to study from various sources. He looked at the brains in a very systematic way and found that the left side—the region that we know is related to language skills—is visibly larger, by about 30 percent, compared to the right side in about seventy to 80 percent of people. He interpreted this as possibly a biological substrate to explain why language is usually represented in the left hemisphere.

Up to that point, I had never held a human brain in my hand. I had never worked on brain tissue, but it seemed to me that this was the missing link that we needed in order to understand how the brain was lateralized.

Anyway, in an academic setting, one always is giving seminars and lectures to various groups, and I enjoyed doing that very much. So, I gave an in-house lecture on brain development, mentioning Geschwind's article. The chairman of anatomy at McMaster, Wazir Pallie, was not able to attend, but heard about it. Because he had become interested in how the brain functioned, not just its anatomy, he called and asked if we could have lunch so that I could tell him about my findings. I said I'd be happy to give him a private version. That conversation led to our collaboration.

Ghaffari: Did you and Dr. Pallie share the same views?

Witelson: In some ways, no. The collaboration was good because I was biased in one direction, while he was biased in the opposite.

Dr. Pallie was very senior in his career and had worked in Malaysia doing thousands of autopsies. He told me he'd never seen any systematic difference between the left and the right hemispheres. I told him that that could be because he never did a study—he only looked at these brains case by case. I was so *sure* that the two hemispheres had to be different that I suggested we skip right to chimpanzees and show that we evolved that way.

It's actually difficult to obtain chimpanzee brains, so we compromised and studied human infant brains to examine whether lateralization was present from birth. As an anatomist, he had access to a nearby hospital for children and was able to obtain the brains of children who had died very soon after birth from non-neurological causes. We also obtained some adult brains to see if we could replicate the findings of Geschwind's paper, which we did very closely.

Ghaffari: Why did he miss finding lateralization in his autopsies?

Witelson: Every brain is as different from another brain as every face is different from another face. There are major variations in the actual brain topography, but unless you're specifically looking for something and documenting what you see, you're not going to notice any general principles. A clinician is dealing with an individual case, and a scientist is trying to get the general principles about an issue. If you are not asking the right question, you'll never find the answer to that question.

When we did this research study, we began with just a small sample of sixteen adult cases and saw that the left side was greater than the right area, replicating the Geschwind results. After we did just thirteen neonates [infants' brains], it was absolutely clear that the asymmetry existed right from the beginning. So we submitted the paper, by mail, to a very excellent journal, and they accepted it, immediately, by return mail.

Ghaffari: Did publication change anything about the way you were seen or treated by your colleagues?

Witelson: Publication of our findings was a very major event for me professionally. It enabled me to win a large, American contract to start the work that I ended up focusing on for the next twenty-five years—namely direct study of the relationship between structure and function in the human brain. I left the field of pure neuropsychological research and moved over into the cognitive neuroanatomical area.

In thinking back, when my brother and I were growing up, I don't remember that my parents treated us differently in any way. The environment seemed sex-irrelevant. I think that's how I have always treated everything, except of course things specifically related to being a woman—romantic and motherhood issues.

One thing that was crucial for me, as I progressed in my career, was the way I responded to people's treatment of me. When I wanted to do this study on neonatal brains, in those days there was an unwritten system that you were supposed to tell the head of the unit where you worked about the study you planned to do.

I went to talk to the head of the unit and, of course, brought Wazir with me as my collaborator. We were not asking for grant money. I explained the proposed study to the head of the unit, who was a psychiatrist. When I finished, he looked at Wazir and asked *him,* "Does this make sense? Do you think you can do it?" I remember thinking, "This guy's so inappropriate! I'm the one who's explaining it. The project is all about language lateralization."

It didn't matter, though. All we needed was the go-ahead, which we got, and we did the project. I realized that maybe he was turning to Wazir because he was an established scientist already. Or maybe because he was a man. Who knows? The point is that I really didn't care—it didn't disturb me at all. All I wanted to do was ensure that we could go ahead—that he wouldn't stand in our way.

It was the same thing as when the department head asked me, "What if you were to have another child?" It just didn't register with me. I just wanted the end result —to be accepted into graduate school.

Ghaffari: When did you start actually building the brain bank at McMaster?

Witelson: In the late 1970s. Winning this contract from the National Institutes of Health was a big coup. It was a lot of money—something like a quarter of a million dollars for each of three years. Subsequently, I was promoted to the rank of full professor in 1977, which was only eight years after I was at the university—a very rapid promotion.

Ghaffari: How would you describe the study?

Witelson: The aim of the study was to see whether this anatomic asymmetry was, in fact, the basis of language lateralization. Our approach was to study people who had metastatic cancer, while they were alive, using neuropsychological tests to find out which hemisphere was the dominant one for language. Most of these research volunteers succumbed to their disease and left their brains to the brain bank. We then related their test results to their pattern of anatomical asymmetry. We studied the gross anatomical pattern and also the microscopic anatomy.

Ghaffari: Is that where you started finding sex differences in brain structure?

Witelson: That's right. By this time, my colleagues in this work were neuroanatomist Dr. Marc Colonnier and research associate Debra Kigar. It happened that, while we were counting the number of cells, we discovered a major difference between men's and women's brains in how the cells were packed together in the language region, the region where there is anatomical asymmetry. We found a sex difference in "cell packing density"—that is the number of cells packed per unit of volume.

That paper got a lot of attention from the media, partially because anything related to sex, whether it's the brain or anything else, gets a lot of attention. That paper was described in an article in the *New York Times* in February 1995.[2]

The *New York Times* piece caught the attention of Dr. Thomas Harvey, a retired pathologist from New Jersey, who had removed and retained Einstein's brain after a clinical autopsy and was looking for someone to study it. That *NYT* article led him to contact me at McMaster. Ultimately, that led me to the opportunity to study Einstein's brain.

In June 1999, we published "The Exceptional Brain of Albert Einstein" in *The Lancet*, the British medical journal. The article discussed what my colleagues and I found when we compared anatomical measurements of the late physicist's brain with those of normal intelligence people whose brains were in our brain bank.

You know, one thing leads to another in any aspect of life, right?

Ghaffari: You've received a number of awards. Are most of these related to your NIH project?

Witelson: The awards related to my work on the development of language lateralization in normal children and in children with dyslexia, neuroanatomical studies of cognition, and sex differences in the brain.

Ghaffari: It looks as if most of your collaborative writing started after this NIH work. Would you agree?

Witelson: Yes, by that time I was working with senior neuroanatomists, a staff of assistants, and a group of PhD graduate students, so it became a much more multidisciplinary research starting in about the 1980s.

Ghaffari: What are the awards or recognitions you value the most, personally?

Witelson: One of the most memorable awards was the one from the American Psychopathological Association in New York City. I remember that well.

I knew somebody from my days as a postdoc and met him at a conference. He told me about the Association, and I said, "Maybe you could invite me to give one of the lectures because then I could also visit New York." So, he invited me to give a talk. I was one of just a few presenters who were not psychiatrists. I was certainly was not part of the group. I was a young neuropsychologist.

---

[2] Gina Kolata, "Man's World, Woman's World? Brain Studies Point to Differences," www.nytimes.com/1995/02/28/science/man-s-world-woman-s-world-brain-studies-point-to-differences.html?pagewanted=1, February 28, 1995.

I gave my talk—I thought it was a good one. The next thing I knew, I received a letter saying that I'd won the award for that year for the best talk and the work behind the presentation. The letter said, "Your award will be sent to you." The next thing I knew, I had to pick this package up at the US-Canadian border. They sent me a beautiful, black-lacquered captain's chair with an inlaid medal with my name and the award inserted in the back of the chair. That was very exciting. Everyone likes to be patted on the back. I still have the chair in my living room.

Then again, to be named a fellow of the Royal Society is the highest honor that a Canadian scientist or scholar can have bestowed on them. So, obviously, that is very, very important to me.

Finally, the other recognition was being invited to be a member of the Dana Alliance for Brain Initiatives in New York because there are only around two hundred and fifty neuroscientists who are members from around the world. At the time I was asked to be a member, about 1997 or '98, there were only six Canadians, so that was exciting.

Ghaffari: What is the Dana Alliance? Do you work with them or is it more a recognition?

Witelson: The Dana Alliance is a nonprofit, volunteer organization committed to advancing public awareness of the progress and promise of brain research and to disseminate information on the brain in an understandable fashion. The Alliance was established by the Dana Foundation, a New York philanthropy dedicated to support activities and publication in science, health, and education, particularly the neurosciences.

I once had the opportunity to speak, along with other scientists, on Capitol Hill, about the importance of research funds for neuroscience. It is hoped that input such as this helps government officials allocate resources.

Ghaffari: You compared Einstein's brain to those in the brain bank and wrote about it in 1999. To how many brains did you compare Einstein's brain?

Witelson: We had about 110 brains in the bank at that time, which we used as a comparison group.

Ghaffari: In the January 2005 presentation that Lawrence Summers gave before the National Bureau of Economic Research,[3] in which he discussed the

---

[3] Lawrence Summers, "Remarks at NBER Conference on Diversifying the Science & Engineering Workforce," www.harvard.edu/president/speeches/summers_2005/nber.php.

issue of women's underrepresentation in tenured positions in science and engineering at top universities and research institutions, was he suggesting that the mental divide between the sexes is more complex and more rooted in the fundamental biology of the brain than many scientists once suspected?

Witelson: Yes, he said that, but no—many scientists have been aware of the sex differences for some time. However, his audience at the NBER was not cognizant of the literature nor were they familiar with the hypotheses he put forward.

Not only are there structural differences between the sexes, but there are also neurochemical and neurophysiological differences between male and female brains. So, it's not just at the structural level, but it's also in the functioning of the brain.

In experimental work with other mammals, it's possible to manipulate things and see the resulting modified behavior—that is, alter the structure of the brain, either by a hormone or some other method, which results in a change of behavior.

For example, the ability to run mazes is better among male rats compared to females. If a hormone, say testosterone, is introduced into the immature brain of a newborn female rat, the result is an improved ability to negotiate mazes (an example of spatial learning) relative to normal rats.

In humans, there are certain tasks that involve spatial learning where men consistently outperform women. Of course, you can't introduce hormones to experiment with humans. But, there are clinical conditions in which the hormonal environment, either *in utero* or early in development, is not typical. Neuropsychological studies of such groups of patients reveal that their ability on some spatial tasks is closer to an average male than to an average female.

In other words, depending on the hormonal changes, there are some conditions where little girls have had more exposure to testosterone, and they show more rough-and-tumble play, better ability with certain kinds of puzzles, which are things more often seen in boys more than in girls.

Ghaffari: Did the press come to you for elaboration on the discussion that followed the Lawrence Summers' comment about "different availability of aptitude at the high end" between the genders?

Witelson: There were several newspaper articles that included me and my research along with other scientists. I was very pleased to be involved in the interview with Gwenn Ifill for the PBS show, *NewsHour with Jim Lehrer.* I was one of three women. The other two disagreed with Dr. Summers' comments. My opinion was and is that he was correct—dead on. I had read the actual transcript of his talk. I thought he was very cautious and deliberate. I re-read part of that transcript to the participants of the recent *Wall Street Journal* "Conference on Women in the Economy." Many were in agreement compared to what they had gleaned from media reports.

The question posed to him was, "Why are there fewer women full-professors with tenure in fields such as math and natural sciences in the top universities in the States?"

Dr. Summers cited three reasons he thought might explain the fact that there are fewer women. Firstly, women, for various reasons, are less likely to want or be able to spend eighty hours a week in their careers. He was criticized by some people who argued that that should not be required to get tenure, but that was not the issue he was addressing. Academia is a competitive arena.

Secondly, he said that in math test scores—measuring quantitative skills—the mean scores for men are slightly higher, but the biggest sex difference is that the distribution is much wider for men. There easily are four or five men who are approximately three or four standard deviations beyond the mean compared to one woman. It would follow that there are more competitive men than women for jobs requiring quantitative skills.

Thirdly, he said there could be effects of different socialization and patterns of discrimination. He was describing, not condoning. Other scientists before and since Dr. Summer's talk have made very similar statements.

Ghaffari: Aren't there also some studies about the different responses of men and women to stressful situations?

Witelson: That's right. There are studies which show that when animals are stressed, the neurons in the hippocampus—the center for learning and memory—undergo structural changes that differ between the sexes. In the male, there is more of an increase in the outgrowth of the neuropil—the little sprouting structures surrounding the cell—which is advantageous for learning. The reverse happens in a female. Therefore, stress has different consequences for behavior in the male and female brain, which may be a fact of biology.

There is inferential evidence that this is true in humans, too. If this is the case, then it would be advantageous for men and women to know this biological reality, rather than to pretend the difference does not exist. A plan of action to deal with this reality would appear warranted.

It can only help men and women in all phases of development to be aware and accept some of the biologically based differences in cognition, behavior, propensities, and to note the female skills for collegiality and their relative discomfort with high-risk competitive situations.

For example, the new International Monetary Fund chief, Christine Lagarde, stated that she's going to deal with her job as a woman. She said, "...the majority of women in [leadership] positions approach power ... in a slightly different manner. Women inject less libido and less testosterone into the equation." It sure sounds to me like Lagarde also thinks men and women deal with things differently, with hormones as part of the causes of the difference.

Ghaffari: Do you think that the opportunity for more girls to participate in sports at a young age on an equal basis, as a result of Title IX, might induce behavioral changes of the type that you're describing?

Witelson: The known differences of which I was speaking earlier are not the ones known to correlate with whether a woman was participating in sports or not. Those are different questions.

For women who are very involved in sports—does this have some effect on their body, on their brain, on their personality, on how they approach life? It may very well be the case because, even though the anatomy and the chemistry of the brain are partially genetically determined, that doesn't mean that environment doesn't have an effect. So, one always has to think of the interplay between nature and nurture.

Ghaffari: Do you think we should be developing different teaching tools to convey science and math information to help women absorb this information and retain such knowledge more effectively?

Witelson: There are some data that show that different approaches might make it easier for women to learn these subjects—especially in quantitative subjects such as physics, chemistry, and math. I don't know enough about the follow-up studies of differential educational programs. But, I don't think that one has to have different programs for the sexes in every aspect.

We have separate gymnastic classes because boys are able to do some physical things based on differences in muscle structure and bone strength. Remember, the brain is an organ sexually differentiated just like muscles and the genitalia, so it makes perfect sense that there might be certain tasks or subjects where it may be beneficial to have different types of teaching.

However, the different educational programs and learning of the material are not going to change the basic biological differences. Behavioral consequences that are the result of sexual differentiation of male and female brains are not going to change. The important thing is to be cognizant or aware of what those differences are because knowledge is power. It's important for a woman to understand not just her intellectual and cognitive strengths, but also to be cognizant of what her temperament is. How comfortable is she with competition? How driven is she to try to reach the top of whatever it is that she wants to do? How important is it for her to have a balanced family life? By dealing with those issues, an individual gets to know who she is and what satisfies her as she is making career choices.

Intelligence and education represent only one facet of an individual's life. We know there are leaking pipelines, with women leaving the professions earlier and in greater number than men, in science, medicine, law, and business. There are similar figures from different surveys. So, what is it that is making many women drop out? This is the issue we must face and be ready to accept nature and nurture factors.

Ghaffari: Aren't there women like you who are defining their economic and scientific world according to the parameters that they find comfortable and acceptable?

Witelson: Yes, but there also are women who work in the world as it exists today. I have a certain amount of competitiveness. I'm comfortable with a certain amount of risk. I'm passionate about the research and don't aim for any preplanned balance.

Ghaffari: Are women "leaking" into the isolation of the home rather than creating satisfactory alternative options that could provide them different environments in terms of stress and competitiveness? Are women constructing, by and for themselves, this alternative universe that is appropriate for them?

Witelson: What I learned at recent conferences is that there are many boutique businesses and law firms that women have developed when they "leaked out" of the mainstream or main institutions. The businesses are very successful, and the women are very happy and productive. That does seem to be happening. While that is one approach, not every woman may choose to do that. My hope would be that more women stay within the current reality because they have a lot to offer and to add to that experience. Maybe they might even modify the current reality a little bit and improve it.

There are studies that show that women are more risk-averse than men. Some of the biggest fortunes have been made by individuals who took big risks, predominantly men. Studies show that women invest more conservatively. Women are less competitive. Studies have followed very talented young math students into maturity. On follow-up, men had higher priorities for discovering a new product or idea, for being at the top. Women aimed for having balance in their lives and good relationships.

I would suggest, as many others have, that on average women are more driven to do things that they consider useful to society or helpful to people. Men, at least relative to women, may be more interested in personal accomplishments and success as measured by financial or power indicators. Very often, in the surveys, becoming wealthy is less of an important priority among women than among men.

So when you put these things together, it seems to me that we're dealing with two different strains within the same species, and the combination makes for a strong species. It's a reality that we have to recognize and understand.

Deanell Reece Tacha

Dean, Pepperdine University School of Law

Born 1946 in Goodland, Kansas.

Deanell Reece Tacha *became the sixth dean of Pepperdine University School of Law in June 2011.*

Raised in the small Midwestern town of Scandia, Kansas, Judge Tacha earned her BA in American studies at the University of Kansas (1968) and her JD from the University of Michigan Law School (1971) in an era when women in law were a rarity.

Following law school, Judge Tacha was named a White House Fellow, where she served as a special assistant to the secretary of labor at the US Department of Labor (1971–1972). Afterwards, she worked in private practice in Washington, DC, first at Hogan & Hartson Associates (1973) and then in Concordia, Kansas, where she was director of the Douglas County Legal Aid Clinic (1974–1977).

Judge Tacha joined the faculty of the University of Kansas School of Law in 1974, and was named associate dean in 1977 and associate vice chancellor in 1979. She served as vice chancellor of Academic Affairs of the University of Kansas from 1981 to 1985.

She was the national president of the KU Alumni Association and received its Fred Ellsworth Medallion for extraordinary service to the university (1992). She also received the KU Distinguished Service Citation (1996).

On October 31, 1985, Judge Tacha was nominated by President Ronald Reagan to a new seat on the US Tenth Circuit Court of Appeals (created by 98 Stat. 333). She was confirmed by the US Senate and received her commission on December 16, 1985.

Judge Tacha served as chief judge of the Tenth Circuit from 2001 to 2007. In 2008, she received the Edward J. Devitt Distinguished Service to Justice Award from the American Judicature Society.

In service to the American Bar Association (ABA), Judge Tacha has been the Judicial Division chair (1995–1996); chair of the US Judicial Conference's Committee on the Judicial Branch (1990–1994 and 2001–2005); and a member of the Commission on Women in the Profession (1991–1994).

Elizabeth Ghaffari: Would you tell me a little about your early years in Kansas?

Deanell Reece Tacha: In January 1946, World War II was just ending and my dad had just gotten out of the Navy. My mother had recently lost her brother in the war and was spending some time with her parents in Kanarado, Kansas—a little town in the northwest corner of the state. While I was born in Goodland, I grew up almost entirely in Scandia, Kansas—another small town with about three hundred and fifty people in the north-central part of the state. I'm the oldest of four girls.

Scandia is a little Scandinavian community. My grandmother was Swedish, like many in the community who had came out west from Chicago. I went to a grade school where classes were so small they fit two classes into one room. I always like to say I was the top 10 percent of my class because I think there were only about 11 people in my high school graduating class. I have always thought that it was one of the best educations I could have possibly gotten because the teachers took great interest in me. For example, my third- and fourth-grade teacher kept me after school every day, and we spelled through the dictionary twice because I wanted to do the spelling bees. I did very well in the spelling bees. We didn't have any frills, but we had very good and dedicated teachers.

Ghaffari: What did your father do for a living?

Tacha: He founded a highway construction company. One of my earliest childhood memories was standing with my father, my grandfather, and then President Eisenhower, near Abilene, Kansas, opening the first stretch of the interstate highway system. My dad, granddad, my uncle, and now my youngest sister, Mary Lou, have all been in the highway construction business.

My mother was the company treasurer, although not really involved in the operations. She was the consummate volunteer and a Republican National committee woman from Kansas for over twenty years. She was very much involved in Republican politics. Her passions were politics and volunteer work.

Ghaffari: Why did you choose Kansas University?

Tacha: I thought I was going east to college. I never really considered any place else. It was affordable, and it was where I was going to go. My major was in American studies.

Both of my parents graduated from Kansas University. My father studied business, and my mother got a degree in journalism in 1942. My grandmother, on my mother's side, went there, too. She was in the first class of nurses from the University of Kansas Hospital in 1903. There were five women in that class, two of whom were sisters.

Ghaffari: Wasn't it a little unusual for a woman to apply to law school in the late 1960s as you did?

Tacha: I was "pinned," which in my fraternity/sorority world meant that I was sort of destined to get engaged and go off to do rather traditional things. But, there was something about that that just didn't feel quite right for me. It wasn't about the man, it was just about me. I thought, "I'm just not through with my education yet. I really want to do more." At that time, you could take the LSAT in your senior year and still get into law school. Unbeknownst to anyone else, including my pinmate and my parents, I took the LSAT, the GRE, and the MedCAT.

I ended up getting my best score on the LSAT—a fact that was startling, to say the least. As you properly observed, I knew *no* women lawyers, let alone women judges. I did, however, know a dean of women—that was typical in those days—at Kansas. Emily Taylor. She was incredibly far ahead of her time—anyone who was at Kansas will tell you that. She was instrumental in helping Title IX[1] get passed. At Kansas, she took a group of fairly traditional young women and convinced us we could do whatever we wanted to do. She kind of made us—she wouldn't take "no" for an answer.

Emily Taylor was the first person I talked to after I passed the LSAT, and she thought it was great. Then I got up my courage to talk with the dean of the law school at the time, James K. Logan. He also encouraged me to go. He ended up being my colleague on the Tenth Circuit Court. I went to see several other people who had been mentors or just good faculty—of

---

[1] For information on Title IX, see www.dol.gov/oasam/regs/statutes/titleix.htm.

course, they were all males. They all encouraged me. Now, as I look back on that, I think, "What a wonderful open attitude they had" because nobody said, "Why would you do such a thing?"

Except my dad, who was very opposed to the idea. I had taken the test and scored well. I had taken my spending money and applied to all of the great law schools in the country. Then, wonder of wonders, I got into most of them. I realized, "I've got to tell people I'm doing this." At the time, I lived in a sorority house at Kansas. One Sunday evening, I called my dad and said, "Well, Dad, you know what? I have something to tell you—I'm going to go to law school!" There was silence on the line. My dad was a wonderful man, but he had a bit of temper. So, I expected an explosion. But there was none. It was quiet. All he said was, "Well, that's interesting." And that seemed to be the end of it.

But, five hours later, which is exactly the time it takes to drive from my little hometown to Lawrence, Kansas, Dad came to the door of the sorority house. He took me out for coffee at four in the morning and, for the next several hours, tried to talk me out of this craziness.

He said, "Deanell, when you could do anything you want to do, why would you pick the one thing you can't succeed at?" He spoke the truth from his own experience. He had never seen a woman lawyer. He had never seen a woman judge. And he really didn't like lawyers because he was a construction guy. His famous quote was, "I never go see the lawyers first. I go afterwards and ask them to get me out of it." His experience with lawyers had been anything but pleasant.

When he realized I wasn't to be deterred, he said, "Well, at least you're going to Kansas, aren't you?" And I had to say, "No, Dad, I've been advised that it would be smart for me to go somewhere else." His last ditch effort was, "But you have to go to a state school." And I said, "Okay, I'll go to Michigan."

Ghaffari: Why did you choose a state school? Was that because of the cost?

Tacha: It was partially about affordability, but remember that this was the late sixties. I had a very traditional family. A lot of things were happening on college campuses—especially on the East Coast. At the time, Michigan seemed like a pretty safe Midwestern state university. But, as it turned out, Michigan ended up being one of the most volatile places in the country!

Ghaffari: What did your mother say when she heard about your plan?

Tacha: She was not as vocal as my father. Clearly, now she applauds it. At the time, she was worried and nervous about me doing something that was so nontraditional. But both of them ended up supporting me and helping me enormously. My dad never got over apologizing. Every time he introduced me, he'd say, "This is the lawyer."

Ghaffari: What did your "pinmate" have to say?

Tacha: Yes, I had to carry this news to the man at the time. He was very nice, but it just didn't work out. It was the wrong time.

Ghaffari: What did you like especially about law school?

Tacha: Everything, even though the first year was very, very trying for several reasons. One thing was that I was such a good undergraduate liberal arts and sciences person, but that wasn't necessarily the best fit for law school. I had to hone my analytical skills in ways I had not anticipated. I was accustomed to knowing everything from the Magna Carta forward. But, in law school, the skill is focusing quite precisely on issues, on problem solving, and on the relevant, supporting material. One certainly doesn't learn that as a liberal arts undergraduate.

The other thing that I have come to realize was difficult—but didn't realize it at the time—was being among so few women. To give you a sense of what I mean, those were the days when, in criminal law, they would call on the women to describe the rape cases. You would have to stand up and give all the details. It was mortifying.

But, quite simply, we just wanted to do well. So, we powered on through it all. One of the best things that happened to me—still, to this day—is that among my dearest friends in life are the three women with whom I lived on campus at Michigan. One of them lives in LA, and we just had dinner together last week.

We were reminiscing about how we came together sight unseen—we didn't know each other. Women couldn't live in the law quadrangle, so the law school just sent out a list of people looking for a place to live. The four of us came together in the tiniest, two-bedroom apartment with one bathroom. The woman who became my roommate probably is six-feet, one- or two-inches tall, while I'm lucky to reach five-feet, one inch. I moved in before she did. Those were the days of short-short skirts, so my first impression of her was that my skirts looked like they belonged on dolls, while her skirts looked excessively long. We hadn't seen each other—we'd only seen each other's clothes.

My roommate and I ended up being fast friends, along with two other women. All four of us get together at least once a year—in fact, we're getting together in two or three weeks.

We studied a little bit together, and we were in the same section, but it was pretty much independent work.

Ghaffari: What did you excel in at law school? Did you have a favorite subject?

Tacha: I really liked it all. As in all education, I think it's dependent on who were the faculty and who were your great professors. Certainly, I ended up with some fabulous professors in my section. There were names like Theodore St. Antoine, who was dean at the time and taught labor law, so I loved labor law. I had Yale Kamisar, who is well known in criminal law, and Grant Nelson for constitutional law. I was very fortunate in that the whole lineup of faculty members was just excellent. I wouldn't say that I excelled or anything, but I just liked what I did.

Well, maybe I did excel at moot court. I did very well at moot court. It was all that practice. I think it must have been second year, before my final moot court arguments, when again I was the only woman in the finals in my section. I wasn't the least worried about my case because I knew my material. But I was a little concerned about two things—my tone of voice and what I would wear. There were no real role models or at least very few that I'd seen. So, I went to a very well-respected male faculty member, and he gave me the best advice of my life. He said, "Be yourself." So I wore a bright green dress, and I won.

Ghaffari: How did you come to be a White House Fellow after law school?

Tacha: The plum job after law school, even then, would have been to clerk for a court of appeals judge. And as it turns out, there had been a couple of women from Michigan prior to me who had clerked. But, no one suggested to me that I apply for a clerkship, so that just wasn't even on my radar screen.

I was taking local government law from Professor Tom Kauper and, to his great credit, he said to me, "You ought to look at this White House Fellowship program. I think you'd be well suited to it." He gave me the application and a brochure. I thought it was a long shot, but I filled it out and was selected. Even though there was a long history of White House Fellowships, my memory is that I was just the seventh woman—and the only Kansan—ever selected.

So, I went off to Washington to be a White House Fellow and a special assistant to the Secretary of Labor, James Hodgson. I worked mostly with the undersecretary, Larry Silberman, who ended up on the DC circuit. White House Fellows are always assigned to a cabinet member, but the actual job that they do varies, depending on the needs of the department and the cabinet officer.

Half of the White House Fellowship is like employment, working as a special assistant to the cabinet officer, while the other half is an educational program. During the course of the year, you meet almost all major leaders of the nation—corporate, government, nonprofit, everybody. And we took two international trips. It was at the height of the Vietnam conflict, so the first trip was to Vietnam and all the border states around China, right before President Nixon's trip to China. The second trip was to Central and East Africa on what was more of a trade mission.

I had become very involved in the work of the Labor Department, and so they asked me to stay on after my fellowship ended. I continued to work as a special assistant to one of the assistant secretaries at the Labor Department for another few months after the second election of Nixon. After that, I went into private practice law at Hogan & Hartson in Washington, DC.

Several law firms talked to me, and I had come to know the partners and hiring partners in a number of firms. I was attracted to Hogan & Hartson because they were doing a lot of communications and securities law, both of which interested me.

Ghaffari: You only spent a year with them. What happened?

Tacha: I loved it, but ever since my first year in law school, I had been dating a high school basketball coach from Concordia, Kansas, whom I met when I was volunteering. As a woman, I couldn't get summer employment and had no money, so I volunteered at a little law firm in Concordia, Kansas, worked part-time for my dad, and lived at home. John Tacha was the basketball coach, a math teacher in the local high school, and was teaching driver's ed. He and his buddy, the editor of the local paper, were driving around one day, when the friend said to John, "Hey, there's a chick over at the law firm. You should go over and check that out." So, we went on a blind date.

You could just imagine it—here I am, pretty "high cotton" from all these years in Ann Arbor, Washington, and international travel. Then there was John, who was going to be a high school basketball coach in Concordia, Kansas. He wasn't going to move, and I said, "I'm not coming back to Kansas." So this goes on for several years. Finally, after I'd gone to the law firm and was really thinking about the rest of my life, I realized, "This is my first priority. I love this man. He's the right partner for me." So, I sent him a singing telegram, in his high school math class, that said, "Yes, September 2."

I moved back to Concordia, Kansas. I must admit that, at the time, I thought I'd given up my career. No one would hire me. But there was one lawyer, Thomas J. Pitner, a sole practitioner, who allowed me to come in with him and use his library. I think he might have even given me some of his clients.

It was absolutely a wonderful experience. I took whatever cases came in off the street—deeds, divorces, you name it—general practice.

I had several great role models. There was one elderly judge, Marvin Brummett, who was something of a legend in Kansas as a great state district court judge. One day, I had my first divorce case before him. I had prepared well and thought I was this hotshot lawyer who knew everything. I was just finishing examining my client, when this very kind, wonderful role model of a judge looked up at me and said, "Counsel, you may wish to ask her where she lives." Well, domicile is the most important thing to establish in a divorce case, but I'd failed to ask it. My client never knew that I failed to do the obvious because the judge just gave me the nicest possible lesson in a wonderfully collegial way.

Yes, good men everywhere. Then, just six months later, the KU Law School called me and wanted to know if I'd teach. Would I drive the three-and-a-half hours to teach a course one day a week? Well, of course, I wanted to do that.

By this time I was pregnant with our first child, so here was this little pregnant lady teaching law. That summer they invited me to be a full-time faculty member—which was a very difficult decision, personally. John was very happy where he was, but I really wanted to accept that job. My memory is we decided we would take turns making the big decisions and that this was my turn. All the big decisions turned out to be about location, not kids or money or any of those things.

I got the chance to go full-time on the faculty. John quit his job. We moved to Lawrence. Ultimately he got another job and ended up with the business that he now owns, but he never went back into teaching or coaching. He owns a business called the Bureau of Lecturers and Concert Artists, which is a booking agency for live entertainment for assembly programs at schools all around the country. He was hired by the man who owned it in September 1974. When that man died the following Thanksgiving, his family decided to get rid of the business and sold it to John. He still owns it. Right now, his market niche is bringing four or five troupes of Chinese or African acrobats into the US.

Ghaffari: Tell me about your family.

Tacha: We were married in 1973. John, our first, was born in 1974, Dave in 1976, Sarah in 1979, and Leah in 1983.

There's no doubt in my mind that my best accomplishments are my four children. I'm so proud of them, and they're such interesting, very different people. They all grew up in the same family with the same dynamics, yet they have gone in such different directions and expressed themselves in such very different ways. None are lawyers.

My older son has just returned to Lawrence to help his dad in the business. My second son is an insurance broker in Denver. My older daughter is teaching third graders in Vancouver, Washington, in a school that one would describe as not very privileged. And she's making such a difference for those little kids. And my younger daughter is an artist in New York, trying to make her way in the arts. They are just totally different children, and I'm very proud of them for that.

Ghaffari: What did you teach at the law school?

Tacha: I taught property and administrative law. Also, I was director of the Douglas Legal Aid Clinic. We actually had a case that ultimately went all the way to the United States Supreme Court. An NCAA scholarship athlete came into the clinic because had been denied a government scholarship known as a BEOG.[2] The NCAA had told him he had to choose between the two. He couldn't take both. I'll *never* forget it. He looked at me and said, "You know, the rich guys on the track team can take the money from their parents *and* their NCAA scholarship. I qualify for the BEOG because I have no money from my parents, but they won't let me take both the BEOG and the NCAA scholarship. It just isn't fair!"

So we sued both the NCAA and the university, among a bunch of other people. It morphed into a much bigger lawsuit, but the bottom line was the determination that athletics programs—NCAA athletics programs—were not state actors. He prevailed at the circuit court level, but unfortunately did not win at the Supreme Court level.

Ghaffari: Why did you move over to the administrative side as associate vice chancellor and then vice chancellor?

Tacha: I've always loved administration and actually that's the reason I'm back in higher education at Pepperdine. I've always loved the challenge, particularly in an educational institution, of balancing all the academic priorities with the interests of the institution, the interests of the alumni and the students, all of the myriad interests in a nonprofit milieu.

You know, you can measure your progress in a for-profit milieu by pretty objective standards, but in the nonprofit—and particularly the academic world—you've got to be in it for the long haul and for the good of future

---

[2] Basic Educational Opportunity Grant.

generations. You cannot see your success in day-by-day increments. No short-term parameters. If you do, you sell the institution and its future short.

I loved administration. I started out as associate dean of the law school, then I went out as chief academic officer of the University of Kansas at a pretty young age.

Ghaffari: What would you say would be some principal accomplishments that come to mind when you remember those days?

Tacha: The most direct accomplishment would be establishing a program called University Scholars. It was at a time when honors programs were falling out of favor—anything that sounded elitist was discouraged. I decided that I was not buying into that at all. I actually patterned the program largely on the White House Fellows' program, but within the university. I took very promising sophomores, assigned them faculty mentors, and then put together an education program on top of the regular academic program in which they would meet some of our best scholars, administrators, just a mixture of leaders. If I remember right, we took about twenty sophomores each year.

The program just celebrated its twenty-fifth anniversary two or three years ago. There was a big reunion, and I got to speak to them. Some of the people who were university scholars went on to just amazing careers. For me, one of the great rewards has been watching the people you help to find their way. You don't make it happen. You can only help people who want to become leaders.

Another memorable accomplishment is one that was not so happy, but still I'm proud of what we did. We had to cut the budgets at the university quite significantly during the time that I was vice chancellor. Sound familiar? I made the decision that we weren't going to do it across the board. Instead, we were going to make the hard choices, and I believe that that served the university well.

Ghaffari: How did President Reagan come to name you to the Tenth Circuit Court of Appeals?

Tacha: As you probably know, the president usually receives recommendations from somebody like the [Senate] Majority Leader at the time, Bob Dole, who's a Kansan, and his sidekick and mine, [former Senator] Nancy Kassebaum, who also was from Kansas. I give full credit to my mother on this. She had been friends and supporters of these politicians for a long time.

I'd like to say it was all on merit, but it also was "the mother's network." They had created a new position in Kansas—there had been only one.

Initially I resisted the offer—feeling it was just too soon in my career. I was very happy at the university, my last child had just been born, and I really didn't want to go onto the bench, yet.

Bob Dole gave me what turned out to be very smart advice. He said, "If you're ever going to do it, you better do it now."

Ghaffari: How did your family feel about the court?

Tacha: They were all very supportive. For my mother, of course, it was great because it kind of thrust me back into government. For my own family, my husband and my children, it was really good even though I traveled a lot. It's very much a personal and individual job, so you could do it night and day, weekends, or whenever. I always had the flexibility to go to their school programs whenever court was not in session. In between court terms, I had great flexibility to be very involved in my children's lives.

I was fortunate, too, that I had a guardian angel—today, we would call her a nanny—who came into our lives when our oldest son was just a baby. She's still in our lives, like a part of our family. She made everything that we did possible. In addition, my husband is just all-world. He has been as much or more a caregiver than I am. So I don't think my kids missed much. You know, occasionally they'd complain when I was gone or something. Still, I think if you ask them today, they'd say, "Well, it didn't affect me much."

Ghaffari: As you look back on that twenty-five-year career on the bench, can you give me a sense of what might have been some of the highlights from your own professional perspective?

Tacha: There's no doubt that the most memorable part of the experience was my colleagues. The people on the federal bench are as good public servants as you'll find anywhere around the world. They are not in it for their personal reward, obviously. They are—without exception—bright, dedicated, hard-working, and very nice people. You are a bit isolated on a court, so you've got to like the people with whom you work because you can't talk to the lawyers and you can't talk to the parties. So, the reward of getting to know a group of people who were federal judges was—for me—just extraordinary. I learned from every single one of them.

I had the great privilege of working with two great chief justices. Chief Justice Rehnquist was my close friend, and more recently, Chief Justice Roberts. I give Chief Justice Rehnquist amazing credit because he appointed me chair of one of the most significant committees for the federal judiciary when I was a pretty new judge, and I'll never forget it. It was the US Judicial Conference Committee on the Judicial Branch, responsible for relationships with the other two branches of government. I chaired that committee twice—once in 1990 to 1994 and again in 2001 to July 2005.

Ghaffari: What did you accomplish on that committee?

Tacha: One of our main responsibilities was to try to increase pay and benefits and accoutrements for the federal judiciary. Now, my colleagues will tell you I was less than successful at that, but we did get one significant pay raise, when my predecessor was chair. We worked very hard on that but, more broadly, our charter was at the junction of relationships among the three branches of the government. When there were issues that needed to be addressed, we were consulted either by Congress or the attorney general or whoever was involved. Most of our efforts were focused on the well-being of the federal judiciary.

Ghaffari: Were there other women justices?

Tacha: There's Dorothy Nelson from the Ninth Circuit. Carolyn King from the Fifth Circuit, who also was the chair of the Executive Committee. Rosemary Barkett is Circuit Judge for the Eleventh Circuit, and Ann Williams of the Seventh Circuit. There are more today than ever before, and several women now hold really important positions in the judiciary, which is sort of surprising considering how recently we all came on our courts. But I give great credit mostly to the chief justices who put those women in those positions. So, yes, I had quite a complement of women leaders in the judiciary.

Instead of doing any kind of inauguration here at Pepperdine, I decided to invite three women federal judges to come here and teach a brief session this September 23, 2011.[3] We're just going to tell war stories. I thought it would be good for young women students to hear what it was like, because they don't know today many of the issues we confronted back then.

Some of these opportunities are precarious. We take them for granted. As the economy gets tight, it's often the people who are in precarious economic straits who will feel the adversities the most. I'm not afraid for myself, but I view myself as speaking in part for the powerless. And I worry terribly about what the effects of the economy are going to be on all these children, on all people on the edge.

Ghaffari: As you look back over twenty-five years, are you able to highlight any decisions that might stand out as particularly memorable?

Tacha: I always resist that question because, to the people involved, they are all important cases. I can say that the capital cases were some of the

---

[3] "Hearing Her Story: Reflections of Women Judges," see: http://law.pepperdine.edu/news-events/events/hearing-her-story/

hardest. All six of the states in the Tenth Circuit, plus the federal government, had the death penalty, so we got a fair amount of capital litigation.

When I was in the circuit, there were a lot of tragedies—horrible things happened. We had the Oklahoma City bombing, the Los Alamos Labs case, and the Columbine case, to name just a few. Even so, it felt as if the time went by in an instant.

Ghaffari: When you were on the American Bar Association's Commission on Women in the Profession, what was that experience like?

Tacha: That was from 1987 to about 1993 or 1994. Hillary Clinton chaired that commission.

That was an unforgettable experience because it was the first time the ABA ever looked at these issues. Hillary and I are almost exactly contemporaries. We each have daughters the same age. At the outset, I have to admit that I didn't realize who Hillary Clinton was, but I certainly saw her skills. We met monthly for all those years, and that commission was an eye-opener for me.

There were three of us who were—to put it not so delicately—the old women of the group. The third was Lynn Hecht Schafran.[4]

Most of the other members were somewhat younger. The three of us felt that maybe some of the battles had already been won and that there was a fair amount of parity and equality in the profession. I remember very vividly some public hearings in Philadelphia where we heard these rather touching stories of women who were trying to raise families and whose law firms weren't flexible enough to give them the kinds of opportunities they needed. We finally began to realize that the profession itself still had a lot of structural impediments. That's what I meant by "precarious"—those opportunities have a tendency to disappear in tight economic times, such as those we are facing today.

Ghaffari: What was the Commission able to accomplish?

Tacha: We did a lot of different things—issued reports, talked to law firms, urged firms to implement flextime and part-time as a normal course of business. We also established an award, the Margaret Brent Women Lawyers of Achievement Award, established in 1991, to recognize and celebrate the accomplishments of women lawyers who have excelled in their field and have

---

[4]Senior vice president of Legal Momentum and the director of Legal Momentum's National Judicial Education Program to Promote Equality for Women and Men in the Courts (NJEP).

paved the way to success for other women lawyers. It's given every year to five or six really outstanding women lawyers or judges.[5]

Ghaffari: How was it that you are a Republican and Hillary Clinton is a Democrat, yet you were able to bridge that gap?

Tacha: Oh, we're friends. We've been friends. We probably don't agree on all issues, but we do agree on the opportunities for women.

Ghaffari: Would you say that your experience with the ABA taught you about governance?

Tacha: Somewhat, but the ABA is very large, and the governing body is a little bit difficult to manage. So, while I did learn from my ABA experience how to work with very, very different kinds of people, still I think I learned most of my governance in higher education.

I've stayed on the Board of Trustees of the KU Endowment Association because I really enjoyed seeing that side of educational governance—the investment and development side.

Ghaffari: How did you happen to become a trustee of St. Paul's School of Theology?

Tacha: I went onto that board right after I went onto the bench, serving as chair of the academic committee. I was there for almost twenty years. As a judge you can't do anything in the for-profit world, and you can't do anything that would be any kind of a conflict of interest. So the only boards that I could serve on were philanthropic or educational. I'd been a long-time United Methodist, and St. Paul's was in Kansas City. I greatly admired the president at the time, Dr. Lovett Weems. He's a well-known Methodist theologian who is now at Wesley Theological Seminary in Washington, DC.

Ghaffari: How did the Pepperdine invitation come about?

Tacha: That you will have to ask them! I had no intention of leaving the judiciary. I was happy. I was eligible for, and took, senior status. It was going to be a nice quiet life—finally a little bit more relaxing life than I'd had up to that point. Then Pepperdine came calling. They had established a search committee. They invited me to apply.

There were many ways in which Pepperdine and I had crossed paths. President Andy Benton, for whom I have the most respect, grew up in Lawrence,

---

[5] For more information on the Margaret Brent Women Lawyers of Achievement Award, see www.americanbar.org/groups/women/initiatives_awards/margaret_brent_awards.html

Kansas, where we still have a home. David Davenport, a previous president here, was my student at the KU Law School. Grant Nelson taught me constitutional law at Michigan.

There were just many ways that I felt called to come back to higher education in a place where values count, where I thought I might have a piece of molding lawyers of the future. When you reach my age, it's not about me—it's about what you might do to help shape a more humane future.

I have become so disenchanted with the cacophony of public life that I am now working around the theme of "lawyer patriots" who model civil discourse, who listen to all sides of an issue, who bring their human values to bear on problem solving. "Lawyer patriots" are those who may—the idealist in me believes—be able to give my grandchildren at least a little bit more of an informed and thoughtful future.

Ghaffari: How do you begin this endeavor?

Tacha: For me it's easy. You get to know people. You get to know the culture a little bit. I spent my first two weeks having about hour-long chats with every faculty member. Maybe, later you might do some tweaking of the culture. Of course, students aren't here yet, so I've been trying, to the extent that I could, to get acquainted with the central administration.

Even though I joined Pepperdine on June 1, I haven't had as much time as I'd like because I was already committed to teaching at Oxford. I had agreed to teach a course for the University of Oklahoma at their Oxford campus, so I couldn't very well back out of that. I taught a course on the meaning and characteristics of the rule of law. The course was only eight days, although their summer program is two months long. I spent the middle weekend in London with the students and faculty of Pepperdine's summer program.

Ghaffari: What do you see on the horizon for legal education?

Tacha: I think that it's an exciting time in legal education. Now some would say it's a crazy time, but I would say it's exciting. The Carnegie Commission Report expressed their views on what needs to happen in law schools. The ABA and the American Association of Law Schools are considering some rather different standards for law schools. The public—mostly the media—is questioning whether law school is worth its salt or worth its dollars. I find these to be fascinating issues. We're having a faculty retreat in a couple of weeks. I've invited one of the authors of the Carnegie Commission Report and one of the most outstanding deans in the country to talk with us about the future of legal education. Then, we're going to form some task forces around those themes.

Ghaffari: Will you be including any of these women's issues that you've talked about earlier, or is that not necessary anymore?

Tacha: I don't know if that's not necessary. I would say that diversity issues generally are extremely important. Also, because this is a Christian law school, I think it's part of the mission to be inclusive and to understand that our future depends on our ability to be tolerant, inclusive, listening, and thoughtful in how we move into a very different culture than we've known.

Ghaffari: You've expressed an interest in enhanced capital funding to retrofit the law school building. What do you have in mind?

Tacha: It's largely about how you build community. This building was state-of-the-art in the seventies. We've learned a lot about building community, and I speak not only of law schools, but of everywhere. Where we put our hallways, our sidewalks, and our access points has a really clear impact on the kind of community we are. We have the most gorgeous location on the face of the earth, but we don't have very many ocean views. The students have even fewer views. We want to be very sensitive to all of the environmental and coastal issues here.

I believe that the community experience could be considerably enhanced by some significant changes in the building. It would not be a new building. It would be retrofitting and change. My favorite thing to say is, "Where's the guy with the pick ax? Get some walls down." At home, I was on the board of a health foundation, and I learned so much from an expert about how you plan communities. For example, my father was instrumental in building the interstate system, but it bypassed and killed many communities. Today, our nephew is working to reroute roads through cities to recapture those opportunities.

A former clerk of mine wrote a wonderful book called *Law's Environment*,[6] where he takes five case studies of what happened on the ground to communities. We learned all about sidewalks in the health foundation. Think about sidewalks. Where do we put them? For years, we put them right by the busiest streets. Kids couldn't walk on them, and people took their cars rather than walk or bicycle. If we had put sidewalks behind the busiest streets and crisscrossed them, we'd have created common space. We're learning these things now, but rebuilding communities is really hard.

A good example of where this is being done is in Stapleton, just outside Denver. My son actually lives there. It's a very sustainable, park-oriented

---

[6] *Law's Environment: How the Law Shapes the Places We Live,* by John Copeland Nagle (Yale University Press, 2010).

community. The houses are close to the street, but back onto a big common area. The kids ride their big wheels. Everybody gets to knows everybody. The mothers write blogs about who they saw in the neighborhood. It's just awesome.

Ghaffari: Your husband is still in Lawrence?

Tacha: Yes. That was the hardest part of this decision. I told you that, along the way, the toughest decisions were all about location. He's always supported me in whatever I wanted to do, whenever I wanted to do it. When I began to think about Pepperdine, he said, "I'm not moving to California." Well, he's five years older than I am. He's got his business, he's got his buddies, he's got a life. We have a place in the country that he just loves. He's been a huge volunteer in the community, the church, and in other areas. I go there when I can. Similarly, when I was at the university, he went when he could. He actually didn't go to very many court functions. And that's been fine. We've been pretty much independent in our social lives, in our sort of day-to-day activities. So, he said, "It's fine with me if you go, and I'll visit sometimes."[7]

One of our agreements has always been that we didn't make each other go to the other's commitments. Still, it's hard to be half a country away. You do worry as you get older about health issues and things like that—but so far, so good. And we'll just see.

Ghaffari: Think back about when you were in law school, when there were no women on the faculty, and there were only fifteen women peers. How do you feel now that you are a woman out there who is an affirmative role model to many young women, not just in the law, but in the court as well as in academia, and now in law school? How do you feel about that leadership role?

Tacha: I feel it's a very, very important responsibility, not because I see myself as a role model, but because I want, to the fullest extent possible, to model opportunity for young people. Not that they should do what I did—because you know, I've probably done way too much—but rather I'd like somehow for my life to tweak another life, for young students to say, "I could do this, I could be this"—whatever it is. I've always resisted stereotypes, because that's what kept my dad from wanting me to go to law school. Stereotypes have molded so many people, men and women alike, for too long. When I think of people of different ethnicities trying to model

---

[7] John Tacha and Dean Tacha's mother flew out to attend her inaugural event September 23, 2011 with the three women circuit court judges mentioned above.

the WASP model, I see it just doesn't work. My old faculty member's advice comes back to me. "Be yourself!"

A student came in here the other day, laughing at me because he read an article from my hometown newspaper on the internet about my Christmas decorations. He said, "You do Christmas decorations?" Well, of course I do. I *love* Christmas decorations. I don't mind being the traditional woman. I love it. I want people to realize that those things that are strong pieces of their personalities are the same things that make them strong leaders.

Ghaffari: Where do you see the greatest opportunities for women today?

Tacha: I see opportunity everywhere. And this is one of the things I love about living as long and seeing as much as I have. I saw a lot of this in the judiciary. Women's role models are very good at organizing playgrounds and universities and government, among other things. I try to resist stereotyping in this area, but I do think there's something in our brain makeup or hormones or whatever, such that women really do like to listen to other people. We really like to learn about other people. We like stories.

I love seeing so many women writers come forward because they speak in stories more than in statistics. As I watch women, I really believe they live their lives in stories much more than they do in objective measurement. I've met an awful lot of good, really powerful women who, when you ask them what the bottom line is, they'll say, "I don't know." But they are really powerful women.

Ghaffari: Where do you see yourself in the next five to ten years?

Tacha: I'll be at Pepperdine for a lot of that time. It's hard for me to think about anything other than continuing to be challenged and interested. I was given very good advice by Darryl Tippens, the provost to whom I report. When I was struggling with this decision, he told me, "You know, my momma taught me that we often have to be re-potted to grow."

I've thought about that many times because it's so true. So, I say to young people all the time, "Reinvent yourself. Just reinvent yourself."

Ghaffari: You've made so very many career choices. Are there any choices that you wouldn't make if you could go back to do it over again?

Tacha: My sisters laugh at me all the time about this. I never look back. I just don't look back. Once I've made a decision, I move on. And I think it's made me very happy.

Ghaffari: As you look at the students here, is there advice that you would give to men that would be different from the advice you would give to women?

Tacha: No, I think that's really important because the "be yourself" advice applies to all of us. In a way, it's almost belittling or stereotyping to think that we categorize people—whether by gender, ethnicity, or religion.

Jennifer Tour Chayes

Managing Director, Microsoft Research New England

Born 1956 in New York, New York.

Dr. Jennifer Tour Chayes *is Distinguished Scientist and Managing Director of Microsoft Research New England in Cambridge, Massachusetts, which she co-founded in 2008 with her husband, Christian Borgs, to integrate mathematics and computer science with other applied sciences.*

Dr. Chayes' research concentration has been in the areas of phase transitions in discrete mathematics and computer science, structural and dynamical properties of self-engineered networks, and algorithmic game theory. She has led research teams in developing innovative solutions in economics and social media, new drug therapies for cancer, and energy conservation in the context of cloud computing.

In 1997, at the invitation of Nathan Myhrvold, then chief technology officer of Microsoft, Dr. Chayes joined Microsoft Research in Redmond, Washington, and co-founded its Theory Group to collaborate with academics and researchers on fundamental problems in mathematics and theoretical computer science. While in Redmond, she was also an affiliate professor of mathematics and physics at the University of Washington in Seattle.

Prior to Microsoft, Dr. Chayes was a professor of mathematics at UCLA, where she taught undergraduate and graduate students. During her tenure, she received the

Distinguished Teaching Award, an honor awarded by the faculty of the university's math department.

Dr. Chayes has co-authored more than one hundred scientific papers and co-invented more than twenty-five patents. She was a member of the Institute for Advanced Study; a fellow of the American Association for the Advancement of Science; a National Associate of the National Academies; a fellow of the Fields Institute; and a fellow of the Association for Computing Machinery.

Serving on numerous institute boards, advisory committees, and editorial boards, she is the chair of the Turing Award Selection Committee of the Association for Computing Machinery, past chair of the Mathematics Section of the American Association for the Advancement of Science, and past vice president of the American Mathematical Society.

She received her BA in biology and physics from Wesleyan University in 1979, graduating first in her class. She received her PhD in mathematical physics at Princeton University in 1983, and did postdoctoral work in the mathematics and physics departments at Harvard and Cornell. She received a National Science Foundation Postdoctoral Fellowship and a Sloan Faculty Fellowship.

In June 2011, Dr. Chayes was recognized with the annual Leadership Award of Cambridge-based Women Entrepreneurs in Science and Technology.

Elizabeth Ghaffari: I've heard some stories about your early interest in math and would like to get a feel for your family as you were growing up— your siblings or any of the influences that might have directed you into the math and physics arena.

Dr. Jennifer Tour Chayes: I've always loved math, although I'm not sure why. There wasn't a lot of math done in my house when I was growing up. Two of the three of us siblings are pretty well-known scientists, but I'm not sure where this came from. There must have been something in the gene pool somewhere.

I was born in Manhattan, raised in Riverdale, the Bronx, and then we moved to White Plains when I was three. By the time I was four or five years old, I had found some neighbors who did math, and I would go over there and ask for math problems—which is kind of a strange thing to seek out. My brothers were going to the same house and asking for candy, yet I was going there asking for math problems.

Ghaffari: How many brothers did you have, and where did you fit in the hierarchy?

Chayes: I'm the oldest—a very typical oldest child. I have two brothers who are close in age. One brother is a year younger than I am, while the other is three years younger. The former is a lawyer, and the latter is a prominent scientist. He's a very well-known chemist—James Tour. He won the Feynman Award and was also one of the ten most-quoted chemists of the last decade.

Ghaffari: What about your parents?

Chayes: My parents are both Persian. My father is a pharmacist, and my mom is a housewife. My father used to do little experiments for us when we were kids. He'd bring stuff home from the drugstore and mix up chemicals, which we found exciting.

Ghaffari: How did you come to choose Wesleyan?

Chayes: At the time I started in 1974, Wesleyan was known more for liberal arts than for sciences. It has very good sciences, but it was known more as a liberal arts school. Actually, it was kind of a hippie school in the early seventies, which I liked. Also, a leftover feature from the sixties was the fact that there were no distribution requirements. I'm really not very good at doing what I'm told—I don't like to have a lot of rules telling me what I'm supposed to do. So, with no requirements, I could build whatever curriculum interested me. I could do whatever I wanted. Even though it was very liberal, artsy school, I ended up taking only two non-science or non-math classes during my entire undergraduate career.

Ghaffari: And I understand that you potentially could have had three majors—biology, physics, and chemistry. Is that right?

Chayes: And math too, actually. I was a physics major and a biology major, with just one course shy of a chemistry major and one course shy of a math major.

Ghaffari: After graduating first in your class, you immediately went on to Princeton University. Why did you choose Princeton?

Chayes: Princeton was supposed to be a great place for doing mathematical physics, so since I loved physics and math, it just seemed like the perfect fit. Our class was very small, just twenty students, so we were all close. We interacted socially as well as in our work. One of my classmates was Nathan Myhrvold, who went on to become chief strategist and chief technology officer of Microsoft Corporation.

Ghaffari: You met your first husband, Lincoln Chayes, at Wesleyan. Is that right?

Chayes: Yes, I married him while I was at Wesleyan. I was nineteen. It was a weird thing to do in 1976, to get married at that young age, but we just decided to do that. We were married for fifteen years, went through undergrad and graduate school and two postdocs together. We got tenure together, and then we split up.

Ghaffari: After Princeton, you did postdoctoral work at Harvard and Cornell. What fellowships were those?

Chayes: From 1983 to 1985, we were at Harvard, the first year in physics, the second year jointly in physics and math. In 1985 to 1987, we were at Cornell, the first year in physics, and the second year jointly again in physics and math. It was the typical postdoc work through the university, but then in the second year at Harvard, I got a National Science Foundation postdoctoral grant, which I took with me to Cornell. Then I added an Army Math Fellowship while at Cornell. The Army had a mathematics center at Cornell.

Ghaffari: Was your transition to UCLA for your work or your husband's work?

Chayes: I guess it was for the both of us—all of our work was joint. We joined the UCLA math department faculty in July 1987. They gave tenure to both of us immediately in 1987, so we never had to do a tenure track, which was nice. We both became full professors in 1990. UCLA has a very good math department, so it was a great environment for us.

I taught undergrad and graduate students there. I ended up teaching a lot of freshman- and sophomore-level courses for non-math majors who needed some concentration in mathematics. Every fall I had about five hundred students, including engineers, mathematicians, and physicists. I'd teach two classes of two hundred and fifty students. I liked teaching the undergrads—that was fun because, if you taught them well, you could get them to love math.

Ghaffari: I guess you taught them well—you won the Distinguished Teaching Award from the math department, right?

Chayes: I liked to teach. You're judged based on student evaluations, and I probably had thousands of those. So, it seemed that the students liked my teaching. The department voted on giving awards to faculty members who had very good teaching recommendations.

Ghaffari: Was there a scarcity of young girls in the UCLA math classes?

Chayes: Oh yes. That was no different from anywhere else I had seen. There probably are more young women in the undergraduate math classes there today. In the four years that I was at Princeton, there was no other woman who got a PhD in math or physics.

Ghaffari: What attracted you to Microsoft and why did you go there?

Chayes: The most important factor was that Nathan Myhrvold made a huge pitch. He's very good at recruitment! At the beginning, I thought it was a really strange thing when he encouraged me to go there. I knew very little about computers. I didn't use computers. I had taken one Fortran class back in 1975, and that was the extent of what I knew about computers. I knew discrete math very well and had begun doing some work that might relate in some way to computer science.

I was looking at a particular problem, and Nathan got it into his head that it would be great if I went to Microsoft and started a group. I thought he was crazy, but I visited Microsoft. I remember my reaction was, "Okay, there are interesting people here." Also, I like to build things.

At UCLA, even though I was tenured, I was still a young faculty member. I wanted interdisciplinary work and had managed to get UCLA to hire some people who did some interdisciplinary work, but I had dreams of forming interdisciplinary groups. It's hard to get an academic system to turn around, especially from that lowly position.

Nathan basically said, "Okay, if you come to Microsoft, we'll give you positions. We'll let you do whatever you want, build whatever kind of group you want." That, to me, was pretty compelling. Most of my colleagues in academia thought I was crazy, because it sounded very risky. And Microsoft sounded like a bizarre place for a pure mathematical physicist to go. But it just seemed interesting to me, and when I visited there, I really liked the people. I thought, "Okay, I have a vision. I say I want to build things, and here somebody is offering me the chance to do that. I should take it."

Chayes: I moved to Microsoft in '97, but I didn't officially leave UCLA until '99.

Ghaffari: What was the problem that you were working on that interested Myhrvold?

Chayes: Most of the time, I was working on phase transitions—when a substance changes its state or phase from, say, water to ice or water to steam or from one crystal structure to another. But I was also working on problems of phase transitions in intractable problems, such as resource-allocation challenges. For example, situations where you have resources but you also have constraints.

A good example is when you're trying to schedule flights. The number of airlines is one given. The resources are your planes and gas. Another consideration is the number of passengers who want to go from one place to another in a given period of time. Those are the constraints. If you have lots of resources and very few constraints, then it's easy to solve the problem. If you have lots of constraints and very few resources, then there's no solution.

It turns out that there's a critical ratio of constraints to resources such that when you pass through that window—when the number of constraints relative to resources is large—you go from the system being solvable to the system being unsolvable. I was studying that in much the same way that a mathematical physicist would study a phase transition in a magnet or a liquid-to-gas transition. Nathan thought this was very cool and interesting, and he said that I should come study this at Microsoft. When I was interviewing, I couldn't see the relevance, but they did—or at least Nathan did. So they hired me.

Ghaffari: You co-founded, with Christian Borgs, the Theory Group, as a framework for interdisciplinary research.

Chayes: Right. That was the thing they let me build, and we called it "theory" because it was such a general name. It included math, physics, and theoretical computer science. Pretty much, it included anything you could do with a pencil and a piece of paper.

Ghaffari: Where did you meet Christian Borgs?

Chayes: In 1984, I attended the six-week physics summer school/conference held just outside of Chamonix in the Swiss Alps, called Les Houches. It's a mathematical physics summer school attended by everyone from new PhDs up through very established professors. The French government runs the conferences, focusing on a wide variety of physics topics. In Europe, the governments typically run and fund these schools. It was a natural thing for me to do at that time, given that I was on the mathematical physics track.

I actually met a great many people at that summer school. Many of the professional colleagues I've come to know throughout all these years, internationally especially, were people I met at that summer school, including my husband, Christian Borgs. We knew each other as colleagues, but didn't get together as a couple until 1992.

Ghaffari: You seem to have produced a tremendous volume of articles that you have co-authored with him. Would you say you collaborate well together?

Chayes: Yes, definitely. The way I manage to have a personal life and work life is to combine them because I get really involved in my work. If I had a spouse who did something different, I would never see him. This is my work–life balance.

Ghaffari: Who leads? Who initiates the research or article topic? Is it you, is it him, is it both?

Chayes: Well, I think it's both. I think these decisions certainly involve collaboration. I tend to jump into things first. I make leaps. But then he's very deep and sees the connections. So, I think we're a good pair that way. When it gets really tough, he's right there. It might take him a little longer to understand a problem, but then he's got great depth and phenomenal comprehension.

I like to think about things in a metaphorical way, so I will see analogies from one field to another field, or I might think that tapping some discipline or approach from one field might be appropriate for another field. It's almost an intuitive kind of thing. So, it's useful to have somebody you work with closely who understands your thinking and with whom you can discuss these things on a very deep level.

Ghaffari: What happened first? Were you the co-founder of the Theory Group or were you an area regional manager for Microsoft?

Chayes: First, I co-founded the Theory Group, and then about six or seven years ago, as Microsoft Research grew, the company instituted an extra layer of management in which there were research area managers who typically managed their own groups and then some other groups as well. I began managing the Crypto Group and oversaw other theoretical areas as well.

Ghaffari: What would you say would be your primary achievements at each level?

Chayes: I think of my achievements as twofold. There are the personal research achievements, and then there's the building of something that maybe helps to inspire other researchers. In both cases, it's a matter of bringing together different fields.

For example, a new branch of probability was formed in our lab, the Theory Group, by bringing together some complex analysis and probability theory. Six years ago, the Fields Medal was given to one of the researchers who participated in this. The Fields Medal is like the Nobel Prize in mathematics. That's just one example within math of bringing together different disciplines that nobody had thought to merge in the past and yet, I'm sure, one hundred years from now, people will still be studying the new field which emerged.

I'm proudest of melding together these different disciplines. And the things for which I'm best known are probably these interdisciplinary endeavors—merging different approaches like the physics of phase transitions and computation, or bringing physics and computation to the biomedical field. These are definite interdisciplinary achievements.

Now, too, after all these years, I think I'm known for being a mentor to the postdoctoral students I've worked with over the past decade. Today, they are now faculty at essentially every top university, at most of the top twenty academic places in the world. Mentoring young people, recognizing which young people are really good and helping them to develop, represents a very satisfying personal achievement.

Ghaffari: Would you say Nathan Myhrvold was a mentor?

Chayes: No, Nathan was not a mentor—we are friends. But he was someone who recognized what was possible for me at Microsoft. He was more of a visionary, both for me and for others. Another amazing friend is Maria Klawe.[1] We are best friends now, but she was the one who pushed me to look at certain things that I wouldn't have looked at before—women's issues, for example. I really didn't want to get involved in women in science or women in technology endeavors. That's not atypical for my generation because we tend to think, "Well, I did just fine without worrying about this. So why should I worry about it now?" In fact, it's been good for me.

Maria and I talk a great deal these days. A few weeks ago, I spent a weekend with her and her family in California. We talked through a lot of problems, challenges that we've both experienced. For example, both of us tend to say exactly what's on our minds. Sometimes, we have to extract our feet from our mouths. Maria really helps me to understand how to learn from mistakes—which is one of her greatest strengths and indeed one of the greatest strengths of many amazing leaders.

Ghaffari: How did you first meet Dr. Maria Klawe?

Chayes: She came to Microsoft to ask for money for the University of British Columbia. We went out to dinner with her—we had many mutual friends. She likes to say—this is probably true—we didn't like each other that much the first time we met. She says we were like two Type A personalities clashing. I mean, I didn't know she didn't like me, and she didn't know I didn't like her, but we knew we didn't like the other one that much.

---

[1] Dr. Maria Klawe is president of Harvey Mudd College. Previously, she was dean of the School of Engineering and Applied Science at Princeton University.

Then, a couple of years later, in the summer of 2001, we were at a theoretical computer science conference together in Crete. She was with her husband, Nick, who is a mathematician and theoretical computer scientist, and I was with my husband, Christian. We ended up talking all evening—probably until five in the morning. We realized we had lots of similarities—it was just uncanny the number of similar things we had done over the years or our shared reactions to things. Now, she tells people that I am her sister. We became and continue to be very good friends.

She introduced me to the Anita Borg[2] people. At first, I didn't understand why I should go to the conferences that they ran, so Maria basically dragged me kicking and screaming to a Grace Hopper Celebration of Women in Computing event. After that, I discovered I liked them and became very involved. I've sat on various committees for them and have done other things with them over the years.

Ghaffari: What made you decide to head back to the East Coast to found the New England research center—Microsoft East?

Chayes: Well, I wanted a challenge—a change. This is another characteristic I have. When most people would just start feeling comfortable, I start feeling bored. When I'm not feeling I'm in over my head, I very quickly start feeling bored. It's strange because when I *am* in over my head, I say to myself, "Oh, why did I do this to myself?" But, then, I start feeling good about it. Anyway, I just wondered what the next challenge was going to be.

I was looking at Microsoft's business, what research could do for Microsoft, and how we defined research. I saw that we were defining research basically to be computer science and mathematical sciences only. We were not yet including a lot about the social sciences, yet the business was very much moving in the direction of social sciences, including economics and business models.

In the past, companies would just think about the technology and slap some business model on top of that. But, if you thought thoroughly about building the technology, you had to consider "What is the business model?" Then you had to include other social aspects. How do people use technology? What are their explicit needs? What are needs they may not even realize they have?

I saw that there were disciplines that were just starting to form at the boundaries of social sciences and the more mathematical sciences—

---

[2] Anita Borg was an American computer scientist who founded the Anita Borg Institute for Women and Technology, one of largest groups advocating for women in technology and engineering. The Institute runs the annual Grace Hopper Conference, which brings together thousands of women technologists.

computer sciences and mathematics. I though there needed to be a combination of the mathematical and socials sciences, and also with design—considering design as an academic as well as applied discipline.

I knew very little about these other areas of inquiry. I started to do a little bit of work in economics and thought about trying to build an economics group in Redmond. I became frustrated because I talked to some of the top economists in the world, and they didn't seem interested in relocating to Redmond, whereas I had been able to get some of the top mathematicians in the world when I started a mathematics group. It turned out that economists were fairly well entrenched in certain areas, one of which was Cambridge due to the confluence of MIT and Harvard and the National Bureau of Economic Research, as well as a host of other strong universities.

It seemed that if I wanted to attract the very top people in economics, then it would be much easier to do it in Cambridge. The same was true in the social sciences—there's the Berkman Center for Internet and Society at Harvard, which started out as part of Harvard Law School. It was a combination of lawyers and technologists who, in the past couple of years, started to be a university-wide institute. There's the Media Lab at MIT. There are all these social scientists with whom it seemed it would be very interesting to interact.

I just thought, "Okay, if I come here and get really smart, open-minded computer scientists, mathematicians, and physicists and put them together with smart anthropologists, smart sociologists, smart economists, then maybe something interesting will happen." So I pitched the idea, showing why I thought Microsoft needed expertise in these areas. I talked about where technology was moving and where Microsoft would want to be moving. I presented the argument about the kinds of people who were located in Cambridge who wouldn't relocate. Surprisingly, it took just a few weeks actually for Bill Gates and Steve Ballmer to say "yes" to the idea. It all happened very quickly.

Ghaffari: Was the idea to set up the New England Research Center largely your initiative or Christian's, would you say?

Chayes: I think this one was more my initiative. Christian was very happy. He was doing well, and we had a great team at the Theory Group. We had wonderful friends and a wonderful house. He said, "What's the matter with you?" I replied, "This is something more, something new and different. Let's do this." I definitely think it was more my impetus.

Realistically, I don't think it would have happened without him. I don't tend to take vacations. He forces me to take vacations. He also forces me to unplug and get rid of my phone for a couple of weeks. It was at the end of one of those vacations—while we were on the Greek Isles—that I thought of this. I came home, wrote up a few pages and started circulating it. People went for it.

Christian enforces the idea that we need to have the space to think about these things, which I think is very important in principle. Even so, I never want to slow down, so he constantly needs to remind me that strategic thinking requires space.

Ghaffari: Are you including anything from the neuroscience fields, such as neuroeconomics research?

Chayes: We're still just thinking about neuro-economics. Interestingly, I was surprised when so many people from the biomedical sciences came to us for help. I should have expected that since Cambridge is the biotech capital of the world, like Silicon Valley is the tech capital of the world. There are literally hundreds of biomedical companies in the area, and all the major drug companies have research outlets here.

Many biotech and biology people came asking for help, so we're now doing some of the physics-inspired algorithms in the context of biomedical problems like gene regulatory networks for cancer. We've started talking with other people who are trying to understand the wiring diagram of the brain. There are many problems of a highly mathematical nature in those fields. They tend to be "messy" in the ways that biology problems can be messy, but they're also, at their heart, really problems of extremely large data sets. We try to understand what the underlying network is in that data set, so that you can make sense of it and, for example, develop drug targets for cancers.

That clearly is an area where we are building some expertise now, adding both postdocs and other collaborators. We don't have somebody in every field in which we're interested. I would like to get behavioral economists and psychologists more involved and at some point that would include neuroeconomists.

Ghaffari: Are you finding the phase transition models have applicability to a lot of the healthcare fields?

Chayes: Absolutely. All of these techniques that we're developing—where we're getting very good results—are based on the fundamental understanding we got from looking at highly constrained systems at the points of their phase transitions.

The algorithms that we're using as we work with Sloan-Kettering trying to come up with drug targets for glioblastoma, which is brain cancer, or ovarian cancer or prostate cancer—all of them are based on studying these phase transitions. Sometimes I find that simply mind-blowing—the scale and variety of things that come out of something that appeared, a priori, to be so unrelated.

We are simply trying to follow where the science takes us. Today, it's taken us to a place where the algorithms that we've developed to this point are probably more powerful than any existing algorithms in solving optimization problems on certain types of very large data sets.

Ghaffari: danah boyd[3] is one example of your group's new emphasis on social networking issues. Is that right?

Chayes: Yes, absolutely. danah is amazing. For years, she has studied "the tribe" represented by US teenagers, which is an incredibly different tribe from their parents. We have had a lot of phenomenal visitors in that space, and we are actually planning on hiring more researchers who understand these social phenomena from an anthropological viewpoint, how different cultures emerge and express themselves through the use of different technologies.

US teenagers have very different social norms around things like privacy and friendship. Understanding where that comes from is extremely important. Many people talk about this, but danah actually goes out and conducts hundreds of interviews with teenagers. Her fieldwork last fall took her to different cities and different socioeconomic backgrounds, studying the ways in which teenagers use technology—how they perceive privacy, friendship and bullying. Her in-depth interviews back up her analysis. Her work is very highly cited because there isn't that much substantive research out there, and hers is truly brilliant.

We have another woman here, Kate Crawford, who's visiting from Sydney, Australia. She advises the government down there about social networks, just as danah is advising the government here about them. You begin to see both similarities and huge cultural differences. Kate just came back from rural India, studying the ways people there use technology.

These are intriguing issues. I find it especially interesting to bring such people together with more mathematical people like me. I have worked on models of social networks and recommendation systems that exist in social networks. When I talk to danah, I'm trying to understand what people are seeking through recommendation systems. When you merge qualitative and quantitative skill sets, it takes a while for each to adapt to the other because

---

[3] The lower case spelling of danah boyd is "how she chooses to identify" herself. See www.danah.org/name.html.

there are language barriers and differences in what we're trying to achieve. When we finally do achieve something jointly, I find that it's usually very good and very deep.

Ghaffari: Do you see danah or Kate's work being spun off as a separate center, or do you think it can be accommodated within the Microsoft Center in New England?

Chayes: I believe it is very important that we do not spin these research areas off into different centers. These fields tend to be a bit like oil and water. We work constantly, on a daily basis, to try to make sure that we are mixing them up, toward the goal of getting a really good emulsion. I think we can gain many more benefits if we have that bigger surface area.

Large companies have many advantages. One advantage is that we can fund large research centers. We can look beyond the very short term. We can bring together very different disciplines. If we work hard to ensure that people are talking to each other, understanding each other's values and interacting, then we're going to achieve things that cannot be achieved in separate isolated centers.

Microsoft does not have "lablets"—a little lab in multiple cities—as many other companies do. Part of that goes back to Nathan's and Bill's philosophy of finding a critical mass for research. I do believe that you get something unique when you have that critical mass. But you can't just let people separate by disciplines because then you end up with the very siloed structure of a university.

You can get amazing things done in a university, but there's no reason for Microsoft to get into the university business. It's cheaper for us to go and fund selected university research or buy some intellectual property from a university. In our own research centers, we can create something by blurring these boundaries—a university usually can't do that as well.

Ghaffari: How does Microsoft benefit from the research conducted in the New England center? How does your work fit into the Microsoft brand?

Chayes: Microsoft owns all of the intellectual property—IP—produced by our lab. Some of our research goes directly into products.

For example, in less than three years—which is quite fast—our lab shipped its first product, the Readmissions Manager, which is now part of our hospital database product, Amalga. The Readmissions Manager helps healthcare organizations improve operations, reduce costs, and increase patient satisfaction by identifying the root causes of preventable hospital readmissions.

Through machine learning analysis of admissions patterns, developed in our lab, this product provides proactive identification of patients who are at high risk for repeat admissions, so that hospital workers can implement the most effective actions to reduce preventable readmissions. The readmissions manager uses data from the patients ER visit, and from databases of thousands of previous visits, to address whether the patient is likely to be readmitted in the next thirty days—very important, since Medicare is planning to institute a policy of not paying for patients who are readmitted.

Some of the work produced in our lab has more of an impact on long-term strategy than on products directly. For example, our empirical economics program produces analyses of current and possible alternative business models for online services, which informs our executives and, therefore, may change the course of the company's business and product planning.

Thus, the work in our lab can impact many Microsoft business units, from online services—where machine learning, social media, and empirical economics have profound effects, to cloud services—where our algorithms help to improve efficiency both environmentally and economically, and to Windows—where our security and cryptography work has an impact. There are many more examples.

Although Microsoft owns the IP developed by the lab, we make most of it freely available for non-commercial use. In fact, there are thousands of academic papers which have built on the work coming out of my groups at Microsoft Research over the past fourteen years. Our groups themselves have produced lots of fantastic ideas and papers, but just as important is the foundation the work has laid for further work in the international academic community. Microsoft Research believes that it is important. In fact, one of our missions is to facilitate such work. For all those reasons, Microsoft makes our IP freely available for non-commercial purposes.

Ghaffari: Are you intentionally changing the name of the Microsoft New England Center to be the NERD Center?

Chayes: Yes, we do officially market ourselves as the NERD Center, which stands for New England Research and Development. Microsoft Research New England is the R in "NERD." There are some wonderful development groups here. For example, there's the SharePoint Workspace group which is part of Office, and there is the Application Virtualization group that is a product group within our Server and Tools business. There are other groups working on the Xbox. So we have some dev groups here and then we have research. We used the name NERD as a joke at first, and then we said, "Well, why not?" It certainly is memorable, isn't it?

Ghaffari: How have you dealt with the demands of work and family?

Chayes: Christian has a son, Claudio, who lived with us for a while when he was growing up. He's twenty-seven now and is a lawyer in Germany. He lived with us in Washington State for a while when he was in high school.

So I have done some parenting. When Claudio moved in with us, he wasn't doing well in school, which is why his mom sent him overseas. I would go over his homework with him every day, making him finish his homework and show it to me. He'd say, "You can't do this to a sixteen-year-old!" Or he'd say, "You can't ground me because you're going to speak at a conference in Italy." And I would say, "Watch me!" I would cancel the conference in Italy, and I would ground him.

His grades went way up. It was just so much easier to get all As than to deal with me—especially because he's very smart. It worked out really well. In a very short period of time, he realized I was at least as stubborn as he was. After that, we were just fine. That was fun, and I think he enjoyed it, too, in the end. Although at the time, he wasn't so sure.

I have a lot of graduate students and postdocs I've mentored over the years. It's starting to feel very much as if they were my children. But, it's almost as if I'm a different species because their "generation time" with me as students was only about four years, so I have great-grandchildren and great-great-grandchildren from all the people I've mentored. It's kind of cool. They're all sending me their kids and then their kids' kids. It's become very incestuous—like lab rats, but really smart lab rats.

Ghaffari: Are you still in touch with your mother-in-law, Antonia Chayes?[4]

Chayes: Yes, Toni is great. She's wonderful. She was my mother-in-law for fifteen years, a very influential fifteen years. I met her when I was seventeen, and Lincoln and I split up when I was thirty-two, so she was really a lot like a mom. To a large extent, I grew up in that household because my family didn't have those kinds of ties or careers. I learned a lot from her, and I still realize that there are times at which I'm applying those lessons. She once said to me, "Oh, you took after me possibly more than my own kids took after me." She was also married at nineteen, but stayed married. And she became an academic.

Ghaffari: How do you guide young women to follow careers in your particular area—how do you motivate and advise them?

---

[4]Antonia Chayes is a visiting professor of international politics and law at the Fletcher School at Tufts University. She also taught at the Harvard Law School and the Kennedy School of Government at Harvard. She chairs the Project on International Institutions and Conflict Management at the Program on Negotiation at the Harvard Law School.

Chayes: I always tell them that they should follow their passion, and I really mean that. I don't think they should try to plan their careers. I think that unplanned careers are so much more interesting than planned careers. If you over-plan, you miss a lot of opportunities. So do something you're passionate about. Work really hard. Don't be afraid of being stupid—ask questions. Mentor other people. And just open your eyes. Don't miss those opportunities. Don't be scared to try things.

Don't be too narrow. Don't think, "Oh, this is too far afield for me," because the far-afield stuff often is the most exciting. So, I tell them to always keep your eyes open for something that grabs your attention and not to worry that you might not yet be an expert in that field.

A lot of women, including me, are not confident. I sound confident, but often I'm not confident. Maria Klawe introduced me to the concept of an "imposter panel"—something she started doing herself. An imposter panel is where you talk about how you feel like an imposter, in spite of great success. When you put together groups of very impressive, very accomplished women, in different stages of their careers, and have them talk one after another about how they feel like imposters, then you begin to realize that—more important than actually having confidence—is knowing how to act with confidence. You have to take the actions that a confident person would take and just take risks, in spite of this voice inside of you telling you that you are going to fail. It's just a voice. Probably wrong, to boot. So you learn to just take risks and act as if you are confident, especially if you simply think you were just lucky. I think sounding confident is a big part of success.

Ghaffari: Do you feel that the imposter panels were effective tools?

Chayes: Very effective, yes. It even helps me to hear those things although I'm pretty far along right now. A few years ago, I did an imposter panel at MIT with about five hundred women in attendance. I've never seen a bunch of people so energized. As we were talking, it was amazing to see all the heads nodding in affirmation and the shock of realization on the faces in the audience. Nod and shock. "Oh my gosh! Somebody else feels this way?" I think the panels are extremely effective because when you hear that someone else who's very successful with the same discouraging voices in their head, suddenly it occurs to you that maybe—if that person has decided she shouldn't listen to those voices—may I shouldn't listen to them, either.

Ghaffari: Do you think that guys need the same advice?

Chayes: I think that many men do need the same advice, although my experience has been—and there's also a lot of documentation to back this up—that women are truly less confident than men. Over the years, I would see all of these talented women students doing really well in my classes. For example, I would see a woman being the top student among two hundred and fifty people in my class. And I would say to her, "Wow, you know, you seem to be very good at math. Maybe you should think about having a career in math," and she would say, "Oh, I'm just lucky."

Then some guys would do badly and would come to my office and tell me why they were just unlucky and how they actually knew so much more than was apparent from their exams. I saw that same pattern again and again and again. I'm not sure why but, in general, women tend to be less confident, so I think they need more encouragement to pursue opportunities in spite of whatever their inner voices might be telling them. Men need this too, but, statistically speaking, women need it more.

Ghaffari: Do you think the social networking that's happening today is fostering this insecurity or resolving it or having any impact whatsoever?

Chayes: I think there are different levels of social networking. To the extent that I understand it, Facebook can foster insecurities because it provides a forum for bullying. In my day, of course there was bullying which fostered insecurity, but it didn't occur on Facebook. For example, when girls were good in math or science, they would often be bullied by both girls and boys who would try to make them feel bad about their achievements and themselves. I know that some of that is taking place online today.

There are other kinds of social networking that are extremely helpful—like mentoring and counseling. Many things that were taking place in other venues are now taking place online, which means that they are just happening at a faster time scale. Both for good and for ill, they're happening at a much quicker pace.

Ghaffari: You're also closer to Harvard and Radcliffe and the work being done there to basically undo the impact of Lawrence Summers' statements to the NBER. Do you see that happening?

Chayes: I'm on the board of the Radcliffe Institute and I have associations with the School of Engineering and Applied Science at Harvard. Yes, some of the damage caused by Larry Summers' statements is certainly being undone—basically by amazing women leaders who have come in, instituted great policies, and also provided fantastic role models. For example, Drew Faust[5] and Cherry Murray[6] are incredible leaders.

---

[5] Drew Gilpin Faust is president of Harvard University.

[6] Cherry A. Murray is dean of the Harvard School of Engineering and Applied Sciences.

Ghaffari: Do you have a vision of where you are going to be yourself in five to ten years?

Chayes: Microsoft Research New England is definitely growing. We have over three hundred short-term visitors a year who spend anywhere from a day to a month per visit. We have a dozen permanent staff members, another dozen two-year postdoc students, and ten sabbatical visitors.

As for myself, I don't know. I'm really torn. I talk to a lot of friends of mine who are university presidents or provosts. On the one hand, I want to run something bigger. On the other hand, I like to be very actively involved as a researcher because I love doing research. More importantly, I think I can also model certain kinds of behaviors that people otherwise might not see.

For example, it's not unusual to hear someone say, "Oh, there's no way you'll get somebody like this to work with somebody like that." My response is, "Watch me." And when I model the behavior, I can often get other people involved in the research, and then I can step away. I'm constantly torn about how deeply I want to be personally involved in research and then how much I want to create new research groups.

Over the next five to ten years, I'm sure that I'll be addressing other problems, doing new and interesting projects. For example, I have a great interest in education and lots of opinions about how it could and should be changed.

While the specific vision isn't clear yet, I can tell you that I won't be bored. I'm going to make sure that I won't be bored.

Kellie A. McElhaney

Founder, Center for Responsible Business, Haas Business School, University of California at Berkeley

---

Born 1966 in Durham, North Carolina.

Kellie A. McElhaney, PhD, *is an adjunct assistant professor, the Margo N. Alexander Faculty Fellow in Corporate Responsibility, and co-faculty director and founder of the Center for Responsible Business at the Haas School of Business, Universit of California at Berkeley. In 2003, she strategically developed, launched, and directed the Center, which now encompasses research, instruction, and experiential learning and outreach programs, including the first-ever student-managed Socially Responsible Investment Fund and the Sustainable Products & Solutions Program.*

Dr. McElhaney teaches multiple courses on strategic corporate social responsibility in MBA and executive education programs at Berkeley. She has been a visiting professor specializing in strategic corporate social responsibility (CSR) at the University of North Carolina Kenan-Flagler School of Business, as well as Institut d'administration des enterprises, Université de Poitiers in France and Escuela de Alta Dirección y Administración (EADA) in Barcelona, Spain.

On the faculty of the Haas School of Business since 2002, Dr. McElhaney's consulting and research are focused on corporate social responsibility strategies and

aligning CSR with business objectives, core competencies, and business value; linkages between diversity and CSR, specifically using CSR as a hook to re-engage women with business as employees, consumers, and investors; and using social technology for good by advancing companies' CSR strategies and impact.

Prior to joining the faculty at Haas, Dr. McElhaney introduced corporate strategy to the (now) Ross School of Business at the University of Michigan in Ann Arbor (1993–2001) and taught corporate communication at the University of Cincinnati (1991–1992). She was a visiting professor in international studies at the Sichuan International Studies University in China (1992–1993). From 1989 to 1992, she was a member of the management team at First Third Bancorp in Cincinnati, where she focused on mergers and acquisitions.

Dr. McElhaney received the Aspen Institute and the World Resources Institute's Faculty Pioneer Award (2005) and the Outstanding Graduate Student Instructor Teaching Award from the University of Michigan (1997). She was nominated three times for the MBA Teaching Excellence Award while at the University of Michigan business school. She was listed among the East Bay Business Times' "40 Under 40" leaders (2004) and was a finalist in Fast Company's "Fast 50" list (2004).

She received her BA in political science and English from the University of North Carolina at Chapel Hill (1988); her MA in organizational communication and organizational behavior from Ohio University in Athens, (1989); and her PhD in higher education with a concentration in business from the University of Michigan in Ann Arbor (1998).

Dr. McElhaney is the author of Just Good Business: The Strategic Guide to Aligning Corporate Responsibility and Brand *(Berrett-Koehler Publishers, 2008), which highlights the business value and opportunities in branding, communication, and CSR.*

Elizabeth Ghaffari: Can you tell me about your early childhood and family influences?

Dr. Kellie McElhaney: I am the youngest of three. I have an older brother who, today, has his own advertising agency and an older sister who is a dentist.

I grew up in a very strong, Italian Catholic family with a strong sense of the need to give back and leave the world a little bit better than we found it.

My father was professionally oriented with high expectations for leadership. He started out on the staff at Duke University as a coach of wrestling and football. He got his master's degree and ultimately became an athletic director at the collegiate level. We were always in a college setting, surrounded by higher education.

My mother was a traditional 1950s stay-at-home mom and housewife who met my father when she was nineteen, got married at twenty-one, and followed his career rather than attend college herself. That was the era. When I went to high school, she went back and got her college degree, then her master's degree, and was incredibly successful. You could tell she was a sponge, just thirsty for development and very probably the smartest member of our family. She worked with severely and multi-handicapped children and was exceedingly happy doing so.

We lived in North Carolina for five years, then we moved to Meadville, Pennsylvania, for my first through seventh grades. My father worked at Allegheny College. Next, we moved to Athens, Ohio, where my father was on the staff at Ohio University. That was when I was in seventh grade to high school.

Ghaffari: How did you end up back at University of North Carolina?

McElhaney: I went to University of North Carolina for my undergraduate degree, majoring in political science and English because I thought I wanted to be a lawyer. I learned early on that I had a fair gift for gab. My parents always told me they never won an argument with me.

When we moved to Pennsylvania, I was plucked out of first grade for what they thought was a speech impediment, but it just turned out to be a Southern accent from my first five years in North Carolina. I got that beaten out of me pretty quickly. Ultimately, I do feel I developed strong communication skills.

Ghaffari: Why did you go on immediately to get your master's rather than pursue the law degree?

McElhaney: I was a junior serving on the UNC student-run judicial system, which supported the school's honor code. I was still quite focused on the law and was looking at law schools when the first case that came before the student court involved a freshman female from an economically disadvantaged background, on a full academic scholarship, whose father had died just two weeks before finals at the end of her freshman year. She plagiarized two paragraphs on an English paper, which was grounds for suspension from UNC and an F in the course. If the court reached that decision, she would lose her academic scholarship. It was a pretty cut-and-dry case, and we had to do it, but I learned from that experience that I don't deal well with a black-and-white world.

Once I turned away from the law, I wasn't really sure what I wanted to do. My father was at Ohio University, so I could get a master's degree there for free. I went back to Athens, where my folks lived, and got my master's degree in organizational communication and organizational behavior. I became focused on leadership and how the organization can influence its people.

Ghaffari: You finished the master's in just one year. That was pretty quick, wasn't it?

McElhaney: Yes, because going back home after having been on my own for four years wasn't all that it was cracked up to be, so I decided to just get in and out fast.

Ghaffari: Tell me about your first job after receiving your master's degree.

McElhaney: Even though I was in the financial community at my first job with Fifth Third Bancorp, I started out more aligned with my communications degree by going into the training and development department. I built and led training seminars for the bank. After about six months, one of the executive VPs took me under his wing and said—I remember this vividly — "You're too smart to be in human resources. I'd like you to come into my group." He led the acquisitions-and-mergers component in the bank.

I started buying small mom-and-pop banks throughout the Midwest and on the East Coast. He would go in and make them highly profitable by changing them from neighborhood fixtures into much more corporate operations. But, I felt that he made their lives relatively miserable.

I was there for about three years. It was fantastic management training, and I learned a great deal about management, financials, and operating P&Ls. It was a sharply run business, but I wasn't very motivated.

Then the University of Cincinnati invited me to teach a course in organizational behavior and communication one evening a week. After just one semester, it became evident that I was uninspired on the mornings of the four days a week that I worked at the bank. But, on the Wednesdays when I taught at University of Cincinnati, I just bounced through the day to get on to my night class.

Also, on Tuesday nights, I worked at a shelter for alcoholics and took on a little sister through the Big Brother and Big Sister program. I realized I was constructing my week so that I filled it with things having nothing to do with finance, but rather with things which helped me get through the week. I had this very split existence with divergent things consuming my energy.

Ghaffari: Were these the things that motivated you more than the business side of banking?

McElhaney: Correct. Also, it was a very difficult time in banking. The Community Reinvestment Act [CRA] had been passed, and banks were having a difficult time figuring out how to buy banks in inner-city areas and operationalize the CRA requirements. Most banks at the time weren't working on real economic development activities in inner-city Cleveland, but rather were focused on protecting their loan portfolios and their profits. At that time, I didn't see any way that I could change that from the inside for a couple of really interesting reasons.

First, I lived the classic split existence where work was work and my passion was anything that happened outside of work. I kind of internalized, early on, that they weren't supposed to be one and the same. And there were very few female leaders—in fact, there was only one—in the bank.

I had a fantastic boss, Bob Niehaus. He and I occasionally would have authentic conversations. I do remember questioning the whole concept of "where are all the women in the bank?" He'd say, "You should go talk to Sandra Lober about being a woman in the bank because obviously I can't give you that perspective." So, I did.

You have to remember that this was in the eighties. She was the *only* woman in the bank. She always wore dark gray suits, shirts buttoned all the way up to the top, and neckties, because that was what was expected in that era. And her hair was always very sharply pulled back into a bun.

Sandra took me to lunch. She was very gracious, kind, and direct. She was married, but opted not to have children for whatever reason. As far as I could see, she didn't have much going on in her world except for trying to rise up into the C-suite of Fifth Third Bank.

Ghaffari: Did she give you any good advice?

McElhaney: Yes. Her advice was, "You can't have it all." I believed she was right, then. Although maybe not so much today.

Growing up as I did in the academic world, my parents often said, "You'd be a fantastic professor." After I ruled out law as my chosen profession, they thought I'd be great in an academic setting. But—just like the classic third kid—I had to do exactly the opposite of their advice, and banking was as opposite as I could find from being a professor or a teacher. For a while, I resisted going back into academia.

As I realized that banking wasn't where I belonged, I started to grapple with these two sides of myself—the happier side vs. the dissatisfied side. I reassessed whether maybe higher education might be right for me. I had been a lot happier in the university setting, so I researched PhD programs. I thought of pursuing leadership, just not in the corporate sector. Maybe I could even be a college president.

I had been living in Cincinnati, Ohio, which—at the time—was an extremely conservative and homogeneous city. On top of that, I was working at a bank, the most conservative profession of all. A defining experience for me was the night that Robert Mapplethorpe, the photographer, held an exhibit of his work at the Cincinnati Art Museum. I went with my one other female friend from the bank who really bucked a lot of the corporate conservatism. We went to the exhibit opening on the night the curator got arrested by the Cincinnati police for exhibiting child porn, among other charges. That pretty well convinced me that Cincinnati wasn't going to be a mind-broadening experience.

I was accepted into the PhD program at Michigan. But, I really had this itch to travel. I had never taken a whole year off to just travel. I think I'd only left the US once to take my grandmother to Ireland for her eightieth birthday. And, too, I had to take on a fair number of college loans. So I decided to de-fer my PhD and accept the opportunity to go to Sichuan, China, to teach at a university there for a year.

Ghaffari: What was that experience like?

McElhaney: Fantastic, mind-blowing, and—for me—really world-opening. It's very odd that it was in China that I fell in love with the corporate world. I had sold everything I owned and was just teaching and detoxing from the banking world for a year. I went to the city of Chongqing, quite an industri-alized city in China, just to have a "cool experience"—nothing deeper than that. But, also, I wanted to see if teaching full-time was something that I would enjoy. I thoroughly enjoyed teaching there.

It was in China that I became obsessed with the fact that I had wiring for electricity in my flat, but it never worked unless some dignitary from some foreign organization came through Chongqing. Then, magically, the electric-ity would somehow be switched on. Or, I couldn't drink the water, but I could buy a Coca-Cola anywhere. I became extremely brand-aware while in China. Companies like Proctor & Gamble and Coke somehow could get their products into the most far-flung mountains and villages inside China on the backs of donkeys, yet the public sector couldn't get clean drinking water or utilities to operate properly.

I became very interested in the power of the corporation to do things that other sectors could not do successfully. I had a lot of time to think in China. This was before the internet. Obviously, I didn't have TV or radio, so there was a lot of time to think and write. I began to think about what if you could harness this power of Coca-Cola to also help get clean drinking water in China. It wasn't that Coca-Cola was inherently bad, but it was the potential to do things that might be a little bit better for society or to meet more of a higher need for China than a sugar-drink carried on the back of a donkey across some far-flung mountain. I felt there was something there in that idea.

Ghaffari: Was it back at Michigan that you developed these ideas further?

McElhaney: I came back and went straight into the PhD program, where my area of concentration was the intersection of education and business. I minored in business within the higher education program. They called it a cognate—a concentration.

There was a lot of happenstance. Early on, I spent more time in the business school than the education school. The classes were more interesting there. It took about a year to finish all of the courses that were required for my PhD, then I became very interested on the educational side of how people construct knowledge. That continues to play heavily into how I teach my own courses today.

One course that was interesting was Women in Work, in the business school. I was interested in a whole range of questions. Do women lead differently than men? Do they have different satisfaction motivations than men? Different challenges than men? It wasn't a typical gender course in the true sense of, "Woe is me. Here are the difficulties of being a woman at work," but rather it was much more about what motivates women, what skill set comes more naturally to them. So that course piqued my interest.

I took another course that really brought things together for me. It was taught by Stuart Hart, who was then just becoming a leader in the sustainable development world, but is now a known leader in that field. In his class, I was able to relate back to my vision of looking at the power of the corporation in the world—how in China, Coca-Cola could get through the entire continent so quickly and efficiently. I ended up studying under Stuart for quite a while.

I also studied the AmeriCorps program, which President Clinton had just implemented. Students could learn economics either in the classroom or by working in an inner-city system and get credit for either experience. You could learn about trickle-down economics in the classroom or you could go live and work in the inner city for a semester and realize that the economic cycle doesn't really reach that far down to inner-city folks at the bottom of the income ladder. I was interested in whether AmeriCorps might be a more effective way of educating kids than just lecturing them in the classroom.

I considered writing my dissertation on it, but it was such a rocky political climate for Clinton that I thought AmeriCorps might die before I finished my dissertation. But I did conclude that this was a far better way to educate students and to make the world a better place. It was a twofer. And I had the opportunity to meet President Clinton and share some of my findings with him.

This was a link back to my banking world—Fifth Third was just super at ratcheting up returns on investment—ROI. We were constantly driven to look at our ROI in everything that we did. When I got into higher ed, in one of my early pedagogical theory courses, I learned this fact: that if you put a kid in a classroom and simply just lecture at him or her, they will retain 10 percent of what they hear. And I remember thinking, "Oh my God. If I had an ROI of 10 percent at Fifth Third, I'd be fired." So I chose early on never to just go into a classroom and lecture straightaway. I was constantly looking at ways to improve the ROI of learning—actually the ROI of anything.

When I studied the AmeriCorps program, I looked at taking kids out of an economics classroom and putting them into an inner-city setting and then looked at their test scores. I had a control group of kids who just took Econ 101 and another group of kids who took Econ 101, but we added this experience in inner cities or any situation where they could see an economic theory in reality. The latter group scored significantly higher on a test. That is how I learned that, in order to improve ROI in education, we had to do things differently.

I was heavily trained as a banker to improve my primary ROI, which for banking was profit. In education, while teaching the kids, I became much more fascinated by how much the idea of improving ROI could help the inner-city community develop fresh thinking for the benefit of these young minds.

The profound effect of some small initiative—just having a University of Michigan student sit side by side with an inner-city kid who had never even thought about college in his or her future—that was very interesting to me.

Ghaffari: How did you come to teach at Michigan?

McElhaney: Stuart Hart was denied tenure at Michigan and had to leave, so we had no professor to teach sustainable development or corporate responsibility. The dean was in a bind because effectively he had lost his best professor on a topic that was really starting to emerge in response to high student demand. I was just finishing my PhD when the dean said, "Will you stay on and teach the courses that Stuart taught or maybe just talk to these students and find out what they want to do?" It was pretty much "just put out the fire."

By then, I had gotten married and was pregnant with my first child, so it seemed like a very attractive offer. Michigan is a fantastic university. I stayed on and tried to understand what the students wanted. There were not yet words like "sustainable development" or "corporate responsibility." Course titles were "nonprofit management" or "philanthropy." We started a club which we called Net Impact. It is huge today. We started a joint-degree program, an environmental MBA to bring the environmental world and business world together. Then we started a master's of science program in environmental science, which I ran. That's how I began doing much more administrative work inside of the university and just a little teaching—one course in business communication.

Somehow, on the side, I was studying ferociously the emerging world of sustainable development, which was much bigger in Europe at the time. I focused on the work of Stuart Hart and John Elkington. There were other pioneers who were really starting to bring all this together—Hunter Lovins and Amory Lovins—those on the vanguard of natural capitalism, "the next industrial revolution." I wondered to myself, "Could I put a course together that would merge all of these ideas to help us understand ways in which we could harness the power of the corporation to make the world a better place?"

I put a course proposal together, and the dean wouldn't even let me take it to the curriculum committee. He said, "No way! It seems like you need to be over in social work or go back to the School of Education, but this is not a business topic." With that, I realized that sustainable development or corporate responsibility wasn't yet acceptable at a business school.

I was really defeated for a while. I taught my communications courses that no one took really seriously. The joint MBA/MS program, meanwhile, continued to grow significantly every year, so I proposed the course again the next year. The dean said, "I'm going to put you into faculty review, so that you can hear from others." I met with a small group of faculty from the review committee. They at least let me meet with them and describe the course. Remember, I'm better at talking than writing.

Their interest was piqued. The conversation went like this: "Should we let her teach it one year? Students will never take it. They'll never want to put this on their transcripts because they'll never get a job with this kind of a course. What will be the value of this course?" Anyway, they let me teach the course. The first time the course was offered, I was put into the smallest classroom in the Business School, but I had forty sign-ups and a waitlist of fifty-eight students.

It was clear that something big was happening—students were much farther ahead of the faculty or the university. The course was something like

Corporate Social Responsibility and Projects. The students would work on a real-life challenge inside of a company. I was lucky to have some great companies surrounding me in Michigan. Dow Chemical Company was an early sponsor, as were Ford Motor Company and Herman Miller. Paul Murray was a fantastic pioneer inside of Herman Miller around the concept of sustainable development. They opted to not use virgin wood or virgin materials, and they recycled chairs once the customer finished with it.

Ghaffari: What made you jump from Michigan to the West Coast?

McElhaney: I had this situation with high student demand, high company demand, and the Business School couldn't really say no. I'd built a joint-degree program at Michigan and developed a new course around the theory of sustainable development and how to apply it—live—in company projects.

The dean of the Haas School of Business at the University of California at Berkeley at the time was a woman named Laura Tyson. She recruited me to do something similar in corporate social responsibility [CSR] at Haas because there were no formal programs there, but there was a lot of student demand.

I was very drawn to Berkeley. I'm always drawn to people that I like, even more than to opportunities. I was fascinated by a female dean. Up to that point, I had been in business and academia roles and never had worked for a female. A big factor in my coming out here was Laura herself.

She'd heard of me because I had done a little bit of writing, nothing major, but it was a small world—there weren't a lot of people doing what I was doing. I was well known in a small crowd. Somebody had recommended me to her. It might have been Stuart Hart.

I came out, did the tour, had a great visit, and a terrific interview. Obviously, I loved Berkeley, always loved the city of San Francisco, the energy of San Francisco. I was intimidated by the cost of living and the fact that I'm an East Coaster or Midwesterner with no family out here.

They were interested in me, but I felt fairly immovable. At the time, I was married and had one child. My husband had just started a company, and it wasn't a good time to move. Berkeley continued to recruit, but didn't find anybody that interested them. Laura came back with another offer the next year. By that time, two things had happened. I was pregnant with our second child, and my husband's company had started to show the early signs of dying. His business was a remote data-monitoring company, telemetry they call it—an idea that has absolutely has taken off now. The business was very tied to monitoring chemicals and gases for the auto industry. Then we went through the recession of 2000 and 2001, and the business just didn't take off because it relied on an industrial economy that was hit first.

Berkeley said, "You're the person we want to lead us, to build something." I came back out for interviews. I was newly pregnant with my second child, but didn't want to tell them. I remember vividly throwing up between each of my interviews due to severe morning sickness.

I took the red eye back, walked into the house at 7 a.m. and threw up in the kitchen sink. When Dave asked, "How did you like it?" I said, "I desperately want to move out there. It's a great opportunity."

Laura Tyson was so very understanding. She called me that week, just a couple of days before Christmas, and said, "Have your baby in Michigan and come out here on a one-year leave. I know you have reservations about being far from family with young children." So, I had my second child and came out the following summer. The bad news was that Laura made her decision to leave Berkeley to head the London Business School. That was a huge factor for me—I wasn't going to have the opportunity to work for this smart, authentic woman.

Ghaffari: Was your family supportive of your decision?

McElhaney: I took a leave from Michigan, and we came out to Berkeley in July—both the kids and my husband. To my mind, after two weeks here, I definitely wanted to stay permanently. As a family, we made the decision to stay permanently by December of that first year. My husband was unemployed for the first six months, which was difficult. He wanted to be an entrepreneur, stay in the startup area, so he ended up taking a job in tech transfer—but it was suboptimal because he had a long commute, and it wasn't what he really wanted to do. So, while his career was shaky and maybe moving in a more circular pattern, mine was really taking off.

You couldn't find a better place than Berkeley to do the kind of work that I'm doing. Michigan had high student demand. Berkeley had higher student demand. Michigan had a few companies that were pioneering. I remember calling my father, who's always been a strong mentor, saying, "My gosh, Dad, you can't swing a dead cat in Berkeley without hitting seven companies who just embrace this whole concept of corporate responsibility." I had a donor, Mike Homer, who had given $1 million to start something, but hadn't developed a clear vision of what it should be. So I had donor support, student support, corporate support, academic support, and management support.

The new dean, Tom Campbell, came in and was very interested in this topic. I really liked Tom a lot, so even though he "inherited me," he really helped to create the environment for success here.

But far and away, without a doubt, my absolute best mentor, advisor, and friend was Mike Homer, the donor who initially gave us $1 million and ultimately $2.5 million. He was an entrepreneur who taught me how to build something. It was just a fun ride working with him.

Mike was a Cal undergrad alum. He worked for Steve Jobs at Apple, GO Corporation, and made his millions as an officer at Netscape. He started companies in the tech sector like Loudcloud, Tellme, and Kontiki.

He had written a check for $1 million, but nobody had asked him what he wanted to see happen, so I went to him and said, "Tell me what your vision is." He said, "I got out of college, was very lucky, worked really hard, made millions, and now I'm thinking about how I want to give back. I would like kids today to get out of college and know that you can do both at the same time—run a good business that makes money and give back from inside the business."

Ghaffari: So, you were the one who implemented his vision.

McElhaney: Very much so. In a way, I was building a business for Mike. He was extremely helpful, and he was tough. I would get frustrated and discouraged by the challenges of trying to do something new and different at Berkeley. Some of the faculty viewed me as a threat and early on tried to get rid of me. Mike would always say, "Where's your fight? Are you just going to let them run you out of town?"

The sad thing is that Mike contracted Creutzfeldt-Jakob disease when he was forty-seven, and he died at forty-nine. But at least he had the opportunity to implement his dream. And I would love to name the center for him at some stage. He was the one who planted the seed. I couldn't have done it without him.

Ghaffari: You were the John C. Whitehead Faculty Fellow and now you are the Margo Alexander Fellow. Who were they? How did these fellowships come your way?

McElhaney: It was Laura Tyson. I had been here for two years and received an offer from University of North Carolina, my alma mater. One of the ways that Laura was able to help Tom Campbell keep me at Haas, even from the London Business School, was to get some funding for the teaching position. I had funding to build a center, but no funding around my own professorship.

Laura was close with Paul Newman and John Whitehead, who were running the Council to Encourage Corporate Philanthropy in New York City. The original money to fund my fellowship came from Paul Newman, but he didn't think that having a Paul Newman fellowship would do wonders for my academic credibility. So they named it for John Whitehead, a former CEO of Goldman Sachs. When Paul Newman passed away, John Whitehead re-upped the gift, as a way of honoring Paul Newman.

They were always term gifts of three years. With this past iteration of the gift, we ran out of Whitehead money, so then we got funding from Margo Alexander, another Cal undergrad alum and a big philanthropist in New York City. Margo was one of the highest-ranking women in sales and trades on Wall Street, after starting out as a securities analyst with PaineWebber.

I'm proud in many ways, and it's kind of interesting to close the loop. Now, my fellowship is named after a female banker. Even though Laura came back to Berkeley from London, she's not active in my program. But, she's part of my personal network and is still a valued mentor and advisor.

Ghaffari: What do you think she saw in you?

McElhaney: Balls. Guts. Courage. Just the fact that I'd been told "no" so many times, yet just kind of created my own path and didn't let the frustrations deter me. I always want to be very authentic. There are many times that I thought, "This program is not going to happen. I'm so sick of being told 'no' by these old white men who don't want to do things differently." There were lots of days I felt as if I were back at the bank, where it was all about ROI and just maximizing profit.

Laura saw that I also could operate in various circles—I had learned that I needed to play the faculty game and also the corporate game. She saw the early signs that we were a public university, but public funds weren't going to be around forever, so we were privatizing as much as we could. I was able to go into a corporation and sell a concept that they'd get behind and fund. I've always been really strong at teaching, so students really loved the concepts and the project work. I bridged academics and the corporate world naturally because it was a better way to teach, but also because we got funding from the corporate world.

Ghaffari: Who were some of the earliest companies that came on board to support your program?

McElhaney: Levi Strauss was a strong early supporter because of Bob Haas and his obvious affiliation with the Haas School, named after his uncle. Levi is a pioneering leader in corporate responsibility. Bob Haas also helped to make sure that I was set up to be successful here.

Ghaffari: Why do you think he wanted you to succeed in particular?

McElhaney: His passion and core belief in corporate responsibility were parts of the equation, but also I think Bob has always, even with his Haas

Fund, fought for the underdog or the marginalized. Not that I myself feel that I'm an underdog or marginalized, but certainly what I was trying to do was a bigger challenge than that faced by others.

Ghaffari: There were two very interesting programs that you developed while at Haas. One was the Socially Responsible Investment Fund, a $1.3 million, student-managed fund, and the other was the Sustainable Products and Solutions Program, a $10 million endeavor program. What are they, how did they get started, and what was your involvement?

McElhaney: The student fund began with a conference in 2006 on the topic of sustainable metrics—measuring the impacts of corporate responsibility. What is the return to the company? What sort of return is there to society, and how can you maximize ROI therein? I met another Cal alum, Charlie Michaels, who runs a hedge fund in New York City, and his wife, Doris. They both attended the conference together just out of their sheer love for Haas and Berkeley. The topic was touching on Charlie's world of investments and what's the return on investing in an environmental or social strategy. I didn't know who they were. I sat next to the two of them in the conference, and we just had an interesting conversation about Charlie's world—hedge fund investing—no focus on social or environmental returns or the conference topic.

I happened to say, "Wouldn't it be great to kind of do something different?" He had an opinion of what was then socially responsible investing, which was based on a strong negative screen-out process—screening out tobacco, firearms, alcohol. Our conversation suggested that that strategy probably limited the way we look at the whole concept of ROI. I wondered if there might be a different way.

I also said, "It's my belief that faculty seldom are the pioneers in the higher-ed space or the academic space. It's typically the students." We wondered if we could run an experiment to see if students could do it better.

That conversation stuck in his mind, and he came back with an initial gift of $250,000 to start a fund with the goal of trying to develop more innovative investment strategies while also trying to maximize ROI. We used that money to attract two other donors.[1]

---

[1] The $1.3 million Haas Socially Responsible Investment Fund was created through gifts from University of California at Berkeley alums Doris and Charlie Michaels, Marguerite and Al Johnson, and Vicky and Larry Johnson.

The fund is very focused on doing things differently and trying to get some metrics and some hard data into Wall Street around this concept of socially responsible investing.

Ghaffari: How are you communicating the concepts of metrics and ROI? Are you publishing them in order to disclose, in a general way, the kinds of metrics you are identifying? Or are you doing it in a proprietary way, communicating your findings to those who are talking with you and donating funds?

McElhaney: Great question. We don't want to be proprietary at all. We're really cognizant of the fact that we're a public institution, and we want to move the needle. In order to do that, you need to be transparent and highly communicative, but we are also incredibly aware that in the investment world, you really can't start talking about any kind of a track record until you have five years under your belt. We're just hitting the five-year mark this year.

In fact, we have had very great results. We've had strong returns. We've beat our indices. And again, I'm the advisor on this, so it's student-run, student-managed. The students really came together. They had the money, while the vision from the donors and myself was, "invest this money in a way that you obviously focus on financial return, but you also produce a positive social and/or environmental return."

Ghaffari: Are you able to write about the performance as a research endeavor or before the five years?

McElhaney: We are. We produce an annual report, but we don't really push it out into the world. It's open and available on our website, showing the criteria that we developed in terms of what the students are looking for in a company. It shows our investments and our exits, so the students have both invested and divested. And it shows our performance and the indices that we track.

Ghaffari: How do you compare yourselves to other socially responsible investment funds, such as Calvert?

McElhaney: We don't track to other socially responsible funds. We track to traditional Russell and S&P indices. Unlike those funds, we don't negatively screen companies out of our fund. We do try to develop a set of criteria for companies in which we want to invest. For example, we have a bucket of criteria around governance structure—like executive compensation, another bucket around transparency and reporting, and another around community engagement or community involvement. Within each bucket are anywhere from ten to fifteen criteria that we're looking at.

The students invest through Charles Schwab as our investment arm. It's almost a hedge strategy, but we're not allowed to use the word "hedge." We really try to go long on companies who closely match our criteria and short on companies who are very far away from our criteria.

Ghaffari: When and how did the Sustainable Products and Solutions Program start?

McElhaney: I had a pre-existing relationship with Dow because of our collaboration at the University of Michigan. Dave Keppler, another Berkeley alum, is the chief sustainability officer for Dow. In 2009, the Dow Chemical Company Foundation made the largest corporate pledge in the Haas School's history—a $10 million, five-year grant to provide students with cutting-edge training in sustainable business strategies.

I was talking with Dave Keppler about the problem with academic research, which in general has a very long lag time to market. We wanted to address that problem in the sustainable development field by improving students' understanding of what it takes to bring socially responsible products to market faster.

Part of the problem is that the academic world is very siloed. For example, a chemist might be working on a great new polymer, but have no concept of how much the cost to produce that polymer might add to the product cycle. So, one thought was to have the chemist collaborate with an economist or a product development person, so they could all benefit from each other's perspective and potentially speed up the product's time to market.

Ghaffari: How are the faculty responding to this new approach?

McElhaney: There was a little pushback when I first got the gift because it was Dow Chemical Company and, at Berkeley, there are some challenges about the perception of taking "dirty money." There are constantly protestors demonstrating at Berkeley who don't really care what the topic is—they just love a good protest. At the time I got the money, there was a big tree-sitting protest going on because Berkeley was tearing down some trees to retrofit the football stadium. The protestors came down from the trees for a couple of days just to protest our gift because it was more comfortable.

The faculty, at first, were unperturbed. It didn't really affect them. It was another source of funding for their research. The PhD students have been more substantively multi-disciplinary than the faculty. The social responsibility arena is more a generational phenomenon—the students seem to be naturally more comfortable with cross-disciplinary work. Some of the best work has come from the students—more from the master's students than even the PhDs.

Ghaffari: You are listed as a co-faculty director for the Center for Responsible Business. Who is the other director and does he/she share your vision for the Center?

McElhaney: Tom Campbell invited Ben Hermalin to co-direct the Center to show that there was a tenured professor in charge. The primary reason I have a co-director is the academic belief that there needs to be a tenured faculty associated with every endeavor at Haas-Berkeley. Ben's a fantastic guy. He has consistently supported our vision and me, but he's not involved really in the day to day. It's more titular. We have a full-time manager now—a woman by the name of Jo Mackness. She is the executive director and really runs the day-to-day maintenance of the Center.

I started the Center and was the executive director. I'm more of a builder than a maintainer. Once the Center was up and running, successfully—at least on a path that I thought was successful, I stepped aside to focus more on my own research, consulting, and teaching.

I've always had a bit of pushback from traditional faculty because I'm not on a tenure track. My subject field historically has not been a tenurable topic. I was always told not to focus on sustainability if I wanted to get tenure. Now, we are starting a PhD program. I could probably get tenure focusing on this topic, today.

Ghaffari: Do you regret not getting tenure? Do you think that will limit you in the long run?

McElhaney: Not at all. If I wanted to be 100 percent in academia, it might. But, my number-one passion is teaching—that's where all my energy is focused. The students don't really care—they don't even look at the difference between tenured and non-tenured teachers.

My second passion is influencing corporate behavior, corporate practice, so my consulting and work inside companies are in no way linked to tenure.

Ghaffari: Currently, what's the mix in your activities among corporate practice, consulting, teaching, and Center administration?

McElhaney: I do very little Center administration, today. I'm more the chief evangelist, getting more corporations engaged. I just recently got ING, the bank, to come on board. I would say my mix is around fifty-fifty teaching or student-driven work and consulting or corporate practice.

I also do a lot of executive education, which is both teaching and corporate practice because executive education takes social responsibility courses directly into the corporate environment. There are several courses, all with the same focus on how to integrate corporate responsibility into a business strategy and how corporate responsibility is linked to value creation for the company.

Ghaffari: Are you finding greater acceptance from the corporate environment today?

McElhaney: Very, very much so. I think that corporations are seeing the business imperative. They're seeing their raw resources and the rising costs associated with depletion of water or energy or clean air or even human talent—all with direct impacts on their business. They're seeing the financial reward or punishment of not focusing on the environment and society. They're seeing employee satisfaction or losing their employees—who today are less interested in the simple focus on profit maximization and more interested in the consequence for society or the environment.

I think we are just at the cusp of having this younger generation of people who are now in management and leadership positions and who really want to use the power of corporations to make the world better.

Ghaffari: You've also said elsewhere that your research is exploring the linkage between diversity and CSR—"using CSR as a hook to re-engage women with business as employees, consumers, and investors."

McElhaney: It is an issue that I'm incredibly passionate about. But I don't want to force it before its time. In other words, I can't lead with that as my research interest. I like to go back to this concept of change management. I want to go in there and be seen as somebody who's helping the company with their business strategy.

ING is a great example of that. They see a big market in women as banking customers and clients. Thus, there's a business reason that they want to attract women. They also want to attract and retain top female talent inside the bank. The financial services industry historically had a difficult time attracting and retaining females. So they have a two-pronged business imperative to really engage women. One, women have become a significant force for income earners and investors in the US. Two, how can they attract and retain top female talent? I help them see how corporate responsibility or refining their focus on financial literacy to include young girls or the female market can help them attract and retain females as consumers and as employees.

Ghaffari: Are there different drivers—different economic motivators—when you talk about consumers vs. the employees within the organization?

McElhaney: There are, for sure. I think that we sometimes try to silo it too much because, at the end of the day, we're all consumers and employees at the same time. When I think back to my years at the bank, as an employee, if I could have combined some of my night work—at the shelter or teaching—into parts of my day job, potentially I might have stayed at the bank. It's this very simple concept of wanting to find meaning in your day work.

I think consumers also want to find meaning in their consumption power or in their ability to influence corporate practices.

Ghaffari: How and why are you moving more into social media?

McElhaney: I'm always looking at ways we can drive corporate behavior more solidly or tell better stories. I guess one of the interesting luxuries for me is that I get to work inside of companies that really are serious about trying to make the world a better place with their corporate power. But in my outside life or when I'm just traveling, sitting on an airplane, I'm consistently surprised by the perception that companies aren't focused on this. So I think there's a big gap between reality vs. perception. And I don't think companies have done a good job of telling their corporate responsibility stories. They're very fearful to talk about these things in public. In my book,[2] I talk about how CSR gives a company an effective brand story or just a story to tell the outside world.

I found social media to be a very powerful brand or communication tool. It's one component in a repertoire of communication tools. Too many companies or people try to make it the be-all-end-all. It shouldn't be the only tool in one's toolbox. There certainly could be a lot more depth in their corporate responsibility stories, including their reports, web site, or other communication tools.

Ghaffari: By writing your book, you used another traditional media—the published book—to communicate your concept. Do you use that as a teaching tool?

McElhaney: I do. One reason for the book was that I was getting into a situation of too much demand and not enough supply of just me, so it was a way to get my message out more broadly, globally, and effectively than me as a person. I also wrote the book with the intention of it being a very practical guide for busy managers.

Ghaffari: Do you envision in the long term that you're going to stay within the academic framework and be able to deliver this, your fundamental message, effectively, or do you see yourself coming up with a different entity,

---

[2] *Just Good Business: The Strategic Guide to Aligning Corporate Responsibility and Brand.* (Berrett-Koehler Publishers, 2008).

whether it's private or public or nonprofit entity, to perhaps bring in more collaborations, more people to satisfy the growing demand? Do you see yourself building a company?

McElhaney: You're catching me right at the nexus of that question—it's been a question that has been both presented to me and in my mind for quite a while. So I'm trying to decide—I have been trying to decide when is the perfect time. I have a strong desire to build something else. I'm a little bit antsy right now. I am looking at a couple of different ideas and concepts to expand my capabilities and my force, so to speak.

Personally, it's been a tumultuous time because I went through a divorce, and my kids are still relatively young. They're almost ten and just turned twelve. They're a handful. As my mother once said, "You got what you deserved." I'm so much kinder toward my mother now that I am a mother. I'm convinced that she went back to work full-time because I was driving her crazy at home.

I'm very comfortable and authentic in talking about my divorce. I think the career trajectory was difficult. A big factor was that my career was ascending while his was swirling. Too, I think the concept of my being a successful female was difficult for him.

He's a fantastic person, and we had a very amicable divorce. This past year, he's finally settled into a new job and now is on a great trajectory, experiencing some great success. He went through three jobs after we came out here, which was not easy on either of us.

Ghaffari: How you describe your decision-making style?

McElhaney: I tend to be very, very practical and look at the data, but at the end of the day, I would say definitively that my decision-making style goes back to more of an authentic, gut feel. I take in information from multiple sources, and I'm trained to be very data-driven, but I never make a decision based solely on the data. I try to match the data to my intuition and to my quiet, meditative inner-feeling.

There have been times when I consistently bucked the data. If I had listened to the data expressed by my former dean at Michigan and faculty saying, "This course will never fly. No one will ever take it," then the program would never have happened. But, I had a gut feel that they were wrong.

But I do know that, in both business and academia, I consistently operate in a data-driven world. And certainly the focus on ROI drivers would suggest that.

Ghaffari: How do you define your success?

McElhaney: I think I've been successful in large part because I've really been successful in motivating and inspiring people, combined with an ability to be solid, logical, and persuasive in presenting arguments about why this will work. But I'm also really good at doing things slightly differently.

I think there's a strong amount of pent-up desire to change the world, but there's also a lot of fear that it's not going to work. Sometimes, the fear wins out. I've noticed there's this kind of group mentality—in big corporations as well as in big academic departments. Some of the most fearful people I encounter are inside those big entities, cowered by a strong group mentality that says, "This is the way it's always been done. This is the way we have to do it. I can't speak up. I can't try it differently. I can't fail."

One of the greatest things I learned from Mike Homer, because he was such an entrepreneur, was his focus on the fact that, "So, who cares if you fail? We'll just figure out another way to do it."

Ghaffari: Do you see yourself as a leader?

McElhaney: I do. In the academic world, I very much lead by designing new ways to teach. I lead in getting the students out of their traditional classroom settings and into the real corporate world. For example, now at Berkeley, we have a requirement that all our MBA students take an experiential learning course that was modeled after my initial courses here.

I lead inside corporations because I just go in and show them possibilities. I talk a lot about best practices and best-case examples so that they don't feel like they're going it alone.

And probably the way I'm most successful is just getting MBA students to come in and experience the joy of combining passion and changing the world at the same time. Once somebody's seen that, they never want to go back—they'll never be comfortable again simply focusing on profit alone.

I'm a bit subversive, I guess. Even within companies, I will say, "This corporate social responsibility strategy will help you to be more profitable," but I really do want to make the world a better place through profit. I just don't always go in and lead with that.

Ghaffari: Where do you see yourself in five to ten years?

McElhaney: I hate that question because I don't know where I'm going to be next week. There are so many influences that can change my path. I'm at a stage in my life where I want to work more collaboratively. My path in the academic world has been a little more solo than I've been happy with. And now there's enough of a critical mass of people working on these issues that I want to start working with people who are constantly pressing my ideas and making them better, asking my opinion, and getting input on their ideas. I'm much happier in that kind of setting. So I do see myself still working and very focused on creating change, but there's something else I need to build. I'm antsy right now to build something.

Ghaffari: There are many social responsibility committees popping up at corporate boards. Do you see yourself in that space?

McElhaney: I'd love to get more into that space. I haven't made a concerted effort to do that. I work on Dow Chemical Company's sustainability board. It's the Sustainability External Advisory Committee, but it is a paid board, and we do report into the C-suite. That's a real progressive move by Dow, and I think other companies are starting to understand the success therein. That committee is one of the most satisfying things I do in my work life, so I'd love to get more involved at that level inside companies, because that's when real long-term sustainable change happens.

But, I can't lie. I'm nervous every now and again. What's my next move? In some respects, I panic every now and again. I don't know what my next move is. That's why the whole five-year question makes my feet shake, because I don't know what my next move is.

Ghaffari: Do you think your two daughters are supportive of what you're trying to do?

McElhaney: Very much so. And I've learned from them. One of my daughters wrote a letter to a CEO about his product packaging. My other daughter constantly tries to save snails and slugs in her pajama drawer. They both have such passion. I do bring them along with me to keynotes and work and class, so they know what I'm doing and are very supportive of what I do. That makes it easier for them to understand why I sometimes have to be away from home, miss their soccer game or science fair project—because they know what I'm trying to do.

Ghaffari: How have you dealt with negative comments about what you're doing?

McElhaney: Other than the early days, when I was told there was no place for CSR in the business world, there have been very few negative comments. There have been few negative comments from people who understand what I'm trying to do.

Ghaffari: What's your advice to women today who are Cal students looking at careers?

McElhaney: Don't leave the power of a corporation. I see so many women "opting out." I do have concerns about the opting-out movement. There are so many women leaving the work world right now—losing out on a lot of power and resources.

I see opting out as a dangerous, limiting move. I think we need to look at how we can opt-in. As I look back at my days in banking, I wonder if I could have changed the bank as opposed to just leaving. I know how exhausting it is to work full-time and raise a family. I think we need to create options— ways that we could work less than full-time for, say, five years or so. I think women tend to opt-out as opposed to trying to change their surroundings.

Ghaffari: Is your advice to women significantly different from your advice to men?

McElhaney: Yes, because I think men just naturally think of suggesting a change if they don't like what's happening. But I would say the same thing to men: "Don't leave the power of a corporation just because you want to change the world. Harness it."

Laura Roden

Founder and Managing Director, VC Privé, LLC

Born in Los Angeles, California.

Laura Roden *is founder and managing director of VC Privé, LLC, a boutique investment bank that, since its establishment in January 2007, has raised money for high-quality, alternative asset funds such as venture capital funds, hedge funds, and distressed debt funds. Her firm specializes in marketing funds to private investors, including high-net-worth individuals, family offices, foundations, endowments, and independent financial advisors. Ms. Roden holds Series 7, 66, and 79 licenses to sell securities and provide investment advisory services.*

Previously, Ms. Roden was managing director of The Angels' Forum, a leading association of individual and corporate early-stage investors, and was president and CEO of the Silicon Valley Association of Startup Entrepreneurs (SVASE), the largest nonprofit in Northern California dedicated to helping technology entrepreneurs. At both entities, she was responsible for dramatic increases in membership, deal flow, events, volunteers, sponsorship, and service offerings. During this period, she was also a lecturer in the Department of Accounting and Finance at the College of Business at San Jose State University (2001–2004).

Earlier in her career, Ms. Roden spent a decade in key executive-management roles at several emerging technology companies, including PowerTV (1997–2001) as chief financial officer and vice president of finance and administration; Whalen & Company (1996) as director of operations for the Western Americas; Vicarious, Inc. (1994–1996) as chief financial officer; and US Media Group (1992–1994) as co-founder and principal.

Ms. Roden began her active involvement in new technologies at Chronicle Publishing Company (1985–1992), where she spent seven years as CFO of the television broadcasting division and general manager of the cellular telephone group.

Earlier, she was a senior management consultant at Touche Ross & Co. (now Deloitte), an associate product manager for new products at HP Hood, and an assistant director of media and market research at Hill Holliday.

Currently, Roden is active in the Harvard Business School Angels and the Angel Capital Association. She is on the steering committee of the San Francisco Jewish Community Federation's Business Leadership Council (BLC) and on the Northern California Education Committee for 100 Women in Hedge Funds.

She was named as one of the "most influential women in Silicon Valley" by the San Jose Business Journal. In August 2011, Ms. Roden was appointed to the board of directors of Heritage Bank of Commerce and its parent corporation, Heritage Commerce Corp., headquartered in California.

Ms. Roden received her undergraduate degree in English Language and Literature from Harvard University (1979) and her MBA from Harvard Business School (1983).

Elizabeth Ghaffari: Can you tell me a little about your early years? Where were you born?

Laura Roden: I was born and raised in Los Angeles and lived there through high school.

Ghaffari: How did you come to go to Harvard?

Roden: I had always heard that Harvard was the best place for an education. I saw an advertisement for a summer school program there, so I went to summer school there and just loved it. I worked in the Boston area in between college and business school, and I stayed for business school.

Ghaffari: How did you get your first job?

Roden: It was a chain of introductions. The year before I graduated from college, I worked in New York during the summer for an ad agency, Compton Advertising. I got that job through a friend who knew that I wanted to work in advertising. There, I met a number of people who were able to give me referrals after I graduated and was looking for a career position in advertising.

One referral was to HP Hood, a big dairy-products company in Boston. They needed someone to do market research for consumer products—

leading focus groups, designing questionnaires, and analyzing results. It was not long after they lost their research manager, and they only needed a few projects done, but I did the work well enough that they recommended me to their ad agency, Hill Holiday Advertising, which also was looking to hire market research people. I spent a few months working there, but a large portion of my time was on the Hood account, so Hood hired me back full-time just to work for them on market research.

My first jobs in market research were very helpful—it's a great background for every business.

Ghaffari: What made you decide to go back to Harvard Business School after the HP Hood assignment?

Roden: I had already been accepted under the deferred admission program, which is a fairly typical route into Harvard Business School for those applying directly out of college and who have not yet established prior work experience.

Ghaffari: What was your first job after business school and how did it come about?

Roden: While I was at Hood and, later, while in the business school, I became very interested in food companies and the food industry. I read an article about a company called Williams-Sonoma that was going into the food business. At the time, they were into housewares only, but the owner had become enamored with the food business. He had acquired US rights to Il Fornaio, the Italian bakery concept, and he was starting to open a chain of restaurants. They began as bakeries and then blossomed into restaurants.

I contacted the owner, Howard Lester, because I was very excited about that concept. I asked if I could come and work with him on that.

He hired me for a summer job in San Francisco. He also had me do some projects for Williams-Sonoma. One job in particular was doing a logistics analysis, studying the movement of goods from warehouse to stores. They ended up hiring Touche Ross & Co. to implement a solution, including a whole new software system. I got to know Touche Ross through the process of helping transition my work to their system. At the end of that project, Touche Ross invited me to come back to work for them in their San Francisco office, which I did for two years.

Ghaffari: How did you get your next job at Chronicle Publishing?

Roden: I was hired by the CFO of the broadcast group at Chronicle Publishing, initially as vice president of planning. And then after a couple of years there, he left, and I became chief financial officer of that group. Then the general manager of the cellular telephone business left, and I took over that job as well.

Ghaffari: So, a little bit of serendipity. Were there any mentors in that evolution of your employment?

Roden: Yes, I would say that both of the people for whom I worked directly definitely were mentors. The CFO of the broadcast group was very helpful and supportive. And then when he left and I was promoted to CFO, the person to whom I reported, the president of the broadcast group, also was very supportive.

Ghaffari: Can you tell me a little about US Media Group and how you came to that position?

Roden: I had been at Chronicle for seven years when the CEO of the broadcast group—to whom I reported—decided to leave. He invited me to join him in starting a new media company. US Media was a content company for interactive television, providing user information content for distribution via interactive television. Three of us left Chronicle to start US Media.

The closest thing, by comparison today, would be what you see with My Yahoo!—where you sign up with Yahoo! to get information on several topics that interest you. You set up your own channel for news and information to be sent to you via the internet. We had an idea to do a similar thing over television.

Ghaffari: What happened to the company?

Roden: This was 1992 to 1994, and we were very much ahead of our time and the technology. We were developing content, but the distribution channels were not yet viable. The actual interactive television infrastructure, the hardware, wasn't available to carry the content we had developed. We ended up shutting the company down after two years.

For the next couple of years, I worked as the chief financial officer of another start-up company called Vicarious, Inc., which was the closest thing to interactive television—educational and entertainment content for interactive CD-ROMs. That was the cutting-edge technology for interactivity at that time.

Ghaffari: Do you consider yourself a leading-edge kind of person?

Roden: Actually, yes. I was going to qualify that by saying "after Chronicle," but at Chronicle I was very deeply involved in the cellular telephone business, which was also very leading edge back then. It was brand-new.

Vicarious was in Silicon Valley. We ended up shutting that company down as well. Too early again.

So I did some CFO consulting for PowerTV, and then The Whalen Group hired me full-time. They were a wireless telecommunications project-management company located in the East Bay of the San Francisco area, but involved in projects all over the world. My responsibility was western North America, including both the western United States and western Canada, and South America. That's where I traveled a lot and gained some global experience.

About six months after I joined Whalen, they sold the company but offered me the job of divisional CFO. Meanwhile, PowerTV was offering me the job to come back and be full-time CFO there. I decided to go back to PowerTV.

Ghaffari: What was the technology at PowerTV? Was it embedded technology or was it content development?

Roden: It was an operating system embedded in set-top boxes. PowerTV was sold to Scientific Atlanta, which was later acquired by Cisco. I was the CFO and VP of finance and administration.

After we sold PowerTV, I made a commitment to Silicon Valley Association of Startup Entrepreneurs to run that organization for a year. At the same time, I started doing some teaching—just for fun—as a lecturer in the finance and accounting department of the business college at San Jose State University. I ended up doing both of those for about four and a half years.

Ghaffari: How did you get that SVASE position?

Roden: I was on the e-mail list for the Forum for Women Entrepreneurs, which had posted an ad for the CEO position at SVASE. I had been one of the founding board members of FWE—which is now called Watermark.

I ended up being CEO/president of SVASE for the next four years. It was a big change to run a nonprofit where a major part of your job is fundraising. That taught me that I was both good at, and enjoyed, fundraising because I understood the customer and believed in the product.

Ghaffari: Was your primary responsibility there in an executive director role? What were some of your key accomplishments?

Roden: Yes. Regarding accomplishments, we tracked several metrics. First of all, sponsorship was an important performance metric. When I started, SVASE was bringing in about $10,000 a year in sponsorship. When I left, it was $300,000 a year. Another key metric was the mailing list. When I started, we had about two thousand people on our e-mail list. When I left, it was about twenty thousand people. When I started, we had about twenty volunteers. When I left, we had about two hundred and fifty volunteers, meaning people actively engaged in running parts of the organization. At the beginning, we were doing two or three events per month. When I left, we were doing ten to twelve events per month.

So, SVASE grew in every way. They had never had an advisory board before, so we created a thirty-member advisory board.

Ghaffari: Would you say that SVASE was the place where you really first started to get involved in meeting the combination of venture capitalists, investors, and entrepreneurs? Did you like this experience? Was it interesting?

Roden: Yes, I would say so. The most important part of this experience, for me, was my exposure to fundraising, which essentially was sales. That was the big difference for me. Before this, I had been an entrepreneur. I had participated in raising money from venture capitalists. Obviously, I connected with venture capitalists on a much broader scale, in terms of the number of interfaces, at SVASE. But the really big difference from anything I had ever done before was what I call sales experience—actually being on the front line raising money. Before that, I had always been in a role that faced internally—counting the money as a CFO. At SVASE, I was down on the front line facing the community and asking for money. That was the really major change.

Ghaffari: That's a very tough job. How did you figure out how to do it well? What were some key factors of your success?

Roden: I think that the key was in really understanding the value proposition for the customer. I understood the value to the entrepreneurs. I understood the value to the banks, to the attorneys, to the accountants. I understood the value proposition to each constituency we were addressing because I had been in their shoes before. So, it was a very natural transition to be able to explain why they should be involved. If it had been in an area where I really didn't understand the value proposition, it would have been impossible. I never could have done it. But it was really based on the experience I had already acquired. I understood why we were offering something valuable.

Ghaffari: Why did you switch to The Angels' Forum?

Roden: One of my advisors when I was at SVASE was a woman who founded The Angels' Forum—Carol Sands. She recruited me for more than a year to come run The Angels' Forum because she had seen the success we had had at SVASE. She thought The Angels' Forum would benefit from that kind of performance improvement. Eventually, she convinced me to switch. It interested me as another new challenge, something different. I had been at SVASE for about four years—they were fairly stable and it was a nice time to try something new. I was managing director there for about two years.

Ghaffari: And tell me some of the metrics of that experience.

Roden: There were two jobs there. My first job was running The Angels' Forum, which had been around for a long time but had gone through its ebbs and flows in popularity. The first goal was to rebuild the membership of the group, meaning the number of angel investors. My second job was to improve the deal flow, meaning the number of quality deals presented to the group. Those two metrics go hand in hand. If you don't have good deals, members won't come, and if you don't have members, deals won't come. So those were my primary goals, and we made very significant improvements in both areas.

We ramped up the number of deals. When I came in, they were having trouble ensuring that members would see at least one interesting new deal per week. When I left, we had four new deals every week, as well as a waiting list. So the deal flow was ramped up.

There were a lot of things we implemented that improved deal flow, but the visible result was that there were more than enough really quality deals to keep everyone quite busy and engaged.

On the membership side, we had a declining number of members when I started—down to the high teens. The goal of the group was twenty-five members, but I rebuilt it to over thirty members with a waiting list.

Ghaffari: What did you do that was of significance to enhance the number of deals and the membership?

Roden: I would say there were two different things. One was pure process improvement, which kind of goes back to my business school and Touche Ross consulting experience. We had problems just with our basic processes. People would apply with deals they wanted to be seen, but their applications would be lost. Deal proposals wouldn't be read by the right people or on a timely basis. Or they wouldn't be read at all. Improvements to those kinds of basic logistical questions made the whole application process flow better. That was just the pure and simple administrative stuff.

The other side of it, the angel side, suffered from the simple fact that there was no one in charge of rebuilding the membership. No real effort had been made. The processes that we put into place first asked for referrals for potential members from existing members. Then we followed up on those referrals and put into place a process to explain The Angels' Forum and its value. We developed a lot of new marketing materials to explain the group to potential members.

Another important piece—partly process, but partly content—involved improving the quality of the experience for members. We put in some guidelines, rules that were targeted at involving people much more deeply in the process, to ensure that every screening committee had a diversity of members on it and that no one was left out of the process. We standardized our term sheets so that there was less confusion. As a result, people felt more empowered to negotiate a deal.

In essence, almost all of our changes were process-oriented, but more importantly, we looked at all the different things that had become impediments to a positive deal experience there. We just removed those obstacles.

Ghaffari: Sometimes it looks logical after you've fixed it. What made you decide to go off on your own and create VC Privé. What triggered that decision?

Roden: A lot of members were interested in investing in venture capital funds, and a lot of people that I interviewed to be potential members were interested in investing in venture capital funds. Even though there was enormous interest, it became apparent that it was very difficult to find out which venture capital funds were available, how to perform due diligence on them, how to invest in them, how to connect with them.

Initially, we thought we might form our own venture capital fund. But, I decided that the real need in the marketplace was for a channel between private investors and venture capital funds. Very much like The Angels' Forum, which was a channel between private investors and individual company deals, VC Privé would be the vehicle to help private investors get into venture capital funds. That was the idea for VC Privé, and the name VC Privé captures that idea because it's a bridge between VC, venture capital funds, and private investors.

I was very excited about the concept. I knew a lot of investors by that time who were very interested in it, so that's why I started it.

Ghaffari: In any of your SVASE or Angels' Forum or VC Privé experience, did you have a large number of women investors or was it mixed gender? Was it dominantly men?

Roden: In terms of investors, there were almost no women.

Ghaffari: How has your business evolved since you founded it?

Roden: When VC Privé first started, our focus was pretty narrow. It was just the bridge between the angel investors, private investors, and VC funds. But once I started doing that, then other funds started calling and saying, "Look, if you raise money for VC funds, why don't you raise money for my fund? I'm a hedge fund, or I've got a real estate fund, or a debt fund." Ultimately, many different kinds of funds came to us, and bit by bit we said, "Okay, that's reasonable" or "No, thank you," but we expanded the variety of funds we represent. And then, on the investor side, when we started all the relationships with private investors, they started introducing me to their money managers, and then the money managers started introducing me to foundations and endowments. So, that side expanded as well in terms of the number and variety of investors we reach out to. But the core original concept is simple. It was just that we are a bridge between investors and funds.

Ghaffari: So you really have grown through reputational expansion because individuals like what you're doing and others want to be part of this relationship.

Roden: Yes, that's exactly how we grew.

Ghaffari: What motivated you at the beginning? Is it different from what motivates you now?

Roden: I have always been motivated by interesting opportunities where I can add special value, make money, and keep intellectually and creatively challenged. Starting VC Privé in 2007 was a new and different challenge. It was the first time I headed a business that I conceptualized, founded, structured, and built, instead of joining a preexisting team. It was the culmination of all my prior years' experiences coming together to help me identify a market need that was not being filled. I started VC Privé with a clear understanding of needs, values, and customers.

Ghaffari: I've seen different numbers that describe the range of your typical investment at VC Privé. How would you describe it?

Roden: One measure is the size of the investment that a typical single investor might put into one fund—that would range from $500,000 to $5 million. That's the size of an individual check, so to speak, that someone might write.

The other measure is the fund size, the total fund, once you get all the investors together. The smallest fund we've represented was $10 million, while the largest fund we've represented was $3.5 billion total fund size.

Ghaffari: How did you build your advisory board?

Roden: That was an interesting process in and of itself because, first of all, I started building the advisory board by selecting people who were experts in the private fundraising industry. But, I was completely turned down by those I invited.

Then I went to a mentor of mine, a friend who gives me good advice. He suggested that I was going about it all wrong—that I shouldn't plan an advisory board of people in my industry because they would feel that they were, in essence, competitors. Instead, I should develop an advisory board of people who were experts in the types of investments we'd be representing. So, I changed that direction and found that it pulled together very rapidly. It was a very good change in approach. We ended up with a lot of very talented expertise to advise us.

Ghaffari: I noticed references to Viant Capital and EB Exchange Funds on your web site—are those examples of the kinds of funds with whom you do business?

Roden: In my business, everyone needs to be licensed by The Financial Industry Regulatory Authority while the Securities Investment Protection Corporation protects investors by providing insurance for brokerage accounts if a firm fails or goes bankrupt or unauthorized trading is suspected.

There are different levels of licenses. I'm licensed at the registered representative level. Viant Capital is licensed at the broker level. Eventually, if VC Privé becomes large enough, we'll be licensed at the broker level, too, but right now it doesn't pay to do that. The cost-effectiveness of that is such that you need to be much larger to have your own brokerage license. Viant has the brokerage license, and we're affiliated with them. That's specifically a regulatory relationship.

EB Exchange Funds was my first client in this business. We raised one of their funds for them. EB Exchange runs a series of private equity exchange funds.

Ghaffari: You call yourself a "boutique investment bank." How large is that industry?

Roden: There are quite a few—maybe a hundred thousand? They go by a number of different names. Many call themselves boutique investment banks, most of whom raise money for companies rather than funds. Each boutique has its niche, and our niche is specifically representing private funds. There are very few that do that.

Ghaffari: You said one of the challenges you faced was being in the middle of a divorce, having a toddler, and managing your career. At what point did you go through that?

Roden: That was right when I was leaving Chronicle to start US Media Group, so it was right in the middle of my first start-up. I had my daughter the last year I was at Chronicle. She was an infant then and then a toddler during the time I was doing the start-ups.

Ghaffari: Any insight as to how to manage that kind of a transition?

Roden: Getting really good help is key. We had a couple living with us, our nanny and her husband, for the first five years of my daughter's life, so it was like having an extended family—almost like having grandparents living with us. It was invaluable.

Ghaffari: Are you married now? Is your husband involved in the company?

Roden: I'm married, but no, he has a completely different career.

Ghaffari: How do you manage family expectations or commitments?

Roden: Generally speaking, I set the expectations and commitments. I am an alpha-dog type, but if a family member wants to do something that I don't want to do, that's fine. I don't try to control or monopolize other people's time, just control my own environment.

Ghaffari: What do you tell your family about your vision, goals, and business interests?

Roden: They hear about them incessantly.

Ghaffari: How do they react?

Roden: Great! The more they understand what I'm doing, the more they feel we have in common. Since I work 80 to 90 percent of the time, if they didn't have this commonality, we would be pretty remote.

Ghaffari: What are the most inspiring positive responses?

Roden: My daughter wanting to get an MBA and pursue a career in finance. My husband and daughter wanting to create businesses together with me.

Ghaffari: How did you address negative reactions, if any?

Roden: Usually if there is a negative reaction, it's because I was too brusque or impatient in communications. I apologize a lot.

Ghaffari: Let's go back to VC Privé. What were some of the key initial strategy decisions you made in starting VC Privé?

Roden: First, the decision to create an "institutional" rather than "sole proprietorship" structure, culture and image, including the decision to *not* name the company after me. Second, taking the time up front to get the securities licenses in place. Third, investing in a polished web site and marketing materials. All of those helped immensely, plus the decisions not to take outside capital from investors and to build an advisory board of industry experts.

Ghaffari: What keeps you up at night? Did you ever want to quit? What kept you going?

Roden: The main issue that concerns me is that there is always so much more to do, with every day and every minute. Our opportunities are huge. There is a constant urgency to prioritize time and resources, moving forward as fast as possible. The market may change, the economy may change, the competition may change—and we need to be ready to take advantage of every moment.

The second thing I'm concerned about is the burden of counterproductive, destructive, misconceived regulatory issues that harm our industry at all levels, for both large and small firms.

Ghaffari: How would you describe your relationship with investors? Or partners? Or colleagues?

Roden: There are no external investors in VC Privé as a company. I have not taken outside money, although there were two offers. I believe service firms such as ours can and should be successfully bootstrapped. They do not need capital to grow. I have no partners. With colleagues, the important issue is always finding a shared strategic vision. How big do we want to grow? Do we want a flat/regional or pyramid/centralized structure? What kind of clients do we want—are we Tiffany's or Wal-Mart?

Ghaffari: How do you view your competition?

Roden: I'd describe my approach to competitive challenges as "disciplined." I evaluate the strength of the competitor and the importance of the challenge critically. Most challenges fail on their own accord, so the ultimate decision is to just keep our eyes focused on our priorities and excellence in execution. Sometimes a challenge opens our eyes to a new way of doing business that we should be considering. In either case, competitive challenges are never ignored.

Ghaffari: What is your view from your current position? Where are you going to be in the next five to ten years with this company?

Roden: You know, I don't want to jinx anything, but at some point I anticipate we'll sell the company. That's typically what happens to companies in this industry. They get bought by larger companies. That might be what could happen—what most likely will happen.

Ghaffari: You also are involved in other outside interests, such as Harvard Angels, Angel Capital Association, and 100 Women in Hedge Funds. Are those the primary ones where you are currently involved?

Roden: Those are the primary ones that are directly related to the investment industry. I'm also very involved in a nonprofit called the Business Leadership Council, which is more philanthropic.

Ghaffari: That's the San Francisco Jewish Community Federation?

Roden: Yes, and their mission is to enable those leaders who are already in business to come together and inspire each other to do more philanthropy.

Ghaffari: In your business, are there many women of wealth who are private investors?

Roden: No, because primarily we deal in a niche that is very much risk capital—alternative assets. The term "alternative assets" refers to investments that are unusual, not mainstream publicly traded stocks and bonds. They are types of investments that are not broadly known or understood. In my experience, the people who invest in these kinds of assets are very comfortable making independent financial decisions. They're very confident in their own ability to assess investments. They are comfortable investing in things that are not mainstream. And those people are almost always men, typically men who are entrepreneurial and who have built their own businesses. These are people who have had success in their lives doing things that are unusual, taking risks, and relying on their own judgment. They feel comfortable applying the same values to their investing.

The women investors that I talk to are much more comfortable dealing with mainstream investments, almost always dealing with financial advisors, and especially some of the businesswomen I know turn over all of their financial decision-making to their husbands because they just don't want to deal with it.

Ghaffari: Would you consider yourself a risk taker? Where are you on the risk spectrum, yourself?

Roden: Yes, I would say I have become much more comfortable with risk, particularly since 1992 when I was in the first start-up—which was a big decision point for me. Ever since then I have been much more comfortable with risk.

Ghaffari: Would you say your business is risky in and of itself in these economic times?

Roden: I don't think my business is particularly more risky in these economic times compared to others. I don't think it's riskier than other businesses. Every new business has to make its own success. Certainly, running an entrepreneurial business is a riskier job than being part of a big company, but I don't see that this business is any riskier than any other small, growing business.

Ghaffari: You're also involved in 100 Women in Hedge Funds. What is the nature of your involvement in that?

Roden: I'm on the education committee for the Northern California region. So, 100 Women in Hedge Funds is like a trade association for women involved in the hedge fund industry. Each region has an education committee that designs and operates the various regional activities.

Unlike The Angels' Forum, which was something like operating a business, 100 Women in Hedge Funds is a trade association more like SVASE, which is all about putting together events, speakers and membership activities.

Ghaffari: Have you continued your involvement with the Forum of Women Entrepreneurs and Executives?

Roden: Not right now, no. I was on the board for many years, but I haven't been on the board for many years. Occasionally I go to an event, but I don't have any other role.

Ghaffari: How would you describe your decision-making style?

Roden: I think I am a very good decision-maker. First, I evaluate the importance of the decision. A decision about "what do we want for lunch?" has very low importance. "Should we hire this sales person" has much higher importance. I allocate a proportionate amount of time to collecting and considering the pros and cons. If I spend more than sixty seconds on a lunch decision, that's too much. If it's a key decision, I may consult many outside data sources, physically write down an outline of the ramifications, sleep on it for a few days, etc.

One shortcoming I have is that once I make a decision, I am very loath to change it. This can be a strength but also a real weakness.

Ghaffari: How do you define success?

Roden: If you feel satisfied with your accomplishments.

Ghaffari: How do you define your position as a leader?

Roden: I think a leader inspires others to action, whether for profit or nonprofit, whether for my mission or their own.

Ghaffari: Would you do anything differently if you were starting out today?

Roden: I would have taken voice lessons to improve the depth and gravitas of my delivery—a key weakness among many women.

Ghaffari: How do you advise women today who face the kinds of challenges you did? How can they work their way through or around them?

Roden: Persevere, persevere, persevere. Do not allow yourself to admit the possibility of defeat. Stay fit and sharp. Try to think six steps ahead on every move—yours and others. Don't take your foot off the dock until you have identified a secure stepping stone.

Absolutely everyone goes through very tough times, so empathize with them. Ask people's advice, but trust your own decisions. Share enough of your difficulties to solicit help, but not so much that it hurts your credibility.

Very importantly: If you really can't afford the luxury of failure, there's a much higher chance you'll succeed.

Don't waste time. Use every moment, either for business or for pleasure, intentionally. Lose your TV. Lose the YouTube URL. Have your assistant update your Facebook with your vacation pictures.

Save every contact that is at all meaningful, with notes on when and how you met, any key points of common interest, etc., in a database you can search by keyword.

If your spouse or partner is unsupportive, stop trying to fix them or blame yourself or deceive yourself or others as to why the relationship isn't happy. You need and deserve support. Make this the ultimatum: "support me or lose me." You would, presumably, do as much for them as well. If you're not supportive of your spouse/partner, you're doing them an injustice.

Ghaffari: What advice, especially, do you have for young women?

Roden: You have much more power than you think. Understand it, learn how to use it as quickly as possible, and find a female mentor who can train you in this.

Ghaffari: What do you see as the areas of greatest opportunity for young women professionals?

Roden: Anything where you are indispensable. The easiest way to get power, money, and position is to do the jobs that other people can't do well—finance and sales. *Avoid* soft, non-measurable jobs like marketing, business development, human resources, PR, etc. You will be totally disposable and under-appreciated. Management may love you now, but management is subject to change without notice, and unless the metrics are there, you are dust.

Myra M. Hart

Professor of Entrepreneurship, Harvard Business School

Born 1940 in Evanston, Illinois.

Dr. Myra Maloney Hart *is a retired professor of entrepreneurship (1995–2007) at Harvard Business School, where she held the Class of 1961 Chair in Entrepreneurship and served as co-chair of the Entrepreneurship faculty from 1999 to 2002.*

Dr. Hart was commended for faculty leadership with the Greenhill Award, given by the dean of Harvard Business School in recognition of outstanding and significant contributions to the school.

While at Harvard Business School, Dr. Hart started MBA courses independently and in collaboration with faculty colleagues, including Starting New Ventures; Women Building Business; and Building Businesses in the Context of a Life.

Dr. Hart, along with her colleague Professor Marco Iansiti, won the Apgar Award for Innovation in Teaching for their Starting New Ventures course. The Apgar Prize recognizes a faculty member "who motivates students' interest, curiosity, and love of learning; proposes and applies new teaching concepts and methods; and serves as a mentor to stimulate students' intellectual development."

Dr. Hart is also responsible for the creation and direction of several entrepreneurial executive programs and HBS alumnae programs for women re-entering the workforce, including Women Leading Business: A New Kind of Conversation; Charting Your Course: Working Options; and A New Path: Setting New Career Directions.

She served as chair/director of the Marjorie Alfus/Committee of 200 Case Writing Initiative (1998), which created more than seventy-five Harvard Business School business case studies with women in the protagonist/leadership role. The goal was to increase the availability of quality teaching materials featuring women as key decision-makers.

Dr. Hart is a member of the Diana Project, a research team of five professors established in 1999 to investigate women entrepreneurs' access to capital and to raise awareness and expectations of women business owners regarding the growth of their firms. Other team members include Dr. Candida Brush (Babson College), Dr. Nancy M. Carter (INSEAD and Catalyst), Dr. Elizabeth J. Gatewood (Wake Forest University), and Dr. Patricia G. Greene (Babson College). The Diana Project was awarded the international 2007 FSF-NUTEK Award, which recognizes those who produce scientific work of outstanding quality and importance related to entrepreneurship. (FSF is the Swedish Foundation for Small Business Research and NUTEK is the Swedish Agency for Economic & Regional Growth.)

Books authored by the Diana Project team include International Growth-Oriented Women Entrepreneurs and Their Businesses: A Global Research Perspective *(Edward Elgar Publishing, 2006);* Women and Entrepreneurship: Contemporary Classics *(Edward Elgar Publishing, 2006); and* Clearing the Hurdles: Women Building High-Growth Businesses *(FT Prentice Hall, 2004).*

Prior to her tenure at Harvard Business School, Dr. Hart was a co-founding officer at Staples (1985–1990); director of marketing at Star Market, a division of the Jewel Company (1983–1985); and general manager of Hart, Shaw & Company, a family-owned residential and commercial real-estate firm.

Dr. Hart serves on the board of directors at Kraft Foods and Office Depot and is on the Smithsonian Institution National Board. She has served as a director on numerous private and entrepreneurial and advisory boards, and as a trustee of several university boards. She was chair of the Springboard Enterprises New England Forum in 2000 and 2001. She was a visiting scholar at The Center for Women's Leadership at Babson College in 2007 and at Stanford University's Clayman Institute for Gender Research in 2008.

She received a doctorate of business administration from Harvard Business School (1995), an MBA from Harvard Business School (1981), and a BA from Cornell University (1961).

Elizabeth Ghaffari: Can you give me a little bit of your background and that of your family?

Dr. Myra M. Hart: I was born in Evanston, Illinois, and was raised in the Chicago suburbs. I have six brothers and one sister. All of us are very close.

Pretty much all of us are actively engaged in business, though in many different dimensions. For example, my youngest brother is a sports writer for Knight Ridder, while my sister started in education but switched to become an obstetrical nurse.

With a family of eight kids, my mom was an at-home mom, while my dad was a small-business man.

My high school had about four thousand students and was co-ed. I was a good student and an ambitious person who looked for opportunities to get the absolute best possible education. I wanted a university that was bigger than my high school. In looking at the range of alternatives available to me, I considered Cornell, Stanford, and Duke. At that time, Cornell and Penn were the only Ivy League schools accepting women. I was not a city girl, so I really did not consider going to a city university. I wanted a totally enclosed campus. Cornell seemed to meet my needs perfectly, so I went there and was extremely happy.

Ghaffari: What was your major at Cornell?

Hart: Government. And I minored in languages. I thought I was going to be a superstar in the Foreign Service. I was wrong about that.

Ghaffari: What was your first job after college?

Hart: I got married right out of college. My husband and I went to Stanford, where he went to law school. I taught in the public school system in California, putting him through law school. We returned to the Chicago area in 1965. When my father-in-law died in 1967, I took over leadership of the family residential and commercial real estate business, Hart, Shaw & Company. The focus of the business then was primarily residential.

I ran Hart, Shaw & Company from 1967 until 1975 when my husband's job change required that we move out of Chicago. We sold the business and moved to Michigan for the next four years.

Ghaffari: How and why did you decide to go back to school at get a business degree?

Hart: I learned at Hart-Shaw that I was really good at business, but I certainly didn't know everything about it. I thought I would be a lot better businessperson and much more credible if I had an MBA from a top-notch business school. After I put my husband though law school, I made a deal with him that one day I would go back to school and get my degree as well.

So I began to lobby that the kids were old enough and that I felt the time was right to pursue the opportunity of going to business school. When we moved to Michigan to follow his career, we agreed that within the next four years I could call the shots on where we would go next. In 1979, we moved to Boston so that I could get my MBA at Harvard.

He switched from working as in-house counsel for Dow Chemical to another chemical company. However, the marriage didn't really survive that long after we got to Boston. We stayed together until I finished my degree. I was fortunate that, when I was off on my own, I was also completely able to take care of myself and my children.

My husband and I had been high school sweethearts. We were married for twenty-two years and had three children. We divorced in 1983, and then I was a single mom for the next eleven years. Then I married someone that I knew as a friend in college, and we've been married seventeen years now. He's a retired physician. He had four children of his own, so together we have seven children.

Ghaffari: What was your first job after your MBA?

Hart: I finished my MBA in 1981 and went into food retailing with the Jewel Company, headquartered in Chicago. I chose the company because I had a great deal of respect for the integrity of the firm, their mission, and the quality of the people running it.

There also were very personal reasons for my choice. Jewel agreed to let me work in the Star Market division, which was headquartered in Cambridge, for the next five years. That allowed me to develop my career without uprooting the family before my youngest graduated from high school. I was very committed to not creating any more disruption or chaos in my children's lives. They had moved to Boston on my behalf. Then, we went through a divorce, which was inevitably disruptive. I promised my kids I wouldn't make them change schools or in any way follow my career.

Jewel was very accommodating, saying, "There's plenty of room for you to develop and become an important part of our organization in Star Market. Whenever you are ready, you can come to Chicago." So that worked out well from the perspective of what I wanted to do as a career. The company was very accommodating.

Ghaffari: Did you go to Chicago with Jewel?

Hart: You can plan all you want, but Jewel was acquired in a hostile takeover in 1984. American Stores bought it, so headquarters were relocated to Salt Lake City. Of course, one of my primary reasons for wanting a Chicago-based company was that my whole family was there. It was a great extended family for me and for my children. I didn't see any advantage to my moving independently to Salt Lake City. While I did have a very good set of career options with the company, I was much more open to the kind of head-hunter calls that I began getting on a regular basis.

I got a call from a colleague whom I had met at Star Market. He had also gone to Harvard as an undergrad and to Harvard Business School, and—though he was younger than I was because he went in a more linear trajectory—he had been at Star for about eight years before I joined the team. He had been in their fast-track management development program and then had left Star to become president of First National Supermarkets in Connecticut. For a variety of reasons, he left First National to start a new business.

His name was Tom Stemberg. He had written a business plan for Staples and was looking for venture capital money. He got push back—not on the concept—but on the idea of who's going to run the company. At first, in a somewhat naïve way, Tom told them, "You know, once I get some money, I'll build my team. Here are some ideas about how I might go there." The venture capitalists replied, "No. Don't you know that it's all about execution, especially in retail? So while we like the idea, we won't invest until we know who's going to be on the founding team."

So Tom called me for a drink. He showed me his business plan. I thought it was fantastic. I didn't think conceptually that there was a problem. I told him, "The only thing that could bring us down is a failure to execute flawlessly." Tom asked me if I would be the vice president of operations. That offer surprised me somewhat because, at that time, I was head of marketing at Star Market. Tom had also been head of marketing before he left to become the president at First National. He had decided to bring on another person who was the VP of marketing for Osco Drugs. So Tom said to me, "You're the one who has the deepest operating experience, so that's what we want you to do."

Next, we found and solidified relationships with two other fellows who joined the founding team. Together, the four of us went back to the venture market. We got the money within six weeks of when we got our team together, and it was a very exciting time.

Needless to say, Staples was quite successful for both the investors and the original players. For me, it was absolutely terrific. I don't think there was anything you could plan. You couldn't say, "And then I'm going to be an entrepreneur in an incredibly successful venture," especially because I have to be very honest and say that I had really thought I would build my career in a corporate environment. I thought I was pretty well suited to that, but when the entrepreneurial opportunity came along, I quickly adapted, and it really worked well. I think I did a great job for them, and they did a great thing for me by giving me that amazing opportunity.

Staples also made us reasonably well-off in a very short time. I was approaching my fiftieth birthday, and my last child had gone off to college. I was still single. And I asked myself, "What would you do with the rest of your life if you didn't have to show up to get a paycheck?" I concluded that I would not be staying at the company, but there were several options open to me.

Probably most of us think deeply about how we want to make a difference in the world. And I felt that I could try to go about it one step at a time or I could try to touch the lives of many people and influence the world through others. I chose the latter path. I thought, "There are a couple of different directions, but I think that my next venture is going to be in teaching. That could take the form of something as frontline as going into the Peace Corps and teaching in a community, teaching the principles of business and being entrepreneurial, but in a very simple and straightforward way. Or, it could be teaching in an academic setting."

I chose the academic direction—to be among the people who were truly going to be leaders around the world, trying to influence, at least in some small way, how they think about strategic issues, diversity issues, and environmental issues. As a teacher, I thought I might not touch everyone I come in contact with, but there certainly would be many I could influence.

So I chose teaching. I chose Harvard Business School, both to get my doctorate and fortunately to be able to be on the faculty.

Ghaffari: Were there any mentors who helped you make that decision?

Hart: I really owe the decision in large part to some of the faculty with whom I worked when I was an MBA student. One in particular, Chris Christensen, supervised my independent study for two years, and he strongly encouraged me to think about life as a faculty member at Harvard Business School. I told him, back then, that I had come to business school in order to generate a lot of personal wealth to support myself and my children. Becoming a faculty member wasn't necessarily the avenue to that goal. And being a student for an additional five years, in order to get my doctorate, was certainly something that was not in my life plan. At Harvard the doctorate is a DBA, a doctor of business administration.

Once Staples went public, there were a couple of things that happened. Each of the officers met with a financial advisor and also with members of the board in order to discuss whether the officers were going to stay or leave. With an IPO, after the six-month hold back, there's a triggering event, and many people have the wherewithal to walk away as I did. I called Chris Christensen and said, "Chris, I think I could afford to become a faculty member now."

Ghaffari: Was Harvard supportive?

Hart: Yes, very! While I made a joke of it, then, I knew that the value of investing in me could be questionable. I asked Chris, "What do you think? Is it still a viable option?" And to be honest, it's a pretty big reach to think about the enormous investment that a university makes in a doctoral student in terms of the dedication of faculty time. As a doctoral student, you are working one-on-one with your thesis advisor and your thesis committee.

It might be a very effective use of their time, but it's not a very efficient use of their time. So, rationally, you'd think they would like to invest in much younger candidates who will have a very long runway in which to utilize that training. I believe it was a great gift that Harvard Business School gave me— to enable me to have that kind of education.

I had a deep connection to the institution, and I had some good business experience, but, honestly, if you look at when I came out of the pipeline, I probably had a maximum of fifteen years of active classroom time available to them. Certainly, it's not just the teaching they're interested in. It's the research pipeline and what you can contribute to the creation of knowledge, as well as dissemination of knowledge. So, it was a great leap of faith on their part that I could make some payback on their investment, and it was absolutely delightful that it worked well. I think it worked well for me and for Harvard Business School. But I never underestimate the value of the gift that I believe they gave me.

Ghaffari: If I could opine here—I think they pretty well got their money's worth.

Hart: I hope so. I hope so.

Ghaffari: You were in the doctoral program from 1990 to 1995, and then you immediately joined the faculty at Harvard Business School. Is that right?

Hart: Yes, and it is rather unusual to join the faculty of the school where you got your doctorate. There are many, many people who get their doctorate, go somewhere else, and then maybe come back later. In my career, I didn't have a huge window of opportunity in which I could go out to prove myself, develop different perspectives, and come back. If I was going to be valuable to the school, it had to be right away.

Fortunately, things worked in my favor, and I think it worked out very well for Harvard as well.

Ghaffari: When you came on the faculty, was there an entrepreneurship program?

Hart: There was indeed. Historically, we would go back and say that the entrepreneurship program was born in the 1940s when some of the returning veterans came to Harvard Business School after World War II. There were many people who couldn't have considered Harvard Business School prior to the GI Bill. They offered the school a whole new perspective on business career paths. Many of the new students were interested in starting their own businesses rather than going into the financial services or Fortune 500 careers as had students and graduates in prior years.

The entrepreneurship program was started with a simple course—a single course—on how to start new ventures. Later, it was significantly enhanced. It became quite a serious program, growing to the point of not being just special course offerings, but actually being a unit or department at Harvard Business School when Howard Stevenson took over its leadership in the early 1980s. And Howard hired and developed a faculty.[1]

When I joined the faculty in '95, there were just a few people associated with entrepreneurship as their primary interest. That would have included Howard Stevenson, Amar Bhide (innovation and entrepreneurship), Teresa Amabile (individual productivity, team creativity, and organizational innovation), and Bill Sahlman (investment and financing decisions in entrepreneurial ventures).

I studied under Howard Stevenson (my thesis advisor), Clay Christensen (technology and business model innovation), Dick Walton (organizational theory), and Bill Sahlman (on my thesis committee). All of them had a very strong interest in entrepreneurship long before I got there.

From 1995 until today, there has been explosive growth in the entrepreneurship faculty, so today there probably are about thirty-five full-time faculty in that area. When I came in 1990 to get my doctorate, I specifically indicated that that's what I wanted to study. At the time, it was under the banner of "business policy." Around 1997, it was spun out and became a separate division. So entrepreneurship has been around for a long time.

Ghaffari: Pretty soon you started to develop some new courses, such as Starting New Ventures.

---

[1] Harvard Business School Alumni Bulletin, "The House that Howard Built," www.alumni.hbs.edu/bulletin/2011/june/stevenson.html, June 2011.

Hart: Yes, Professor Marco Iansiti and I co-developed and co-led Starting New Ventures as a new course, but in a way it was a new version of a much older course that had its origins back in the forties. That eventually morphed into entrepreneurial management, which looked at entrepreneurial behavior in many different settings. For example, it examined the idea that you could become very entrepreneurial within a structured corporate environment or in a nonprofit. We did take a look at this subset of entrepreneurship that was strictly about building a new company.

I'd say we did a little bit of refocusing. We said, "Entrepreneurship is very broad. It can be practiced in many different places, but some of our students are interested in the specifics of starting a business from scratch so let's focus not only on the strategic, but also on the mechanical, issues of how you start a new venture." We developed many courses focused on even more specific aspects: building human resources in an entrepreneurial venture, compensation in new ventures, building financial resources, and venture capital/private equity courses.

Ghaffari: What would you say was your primary contribution at Harvard?

Hart: The one thing that I would identify as unique to my experience at Harvard is that, after a couple of years, I began to focus on women—a focus that came out of a survey I conducted of our graduates in order to identify how many of them actually did start new ventures or joined startup ventures over the course of their careers. Harvard keeps very good data on our graduates, but we had not always followed exactly what they're doing five and ten years later. So I began to conduct those long-term surveys.

I developed many hypotheses about what graduates might be doing. It turns out that Harvard Business School graduates are very, very entrepreneurial. More than half identified themselves as entrepreneurs, and 40 percent are involved in a startup or a privately-held business. They typically don't do it right after graduation, but they gravitate to entrepreneurship later in their careers. The really interesting question for me was, "What do women graduates do? Are they more or less likely to become entrepreneurs?"

I would have expected they were more likely to become entrepreneurial, but I was terrifically surprised that women seem to be substantially less likely than men to either start or join an entrepreneurial venture. The survey data showed that some commonly held beliefs just weren't true.

After that, I began to focus on women and entrepreneurial choices. I became very interested in professional businesswomen's careers and how their choices were different over time from those of men. I also wanted to move away from the obvious issues such as, "Oh, they have children. Perhaps they tank their own careers in order to either go on a Mommy track or leave the business world altogether." I wanted to go much deeper than that while developing the courses, the executive programs, and the case research that I did while I was at Harvard.

It had never been my intention to be a gender specialist—not when I went to the doctoral program and not when I started on the faculty. In fact, I do not consider myself a gender specialist at all because I did not come to this topic from the perspective of the differences between men and women. I approached the study much more from the view of business and how business plays out in different ways. So, I came in from the other side of the equation, but it still brought me to a focus very much on courses for women MBAs, women executives, and led me to a very large case-writing initiative to create more teaching materials in which business leaders happen to be female. Eventually, all that became the genesis for my involvement in the Diana Project.

Ghaffari: When you surveyed the graduates, did you do it in one year or multiple years?

Hart: I did the surveys for five years. I followed the reunion classes, so they were graduates who were five, ten, fifteen, twenty, and twenty-five years out. I chose that approach because reunions are the times when alumnae usually think about coming back—they feel a little more nostalgic. They might be a little more willing to do a survey. I promised that if they did complete the survey, I would share the results with them at the reunion. So I got very good participation.

I discovered a great deal about how careers really transition. The surveys were separate snapshots of different people, rather than a longitudinal study following a single group throughout their life, which is research that is very valuable, but extremely time-consuming. One of my colleagues, John Kotter, actually does that. He's followed the same group since the late 1970s. But my surveys were of a group of people who were queued up for their reunions. Each set of surveys was discrete, yet the findings were relatively consistent over the years.

In the beginning, I had no gender interest whatsoever. Gender was just one of the demographics or data points that I was collecting. The core of the study was about whether Harvard Business School was instrumental in their professional success—the answer, of course, was yes. Whether or not Harvard Business School was instrumental in their personal happiness, that answer was a little more mixed. I finally decided to sort this out.

Well over 90 percent of the men thought that Harvard Business School was a substantial contributor to their personal happiness and success. But the women were a little bit less so, and I was interested in why that was the case. Were they disappointed in their career opportunities? Were they no longer using their Harvard Business School education? This was interesting. I thought, "Oh, this is kind of surprising, so let me go out and talk to the people."

Ghaffari: How extensive were your interviews with alumnae?

Hart: With the help of our alumni office, I set up interviews with small groups of women alumnae in San Francisco, New York, Washington, Chicago, and all over the country, trying to find out what were the stories behind these survey answers and to learn what the aggregated data was telling me. I really wanted to hear their personal case studies of what was going on.

The interviews told me and, ultimately the school, that perhaps our women alumnae needed some different kinds of attention. It wasn't so much about professional success, but much more about how you make a contribution in life in a much broader way.

Women who attend professional schools are highly likely to marry or partner with another professional, which usually means they constitute a pretty high-income household. They are the fortunate people who have more choice about whether they're going to work for money or not. Often, they are in a household where they could live on one income. And in the United States, I would guess that about 80 percent of our households have both partners working because they actually need to work and provide for their family. There is a subset of professionally trained and professionally employed people for whom it's possible to live on a single income. It might be some sacrifice, but it's feasible.

There's good news and bad news about this. The good news is that it presents choices, and it usually is the woman who weighs the choices. In about 5 percent of the cases, I found that it was the man who made the choice to stay home and follow the woman's career, but typically it's the woman. Yet, the women are not really staying at home. They're totally engaged in community and nonprofits, and they're working at them just as hard as a business. They make that choice because it gives them a little more discretion about what hours they work and when they are engaged in the work.

Another situation might be when a woman decided to take time off or pull back from her career—staying engaged but doing the job maybe on a little less competitive basis. I asked if they planned to come back to the paid workforce. What did they do strategically to enable them to keep their connections alive and their knowledge of the industry and their network active? Essentially, how did they come back?

I discovered that these life decisions were quite strategic and that women should be thinking about them before they actually made the decision rather than thinking about them only in the heat of the moment when they make the decision.

So we introduced some courses at the business school originally for women to help them think about life planning as a part of career planning. It turned out that there were so many men who were interested so we changed the title of the course from Women Building Business to Building Business in the Context of Life. And when we did that, the enrollment went up to more than 50 percent male, attracting all students who were deeply interested in planning their professional career success as well as their personal life success. The class helped them focus on how to think about those options, develop early dialogues with intended partners, make choices about the industry or job channels, as well as how to negotiate these things before they actually were faced with the decision to do it.

Ghaffari: Was the original course the one that you developed with Professor Lynda Applegate in 1999? When did it change? Did she concur?

Hart: Yes, Women Building Business was the first course. It was renamed about 2002 or 2003. She was no longer jointly teaching it at the time that I converted the course to Building Business in the Context of a Life. When I took over the course on my own, maybe around 2002 or 2003, I had two men signed up whose wives were in the class. They said, "These issues are just as important to us. It was pretty hard for us to sign up given the course name, but not only are we interested, but there are a lot of others who are interested." So we talked it over and decided it's really about career issues, but it's also about putting those choices in the context of the full life you want to live.

Ghaffari: You were also developing some executive education courses. Was the same thing happening in that environment—that men as well as women were interested?

Hart: In fact, the executive education courses were leading the way. Around 1996 or 1997, The Committee of 200 came to Harvard Business School. They are an international, nonprofit organization of more than four hundred, today, of the most powerful women who own and run companies. Most of The Committee of 200 are self-made women from the entrepreneurial side. They wanted to make a major philanthropic gift that would really assist and promote women in business and entrepreneurship, in particular.

They were thinking how best to invest $500,000 from their foundation in ways that might enable this. Not unlike my earlier decision to go into teaching, they tried to assess where they'd have the greatest impact. They considered fellowships, scholarships or a named professorship. I told them, "Each of those options will have influence. With scholarships from that amount of money, you could help maybe two or three women a year going through an MBA program. Endow a professorship and maybe the business school has some influence through that research. But, even though you endow a chair, you cannot actually control who gets it or what their perspective might be. There's another way you could reach the broadest possible audience. That is, if you could influence the cases that are used in business schools, you could have a truly significant impact."

The Harvard Business School publishing company totally dominates the dissemination of case studies to probably three hundred business schools around the world. Those cases are read by almost every business school student. If you could change, in some way, the perspective of students through the cases, you could really touch thousands and thousands of people every year.

When The Committee of 200 came to Harvard, Dean Kim B. Clark of the Business School said he would match their gift from the Dean's Fund. So instead of merely $500,000, there would be $1 million devoted to the case-writing initiative to develop cases across the whole universe of courses that Harvard covered, with the common theme that the protagonists were all women. The issue was not about gender—it was about leadership.

These cases would add to the inventory of leadership studies, but the leaders would be women—authentic and extraordinary. In every way, this would be just a subtle signal: "Hey, women are in these places. They're making these kinds of decisions." Once you develop a lot of information about the persona of the case protagonist, you get a lot more insight into what issues women take into consideration that men don't—or that men do take into consideration, but that issue never made it into the cases.

Ghaffari: How was Marjorie Alfus involved in the development of case studies?

Hart: She was the fire in the belly of The Committee of 200 because she said, "We have this foundation. We raise a certain amount of money every year from the members. We distribute it in bits and pieces. We really need to make a bigger statement." Marjorie probably channeled her money through the foundation, but she was the lead giver. She stood up and said, "I'm going to put my money where my mouth is. We have to make this big gift. We have to make it in a very public way. We have to make a statement to the world that The Committee of 200 is not just interested in itself and its members. We're interested in women in business everywhere."

It was going to be the fifteenth anniversary of the founding of The Committee of 200, so Marjorie put up the first $250,000, and the next $250,000 came from the foundation.[2]

We were very successful in developing about seventy-five cases but, in the process, we also educated our faculty that these were important things to think about on the grid of issues that you consider when you're building new case material. Another fifty to one hundred new cases were introduced into the curriculum beyond those actually funded by this initiative. Faculty were inspired by this initiative. They were writing cases under their own research budget but were now asking me, "Help me identify women candidates that I could study." They'd give me the specs of what they needed—the financial services, this kind of a situation. Suddenly, they all wanted names of women for case studies.

Ghaffari: Are these kinds of women in leadership cases still being developed?

Hart: Oh, yes. In fact, I think in some ways there's no need whatsoever for the initiative anymore. The initiative was not an endowment—a portion was spent every year. Each case probably cost between $25,000 to $30,000, so the million dollars was used up pretty quickly. But the impact is enduring.

Today, it is a very high priority, with our dean and faculty, to have cases that reflect the kinds of protagonists that you see in the classroom. As we look around the room, we see that 40 percent of the students are female and about 35 percent are international students, so our cases need to address situations in which those people play a major role.

Clearly we have migrated from thinking, "Well, this is nice to do." Or, "It would be politically correct to do this." Now we are at the point where we think, "Well, of course, this is what we do."

Ghaffari: How did you get involved in the Diana Project?[3]

Hart: I had met the two original parties, Candida Brush and Patricia Green, at a doctoral research program in France in 1992 or 1993. We learned that we had very similar interests in the entrepreneurship area and that our research was quite complementary. I went to another research seminar where Patty and Candy were presenting another paper they'd written together. I

---

[2] Harvard University Gazette, "New Initiative at HBS Focuses on Women in Business," http://news.harvard.edu/gazette/1998/01.15/NewInitiativeat.html, January 15, 1998.

[3] The Diana Project was established in 1999 to raise awareness and expectations of women business owners regarding the growth of their firms. For more information, visit www.esbri.se/diana.asp.

was already working on a very similar paper. Afterwards I spoke to them, told them I was interested in the same topic and that maybe we could collaborate.

So we wrote a paper together called "Toward A Research-Based Theory of Entrepreneurship" [1995]—actually a very popular paper even today. We discovered that we worked well together and had a lot of fun at the same time. As my work began to pick up at Harvard, beginning about 1997, focusing more on women, I brought them right into this. This was a whole field that nobody had explored in a systematic way, although Candy Brush had been involved in studying women in entrepreneurship since the early '80s. Maybe it was because the field didn't exist or maybe there weren't enough people demanding information. So we started to think seriously about the topic and wrote another paper at a conference.

Two other women academicians whom we knew, Nancy Carter and Elizabeth Gatewood, said they too would like to join the group. They had done selectively different kinds of papers.

I have to say that a research group of five is hard to manage, but we decided to try it out. Since we were at five different schools, at least four of us were going to have to travel someplace in order to meet. We decided we'd all travel to Santa Fe because of Georgia O'Keefe. We wanted to work in a place where a woman's persona dominated the atmosphere.

We spent a week, working for about six to eight hours every day, scoping out the questions that we had and what we could explore. How will we go about this? Of course, like the academics we were, we decided, "The first thing we have to do is understand everything that's already been done so that we don't recreate the wheel." As our very first project, we outlined an exhaustive survey of the literature in which entrepreneurship and women might intersect, even though it might not be about women in entrepreneurship. We also looked very exhaustively at the gender research and assembled an annotated bibliography of all the existing work on women in entrepreneurship. That was our very first project.

Ghaffari: Was there anybody else, besides the five of you, interested in this subject?

Hart: We weren't at all sure there was a high demand for it, but we found Magnus Erikson, managing director of the Entrepreneurship and Small Business Research Institute, a research institute in Stockholm, Sweden. He was very interested in our work and offered to publish our research if we would come to Stockholm and spend some time with the Swedish community, talking about entrepreneurship in general and focusing in particular on women in entrepreneurship. And that was the beginning of our big collaboration.

Now, when you have five academics—and luckily we had all been promoted, so it wasn't as if we were jockeying for tenure and tenure review—the big question is always, "Whose name should go first?" I think our solution was very feminine. We decided to make it clear that no one person was the lead writer, but that all of the work that was produced was a collaborative effort from all of us.

We decided that we would always list our names in alphabetical order. And we would call ourselves the Diana group so that it was very clear this was not Candy Brush's group, nor Myra Hart's group, or Patty Greene's. It wasn't a leader and four followers, and not even a shifting leader with four followers. There were five people who worked together, and we called it Diana. We chose Diana, the goddess of the hunt, because we said our work was about women in the hunt for money since were primarily focused on women entrepreneurs. We named it Diana so that we didn't have to go through five names every time, and we didn't have to explain who was in charge.

For us, this just solved a lot of problems like "Who was the lead writer?" We didn't need that—it wasn't important to our careers at that point in our lives. If you're a junior faculty member, it's very important that you be the lead author. It wasn't critical to our success as academics. We had already been over that hurdle.

Ghaffari: I've identified at least four books. One was *Assuming Control*. That was the first one.

Hart: Well, *Assuming Control* is not actually finished, I would say, so you won't find that one. It was one that Candy, Patty, and I worked on separately. Because of my other commitments, it took a back burner for me. Meanwhile, Patty's career had gone in a different direction. She became the provost at Babson, so that probably will never be anything more than an article.

Ghaffari: As a team, you've published a number of books.

Hart: Our very first one was the annotated bibliography. We have several collected works that are studies of the literature or collected from the Diana Symposium. We had *Clearing the Hurdles* and many research papers like "Women Business Owners and Equity Capital" and "The Gatekeepers." Because of the way we work, sometimes one person would work on it, but everybody would get credit. I had far less of a hand in some of these books compared to others.

Ghaffari: What is the status of the Diana Project, currently, either for yourself or in general?

Hart: That's a great question. All of our Diana research to that point had focused on women entrepreneurs in the United States—we just didn't have the time or the resources to look at women entrepreneurs around the world. While entrepreneurs by their nature are not very global until they've grown to a sufficient size to cross international borders, we thought there were a lot of commonalities, globally. There also were a great many benefits if we could share research methods. So we decided to facilitate the international research by broadening our cooperative effort.

We moved into the global research space in 2003 when the first Diana International Conference was held in Stockholm, Sweden, at the suggestion of Magnus Erikson who said "Let's think about hosting a conference for other researchers who are interested in women entrepreneurs." The fact that about thirty men and women academicians came to the conference confirmed out belief that there was interest internationally.

The second international conference was held in 2004. The third in 2007 in Belfast, Ireland. The fourth in 2010 in Banff, Canada. By about 2007, we had really gotten a nucleus of very interested women and men from all around the world with a very robust group of leaders. When we started, just fourteen countries were interested, a large portion of them Nordic countries, but also from South Africa, Asia, and Australia.

Next year, the conference will be held in Perth, Australia. So the work continues on a global scale under the leadership of Diana International where Karen Hughes and Jennifer Jennings have embraced the leadership mantle.

On a personal level, the five of us have essentially disbanded as a research group. And I have retired, although I serve on the boards of directors of companies like Kraft Foods and Office Depot.

Ghaffari: Do you think that the issues change dramatically once you move from a North American business perspective into the international world?

Hart: Yes. There still are many people in Diana International who are US- and Canadian-based. They're looking at issues that are similar and those that are different because the context of their economy is different.

Nordic countries are completely different situations politically, economically, and in the nature of business. If you're in microfinance as compared to venture capital, there are totally different issues. But the people who are interested in these issues are learning across borders.

There are common concerns such as research methodology or what people are doing who are the next rung up on developing their economy. What's the transition from micro-entrepreneurship in Africa or Latin America? How do you scale micro-entrepreneurship up to the next step? How about Central and Eastern Europe, where the economies have changed so radically in the past fifteen years? How receptive are those economies to entrepreneurship? Very receptive, it turns out. How much history do they have that they can actually learn from? Not very much. So, they have to learn what's going on in other countries.

There is a great advantage for those who are part of Diana International in sharing knowledge. Even though the research that they're doing might be focused very much within their own country, they are learning a great deal across country borders. Some of them collaborate, and some of them don't. In any academic conference, you can attend and learn from others there, but you don't necessarily have to do what they did.

Ghaffari: You, personally, have been involved in generating new businesses yourself, through programs like Springboard Enterprises. How did you get involved in that?

Hart: Springboard actually started in 1999. Kay Koplovitz was the inspiration for Springboard when she was chair of the National Women's Business Council. She accepted President Clinton's appointment to that position only under specific conditions: "I want to stimulate not just small business, but potentially large business. I want to focus on potentially venture-funded businesses led by women."

She and Amy Millman, the executive director of the National Women's Business Council, came up with the idea of Springboard. Their goal was to convince the naysayers that there were a lot of women who had the ability, the knowledge, and the ideas to run big and scalable businesses and, thus, they deserved the attention of the venture capitalist community.

When you talked to venture capitalists, they would say, "Our money is gender-blind. It just goes where the great opportunities are." But, essentially, you could tell that they had some preset ideas about who they were seeing and how they were approaching the dialog.

I take no credit for Springboard. Like Staples, it came to me as an idea that was fully developed by somebody else. Kay and Amy had the idea to put out a call for women entrepreneurs to present their business plans. At the initial screening, maybe about five hundred business plans were presented. They looked at them every which way from Sunday and chose about the one hundred best in terms of the business concept. Then they brought those people in and talked with them as the talent behind the idea.

Finally, they chose about twenty-five whom they thought really had a track record as business leaders, good fundamental concepts, good management teams, and who credibly could start a really big, scalable business. They coached them well because many of these women did not have any experience in how to do the pitch, how to engage that conversation, how to do "the push and pull" required in the venture community.

Springboard held the first event in San Francisco at Oracle because Kay Koplovitz at the time was on the board there and was able to convince Larry Ellison that that was a good thing. When they planned to come to New England, they asked me if Harvard Business School would be willing to host it. That was a big step for Harvard Business School because they primarily host things that are Harvard-related. Harvard seldom gets involved with outside nonprofits that are supported by individual members of the faculty or the staff here. You can understand why—they could be inundated with these things.

Fortunately, our dean felt that this was very much in concert with our effort to reach out to women entrepreneurs and women in business. So, Harvard Business School hosted it for the first two years in New England, and I chaired it.

Ghaffari: Was the Diana research group involved in Springboard?

Hart: After me, the chairmanship stayed within the Diana group because of all our interest in women entrepreneurs. It went to Candida Brush who was then at Boston University. And the Diana group actually has kept close ties with Springboard because we used that as a research database, following up with all the women who had applied to Springboard or who had presented to Springboard to see how their professional life progressed and whether they got money, how they were doing in business, and what their next steps were. On an individual basis, we became involved with some of the entrepreneurs to try to help them by counseling them on an ongoing basis.

Ghaffari: You've been on a couple of the boards of entrepreneurial firms as well as major entities like Office Depot and Kraft. Are the roles significantly different?

Hart: It is a different focus. Now I'm more actively engaged in "things of the moment," and I'm not so enmeshed in the research.

Ghaffari: Do you see any irony in your being a board member of Office Depot, a direct competitor to Staples?

Hart: Not really. I had not been involved with Staples at all after I left in 1990. I totally diversified my Staples portfolio the day that I walked out.

If you follow the industry, Staples and Office Depot tried to merge in 1996, but the Federal Trade Commission blocked it because they thought it would concentrate too much power in one business entity and that could result in increased prices for office supply products. The eighteen months of discussions, court review, and the failure of the merger had a greater impact on Office Depot than on Staples.

As for the industry, I've always believed in competition—the industry absolutely has to have good competition. Even in the days when I was an officer at Staples, I always said that Office Depot was one of the best things that ever happened to us because it made us so much better and it—absolutely—always was a good competitor. I was interested in the industry.

James Heskett, a colleague at Harvard Business School, was on the Office Depot board. In 2004, he asked me if I would consider going on that board. I personally considered it an enormous entrepreneurial opportunity in that Office Depot had been having some recovery difficulties, and I thought it was an opportunity to try to kind of get it back together.

Ghaffari: Was Office Depot your very first public company board?

Hart: Yes, but I had served on a number of private company boards for quite some time. Some of those come about through my professorship at Harvard, but certainly not all of them. For instance, Orchid Partners was started by Todd Krasner, who was at Staples. When he left Staples, he started Zoots, in which I was an investor. Later on, he started Orchid Partners as a venture fund. He invited me to be on his advisory board.

There's a clear distinction between being on the board of directors vs. an advisory board. An advisory board is much easier, and you can serve on many more of them concurrently. You have no fiduciary responsibility, no legal liability. A board of directors is a much more demanding position. For my students, I would almost always be willing to be on their board of advisors, at least for the first two years—until they were able to field a board of directors. However, I did not want to take on the liability or the extent of responsibility as a member of their board of directors.

Ghaffari: When did you go on the Kraft Foods board?

Hart: December 2007. It was just made public today that Kraft is going to be splitting into two companies. That will be very interesting and really a big challenge.

Earlier, I'd been on the board of other big companies, including Royal Ahold N.V., a Dutch retail company in the food business. They own Stop & Shop and Giant Foods in the United States and Albert Heijn in the Netherlands, probably the single biggest supermarket chain there. The international experience was very interesting. When I joined Kraft, I had to leave the Ahold board because they are a big customer of Kraft, and you can't be on both sides of the deal.

I was also on the board of Summer Infant, which is a much smaller local company that went public about four years ago. I was on the board to help them through the process of understanding governance in a public company and to help them figure out not only how to build a board but to help them conduct themselves in a much more professionalized way as a public company rather than a private company.

Also, I've done a host of nonprofits. I'm now on the board of the Smithsonian, which is really an extraordinary and a wonderful experience. I have been a trustee of Cornell and of Babson. Those were great opportunities for me to provide the business skills and oversights to a nonprofit that I learned elsewhere. It's been great fun.

Ghaffari: As you look at women today in the professions, are you optimistic or pessimistic? What do you see are the great challenges? What do you see as the big picture?

Hart: Well, first of all I'm very optimistic because women are, by far and away, the better educated segment of our population. About 58 percent of the undergraduate degrees go to women, and about 50 percent of the graduate degrees go to women.

Many organizations and business and professional services firm now recognize that—because their talent pipeline coming in is so heavily weighted to the female side—they had better figure out how to make it attractive to those people to stay with them, perform well, and become leaders.

I am on the advisory board of Deloitte, and I think the world of the way that they are approaching this challenge. All of the accounting/consulting firms have figured out that if they are hiring 50 or 60 percent of the college graduates who are female, yet the women leave, then companies are going to have to find leaders from only 40 percent of their recruits. That doesn't make any sense at all. It's not smart. So instead, they want to make sure that they actually nurture, recognize, and develop the women in their workforce. And they want to make sure that they don't have hidden barriers in either expectations or opportunities for the women. So I'm very optimistic.

On the other hand, I'm unhappy about how slowly it's going. Actually, the number of women on corporate boards is still kind of pitiful—about 17 to 18 percent. In large part, women directors are drawn from the C-suite of existing businesses, and that's an even worse number. So there's still a really great deal of work to be done.

The other thing that frightens me a bit is that I don't think that young women recognize the amount of challenge that still remains. I think that because of Title IX and some other initiatives, life is pretty smooth-sailing for young women coming through our K-through-12 experience in terms of opportunities and availability of the options for them.

Obviously, the undergraduate experience is dominated by women. Young women who got out into the workforce and even young women who come to get their MBAs are very optimistic that this same kind of equality awaits them going forward. Then they're a little blindsided when they find out later—as a result either of their own internalized expectations about family or external expectations that it is difficult—that they have to make a greater effort, compared to their male colleagues, in order to really become very successful in their professional careers. The greater effort required is concentrated in how they will have to integrate all aspects of their lives because society still has programmed us to think about roles, expectations, and socialization for women that aren't always consistent with a really high-flying, great career for women.

Ghaffari: When you were coming up your career path, it was quite difficult. Would you say you understood the challenges?

Hart: I totally understood it. I think that young women are not at all aware of the difficulty in managing themselves and some of the issues that may be external to themselves that they will also have to manage.

When women come into the workplace today, they're given opportunities and then when they meet the challenges, they are surprised and shocked in many ways. They're a little bit inured to the challenge by the fact that we've pretty much taken care of the early part. Not totally—I could point to the choices that young women make with regard to math and science that are still kind of lurking out there in the cultural expectations about what girls are good at and what boys are good at or what careers are attractive.

There are still some land mines and booby traps along the way, even though there are many people who are sincerely devoted to changing that. Sally Ride has a whole organization that is structured to keep young women—and young men as well, but especially young women—engaged in science and math at the junior high and high school level when many of them take themselves out of that game.

My research has not reached back to the K-through-12 experience. I am letting other people deal with that. I've been much more focused on the young women post-college and in their early career. That includes women in their forties who are returning to the workforce after a hiatus.

Catherine Bromilow

Partner, PwC LLP

Born 1963 in Kapuskasing, Ontario, Canada.

Catherine Bromilow, a partner with the PwC Center for Board Governance, works with the boards of directors and audit committees of major companies and institutions, both in the United States and abroad, providing insight on developments in governance and company compliance regulations and expectations. She also benchmarks corporate and committee processes against leading practices.

Ms. Bromilow is an authority on corporate governance practices and is frequently a guest speaker at conferences and seminars for PwC, the National Association of Corporate Directors (NACD), The Conference Board, and the Practising Law Institute. She also lectures at universities.

Ms. Bromilow is the principal author of Audit Committee Effectiveness—What Works Best, Fourth Edition (The Institute of Internal Auditors Research Foundation, 2011), a guide that helps audit committees understand leading practices in discharging complex responsibilities. She coauthored the book's second and third editions. Ms. Bromilow is also principal author of the companion report, Board Effectiveness—What Works Best, Second Edition (The IIA Research Foundation, 2011); coauthoring the first edition in 2000. She also leads periodic PwC studies and reports, including the Annual Corporate Directors' Survey.

At a NACD/PwC forum held in New York City in 2011, Ms. Bromilow moderated a panel discussion on opportunities for women in the boardroom. More than one hundred women corporate directors and executives attended the event, reinforcing the importance of strong, diverse corporate boards of directors.

In 2011, for the fifth consecutive year, NACD Directorship named Ms. Bromilow among the "100 Most Influential People in Corporate Governance."

Ms. Bromilow is a certified public accountant (licensed in New Jersey) and a chartered accountant in Canada. She has both an undergraduate degree (Honours Chartered Accountancy Studies) and a graduate degree in accounting from the University of Waterloo in Canada.

Elizabeth Ghaffari: Where were you born and may I ask the year?

Catherine Bromilow: Certainly. I was born in 1963 in a small town in northern Ontario called Kapuskasing, approximately five hundred miles north of Toronto. It's very cold up there. It wasn't until I left for university that I learned you could buy a car without a block heater. All cars in my hometown had electrical cords to plug in during the winter so they would start when it got really cold.

Ghaffari: Tell me a little bit about your family. What were some of the influential factors in your upbringing?

Bromilow: My parents always worked really hard. My dad was an electrician at the paper mill, and my mother stayed home and raised us. They always set a great example of hard, diligent, and thorough work. They never left things half done. They taught us that, if you were going to take on a task, you do it well and do it with quality. My parents were not big spenders. They always saved so they could pay cash for any major purchase. I always knew that I wanted to do something career-wise that was going to enable me to provide for myself. I never wanted to have to depend on anyone. I thought the best path to financial self-sufficiency was to be a professional of some kind. So, those ideas about hard work and self-sufficiency have fueled my work ethic throughout my career.

Ghaffari: How large a family did you have?

Bromilow: There were three of us children, and I was the youngest and the first to go away to university.

Ghaffari: What made you decide to get that level of education?

Bromilow: When I was in high school, I took some accounting courses, which in retrospect were really just bookkeeping courses, but I really liked the order that they imposed—the idea that there was a right way of doing things, and one right answer, and that events could be reported and fit into a framework. Even though the bookkeeping we studied was not really accounting, it did have an appeal to me.

At one point, I was trying to decide which path I wanted to follow—medicine or accounting—and where I wanted to go to university. Then I heard that the University of Waterloo had a co-operative program, where you could be on campus for four months and then work in your field for four months. You repeated that study-work pattern until graduation. I thought that would be a great way to help pay my way through school, while also getting early work experience in the profession I wanted to enter. By the time I graduated from university, I would already have a fair amount of practical experience. And so I selected Waterloo and decided that I was going to become a chartered accountant.

Ghaffari: Your degree was a bachelor of arts in accounting. When did you get your degree?

Bromilow: I got both my undergrad and my master's degrees in accounting in 1987, within just a few months of each other. When I started at Waterloo, they had just introduced a new master's accounting program, where you did two years of undergrad study after which you could apply to the master's school. It was a great opportunity. The masters program entailed twelve straight months of study on campus, followed by twelve months off campus, working, and then twelve months back on campus. By the time you graduated, you finished with a master's degree and could go directly to take your chartered accountancy exams, without having to get a few years of additional experience after graduation. It was a bit of a fast track. I passed my chartered accountancy exams the first time I took them.

Ghaffari: Can you give me a sense of how many other women there might have been at Waterloo out of how large a total class size?

Bromilow: When I got into the master's program itself, I think there were probably only fifty or sixty of us who went through the entire program of the twelve months off and twelve on over a three-year period. Only about thirty-five of us ended up graduating. And I'd estimate that 40% percent of the class was women.

Ghaffari: What were your best subjects?

Bromilow: This may sound funny, but the best skill I picked up in high school was touch typing. I do a tremendous amount of writing, so knowing the keyboard has been extremely useful.

At Waterloo we covered a wide array of subjects. We had in-depth classes on taxation, management accounting, financial accounting, auditing, law, and ethics. Among all these great classes, I remember one instructor in particular—Sally Gunz. She taught us two semesters on communications, both written and verbal, which included a semester dedicated to giving presentations. That semester, in many ways, was absolutely horrifying because we had to stand up, give speeches, and then work with other students to deliver presentations to executives from the local business community. I don't think any of us liked making those verbal presentations.

But, now that I look back on the experience, I can see that her having forced us to stand up in front of other people and talk probably had a fundamental and positive impact on my career. That is especially true today in light of all the public speaking and interactions with boards that my work entails.

So, when I reflect on everything I learned at university, there are two types of lessons that were among the most important. First was the ability to apply logic, reason, and critical thinking. Second, and equally important, was the ability to stand up and speak in front of people. I never do it without some level of unease, but at least I can do it without being paralyzed.

Ghaffari: What was your first job after graduating and how did you get it?

Bromilow: I started working with Ernst & Young, one of the big accounting firms in Toronto. I had worked with them during one of my co-op terms when I had a twelve-month, off-campus job. I worked in one of their satellite Toronto offices. After I passed my CA exam, I started with them in their downtown Toronto office.

Ghaffari: Was it a big shock to be a little girl from the north working in the major metropolis of Toronto?

Bromilow: Well, it was a shock just to go to the University of Waterloo because the enrollment on that campus was twice the size of my hometown. It just all seemed so big and new for me. For my entire first month at Waterloo, I think I just looked at the ground—I was so shy. Then, thank goodness, people started talking to me.

Ghaffari: But you were bold and fearless.

Bromilow: Well, maybe I didn't know what I didn't know. Sometimes that protects us. I loved Toronto. I lived there for years, and I absolutely love Toronto.

Ghaffari: How long were you with Ernst & Young in Toronto?

Bromilow: I was with Ernst & Young from '87 until '92 or '93. Then I left public accounting. Many of the students who were in the master's program with me were certain we were never going to become Big Eight accounting firm partners—it was Big Eight back then. We thought we'd get our chartered accountancy designations and go on to bigger and better things. So I left Ernst & Young and joined Toronto Dominion Bank in their internal audit function. I really enjoyed it and learned a great deal about banking and how banking back offices worked, and—from a client perspective—what worked well interacting with professional services firms.

It was a great team and a really credentialed group. I had some amazing bosses there. Quite honestly, I would just look at them and try to figure out what their secret was. And we had a lot of fun.

After about three years there, I began thinking about what my next career might be or my next career move. One of the challenges with the banks is that most managers progress out of the inspection function [their internal audit] into managing a back-office function. That didn't necessarily have a lot of appeal to me. Then, it happened that one of my very good friends, Carol Brandt, with whom I had worked at Ernst & Young, had moved to Price Waterhouse. I was talking to her, and she said, "Well, why don't you come and work with us?" And so I ended up back in an accounting firm working for PW in Toronto.

Ghaffari: Was there anything different that you observed about the Price Waterhouse experience?

Bromilow: I don't know if it was because I was more mature by that time, but the partners seemed more approachable. There was a different culture—one that seemed more inclusive. Work-wise, I started doing control self-assessment implementations for our clients, which was right up my alley because I had a good understanding of controls, systems, and processes from my internal audit experience.

Based on that experience, PW asked me to participate in similar client work in the US. I went down for my first assignment and, at the very end, as I was sitting in the airport waiting for the plane, one of the partners said to me, "Why don't you come and work with us in the US?"

Ghaffari: When you left Toronto, where did you go to in the US?

Bromilow: I transferred down to the U.S. firm at the start of 1998. The group I joined was a virtual group: a few partners were in New Jersey, and the senior managers were in various cities: Chicago, Washington DC, and Boston. PW also had a formal telecommuting policy. So I was able to work out an arrangement where I didn't actually move from Toronto. I lived in Toronto and either worked from home or flew to wherever I was needed, wherever our clients or projects were located. That actually was brilliant because, quite honestly, I didn't know whether I was going to be able to cut it in the United States.

Ghaffari: Why would you think that?

Bromilow: It's a very different business culture than Canada. The partner for whom I worked, after the first few client meetings we attended, would tell me that I needed to talk more in the meetings. I told him that I didn't really have anything different to say. He pressed on, "It doesn't matter. You just need to talk." That's very different from typical Canadian business situations where, if you don't have something new to say, you don't talk. This partner was a New Yorker, and, to put it as nicely as possible, he never could leave an opinion unexpressed.

So, I was sure that it was a really good thing I didn't move down to the US because I didn't believe there was any way that I was going to last six months.

Interestingly—and luckily—enough, the first big assignment they asked me to do at the start of 1998 was to manage some research into corporate governance. PW had won a contract to research and write a corporate governance book.

At that time, Canada had some of the leading governance standards in the world, with the Dey Report.[1] So the partners thought I would be perfect to undertake this international governance research project. In the end, we produced two books, *Corporate Governance and the Board—What Works Best* and the second edition of *Audit Committee Effectiveness—What Works Best*. We issued both books in 2000.

Unexpectedly, governance became my primary focus, and it was absolute serendipity, as I have stayed in governance ever since. Without ever planning it, governance just became my career.

Ghaffari: When and why did you finally move down to New Jersey?

Bromilow: I telecommuted for seven years, until my visa ran out. Then I had to apply for a green card or not work in the US any longer. That was

---

[1] The Dey Report, also known as The Toronto Report, is a study of Canadian corporate governance. It is completed by the Toronto Stock Exchange (TSX) committee, chaired by Peter Dey. The report contains fourteen recommendations to assist TSX-listed companies in their approach to corporate governance.

not palatable because I really love working in the US—once I adapted to the different business culture. We moved to New Jersey at the start of 1995.

Quite honestly, once I became more of an expert in governance, then I *did* have something original to say and contribute—something that other people weren't saying in meetings. So I became a lot more confident and comfortable with my contributions.

Today, I'm based in the Center for Board Governance, which is housed in PwC's[2] national office. The national office provides support to our assurance teams from across the country, answering questions about complex accounting or auditing issues.

Ghaffari: How did you become a partner?

Bromilow: My path to partnership was a long process that emerged slowly as I gained more experience and added more credentials. Another factor was that the external environment for boards was changing. The Sarbanes-Oxley Act was passed after the Enron and WorldCom financial reporting scandals, and that brought an intense focus on audit committees. Also, there were new rules from the New York Stock Exchange and NASDAQ that had a fundamental and transformational impact on boards of directors. As a result, there was a stronger case for me to make partner, focusing on corporate governance.

In our firm, we don't view partnership as a promotion following a period of excellent service. Instead, it's an admission to the partnership. There needs to be a carefully articulated business case as to why someone should be a partner, what value they bring to the firm, and why they need to be a partner to bring that value forward.

When I made partner, I made it with a corporate governance business case, which was unique. In many ways, I'm a bit of an unusual creature in that much of my business case related to enhancing PwC's thought leadership around governance, as well as building and improving high-value relationships with boards of directors and audit committees.

Ghaffari: You didn't make partner the first time you tried. Is that right?

Bromilow: I made partner in 2004, but had gone through the process unsuccessfully the year before. I just didn't have a strong enough business case in the prior year, and I didn't know how to approach the interview. Maybe it

---

[2] Price Waterhouse became PricewaterhouseCoopers in 1998 as a result of the merger with Coopers & Lybrand. The PwC brand name came into existence in 2010.

was the typical woman thing, but I tended to talk more about what our team had accomplished. My discussion was largely about "we." The feedback I received said that it sounded as if *I* hadn't done anything.

Ghaffari: Did you get any help the second time around?

Bromilow: The next year, when I was about to go through the process again, one PwC partner, Bud Thomas, called me for a meeting, out of the blue. He asked about my candidacy and had me tell him about myself, which I did. He gave me wonderful coaching, especially in terms of how to present myself. Then he shared with me a whole list of possible questions to think through, and he gave me some generous advice on how to approach the interview, how to articulate answers, and how to succeed. I still think the world of him. You don't know what you don't know, and if you're not getting coaching on how to go through these processes, you just can't know how to do it well.

As a result of Bud's outreach and generosity, ever since I became partner, I've done the same sort of thing to counsel both men and women as they prepare for partnership, with a particular focus on the women I've known who are going through the process. I've coached candidates on how to prepare for the questions, think through their answers, articulate their value, and how to use the word "I" without making it sound like they run the entire firm single-handedly. There's always a tough balance, but I think women have to own our own success, our accomplishments, and our contributions more than perhaps we are comfortable doing.

Ghaffari: Did you write the business case or did somebody else write it for you?

Bromilow: The first year, my unsuccessful year, I wrote it with a partner with whom I was working. When he retired, the following year, there was another partner, Gary Stauffer, who was sponsoring me. He barely knew me, but he had a strong track record of supporting new partners. I'm so thankful to him—he completely rewrote my business case and articulated it in much better business terms.

Also, by then, we had another year of post-Sarbanes-Oxley experience, so the environment had changed, and governance was more crucial. I also got good coaching from some of the other, newer female partners who had a less traditional business case, as I had. By the time I went into the interview, I had a good view of the information I wanted to get across.

I even redirected the interview at the outset by saying, "I'm happy to answer your questions, but maybe, before we get started, would it help if I shared with you some perspectives on what the environment is like out there from a governance perspective?" And they said "yes," so I talked about the pressure directors were under, the amount of change they were facing, and how they were looking for sound advice, counsel, and help. I was able to articulate how what I was doing and contributing played directly into helping directors deal with those issues.

Ghaffari: How did they respond to that?

Bromilow: Amazingly, it was a pretty concise interview process lasting maybe an hour. It was with two partners, but, now, I was so much more strategic, because of the good coaching, so I understood who the interviewing partners were, what clients they served, and the issues their clients were facing. I approached the whole process in a different way. I couldn't have done that the first year because I had no inkling of what I should do.

Ghaffari: Did you ever feel like you wanted to give up or quit?

Bromilow: Quite honestly, the year I didn't make partner the first time was pretty traumatic. The partner who led the national office was the one who told me that I wasn't making partner. It was obviously unwelcome news. I asked about next steps. He said, "I think we can reshape your candidacy and get you admitted next year." I asked whether that was realistic. And he said, "Well, shame on us if we don't do it." I remember thinking, "Well, it may be 'shame on you' if you don't do it, but *I'm* the one who's going to suffer if it doesn't happen."

I remembered the words of a woman partner in a law firm in Toronto— Carol Hansell. She had been deeply involved in corporate governance for years. I remember we were talking over lunch one day when she told me something that probably made the difference between my still being here and being a partner and my not being here—and I do pass it along to other women.

She said that she saw so many great and really bright young women at her law firm who just didn't stick it out. Her view was, "They just don't understand how really great it is to be partner. Sometimes, you just have to stick with it for another few years."

That advice really stayed with me. It is true that we all go through bumps in our careers, and it's not always the upward trajectory we would wish. But her advice was on target and just at the right time. When I didn't make partner as quickly as I would have liked, staying the course and working at it until I did make partner was essential.

Just after I got the bad news, I ran into a PwC partner I worked with, who knew I hadn't made it. I told her, "I thought that they would just have realized how bright I was and how much I have to contribute." And she said, "You've got to realize that by the time you get to the point where they're considering you for partnership, *everyone* is bright. You are dealing with the cream of the cream of the crop. So you have to do something different to differentiate yourself. It's not that you're not bright, it's just that everyone is exceptional by the time they get to that stage of their career."

Next, I did the whole typical woman thing which is absolutely to overanalyze everything, including all my options. I went home and did all the analysis of, "Okay, well, I could stick it out for another year and maybe make partner, which would be wonderful, or I could wait until I get paid my bonus in the fall and then quit, or I could quit now or . . ." I went through all the pros and cons and kept in mind what my friend Carol Hansell said about just sticking it out. I'm really glad I followed her advice.

Ghaffari: Would you consider Carol Hansell a mentor?

Bromilow: I just think the world of her. She's just amazing. She's a senior partner with Davies Ward Phillips & Vineberg in Toronto. She's been the only non-American to chair the American Bar Association's Corporate Governance Committee. Probably unknown to her, she has had a major role in my career.

Now, I'm absolutely delighted I'm a partner at PwC. It's hard when you're younger because a setback of one or two more years feels like a lifetime. But when you look back on it after many years have passed, you realize that it really wasn't that much time after all. Carol was right—there's never any guarantee that if you simply put in those years that you will succeed, but you definitely won't succeed if you don't put them in.

Ghaffari: So you've had quite a collection of women counsel and coach you.

Bromilow: Yes. Some of my really good friends from my Ernst & Young days have been very successful in business. They've gone on to do just amazing things. But they remain the kind of people that I can bounce ideas and questions off of, and I really value their input. Sometimes I look at them and just have no idea how they do it all. I'm in awe of so many wonderful women I've worked with over the years.

Ghaffari: Have you been presented with any opportunities that you've turned down?

Bromilow: Yes. I've had headhunters reach out to me to interview to run other governance organizations, and people I've worked with in the governance field have asked me if I wanted a governance job. For the time being, I'm very happy with PwC.

Ghaffari: When did you first become involved in teaching governance?

Bromilow: Around the time of Sarbanes-Oxley, about 2001 or 2002, we started to do a lot more teaching and training. For about five years, ending in 2008, PwC collaborated with the University of Delaware and Charles Elson in running the Director's College there.

Then I was on the faculty of several other organizations, like the Conference Board, which runs the Director's Institute. I taught courses at the Practising Law Institute and have been the co-chair of PLI's audit committee roundtable session for two years now, and I'll be there again next year. Off and on over the years, I've spoken at the NACD's annual conference and other meetings, and I've taped a number of webcasts for both NACD's BoardVision and Corporate Board Member's "This Week in the Boardroom" series.

In mid-September, PwC and the NACD organized a Women in Boardrooms event in New York that was attended by one hundred and ten senior women, half of whom were corporate directors and the other half were C-suite women. We had a really good afternoon together talking in two key panels. The first panel discussed the key challenges that directors face today. The second discussed the challenges women face in the boardroom. I moderated that second panel, which dealt with getting on boards, being successful as a new director, and general advice for women executives as they interact with their board of directors as an executive—hints as to how to be effective in that role.

I've also been asked into discussions and sessions with our clients' audit committees and directors in their boardrooms. And that's been part of the fun—one of the ways I've gotten to travel was simply responding to requests to meet with boards and directors all over the world.

Ghaffari: You've have been involved with Women in the Boardroom[3] as one of their panelists, right?

Bromilow: Yes. This year, I'm speaking on two panels with them: one in New York and the other in Denver.

Ghaffari: Do you think the coaching and counseling you received in your career still has relevance for today's women executives?

---

[3] Women in the Boardroom are annual executive leadership events focused on preparing women business leaders for corporate board service. See www.womenintheboardroom.com for more information.

Bromilow: Yes. Another example of really good coaching, from another of my women PwC partners, was how to read your audience effectively and modify your strategy to get to their comfort zone sooner. I was having a struggle connecting and communicating with one of my partners. Then a woman partner who had worked with him told me, "You've got to remember, he's a transactions guy. So, you've got to get to the point really quickly. He doesn't care about all the process."

That really stayed with me because I have a bit of an academic bent—my more comfortable approach would be to outline everything that I went through to reach a conclusion and mention who I consulted to develop my recommendation. Now, I focus on just trying to get the bottom line across and then let people ask me how I got there if they want more insight. Just get to the point quickly, and let them ask their questions.

Ghaffari: Do you have a long-term strategy for your career?

Bromilow: It's more a long-term strategy for my life. Under the terms of the partnership agreement, there is an age-limit of sixty years, which is relatively young. It's not unusual for partners to leave and retire earlier.

My husband and I have a very small farm up in Canada, and he's planning to go up and start farming full-time within the next few years.

So I'm thinking about what else I would like to do after I retire from PwC. I suspect that will involve teaching—there's a great university close to our farm.

Also, I think it would be fascinating to start applying all of the governance knowledge that I've acquired over the years by joining a company's board. I think that would be very interesting—providing a fuller picture of what it takes to be on a board and to work with fellow directors and the management team to grow the shareholder value. I think that would be fascinating, actually.

Nevertheless, I do know that it's incredibly difficult to get on your first corporate board. That's one of the messages we share with women during our events—the different possible strategies for getting on boards.

Ghaffari: I cannot imagine that you are not on everybody's short list as a director candidate.

Bromilow: Well, that's nice to think and very nice of you to say, but one of the things we tell women who have aspirations to go on boards is that having real core operational and P&L experience is vital. I manage major projects and teams, but not a P&L, in the corporate sense. I could qualify as a financial expert for an audit committee role because of my understanding of controls. But clearly, everyone recognizes that a director role is not the kind of job where you simply apply. It's very much like our partnership. You're invited to join the partnership. You're also invited into the boardroom.

Ghaffari: Where did you meet your husband and when did you get married?

Bromilow: I met my husband, Doug Brooks, right after I finished university. I was sharing a house in Toronto with a friend who went to university with Doug. My friend introduced us, we started dating, and we married in 1994.

Doug has been absolutely wonderful and hugely supportive. We both really love Toronto. He was born there, and much of his family is in the area. But with my visa running out and my need to move to the US to get my green card, I was considering the options. One of those was to get a condo in New Jersey and commute back to Toronto on weekends. I give Doug all the credit in the world because he was the one who said, "No, let's just move to New Jersey."

Ghaffari: What does your husband do?

Bromilow: He's a finance manager at Hewlett Packard Financial Services. He was with HP up in Canada, and, fortunately, HP had their financing division fairly close to where my office is in New Jersey. So he came down, had an interview, and they hired him. It worked out wonderfully for him in terms of being able to continue with his company.

Ghaffari: Have you shared with him your vision as you were becoming partner? How did he respond to your aspirations in that area?

Bromilow: He's just always been phenomenally supportive. On the down days, he counsels me and bucks me up.

Ghaffari: Do you see a lot of opportunities for women in your field as an accounting firm partner or in the governance arena?

Bromilow: I'd say yes, definitely. We have a lot of really bright young women professionals in our firm. Every year, more and more women are being admitted as partners. Part of advancement does come with having the endurance to stick it out even if it takes one more year.

I'm glad to see that it has changed noticeably over the last few years. But for much of my career working in governance, it wasn't unusual that I would be the only woman in the room. I'd be the one woman among male directors, male members of company management, and male partners from our firm. I've always looked at that as a real opportunity.

You can go one of two ways. You could get angry that there aren't more women there or you could say, "I've got some pretty unique access here. I can just appreciate that I'm getting to see something and be able to learn in ways that very few other people—men or women—are able to do. And I can work to ensure and encourage more women to participate in the conversation."

That situation also makes it even more vital that you always put your best foot forward, because they see you as the only woman there. I've always tried to have my best foot forward just because I want to provide the best possible services to clients and help boards succeed.

I also find that governance has been interesting because I seem to run into so many absolutely wonderful women in that field, whether they are corporate counsel or work with institutional investors. There also are many women at not-for-profit organizations that provide services to directors. There are an amazing number of women in this field. It is a good area to work in, but it's also important to decide how you want to do governance—there are so many different facets of the work. Governance might be the research and thought leadership, or it could be corporate law, shaping boardroom agendas. There are some great options.

Ghaffari: We see a lot of women guiding nonprofits or businesses that critique boards and directors. Are we also seeing more women building businesses where they have the opportunity to demonstrate what they think are better governance practices within the firms that they establish? Are you seeing any evidence of that?

Bromilow: That's a hard question. Let me try to answer it in two ways. My sense is that there are more women than ever out there building businesses.

When you're an early-stage founder and sole entrepreneur of a private company, you do whatever makes sense to you as an individual from the governance perspective. Technically, you might need a board, but it might just be you and the lawyer who helped you incorporate. That's not unusual at all. It's only when you're ready to go to the next step, say considering aggressive growth, or an IPO or similar transaction, that you build a more traditional board.

It is interesting, though, what we do see—and Spencer Stuart has some great statistics on this in their annual board index—for the larger companies and larger public companies in particular, that having a woman or a racial minority as CEO tends to have a positive influence on the number of women and/or minorities on the board. So, perhaps it's a question of cracking into the leadership and into the upper echelons of the larger public companies, where it does tend to have a more positive impact in getting more women and other diverse director candidates onto boards than we've seen in the past.

Based on studying this since '98, in my view, the most important consideration in making a board effective is how the directors interact with one another and with management behind closed doors. Nobody from outside the company can get any real insight into that interaction or truly judge it. Regulators and shareholders have suggested structural surrogates that they hope will produce good governance. And a board might look brilliant on paper. But, if behind closed doors the directors are not engaging in dialogue, if they're not preparing diligently before meetings, if they're not coming to the meeting willing to challenge management and each other, then it doesn't matter what they look like on paper. They're not going to be a good board.

Conversely, I've worked with boards where on paper you might not think the directors would be particularly independent, and they might not look particularly diverse. But, they come to the boardroom with a view of, "What's good for shareholders? Our role is to make sure management keeps shareholder focus front and center." That can be a really effective board. The problem is, from the outside, you can't judge any of that.

Ghaffari: In the next five to ten years, do you see yourself slowing down, speeding up, more involved?

Bromilow: I expect that by the time I'm in my late fifties, we will have moved back to Canada. I like to bake, so my husband has spotted this little closed café not too far from our farm. Every time we drive past, he jokes, "You could turn that into a bakery." So, he's got me teaching at university, helping run our farm, running a bakery, and serving on corporate boards. Meanwhile, I hope that I will be slowing down, but I can't imagine ever doing nothing. I think it's a question of maybe shifting priorities and efforts.

This year has been especially busy because we did the fourth edition of *Audit Committee Effectiveness* and the second edition of *Board Effectiveness*. All of this has come on top of all my regular work, which typically is extremely busy.

Ghaffari: Do you see yourself as a leader?

Bromilow: Yes and no. I think that goes back to the fact that I'm uncomfortable claiming a lot of credit. Many other women face that same challenge.

Maybe this story sort of illustrates what I mean. One of the times that I was reapplying for my work visa, before I went through the green-card process, the INS inspector asked me, "Since your visa application is for a manager role, how many staff do you have?" I replied, "I don't have any staff." He countered, "Well, how can you be a manager if you don't have any people to manage?" I realized that was a really good question. So, I articulated to him that I actually manage projects and bring people together as needed to fulfill projects.

So, my answer is that I tend to think of myself more as a leader of initiatives and projects and teams.

Barbara J. Beck

Chief Executive Officer, Learning Care Group

Born May 19, 1960, in Princeton, New Jersey.

Barbara J. Beck *is chief executive officer of the Learning Care Group, the sec-ond-largest for-profit early childhood education company in the United States. The Learning Care Group has five brands and 1,050 schools serving children aged six weeks to twelve years in thirty-six states and three international countries. Ms. Beck has held this position since March 2011.*

From 2002 through 2005, Ms. Beck was an executive vice president with Man-power, Inc., where she oversaw the $3 billion North American business unit. From 2006 until 2011, she was based in London, England, as Manpower's company president in charge of Europe, the Middle East, and Africa (EMEA). Over that pe-riod, her team brought the unit's revenues to close to $9 billion, doubling profit percentages.

Ms. Beck spent fifteen years (1985–2000) with Sprint, the global communications provider, in a variety of roles, including area vice president and general manager for the western region of the United States. Her tenure included leadership postions in technical sales and applications engineering, business development, customer service, operations, technical support, and program management.

In between her assignments at Sprint and Manpower, Ms. Beck spent a year run-ning her own business consultancy, Beck and Associates, advising companies on leadership topics.

In 2007, she was named to the World Economic Forum's Women Leaders Board, an organization dedicated to establishing strategies that address women's issues on a global basis. That same year, she was invited to become a member of The

Women's Leadership Board at Harvard University's John F. Kennedy School of Government. She was also a founding member of Catalyst Europe's Board of Advisors and was an advisory board member of the Cherie Blair Foundation.

Ms. Beck received the prestigious 2008 Ruban d'Honneur, Business Leader of the Year award, at the European Business Awards. The same year she was also chosen as one of PINK magazine's Top 15 Women in Business for innovations that "turn ideas into earnings."

She has served on the Ecolab board of directors since 2008. Ecolab is a NYSE-listed company based in St. Paul, Minnesota, which develops and markets products and services for the hospitality, foodservice, health care, and industrial markets.

Ms. Beck holds a bachelor of science degree in education (with honors) from the University of Colorado (1982) and has completed executive leadership programs at INSEAD in Fontainebleau, France, the University of Chicago, and Yale University School of Business.

Elizabeth Ghaffari: Was there anything about your family or upbringing that might have contributed to your pursuit of this particular position or career?

Barbara J. Beck: Yes, there is a strong link between my family background and the reason that I have gravitated throughout my career toward service-sector positions. My father was completing his seminary work to become a Presbyterian minister at Princeton when I was born. As he began serving churches in the Northeast, I was raised with a very strong service orientation. My parents held dual careers—my father was the minister of the church and my mother was the church secretary, the choir director, and the Sunday school teacher. Our life revolved around serving others—the importance of that was paramount in my upbringing. As I grew and expanded both my personal life and my professional career, this core value of serving has always been a very significant part of those experiences.

Ghaffari: Were there other siblings?

Beck: I was the youngest of three daughters—one sister was born in 1956, while the other was born in 1958, then I came along in 1960.

Ghaffari: How did it feel to be the youngest?

Beck: I loved having two older sisters—I watched and learned far more than I should have! I played the role of the annoying, tag-along little sister quite well. I was also fortunate that my parents believed each child was a unique individual. We were encouraged to develop ourselves by following our own path. My passion happened to be academics and current events—I was a news and political junkie starting in the third grade! But I was also very social. I was active in youth groups, Scouts, student council, choirs, middle and high school cheerleading, you name it. Rather than push me, my parents actually worried about ratcheting me back a bit—but I genuinely believe the time-management skills I acquired in my youth juggling all my commitments and studies laid the foundation for my ability to do the same as an executive. It was also in my childhood I became addicted to taking on new challenges and experiencing change.

We relocated quite often in my youth because of my father's profession. That also planted a seed—I came to enjoy the whole relocation experience. By the time I was eight years old, we had moved four different times as a family. Then in 1968, we settled in Denver, Colorado, and I ended up completing my elementary, middle school, and high school years there. I went on to the University of Colorado, in Boulder, to complete my undergraduate education.

Ghaffari: Your bachelor's degree in education—what level of education did it represent?

Beck: My degree was in elementary education, kindergarten through eighth grade. Initially, I intended to teach middle school.

Ghaffari: What did you do immediately after college? What was your first job and how did you get it?

Beck: Directly upon graduation from college, I accepted a teaching position at a private school. The only available position at that time was in kindergarten. I had intended to teach kids at the middle school level, but accepted the kindergarten position because I was so excited to begin a teaching career. Midway through my first year, based on a relationship that I was in, I relocated to Atlanta, Georgia, early in 1983. Since I was not certified to teach in Georgia, I began pursuing courses that would lead to my certification. At the same time, I accepted an entry-level business position with an architectural firm. I've been in business ever since that day.

That first position led to a job with an Atlanta telecommunications firm, now known as Sprint. Once again, I accepted an entry-level position at Sprint's national operations control center from 1985 to 1987. In the beginning of 1987, I was offered the opportunity to move to Southern California and take on a field-based service role.

Over the course of the following years, until 2000, I was promoted rapidly through the Sprint organization. I took on my first leadership role, with direct responsibility for managing others, in the 1987 to 1988 timeframe. Leadership clicked for me—from that day forward, I've always held leadership roles of increasing levels of responsibility.

Ghaffari: Where were you located in California?

Beck: Originally, I was based in San Diego. A year later, I accepted a promotion and transfer to San Francisco. Three years later, I was promoted into a position based in Orange County. Finally, I concluded my Sprint career back in San Diego after being promoted into an area vice president position, responsible for the western United States.

Ghaffari: The breadth of your technical experience at Sprint was quite wide, wasn't it?

Beck: Yes, it encompassed technical sales, applications engineering, business development, customer service, operations, technical support, and program management.

Ghaffari: Were there bosses, mentors, or leaders at Sprint who helped you climb this particular career ladder?

Beck: There were many bosses who were always willing to offer new promotional opportunities based on results. One of the noteworthy aspects of Sprint during my fifteen years there was that the company was truly a meritocracy. Promotions were offered based on an individual's ability to deliver strong performance and results. I was fortunate enough to be a part of the National Account/Sprint Business organization, so I was interacting with *Fortune* 500 clients during the rise of data communications. My entire fifteen-year Sprint career was devoted to selling to and servicing some of the most prominent companies of the era.

That was the heyday of telecommunications, during the explosion of enabling technologies, emerging technologies, and the dot-com era. Telecommunications was growing and evolving at a very rapid pace, as was Sprint. If you delivered results, you had an opportunity for promotion.

A key career lesson for me was that most promotions came with the need to relocate. And I was almost always willing to relocate. That allowed me a very rapid succession up through the organization. It offered me many opportunities that others, quite frankly, turned down for legitimate, yet typically personal, reasons.

Ghaffari: When and why did you decide to leave Sprint?

Beck: Late in 1999, Sprint Corporation and MCI WorldCom announced they were going to merge. The deal fell through because of pressure from the US Department of Justice and the European Union over concerns that the combined entity would create a monopoly and be anti-competitive. About mid-2000, the merger was jointly terminated.

Sprint began consolidating leadership positions from my business unit back into corporate headquarters in Kansas. So again, opportunity came knocking with a requirement to relocate. However, this time the "relo" would have completely disrupted my husband's career, which was firmly rooted in the music industry in Southern California.

So, we made a family decision to allow my husband's career to take precedence, and I remember driving up the coast to meet my brand-new boss not only to turn down the job offer, but also to resign from the company. I felt really badly for him. He had been recruited from outside the company and had been in his new role for a matter of weeks. In a twist of irony, I learned several years later he also left Kansas to relocate to San Diego with a different company. I'm guessing he understood my decision!

Ghaffari: Would you tell me a little about your family?

Beck: My husband, Randy, and I married in 1989. We had our first baby girl in San Francisco in 1991 and our second baby girl in San Diego in 1993. Both my sisters settled with their families in California as well, one in San Diego and one in Carmel, so our daughter's early years were filled with beaches, sunshine, family, critters, travel, and hard-working executive parents! Fast-forward to summer of 2000, after resigning from Sprint, I decided to start a consulting business, travel less, and create more flexibility so I could devote more time to my daughters. They were nine and seven years old then, and I wanted to experience volunteering in their schools and actually being in town to attend their weekday events. Looking back, even though it only lasted eighteen months, I wouldn't change a thing.

Ghaffari: When and why did you transition to Manpower?

Beck: I was headhunted for the Manpower position in August of 2001, just prior to 9/11. Understandably, the interview process stopped for a time, and we finalized terms over Christmas. I joined Manpower in January 2002 as the executive vice president of North America. It was a $3 billion business unit with responsibilities throughout the US and Canada.

Ghaffari: Where was that job located?

Beck: This is where irony comes into play. Recall that I had turned down moving to the Midwest with Sprint, so I suppose it was destiny that eighteen months later I would be headhunted for another position that also was in the Midwest—Milwaukee, Wisconsin.

Ghaffari: Did your family move with you?

Beck: Yes, but not until the end of the school year, so for the first six months, I commuted. Mondays through Fridays were 100 percent devoted to the new job. Weekends were one hundred percent devoted to my family. This is a very typical arrangement for newly relocated executives, and I would argue there's a tremendous benefit to having zero distractions when you're on-boarding into a top role. Once we sold the house and fully relocated to Wisconsin, it was my husband's turn to commute back to California for the workweek. We made the best of it, renting him an apartment overlooking the beach and visiting as often as possible during the Wisconsin winters!

The dual residence worked well as I led the North American business unit. However, early in 2005, my boss, the CEO and chairman of the company, approached me with an unexpected opportunity—a move to London to become the president of Manpower's largest business unit, Europe, the Middle East, and Africa—EMEA. It was my dream job, running a business unit that spanned thirty markets from the UK to Europe to South Africa to Russia. I went home to have yet another family discussion about a move—and I remember my husband and daughters saying "yes" before I could even finish the story. The girls were teenagers, and the fantasy of living in London encompassed their love of fashion, boys with British accents, and extensive travel.

The consequence was that my husband then had to disengage from his position since there was no feasible way for him to commute from London back to California. We thought we had plenty of time to work through the details, targeting August for the move so the girls could begin their new international school on time. Unexpectedly, the paperwork associated with four visas, work permits, international transport of household items, and pet passports took us through a mad scramble into the final hours to accomplish it all in time. Anyone who has ever relocated to the UK will tell you the most daunting part of the process is getting your critters onto the island—and once they land, due to quarantine requirements, they aren't leaving until the day you move home! Finally, in late August of 2005, our great EMEA adventure began.

Ghaffari: How did you prepare your daughters for such major transitions?

Beck: We're really fortunate—our girls are both flexible and adaptable to change. One of the parental roles Randy and I took very seriously was our need to prepare our girls for the world they would grow up in and have to live in as adults—one of constant change. So from an early age, our daughters experienced a fair amount of change: new cities, new homes, new schools, new country and cultures. They were very young when we moved three times within California and were still in elementary school when we moved them to Wisconsin. When it was time to have the discussion about London, we weren't terribly surprised they embraced it as much as they did, but we were really proud of them. Our oldest daughter was just beginning high school, our youngest, middle school, so it could have been a very tough transition. We never went through the "you ruined my life" tantrums that many of our new expat friends experienced.

Ghaffari: What it was like to be president of EMEA?

Beck: My one-word answer would be *astounding*. And the word that follows closely is *challenging*. When I took on that role, I represented three very distinct things to the leadership team in EMEA. Number one, I was an American. In the 2005 to 2006 timeframe, Americans were not wildly popular throughout Europe. Number two, I represented an executive from the corporate headquarters location. And this was a very proud, field-based organization that really enjoyed their autonomy. Number three, I was a woman. I was stepping into a leadership team that was very tenured and very male-dominated.

In addition, I was also taking on a business unit that had some immediate business challenges. When I stepped into the role, the business was producing approximately $5 billion in revenues, but profitability was far too low. Working through some changes in the leadership team, promoting from within, as well as bringing in some new talent, and introducing several new business models and ideas, within a three-year period, our leadership team grew revenues to almost $9 billion a year, and we doubled the profit percentage.

One of the most exciting aspects of the job was the breadth and depth of the position. We provided our business offerings to about thirty markets across a vast geography. On top of that, there were some specialty stand-alone businesses, like our IT staffing entity, that offered unique services across seventeen countries.

For five and a half years, I had the opportunity to travel extensively throughout Europe, the Middle East, South Africa, and Russia and was able to experience these cultures from the eyes of the locals. This afforded me a clear opportunity to embrace the need for what I describe as a "power-through" as opposed to a "power-over" style of leadership.

It was absolutely imperative, as I stepped into so many different countries, to understand the aspects of the culture that drove the behavior that I witnessed. Each culture is unique, and there is a tremendous amount of national pride. Understanding the nuances and the unique nature of every culture allowed a power-through leadership style to evolve. Collaboration, networking, and working through the individuals who were responsible for the businesses within their own countries—all of these factors became critically important.

Remember, in this timeframe there was a great deal of skepticism about Americans and American leadership. In many countries, there were expressions of outright anti-American sentiment, which required even more commitment to working through people, in collaboration, rather than trying to power over them. If you tried to overpower them, they would just shut down.

Ghaffari: Can you give me a specific example of this?

Beck: I'll give an example of a business offering that my team worked very diligently on requiring tremendous collaboration. Manpower is an employment services company, so the objective is to match people to jobs. Primarily, that means placing people into contingent work or temporary jobs, but, in addition, it's also helping people find full-time work and meaningful work. There were some real challenges in Europe in regards to the skills gap—in essence, how to match the right skills to the right job in the right place at the right time. Despite high unemployment in most countries, many jobs remain unfilled due to a skills mismatch. Europe will continue to experience this gap as the rapid aging of the population changes the underlying demographics. One solution would allow for the migration of workers with particular skills to locate where those skills were required.

Therefore, my team worked in collaboration across multiple countries to identify where skill gaps existed and where workers with those particular skills were located. We coordinated with multiple entities to migrate large numbers of people from one country to the next, to get the right skills to the right place. Whether migrating engineers to Norway where the engineering unemployment rate was 0 percent or sending butchers to Scandinavia, it was a prime example of "power through." We were required to work across cultures, borders, industries, local employers, governments, and licensing bodies to ensure that groups of skilled workers were migrated across countries—creating a solution that worked for all sides of the equation.

Ghaffari: During this later period as president of Manpower EMEA, you started to take on some outside, but complementary, roles and responsibilities. Can you tell me a little about these?

Beck: Yes. It was during the timeframe that I was offered the opportunity to serve on the Ecolab board of directors. I've been there since 2008, specifically as a member of the finance committee and the compensation committee.

In addition, I was introduced to some very powerful nonprofit organizations that happen to specialize in an area of passion for me —empowerment of women and enabling women and girls across the globe to reach their aspirations.

Ghaffari: Which ones came first, and how did you get connected to those?

Beck: As a member of the Manpower executive team, I began attending the annual meeting of the World Economic Forum beginning in 2005. The WEF takes place each January in an idyllic Alpine ski village in Davos, Switzerland. It's a remarkable forum that brings together the world's top business leaders, economists, government and educational leaders. My role at Davos each year was to represent the impact of current labor trends on economies across the globe. Through my work at the World Economic Forum, I was exposed to many prominent leaders who subsequently would offer me opportunities to engage in board work.

In 2007, I was named to the advisory board of the World Economic Forum's Women Leaders Programme, which is dedicated to establishing strategies that address women's issues on a global basis.[1] Through Davos, I had the opportunity to spend time with some of the leaders of The Women's Leadership Board[2] at Harvard University's John F. Kennedy School of Government and was invited to join the WLB as a member. Also, at the World Economic Forum, I engaged in a panel discussion with Tony Blair's wife, Cherie, just at the time she was launching the Cherie Blair Foundation,[3] and she invited me to join her advisory council.

So, really, Davos was the launching pad for a lot of the philanthropic and board work that I embraced, starting around the 2007 and 2008 timeframe, all linked toward the common goal of improving the lives of women and girls across the globe.

Ghaffari: How did you get the nomination to the Ecolab board?

Beck: I was recruited by a corporate board search firm. Ecolab was searching for a board candidate who was currently serving in a global operational

---

[1] Through the Women Leaders and Gender Parity Programme, the World Economic Forum advances women's leadership and efforts to close the global gender gap. See www.weforum.org/women-leaders-and-gender-parity.

[2] The Women's Leadership Board is a body of 150 corporate and individual members and influential leaders advancing issues related to women at the Harvard Kennedy School and throughout the world. See www.hkswomensleadershipboard.org/

[3] The Cherie Blair Foundation for Women, founded in September 2008, invests in and mentors women entrepreneurs, primarily in Africa, the Middle East, and South Asia. See www.cherieblairfoundation.org/

role because they were rapidly expanding throughout Europe, the Middle East, and Africa. At the time, I was the in the Manpower EMEA role. So I was recruited to bring some additional global perspective to their board of directors.

Ghaffari: How did you happen to return to early childhood education at the Learning Care Group?

Beck: I received a prompt from a recruiter in late 2010. The nature of the CEO position at the Learning Care Group was intriguing to me precisely because it was in early childhood education. My expat assignment in Europe was coming to an end, so the timing was literally divine. Since my undergraduate degree was in elementary education, and the timing was perfect for a change, I began a very quick interview process for the job, accepted the position, and started my role here, March 1, 2011.

Ghaffari: Do you know where the headhunter learned about you, or had you had earlier contact with the search firm?

Beck: I had not worked with this particular search firm in the past, so I asked that very question myself. It turned out to be a combination of my particular experience and recommendations from their network of executives.

Ghaffari: Did you bring your family back home to the Midwest?

Beck: Actually, even when we relocated to London, we never gave up our home in Wisconsin. We had made a commitment to our daughters that they could return from London and graduate from their US high school if they chose. In my third year in EMEA, my husband and daughters relocated back to our Wisconsin home so the girls could graduate in the US. During that timeframe, I did a reverse commute from London. So when the LCG position was offered, I already had a home base back in the US.

As I said earlier, relocation/commuting have been a part of my experience from the very beginning of my life, and I take it in stride. Nevertheless, it's not until I conduct an interview, answering questions like these, that I realize how prevalent it's been. Geographic flexibility truly has been a defining experience. Had I not agreed to many relocations, I'm certain my career would be entirely different than it is today.

Ghaffari: Are your daughters in college now?

Beck: Yes. My life has gone full circle in many ways. Both of my daughters chose to attend the University of Colorado in Boulder. They are both in Boulder now. My oldest is a junior, and my youngest is a freshman. The travel bug and the embracing of change are well-ingrained in both of them.

My oldest daughter will be heading off to Paris next semester to study abroad.

Ghaffari: You went to get some advanced executive education at both IN-SEAD[4] and the University of Chicago. What persuaded you to do that?

Beck: I recognized that I needed and wanted some formal executive development. INSEAD in Fontainebleau, France, was very geared toward conducting business in a global economy and provided me some great insights into global business strategies. Over the course of five years, I attended three separate INSEAD courses.

There was another weeklong course offered by the University of Chicago covering advanced financial management for senior executives—an area that I felt would enhance my performance.

As I said, I'm very passionate about lifelong learning and training. When I was named to the Ecolab board, I took the opportunity to attend Harvard's board of directors training and received board certification from a course that was directly oriented toward corporate board directors.

Another very interesting program was offered by Yale University in their School of Management—the Leadership Exchange and Analysis Program[5]—which focused on enhancing leadership skills. The course was for senior executives who aspired to be CEOs at some point in their career. It was led by Jeffrey Sonnenfeld, the associate dean of business at Yale. It was truly a wonderful experience to attend a course with fellow C-level executives from across the country—representing different segments, different industries, different companies—and to focus on senior executive leadership skills, case studies, and enhancing those skills.

The Yale experience came in 2004, close to the end of my role as executive vice president of Manpower's US and Canada business unit. The LEAP curriculum was followed by a very interesting two-day forum where CEOs from across the country gathered and spoke in a very open dialog about their current businesses and how they addressed and overcame the challenges they faced. The CEOs had the opportunity to ask questions of each other, as well as seek and give each other advice. Those of us who had attended the LEAP program were allowed to listen in on those discussions.

---

[4] INSEAD stands for Institut Européen d'Administration des Affaires, which translates to the European Institute of Business Administration. It is an international, graduate business school and research institution.

[5] LEAP is now called The Chief Executive Leadership Institute at the Yale School of Management. See http://celi.som.yale.edu.

That course provided me the opportunity to think about my own personal goals, objectives, and aspirations. It solidified my personal commitment to aspire to a CEO-level position at the right time in my career.

Ghaffari: What aspect of the course or the experience inspired you in that way?

Beck: The interaction with the other CEOs. It became apparent to me that I needed global experience. In my own mind, in order to be an effective CEO, I needed to become a truly global executive, going beyond merely conducting business from an American base. I began to understand how I could greatly enhance my skills if I actually lived overseas, became an expat, and ran, at the ground level, a non-American business unit. So the Yale experience was very important to me, first, by affirming to me that I needed a genuine international assignment and, second, by confirming to me that—at the end of an international assignment—I would feel more confident and prepared to take on a CEO role. That is exactly how things evolved.

Ghaffari: When you saw the opportunity as CEO of Learning Care, did you in any way connect this position with the discussions that you might have had about employees' searches for childcare options, childcare services, and businesses' challenge of keeping women in the pipeline?

Beck: I think you've summed it up beautifully. Having been a working mom for my entire executive career, I understood the unique challenges that parents go through trying to fulfill the needs of their family, the needs of their children's educational experience, as well as the needs of their career. So when I was headhunted for the CEO position, first, it appealed to my very early desire to be in early childhood education. Second, it was a subject matter or life issue that I had experienced firsthand and knew very well. Third, it was an opportunity to fulfill one of my own personal goals, which was to lead a company at the CEO level. Once I began the CEO role, I've had an opportunity to spend a significant amount of time in our schools across the country and see, firsthand, the positive impact we have on the children we serve and their families.

Learning Care Group[6] has five different brands in thirty-six states and three countries. We are the parent company for La Petite Academy, Montessori Unlimited, Tutor Time, Childtime, and the Children's Courtyard. We have 1,035 schools across the US or 1,050 schools system-wide, including corporate-owned and franchises. Within those schools, we have the capacity to serve, to touch, to interact with, and to care for 156,000 children each year.

---

[6] For more information, see www.learningcaregroup.com.

Tutor Time is the brand within our portfolio that was built upon a franchise model. The schools located in Hong Kong, Indonesia, and Portugal are within the franchised community.

This position links together my commitment to early childhood education with my passion for lifelong learning. At its very core, this job is an opportunity to instill a love of learning in the minds and hearts of thousands of children across the country. The more time I spend in the field, visiting different schools and spending significant amounts of time with our field-based organizations, the more passion I discover out there—teachers' love for education and our staff's love for the children.

This goes well beyond just day care centers for kids—our schools are early childhood learning centers. The strong focus on curriculum appeals to me personally based on my educational roots, on my own background, and my own personal passion for learning.

Ghaffari: I read about the Journey Curriculum offered by La Petite Academy. Is that applied across other brands or is it a unique curriculum offered only within La Petite Academy?

Beck: Each brand has a unique curriculum, each based upon different philosophies. The Montessori Unlimited curriculum is based on Dr. Montessori's methods of self-motivated learning. The La Petite Academy has the Journey Curriculum, which provides a holistic approach to supporting children's learning and development, based on developmentally appropriate objectives. The Children's Courtyard are beautiful campuses located throughout Texas, which offer a curriculum that's specifically oriented to the High/Scope model. Tutor Time has the LifeSmart curriculum, which is framed by the theory of multiple intelligences and based on the concept that all children are smart in their own way and the learning evolves based on that premise. Childtime Learning Centers—which is derived from Gerber's program, one of the earliest—offers the Empowered Child curriculum, based on the Reggio Emilia approach, providing preschool-age children with both guidance and freedom to acquire knowledge in ways most meaningful to them.

Ghaffari: It's not unlike what you did for EMEA and unique cultures, is it?

Beck: Exactly. Each brand has its own unique culture. Additionally, we are constantly evaluating the portfolio to determine if schools remain in the appropriate location, based on demographics. For example, in Southern California in particular, we have a significant number of La Petite Academies, our dominant brand in California. Based on our very specific demographic studies, we evaluate where opportunities might arise, where we might have new growth potential, to determine where schools would best be located.

We do demographic studies as leases expire on the buildings. So, we may discover that a school is located in an area that fifteen years ago had a very large population of families living within a three-mile radius, but, today, that concentration of families may no longer be the case. That may present an opportunity to not renew the lease in that location, but instead relocate to a different area with young families. Our existing children still attending the original school could be migrated to a school we have in the vicinity.

Ghaffari: Have you centralized the demographic analytic capability?

Beck: Yes, we have some very talented people in the Learning Care Group corporate office, here in Novi, Michigan. They spend a significant amount of time looking at demographics, down to the per-school basis for the entire portfolio across the country.

Ghaffari: One way to identify your schools is as either corporate-owned or franchised.

Beck: Yes, the portfolio is dominated by corporate-owned schools, but there are still Tutor Time centers, which are franchises owned by others.

Ghaffari: You also have schools that are located within a company, hospital, university, or government entity.

Beck: Yes. A number of centers or schools are co-located or based on-site in particular facilities. The majority of the schools are in standalone buildings within the corporate-owned school portfolio.

Ghaffari: Can you give me the distribution between franchise vs. corporate-owned schools?

Beck: Approximately 65 of our 1,050 schools are franchise-owned.

Ghaffari: Do you see Learning Care Group taking the top position in terms of number of facilities and size of facilities?

Beck: We are working through a strategic planning process right now, and part of that is taking a look at where we'd like to be in the next one, three, and five years. I think it's safe to say that any company would like to be in the number-one position within their industry, within their sector. So let me just say that we have a very talented group of people who see some opportunities for expansion and growth.

Ghaffari: How many direct reports do you have?

Beck: Learning Care Group has a typical executive structure, meaning the primary disciplines of the business report directly to the chief executive officer. These include leaders of finance, operations, marketing, human resources, legal, and technology.

Ghaffari: How many of those are women?

Beck: I'm very proud that the majority of the employees—over 90 percent—in the LCG organization are women, and women are fully represented at the C-level. The chief operating officer, chief marketing officer, and the chief executive officer are all woman. The chief financial officer, chief human resources officer, chief information officer, and legal officer are men.

Ghaffari: A certain portion of the company was sold off to Morgan Stanley Private Equity. Is that still the case?

Beck: Yes, Morgan Stanley Private Equity is the majority owner of the company. I report directly to Jim Howland, managing director of MSPE and chairman of LCG. Additionally, Jim was interim CEO for almost a year before I joined the company.

Ghaffari: Does MS Private Equity get closely involved in the operations?

Beck: As appropriate. Jim has a lot of faith in management to run the day-to-day operation. I find it extremely helpful that he understands the business and the company to the extent he does due to his stint as interim CEO. His insight was very helpful to me as I moved into the CEO position.

Ghaffari: Can you give me a sense for any of the bosses or mentors that have had the biggest impact on you?

Beck: Early in my career, going back to my time at Sprint, I was working within the national sales organization and had an opportunity to directly report to the president of Sprint Business, Patti Manuel, now Patti Hart. She promoted me into my first executive position in 1996. Patti demonstrated that she was courageous enough to reach into the organization, a very male-dominated company, to identify high potential women who would benefit from specific areas of training and experience in order to be considered for more senior executive positions someday. Quietly, behind the scenes and over a period of time, she worked with other executives in the company to identify a number of women across the organization that she felt should be given an opportunity to take on increasing levels of responsibility.

All of that was unbeknownst to me. My first true interaction with her was in 1996 when I was interviewing for my first vice president–level position. The interview process for the VP position was extensive, involving five different executives who had to weigh in on the decision. Once I was selected for the role and began reporting directly to her, she became a true mentor with whom I had more regular interaction. I actually worked directly for her for only a year. She was then promoted and became my boss's boss. After a couple years, she left Sprint for a CEO role in the Silicon Valley.

Patti has served an interesting role in my life. Number one, she inspired me to identify and assist talented people, both men and women, and move them to areas where they can gain different experience and broaden their skills. Number two, her leadership style was very much about "power through"—relying on collaboration and networking. That style was a natural for me and laid the foundation for the leadership style I would use throughout my career.

Number three, Patti has always been ahead of me in my career, and I think it's important for everyone to have a mentor in their life who actually precedes them in taking a leap, whether it's leaving the company, taking on a promotional opportunity, or staying within the company and taking on more responsibilities. It's wonderful to have someone whom you can look to and who carves out a path that allows you to decide if that's a path that's appropriate for you. After Sprint, Patti took on CEO roles of both publicly traded and privately held companies. She accepted board roles and built an incredible network of business leaders. Over the years, I've felt free to speak with her about those experiences, and it's been a helpful way for me to define very specifically what I aspire to and what is right for me. Our friendship and our interaction continue to this very day.

Ghaffari: How would you describe your own decision-making style?

Beck: Fact-based and timely, by relying on input from those most knowledgeable about the topic.

Ghaffari: Does your corporate strategy include a succession-planning strategy within the organization?

Beck: Definitely yes. I've learned throughout my executive career that a business strategy must be married to a talent strategy. And succession planning is an important component of that. When the team builds a five-year strategic plan, we also have to ask, "What are the skills and positions required to deliver against that strategy?" It's a separate, extensive exercise to go through the existing talent of the organization and inventory what skills exist, what skills are needed, what are the gaps between those two, and how we are going to develop our existing team to bridge that gap. Will there be a need for any outside expertise to come into the company to make certain that we have what we need to deliver against the strategy? So, the two processes operate in parallel, if you will. One is defining, "Here is where we are today. Where do we want to go over the next one, three, and five years?" And then there's the separate, tandem exercise that says, "Okay, now let's take a look at the talent. Do we have what we need? Are there gaps? How are we going to fill those gaps? And let's make certain that we're confident that our talent can actually achieve what we're setting out in this strategy."

Ghaffari: How do you define your personal success?

Beck: Achievement of my goals. I think a fundamental reason for any success we've experienced as a family is that we have embraced opportunities and change. That is coupled with a wonderful open relationship with my husband and daughters, who are equally as flexible and willing to take on change.

We've actually talked about this as a family. We feel incredibly blessed. We've had this great experience and an incredible life. Especially now that my girls have gone off to college, we reflect on the eighteen years that they lived at home. Our experience has been just so broad and deep—we've had a very big life. I genuinely believe that the reason for that success is that we've been open to, and embraced, change—we've said "yes" when opportunities came our way. And, honestly, our life has been incredibly enhanced because of that.

Ghaffari: What do you see yourself doing over the next five to ten years?

Beck: I certainly hope I'll continue in my CEO role while serving on boards. Retirement will entail a combination of corporate board work and philanthropy.

Ghaffari: As you look out at the marketplace today for young professional women, where do you see the greatest opportunities for them?

Beck: This is a very tough job market. And I talk to many young women. Having a daughter who is a junior in college, I speak to a lot of her friends, and I'm increasingly concerned at the perception that our college students have today about their prospects and their future. There's a lot of fear about this job market and where they will find opportunity.

The advice that I give to these kids as we're having these conversations is that there are opportunities throughout the world for individuals who are willing to take entry-level positions and work very hard, prove themselves, and remain flexible. Be willing to go where the jobs are. There are jobs, but it doesn't necessarily mean that your first job is going to be exactly where you want it, in the exact company that you want. I'm a big advocate of students working in their college years toward internships. I really encourage them to just get the experience—it doesn't matter if they're paid or not. Take it. Try it. These days, you have to work really hard to package yourself and sell yourself.

And I also encourage young women graduating from college to consider sales as a starting point. One of the benefits of sales is that it brings a whole wealth of understanding about the business, overall. It's also a real confidence booster. It is a tough job, but a great way to learn to push yourself out of your comfort zone. Once you actually master the art of sales, you can apply it to every aspect of your career.

Another important piece of advice that I find myself giving to women at all stages of their career: at some point, take on a role that allows you responsibility for the profit and loss of a business unit.

One area where the perception of women's skills is misunderstood is their ability to take on roles that require strong knowledge of finances and financial statements. Running your own P&L business segment demonstrates that you understand the financial aspects of the corporation. It allows women a chance to show they can deliver results. When it comes time to assess women for senior-level executive positions, the biggest challenge they face is whether or not they've ever had P&L experience. If the answer is "no," women will not be in line for executive-level promotions.

When it comes to C-level positions, it's imperative that there is an understanding of financial reporting and the financial aspects of running a business. For women who aspire to sit on boards of directors for publicly or privately held companies, there is always a requirement that the financial aspects of a business be understood and that there is a track record of demonstrating ability for the full P&L of the business unit.

Ghaffari: Do you think there's any difference in the advice that should be given to men vs. women?

Beck: As you know from the statistics, a slightly higher percentage of women are graduating from college now compared to men. There is one area that women need to hear some very specific advice and that is demanding what you're worth during the interview process for a new role. Study after study has shown that women are far more likely to accept the first financial number thrown on the table when being offered a job, whereas men tend to demand more and negotiate for a higher starting rate. Pay equity is still a very real issue, and there's still a gap, as many studies have shown. Women, especially those graduating from college, must have the confidence to negotiate. If you're not comfortable negotiating, go take a class—because I think the ability to get what you deserve is critical. I would like to see women stronger in that area.

I also think that women have to stop selling themselves short. I'll give you a real example that has happened many times in my career. I offer a woman a promotion—a significant promotion, one that I wouldn't be offering her if I didn't know that she was extremely qualified. I have full confidence that she could do the job, and I assume she will be wildly successful. Numerous times women have looked at me and said, "Oh, I don't think I'm ready for that. I don't think I should take that promotion." I must tell you that, in my entire career, I have never offered a man a promotion that he didn't accept on the spot. So yes, I do think that women need to be very comfortable in asking for what they deserve and accepting opportunity when it is provided to them.

Finally, I'm going to repeat the message that has pervaded this conversation. That is the topic of women being open to relocation. I *know* it can be hard, very impactful on family lives, for all the reasons that you heard in my own background. I did have one point in time when I chose not to relocate. But, the majority of the time, I have said "yes" to a relocation offer, and it's always resulted not only in a wonderful promotion but also in a life-altering and enriching experience.

Ghaffari: Do you think Learning Care Group is helping young women to develop more confidence and to be willing to take on a little more risk if they have greater confidence? Is that part of the curriculum?

Beck: We are absolutely fostering self-confidence. We serve children from the age of six weeks to twelve years. We are very focused through our curriculum on building self-esteem, self-awareness, and self-confidence, and—over and above all else—instilling a love of education. If we do our job properly, we will have inspired children to want to learn for the rest of their lives.

Ghaffari: Maybe not this year, but for the long term, whatever president gets into office, if they knocked on your door and said, "I want you to initiate some leadership programs for K-through-12 children to help American children better prepare themselves for the future," is that an opportunity that you would say yes to?

Beck: That's a great question. I would welcome the opportunity to impact the educational needs of kids in America. I'm going to stop short of saying that I would take a particular role or take a particular job, but I will emphasize that I'm extremely passionate about education, and I'm extremely focused on inspiring lifelong learning because I do worry about the current state of the American school system.

We've talked at length about the important work that is being done in forums such as the World Economic Forum, the Clinton Initiative, and the work that Bill and Melinda Gates are doing through their foundation right now. There is a tremendous emphasis on what is happening in the American school system. But, the results are that our test scores are falling, our competitive edge is falling, and our rankings in the world are falling. So, anything that I could do through my current role or personally to help improve that situation, I would welcome.

Jeanette Horan

Chief Information Officer, IBM

Born 1955 in Dover, England.

Jeanette Horan is CIO of IBM, a position she has held since May 2011. She has been a leader at IBM since 1998, when she began taking on portfolios of responsibility at the vice president level. She was in charge of development of the Lotus brand (1998–2002), followed by strategy for the Software Group (2003–2004), and then information management (2004–2006). She became vice president of Business Process and Architecture Integration (2006–2007) and then headed Enterprise Business Transformation (through April 2011).

Before coming to IBM, Ms. Horan was vice president of the Software Group and the AltaVista business unit at Digital Equipment Corporation (DEC; 1994–1998). She was also vice president of Development and Engineering at the Open Software Foundation (1989–1994).

Ms. Horan has been a member of the board of directors of MicroVision in Redmond, Washington, since July 2006 and serves on the Audit and Compensation Committees. She is also in great demand as a keynote speaker and expert on corporate IT, CIO strategies and responsibilities, and women in leadership topics. Recent speaking engagements have included the CIO Executive Leadership Summit in Greenwich, Connecticut; the CIO Executive Summit in Dallas, Texas; the Global Women's International Networking Conference in Rome, Italy; Canada's Government Technology Exhibition and Conference in Ottawa, Canada; and Forrester Research's CIO-CMO Forum in Boston, Massachusetts to mention just a few recent examples.

In her early career, Ms. Horan worked for EMI (1976–1979), Singer-Link (1979–1981), and Gould Computer Systems (1981–1989).

Ms. Horan received an MBA from Boston University's School of Management Executive Education Program (1993) and a BS in mathematics from the University of London (1976).

Elizabeth Ghaffari: Can you tell me a little about your family—your parents and siblings?

Jeanette Horan: I grew up in the south of England where my parents both grew up. My father was a sales manager and my mother was a bookkeeper. I have one brother and one sister.

Ghaffari: You pursued a bachelor's of mathematics at the University of London. What were some of the factors that might have influenced your interest in math?

Horan: I knew I was good at math and that I enjoyed it. It's probably accurate to say that I didn't know any better. I just decided it was a good grounding for any career that I might want to go into subsequently.

When I was at high school, I had something of a natural aptitude for math, and it happened that the headmistress of our school was a math teacher herself, so she was very encouraging to those with that aptitude.

Ghaffari: Any particular reason why you chose to attend University of London?

Horan: The higher-education application process in England has you select and prioritize six places in which you're interested. Different colleges specialize in different fields. I went to Royal Holloway College, within the University of London, which was known for math, music, history, and zoology. It is an interesting mix.

Ghaffari: Did you have interest beyond math?

Horan: No, I did three straight years of math classes, graduating in 1976.

Ghaffari: What was your first job?

Horan: I went to work for EMI, which you may know as a music company. I got the job through what they fondly call in England the "milk round," which is when companies come on campus to recruit. At the time, EMI was much more of an industrial conglomerate. I was hired by their central research lab to work on medical ultrasound research doing digital signal processing.

I liked the field because it gave me my first substantive exposure to computers. Up until then, my experience with computers in college meant getting a bunch of punch cards and handing them over to the data center people. The work at EMI was much more hands-on, using minicomputers and working at the assembler language level. That's where I first became interested in the whole field of computer technology and in technology applications.

I stayed at EMI for only two and a half years, because they were going through a lot of business changes and had concluded that they did not want to stay in this area. I started to look around and spotted an advert in one of the computer papers for a company called Singer-Link, which built flight simulators used to train pilots. That was a huge amount of fun. My work there had a lot to do with keeping the systems operational in real time. The technology of the day was the 16-bit PDP11 from Digital Equipment Corporation, which had a very small amount of memory. That presented a pretty interesting set of technical challenges.

I was at Singer-Link from early 1979 until late 1981. I began working on systems from a company called Gould Computer Systems—one of the minicomputer manufacturers that was very strong in the real-time space. I developed a good understanding of their operating systems and core technologies and ended up moving to the United States to work for Gould.

That was an important turning point in my life.

Ghaffari: How long were you with Gould and why was it a transition?

Horan: I worked for Gould from 1981 to 1989. There were two things that made that period significant for me. One was that my two daughters were born during that time. The other thing was that I got my first management position. Gould was a company big enough to have a good management training and education program. I was very lucky to get that kind of exposure during a formative part of my career.

Ghaffari: Why do you think Gould thought you were good management material?

Horan: I had been in project leadership positions, but without the people management decisions. By the time I was promoted to my first management position, the company was growing very rapidly, expanding and hiring new people. I had developed or demonstrated some leadership capabilities through those project leadership experiences.

Ghaffari: Where did you meet your husband? When were your girls born?

Horan: I met my husband when I was working at Singer-Link in England. We worked in the same field. My daughters were born in 1983 and 1985, while I worked at Gould. They're now both PhD students. One is studying advanced developmental psychology, while the other one is in pure mathematics, doing research sponsored by the federal government.

Ghaffari: Family considerations were included in your decision to relocate to Cambridge, Massachusetts. Is that correct?

Horan: Yes, that's correct. Toward the end of 1989, Gould was sold to a Japanese company, and the Computer Systems Division was spun off due to the amount of federal government contract work. There was a lot of churn in the organization. My oldest daughter was just starting the first grade, and we decided that it was probably a good time to make a move both professionally and personally.

It happened that the same manager, Roger Gourd, who had hired me at Gould to relocate to the US from England, had left Gould, done some other work, and then ended up at the Open Software Foundation [OSF][1] in Cambridge, Massachusetts. He recruited me to work for him, and my family relocated to Sudbury, Massachusetts.

Ghaffari: Do you consider Roger Gourd a mentor?

Horan: Yes, very definitely. Even after I left OSF, he still was somebody that I would go to for different kinds of advice at different points in time. I'd ask his advice on career choices or job changes. I consider him a good friend, as well.

After I left OSF, I went to work for Digital Equipment Corporation at a time when they appeared to have hit bottom and were bouncing back up, but then they took another downturn. I ended up leaving when Compaq acquired them. That was a very rocky period. It was very good to have somebody like Roger to whom I could talk about both the choices I was making around options within Digital and about my ultimate decision to leave.

Ghaffari: You were an engineering vice president and then a development vice president at OSF. What did those jobs entail?

Horan: They were primarily product development roles. The work included everything from development of strategy; for example, making decisions about what kinds of product we were going to build, what features would be

---

[1] Open Software Foundation (OSF) was founded in 1988 to create an open standard for implementation of the UNIX operating system.

included, and what the capabilities would be to delivery of the final product. And finally, figuring out how we'd deliver those products to market.

Ghaffari: How large a staff did you have?

Horan: When I was at Gould, I had a staff of about 150 people. When I was at the Open Software Foundation, it was about 300 people.

Ghaffari: Was OSF a not-for-profit entity?

Horan: Yes, OSF was an organization sponsored by a number of big companies in the industry. The business model is a shared R&D center, where several big companies were investing because they all wanted to use the same kind of technology, and it wasn't something that they expected they were going to compete on. That structure provided a way to amortize the R&D cost across several different companies. It was quite a visionary concept and in many ways a precursor to today's "open source software movement"—a way of sharing and disseminating knowledge. The idea has had its successes and its challenges as a business model.

Ghaffari: What is the story behind your move to Digital?

Horan: As I moved up into senior leadership roles at OSF, I began to realize that I was sitting at the table more and more with marketing, finance, and sales people, and not just other engineering people. I also began to realize that up to this point, I had been focused on engineering and that my knowledge was very deep, but also narrow. I decided I wanted to understand more about business, and so went for my MBA—an executive MBA at Boston University.

While in that program, a friend and classmate told me her husband was a vice president at Digital. He said to me, "If you ever decide you want to move, give me a call and come join Digital." I thought it would be interesting to figure out how to operate in a larger company. Most of the companies where I'd worked before were relatively small. Digital, at that point, had about 125,000 employees. So, I took him up on his offer to arrange an introduction to Digital.

I stayed at Digital from April 1994 to May 1998, four years during which I had three different jobs and seven different bosses. I was a vice president in charge of the Software Group Strategy and then development for the AltaVista business unit. Those were the very early days of the internet. Digital had an e-mail product, a firewall product, and several other products related to the internet, including the search engine, all in the AltaVista business unit. The search engine became most closely linked to the AltaVista name.

It was a very tumultuous period in Digital's history, which culminated in the sale of the company to Compaq Computer Company in 1998.

Ghaffari: Did you observe that there were many women along the way in your career in technology?

Horan: Now, that's a really interesting question. Early on, no—there were very few women. When I was at EMI, there were two women in a research department of about fifty people. At Singer-Link, I think were four women among a staff of one hundred. So in both cases women were about 4 percent of the technical workforce in that department. When I came to the US, there were more, but it was still pretty small as a percentage.

Beginning with OSF, I noticed that there were beginning to be more women on staff, as well as women in management and leadership roles. I'm not sure whether that says something about Massachusetts or the fact that it was a collaborative environment or whether it was just the time and the place.

By the time I was at DEC, it just didn't seem to be as big an issue anymore. Progress was beginning to emerge.

Ghaffari: After Digital sold itself to Compaq, how did you make the transition to IBM?

Horan: I had been introduced by a friend to some of the people who were leaders in an organization called Iris Associates,[2] the wholly owned subsidiary of Lotus Development Corporation. When Lotus was looking for a new vice president to run some departments of their organization, the people at Iris introduced me to Lotus, saying, "You should talk to Jeanette."

I wasn't actively out looking for a job. That was just before the acquisition of DEC by Compaq, so I was receptive to an opportunity and then decided to join.

There were a couple of things that interested me. To be honest, on the personal front, the job meant I could continue to live in the same place. I didn't have to move again, which was attractive to me since my children would not have to uproot themselves from school. Also, I was absolutely intrigued by the products, which presented a whole new paradigm about collaboration with Lotus Notes and Domino among other software developments. It was very appealing to me from a technology perspective. I became vice president

---

[2] Iris Associates was a software development company founded in late 1984 by Ray Ozzie to build the collaborative "groupware" and e-mail software product known as Lotus Notes. IBM purchased Lotus in 1995.

of Development of IBM in charge of the Lotus brand and led worldwide product management, development, and technical support.

Ghaffari: You made quite a progression from nuts-and-bolts software engineering to strategic software development. How did that transformation happen?

Horan: Yes, it's interesting that I started out truly working on the bits and bytes of computers. Then I moved into operating systems and device drivers, which still were close to the hardware. AltaVista and Lotus Notes were more collaborative tools—information resources that allowed for searching and sharing across departments and, ultimately, companies. I definitely started to see possibilities—I think it was the advent of the internet that started me thinking, "Wait a minute. There's a whole new proposition here and some interesting opportunities to explore new areas."

Ghaffari: Tell me how your people management responsibilities grew.

Horan: At Lotus, from May 1998 to December 2002, I had about three thousand people. I had all of product development and the technical support organization—all the people you call on the phone if you have a technical product question. The following year, I became vice president of strategy for the IBM Software Group. As vice president of all information management, over the next two and a half years, I was responsible for a staff of about four thousand people.

These were global roles. As the teams became more and more distributed, I had product development teams in China, Germany, and Canada, as well as throughout the US.

Ghaffari: So how did you feel about that international demand on your time and your physical stamina?

Horan: I actually found it to be great. I felt energized by having teams all over the place. Obviously, it made it tougher to manage a family if you're traveling that much, but it was something that we figured out how to work through, and everybody understood that it was something that was important. So, that's what we did.

Ghaffari: What are some of the key things you did to work that out, would you say?

Horan: Well, living three thousand miles away from my own family in the UK meant that I didn't have that kind of close-knit support network. But, my husband and I would figure out mutual travel schedules. If I had to go somewhere, was he going somewhere? And how would we manage that? I did have a small network of friends whom we could call upon in an absolute emergency, and we had a nanny until my eldest daughter was fourteen years old. By that time, she was much more of a chauffeur than a nanny. I think you have to build your own kind of support network in order to be able to manage that kind of work.

Ghaffari: After about eight years, you moved into what they call enterprise business transformation. How would you describe that?

Horan: This was a role working for the IBM CIO. One of the things that the CIO does is not just manage data centers and the technology, but at IBM, we actually call it business transformation and information technology. That role requires working with both operations and the business to understand what the corporate strategy is and how we will implement the IT systems and the business processes supported by the IT systems.

When I moved into that role, our corporate strategy was evolving quite a bit. IBM had divested itself of commodity products, such as the ThinkPads and PCs, in order to move forward. We acquired a lot more software companies. We'd bought PricewaterhouseCooper's Consulting, which took us into a whole new services business. There was a genuine need to make changes to our business processes to be able to support that new corporate strategy. So my role, first, was to help our senior executives understand our current limitations and why we needed to make a change. Then, having convinced them that we needed to do something different, they said, "Okay, that's great. Now, you go run the project to actually do that."

When I came into that role, I thought I was going to do my eighteen-month tour through corporate that everybody in a large company has to do. Then I thought I'd just go back to a role in a business unit. I've been here five years, now, and I absolutely love it. It's great.

Ghaffari: Did you pursue the role of the CIO?

Horan: As a part of my enterprise business transformation role, we were deploying a re-implementation of SAP,[3] which was our core ERP system. We'd been a customer of SAP for a long time, but we decided that a re-implementation and expansion of the SAP footprint would better support our corporate strategy. I was leading that project, which went live with our

---

[3] SAP is an international company based in Germany that provides business management software, solutions and services—most prominently ERP (enterprise resource planning) software that firms use to manage and integrate multiple sources of management information including finance, accounting, manufacturing, sales and service, and customer relationship management.

first rollout in China at the beginning of 2011. Right after that, Pat Toole, who was CIO at the time, was asked to become a general manager in IBM's Global Technology Services. With the success of the project rollout and my knowledge of what was happening within IBM's IT environment, the decision was made to offer me a promotion into the job of the CIO.

IBM does a very good job about career and succession planning. I had had discussions over the past five years with Linda Sanford, who is senior vice president for Enterprise Transformation at IBM and to whom I report now. She had asked me if the CIO role was something that would ever interest me, to which I answered, "yes."

Ghaffari: Would you consider Linda Sanford a mentor?

Horan: Yes, very definitely. IBM is a very large, complex operation. I think having somebody who can help you understand the background, nuances, and how to navigate this kind of organization is very helpful. I'm somewhat unusual in that I'm not an IBM exec who spent my whole career here. Many executives have been at IBM their entire career and grew up knowing who's who and where the important opportunities are situated. So, having someone who can help with that navigation is invaluable.

Ghaffari: You've been on this job just a few months. How is it different from what you were doing before?

Horan: Let me try to answer that in a couple of ways. That one transformation program that I was running before—it was called Blue Harmony—was possibly one of the most complex and strategic projects that IBM has ever undertaken. I've spent the last three years focused on it—a very large and complex project. Every day, I'd get up and think, "What's happening with the Blue Harmony project today?" By design, I had a relatively small staff—about fifty people on my direct team out of a total project team of about fifteen hundred people in a very matrixed structure.

Now, in this new position, I still have responsibility for that project, but it's now one project in a very large portfolio. I have responsibility for a lot more things as well. I have full responsibility to make sure that all of IBM's IT systems are up and running. The scope of my responsibility is much, much broader. Today, I can have twelve different meetings on separate and individual projects. The content switching is really quite incredible.

My direct staff today comes to about five thousand people, so I'm now managing much larger teams and all of the processes that go along with that increase. About 60 percent of my staff is located in the US, with 40 percent located all around the world.

Ghaffari: Do you still do a lot of traveling?

Horan: That is accurate. Something else that's interesting about this job, and I imagine it's unique for a CIO, is that I spend about 30 percent of my time with IBM clients because we are in the business of IT. Many of our clients want to know if "we are eating our own cooking"—are we deploying the same technologies or new services inside IBM that we are selling to our clients. That produces a fair amount of travel.

Ghaffari: What would you say were the most significant turning points in your career, as you look back over all the changes?

Horan: Obviously, the decision to come to the US was very definitely a significant turning point. It began as a tentative decision. We said, "Maybe we'll go for two years and then see if we like it." We never went back. That was a very big decision for me.

I think that had I stayed in the UK and wanted to have children, I probably would not have kept working because I don't think that was as socially acceptable in England at that time. The quality day care that would be needed just wasn't available there. So, that's one reason why that was a huge turning point for me.

Another big turning point was the decision to stay at IBM. For most of my career, I had worked for about four years and then moved on. At the time I was having my children, I stayed at the firm for eight years. When I came to IBM, I fully expected that I'd be here for about four years and then would move on. But once I got to know the company, I realized that you could do a variety of interesting things all within the context of this one large company without having to leave for somewhere else. I think that was probably another really big turning point for me.

Ghaffari: Anything keep you up at night? Was there anything that might have persuaded you to think of quitting? What kept you going during some of those tough times?

Horan: I will say that working full-time in a demanding career with two toddlers is not easy. There definitely was a period there when I seriously thought about working part-time or even quitting for a while. Definitely, the toddler years were the toughest just because of the physical demands from them. But, then I got a promotion, so I said, "Well, maybe it's not the right time." I figured out how to plow through that challenge. Then, as the girls got a little older, they became more self-sufficient.

The other challenging time was at Digital, but that was a different type—it was corporate tumult. It was a tough time because I really didn't know where I was going or how I fit in. I've never been one to say, "Look. I'm just here for a paycheck." My job really has to have content, something that gets me up and excited in the morning. When Digital finally decided they were going to do something with the AltaVista business and the internet, then I was able to settle down and find another little niche for myself there. That was another tough period.

Ghaffari: You've mentioned quite a few very positive, collegial relationships at IBM. Do you see IBM as a place that helps women like yourself, with families, advance their career?

Horan: Yes, I definitely think that is the case. IBM provides a variety of benefits to women, including work-from-home options, benefits relating to access to resources, and help with finding day care–type things. The environment and culture of the company are very respectful of the individual. They understand that managing your work and your life are important and that if you're not happy in your home life, you probably will not be as productive as an employee. So the culture is very supportive from that perspective.

Also, I believe the company has definitely made a push for diversity groups in general—not just women, but other minorities as well. In the company's career and succession planning, I see a definite focus on ensuring that, when there are executive position openings, a diverse slate of candidates is presented. People truly are being given the opportunity to compete for leadership positions. I think that's definitely a positive part of the IBM culture.

Ghaffari: How did you come to be a director at MicroVision?

Horan: I was in San Jose, California, in 2006 when I got a call from some people I knew in Boston. They told me, "There's a small company that's looking for some new directors. They want to gain some diversity on their board, and they're looking for somebody in technology. Are you interested in meeting with them?"

At that time, a board seat wasn't really on my radar, but I was intrigued by the idea as well as the technology space of the company. MicroVision produces technology for "pico projectors,"[4] which envisions embedding a projector within a cell phone or another mobile device, so that you could project content onto a wall or a flat screen to share with colleagues rather than everybody trying to crowd around little two- or three-inch screens. It's a great company and a great vision. Obviously, I had to get permission from IBM, which included proving the company was not competitive with IBM,

---

[4] Compact portable projection devices

and also from my direct manager to concur that I could dedicate the time to do this.

I think this is another example of the IBM culture at work, because they see this experience as one that will help broaden my perspective. Furthermore, the experiences I gain in this board position ultimately will help me function in my current business position, as well as understand the broader business world better.

Ghaffari: Who referred you from Boston?

Horan: It was The Boston Club—a women's networking group in Boston. I had belonged to it when I lived there. Part of their mission is to try to help place women on boards. When MicroVision came to them looking for a search candidate, they remembered me and thought I fit the profile. Micro-Vision is in Seattle.

Ghaffari: Were there any big surprises or mistakes that you remember?

Horan: I suppose a big surprise was when I moved from a company where, literally, everyone's in the same building, to another company where you're now part of a global organization and half the people have never met the other half. IBM and Digital were both sponsors of the Open Software Foundation, and I always used to laugh when people from IBM would show up at a meeting and that would be the first time they had met each other. Once I got here, I realized that was the norm at IBM because there are four hundred thousand of us, so how can you possibly know all of them? The big surprise was that you had to figure out how to work in a large company and navigate your way around—learn the importance of building a network within the organization.

Mistakes, I don't know. I could say that my experience of being at Digital was simply the wrong time to make the decision to go there. In hindsight, I might not have made that move. But on the other hand, that experience was something that I was able to leverage into joining IBM, so I can't really regret it that much.

Ghaffari: How would you describe you own decision-making style?

Horan: I am definitely a very analytical person, which comes from my math background. I like to understand enough of the details to get myself comfortable. I do think that I am collaborative in the sense that I listen to other people's opinions, but I am not afraid of making tough decisions. I will weigh the facts and then make the decision.

Ghaffari: Where do you see yourself over the next five to ten years?

Horan: One of the things I've come to appreciate about being on the board of MicroVision is a thought that in retirement I could potentially be on two or three company boards. I think that that would be a fun thing to do and would keep the brain cells working.

Another thought would be to pursue more opportunities to give back to the community. I've recently joined the board of a local nonprofit here in Connecticut. I'd like to be able to do work in that regard as well, while also taking some time to relax and travel—to visit some of those places that I've flown into and out of for corporate meetings but never actually stayed and visited.

Ghaffari: What's the nonprofit in Connecticut?

Horan: It's an organization called Jane Doe No More. Their mission is around raising awareness of the trauma that victims of sexual assault go through and helping them through that trauma, removing the stigma of being a victim.

Ghaffari: When you talk to your family about changing the ball game and moving into a new career, how have they responded to those goals and vision and your business interests?

Horan: My family back in England had little knowledge of what I do. My role is something outside of my parents' sphere of experience. But, they are proud of me when I'm excited about changing roles. My brother, though, works in a similar field, so he has a better understanding.

From my daughters' perspectives, it took them until they went away to college to realize the significance of my work. You're always "just Mom" to your daughters. But, as they started to talk with other people and their professors about careers, they began to be more aware of what their parents do. At that point, I think they developed a much better understanding of my work.

Ghaffari: As you look at young professional women today, what kind of advice do you have for them?

Horan: Everybody's situation, obviously, is unique. But the thing I always try to advise people is don't focus yourself totally on some career goal or career path and have that be a maniacal focus because you might miss some interesting opportunities.

I look at my decisions: what if I had not come to the United States, or if I had not moved to Massachusetts, or if I hadn't come to IBM, or if I hadn't moved to the CIO office? All those things were not necessarily part of a natural, logical progression, but altogether they represent a whole lot of opportunities.

I think one of the most important things is to keep your options open, to evaluate each opportunity as it comes along, and to listen to input that comes your way.

Ghaffari: Do you do speaking events for young professional women?

Horan: I have given presentations at different times and on different topics. Next month, I've been invited to speak at the Women's International Networking Conference in Rome, Italy. It's an event about careers and opportunities. I certainly have done a lot of that.

We have a number of diversity networks at IBM. Periodically I've been asked to speak to a group about my career, the decisions I've made, and why I've made them.

Ghaffari: We say a lot about this concept of being open to opportunities. How do you balance simply responding to random serendipity vs. a controlled selection of opportunities?

Horan: You have to think about the totality of your experiences and not put yourself in a box. One of the things that I try to say to people for whom I am a mentor is, "We all can do a lot of things, but what do *you* want to do? What makes you excited?"

I think that's what's truly important. Maybe an opportunity comes your way, or you hear about something, or maybe you're thinking, "I'm ready for a change. Let me do a scan of the horizon and see what's out there." You have to evaluate each situation at that point in time. It's never *just* a work decision—it's a life decision. You have to figure out where you are with respect to children and family. If it's a job that will have a lot of travel, can you handle that? Once you put the opportunity into your own perspective, maybe it will be the right time for that job or maybe it won't. But, you know you will have weighed it all—considered everything. That's what matters.

Ghaffari: Do you give the same type of advice to men as you give to women?

Horan: I do.

Ghaffari: Where do you think is the area of greatest opportunity for careers for, especially for women at this point?

Horan: I really do think that women can choose to do anything they want to do these days. Sure, the glass ceiling does still exist in some industries, but I don't think that should necessarily stop you if that's something you have a passion for. When I look around a company like IBM or any of the many companies that I do business with, there are women in senior leadership positions in many industries these days. I've actually been quite pleasantly surprised by the number of women CIOs that I've met in just the last four months. Technology—a field that traditionally has been considered something of a male domain—is now wide open. These days, I don't see any barriers to women. If you've got the basic technology background and an interest in the business, you can do it.

Ghaffari: Do you consider yourself a leader?

Horan: I do. I see that my role here is to paint the vision, for the organization, of where we need to go to be able support the business and to make sure that I have the best people in the roles to actually deliver on that vision. My role is to help the organization understand how what we do contributes to the corporate results and the corporate strategy. For me, it's all about making good decisions in the context of that business strategy.

Ghaffari: Do you see yourself stepping beyond the CIO role into a president/chairman role of a corporation?

Horan: I like being the IBM CIO—it's a fabulous job and a great job—but I think maybe I'd like to have a P&L role in one of our lines of business as well. I think that's something that would be fun to do.

I must admit that when I think about how I went from medical ultrasound and flight simulators to being a CIO, it's not a natural nor a straightforward journey, but it was a great trip, and a fun one, too. I look forward to some more of the same in the future.

Karen S. Guice

Principal Deputy Assistant Secretary of Defense for Health Affairs, US Department of Defense

Born 1951 in El Paso, Texas.

Dr. Karen Sue Guice *serves in two prominent policy roles assisting US military leadership in developing strategies to achieve the health mission of the Military Health System (MHS).*

As the principal deputy assistant secretary of defense for Health Affairs, US Department of Defense, Dr. Guice helps formulate, develop, oversee, and advocate the policies of the Office of the Secretary of Defense regarding all military health concerns. She also acts as a liaison for other offices within the Office of the Secretary of Defense, the military departments, Congress, and other executive branch agencies to develop, coordinate, and integrate health care policies with departmental priorities and initiatives.

The Office of Health Affairs is responsible for providing a cost effective, quality health benefit to 9.6 million active-duty, uniformed service members, retirees, survivors, and their families. The Military Health Service has a $53 billion annual budget and consists of a worldwide network of 56 military hospitals, 363 health clinics, 282 dental clinics, private-sector health business partners, and the Uniformed Services University.

As the principal deputy director of TRICARE Management Activity (TMA), Dr. Guice oversees the civilian health benefit program serving military personnel, military retirees, and their dependents, including some members of the Reserve component.

For three years prior to this assignment, Dr. Guice was executive director of the Federal Recovery Coordination Program (FRCP) within the Central Office of the Department of Veterans Affairs. FRCP is a joint program of the Departments of Defense and Veterans Affairs to coordinate the clinical and nonclinical services needed by severely wounded, ill, and injured service members and veterans.

From January 2011 to May 2011, Dr. Guice served as a co-chair of the Department of Defense Recovering Warrior Task Force. In 2007, she was the deputy director for the President's Commission on Care for America's Returning Wounded Warriors, also known as the Dole-Shalala Commission.

Dr. Guice served as program director of the Outcomes and Clinical Trials Center for the American Pediatric Surgical Association (2002–2006), director of the Fellowship Department of the American College of Surgeons (February 1999–June 2002), and health policy advisor to the Labor and Human Resources Committee of the United States Senate (1997–1998), chaired by Senator James M. Jeffords (D-VT), a position that was a continuation of a health policy fellowship she received from the Robert Wood Johnson Foundation the previous year.

Dr. Guice has been a clinical professor of surgery at the Medical College of Wisconsin in Milwaukee (since 1999). She was an associate (1991–1993) and professor (1993–1998) of surgery at the Duke University Medical Center in Durham, North Carolina. She was an assistant (1985–1990) and associate professor of surgery (1990–1991) in general surgery at the University of Michigan in Ann Arbor. She was an instructor (1983–1984) and assistant professor of surgery (1984–1985) at the University of Texas Medical Branch in Galveston.

Dr. Guice has received more than $3.7 million in grants for several research projects undertaken from 1984 to 2008, including studies for the US Department of Health & Human Services' Maternal and Child Health Bureau and the National Institutes of Health (NIH).

She has authored or co-authored more than 70 research articles published in peer-reviewed journals and has written several book chapters.

Dr. Guice has received many awards and recognitions, including the Olga Jonasson Distinguished Member Award (1999) presented by the Association of Women Surgeons to a member surgeon who exemplifies the ideals and mission of the organization; the Award for Outstanding Achievement from the Office of the Secretary of Defense (2007) for her work on the President's Commission; and a Commendation from the Department of Veterans Affairs (2009) for her service as the executive director of the Federal Recovery Coordination Program.

She received a bachelor of science degree from New Mexico State University in Las Cruces (1972) and an MD from the School of Medicine at University of New

Mexico in Albuquerque (1977). Her medical internship and residency were in the Department of Surgery at the University of Washington, Seattle (1977–1982). She received a post-graduate research fellowship from the Department of Pediatric Surgery at Children's Hospital Medical Center in Cincinnati, Ohio (1982–1983). She received a master's degree from the Sanford Institute of Public Policy at Duke University in Durham, North Carolina (1996).

Elizabeth Ghaffari: Was there anything in your family background that led you into medicine?

Karen Guice: No. I'm still not quite sure why I became interested in medicine, but when I was about thirteen years old, I announced that I wanted to be a physician and had some interest in research as well.

Ghaffari: Would you tell me a little bit about your family. Was it large? What did your folks do?

Guice: My own family was just my mother, my father, and my brother. But my mother's family was large—she was one of ten children, so I had a very large extended family with lots of cousins, aunts, and uncles in Las Cruces, New Mexico, which is where we lived. My father's family was from Louisiana. Most of them had stayed in the South, so I would not see them on a regular basis. My mother's family had a profound influence on me and my growth as a person.

My mother finished high school in the post–Depression era, then immediately went to work as a secretary. During the war, she supported her mother and her younger brother. Her father died when she was thirteen, so she grew up without a father for most of her life. She was ninth in a family of ten. My own father died when I was nine. My mother went back to school after his death. She probably had the most influence on me because she was a strong woman who went back to college and graduated in three years with honors. She was a pretty fierce woman. She decided she wanted to teach school, so that her schedule would be better synchronized with ours—she could have summers off and was able to take time off for school vacations with us. She did that basically to have a closer interaction with her kids.

Ghaffari: Would you tell me a bit about your college education?

Guice: I went to Baylor University in Waco, Texas, for my first year in college, but I got sick over that first summer—something called coccidioidomycosis, a fungus infection in my lung that is prevalent in the Southwest. I was in the hospital for a couple of weeks, and my internist said, "Why don't you stay at home for the next semester? You're going to feel weak. You should take a lighter load in school." So, I decided to transfer entirely to New Mexico State University in Las Cruces. I earned a bachelor of science in chemistry, finishing early—in December of my senior year. I immediately began graduate school because, at that point, I had not yet been accepted to medical school.

Ghaffari: What made you choose New Mexico School of Medicine?

Guice: It may have been the only place I applied—close to home and all that. I was admitted to medical school after I had started graduate school in the spring semester. I went to the University of New Mexico that fall for four years of medical school.

Ghaffari: Where did you go after medical school?

Guice: I knew I wanted to do surgery and had applied to several surgery programs. The process is that you go around, interview, and send in your rank-ordered list of preferences. The surgery programs do the same for the candidates. Somehow, the matchmaking happens. I was lucky enough to have been selected to join the internship class for the Department of Surgery at the University of Washington in Seattle. So I headed off to the Pacific Northwest and spent the next five years doing a surgery residency program.

My residency, from 1977 to 1982, was just a typical hard-core surgery residency—taking care of patients, learning by doing, but in a tiered way, so you have progressive responsibility until you become the chief resident, and you're the boss. It's something like an old-fashioned apprenticeship.

In my fourth year, I began dating another surgical resident, Keith Oldham. We fell in love. He proposed, and we got married all in the space of four months. He was one year ahead of me, a chief resident, who was going off to Cincinnati, Ohio, to do a pediatric surgery fellowship. We spent the first year of our marriage apart—he in Cincinnati and I in Seattle. As newlyweds, we were pretty strapped for cash, so we saw each other just a handful of times over the year.

After my residency, I joined him in Cincinnati, where I was a research fellow from '82 to '83 for the Pediatric Surgery Division of Children's Hospital. I think Keith and I had at least two publications accepted during that year by peer-reviewed journals. Also, I took classes at the University of Cincinnati—some courses in electron microscopy, among others. It was just a case of "I'm interested in learning" as opposed to having to do it for a degree. It was an opportunity. Then we both had to look for "real jobs."

Our first foray into the working world had us both on the faculty of University of Texas's Medical Branch in Galveston. I was an instructor, then assistant professor, in the surgery department there. Keith was recruited to go to the University of Michigan in Ann Arbor. We were there for six years, during which time I rose from an assistant to an associate professor of surgery.

We were recruited by Duke University Medical Center to join their faculty in 1991. I was planning to take a sabbatical while I was at Duke University. While we were getting our laboratory squared away, I found something called the Sanford Institute for Public Policy, named for Terry Sanford, the former president of Duke and former governor, and former senator, of North Carolina. This was the beginning of the Clinton health care reform era. I really just got tired of sitting around the cafeteria with everyone whining about how bad health care was. I thought, "You can't complain if you're not willing to be part of the solution." So I thought one thing I could do was to go to policy school. I talked to the admissions people, thinking—of course—that surgeons can do everything. Audaciously, I said to them, "I can be a full-time surgeon and do this program."

Helen "Sunny" Ladd, the dean of the school, said, "No, you can't. We won't let you." But I was intrigued, and after several years, I just went ahead and applied anyway, thinking, "Okay, if I get accepted, then I'll figure it out from there." I did—they accepted me into a one-year program. I got permission from the Department of Surgery chair to take a year's leave of absence. It was a combined-degree program, and they counted my medical degree as one of the degrees, even though it was received years earlier. They let me do a master's degree in public policy in a year.

Ghaffari: You also became a full professor at Duke. Is that right?

Guice: I was the first woman to be appointed professor of surgery at Duke.

Ghaffari: What was the surgery-related work you did while on the Duke faculty?

Guice: When I was on the Duke faculty, most of my time was spent doing clinical care, practicing surgery, and bench research.

Ghaffari: What is "bench research"?

Guice: In clinical research, you use clinical materials such as your patients' or patient records, to try to solve clinical questions. Bench research is different—it is research done in a controlled laboratory setting using nonhuman subjects. My area of research—beginning when I was in Galveston—was gastrointestinal diseases. I started with a model of acute pancreatitis, trying to understand that better. When I was at Michigan, my focus changed a little bit because a mentor of mine there was a pulmonary expert. We changed the model to one where I could induce a form of respiratory failure. It's called pulmonary inflammatory response, where your lungs get damaged because of a biological process elsewhere. I developed an animal model of respiratory insufficiency induced by pancreatitis in order to look at the mechanisms by which the pancreas could make the lungs fail.

Ghaffari: Who was your mentor at Michigan?

Guice: It was Dr. Peter Ward, the chair of pathology there. He was just a wonderful guy—very welcoming and really interested in fostering intellectual curiosity. He said, "Come. Here's my lab. You can work in it. Here are the things I can help you with." He was very supportive, and while we were there, I successfully competed for and obtained an NIH grant for that particular field of study.

Ghaffari: How did you happen to get the health policy fellowship at the Robert Wood Johnson Foundation?

Guice: I was halfway through the public policy master's program when I got a call from a friend of mine, Dr. Charles Rice, who had been on the faculty of the University of Washington when I was an intern. He's currently the chancellor at USUSH.[1] He said, "You can't do this public policy degree program without some sort of a practical experience. I think you should apply for the Robert Wood Johnson Foundation Health Policy fellowship," as he had done several years before. So, I used the same philosophy, "Well, I'll apply. If they don't accept me, that's okay, too." And I was fortunate enough to be selected.

It was one-year fellowship. I was working for Senator James M. Jeffords, who was chair of the Senate Labor Committee—currently called the Senate Committee on Health, Education, and Labor. He asked me to stay on for an additional year so that I would have one full Congressional cycle covering two years in Washington, DC—from '96 to '97.

Ghaffari: That was your first public policy experience, was it not? Did you like it?

Guice: It was my very first exposure to practical public policy work. You go to school to learn all the tricks of the trade, and fortunately for me, I got to put that into practice in a very meaningful way. My focus was on health care quality. We had a couple of legislative proposals with Senator Lieberman. I think I still have a bill somewhere that I wrote for the senator, and he autographed it for me at the top.

---

[1] Uniformed Services University of the Health Sciences.

Then my husband decided to accept a job at the Medical College at Wisconsin in 1999. We had two small children—two boys. Christian was born in '89 while we were at Ann Arbor, and Brian was born in '92 while we were at Duke. When they were still little tykes, it was relatively easy for me to commute back and forth to DC from Durham. It would have been a little more challenging to fly halfway across the country to DC from Wisconsin. So, for a lot of reasons, we decided that I would rejoin the family in Milwaukee, which is what I did.

Ghaffari: You didn't yet have a job in Wisconsin, so what did you do?

Guice: Our professional society, the American College of Surgeons, is located in Chicago. I started working with them and became the director of fellowship. I would commute down to Chicago and back home every day, three hours on a train. That position gave me a good understanding of how the professional society worked.

Ghaffari: How did you handle the two young tykes, the work, and the commute?

Guice: We had one nanny for the whole time we were in North Carolina. That consistency of child care was extraordinarily valuable. However, she did not make the move with us to Wisconsin—she didn't want to go where the snow flew. So, we started over with new nannies. One night, the family was having dinner when we mentioned that we'd had to dismiss the current nanny for some reason I can't remember. Our older son, Christian, said, "Well, there goes number nine!"

I said, "It can't be nine." And he just ticked them off. He said, "There was so-and-so and so-and-so and so-and-so and so-and-so." Keith and I looked at each other and said, "We're probably going to need to chat." So we got the boys off to bed and said, "You know, this probably isn't a good idea for them. They're at the age where they need more consistency." We were looking to replace the wonderful person we'd left behind in North Carolina and just couldn't find anybody to measure up to her standards. She really had spoiled us. At that point, I decided to leave the job in Chicago and the commute. It just wasn't fitting well with our family and what the family needed at the time.

So, I started doing some health services research, specifically looking at children's surgery and working on a national trauma database for children. The research was assessing what were the unique requirements for pediatric trauma and then what was being done for pediatric trauma across the country, trying to come up with guidelines about what and where children should be taken for trauma. The key concern was, "Are their needs different than adults?" I did that through a grant from HRSA[2] for a program for emergency medical services for children from 2002 to 2007.

The nature of this research allowed me to be more flexible with my hours—working while the boys were at school during the day. I got to take them to school and pick them up frequently and go to their events. It met the family needs while they were impressionable young men.

Ghaffari: When and how did you come to serve on the Dole-Shalala Commission?[3]

Guice: That was from March through July of 2007. During the time I was working on the Robert Wood Johnson policy fellowship in DC, I got to know a woman by the name of Marie Michnich, who was a former RWJ fellow working for the American College of Cardiology. Do you know how it is with some people that you immediately hit it off? And she and I hit it off and developed a very nice friendship. In fact, our families started going on vacations together. Marie and her husband, Brian, had a daughter in between my son's ages, so both families would go on a rafting trip down the Rogue River or America's Creek in Alaska or take a sailboat vacation to the Queen Charlotte Islands. We had a little network of friends with kids that would join together to do these adventure things. It was fun for the kids, and the parents had a good time, too. I came to know Marie and her family very well.

My family was on a vacation when I received an e-mail from Marie telling me that she had just been named the executive director of the president's commission and that she was looking for a deputy director. I remember distinctly going to talk to my husband—I think he was shaving—to say, "What would you say if I told her, 'Well, if you're asking, I'll accept.'" And he said, "If that's what you want to do, that's fine."

So that's what I did. I told Marie, "Your search is over—congratulations!" And she replied, "I was hoping you'd say that. I was baiting you a little bit." I did the commission with Marie, and that led to a whole series of new adventures.

Ghaffari: Did you relocate to Washington?

---

[2] The Health Resources and Services Administration, an agency of the US Department of Health and Human Services.

[3] President George W. Bush's Commission on Care for America's Wounded Warriors, co-chaired by former Senator Robert Dole (R-KS) and former Secretary of Health and Human Services Donna Shalala, to investigate and recommend improvements to the effectiveness and quality of health care provided to service members, particularly after serious problems were identified at the Walter Reed Army Medical Center in Washington, DC.

Guice: No, it was just for four months. I was going back and forth between DC and Wisconsin. The other thing that happened when I was doing my health services research, before the president's commission role, was that my mother had had a fairly debilitating stroke and was living with us in Milwaukee. She was paralyzed on the left side, so that meant balancing in my mother's medical needs. The boys were a little older and were able to help out somewhat. That's how we worked through the four months. Afterwards, I went back to Wisconsin and picked up my research.

Ghaffari: What were the next series of new adventures?

Guice: Keith and Christian had decided to climb Mount Denali in Alaska, so they had gone off that summer to go mountain climbing. It was in July of '08, and I was working alone at home when the phone rang. It was Secretary of Veterans Affairs James Peake. He said, "I need you to come run a program." I responded, "Okay. What is it and what do you want me to do?" We talked a little about the assignment, and then I asked, "If I say 'yes' to this, sir, when would you want me?" he said, "Tomorrow." I distinctly remember saying, "Well, sir, my husband and I generally talk about major career moves, and I can't reach him until he comes down from the mountain. So you're going to have to wait a few days." He thought that would be fine.

Keith and Christian successfully scaled Denali, came back down, and we had our little chat. Again, my husband, who's been very patient with all of this, said, "If that's what you want to do, okay. It's fine with me." That's how I wound up back in Washington, and I've been here ever since.

Ghaffari: What was the assignment from Secretary Peake?

Guice: It was the role of executive director of the Federal Recovery Coordination Program—my first foray into the Veterans Affairs field, although I had worked in VA medical centers during my residency and as a surgical faculty member. I knew the VA, but from the practitioner's side. This was my first exposure to working within the big bureaucracy of a federal agency like the VA or the Department of Defense.

Ghaffari: What part of your background did they recognize that would be valuable to them?

Guice: The recommendation came out of my time with the Dole-Shalala commission. I think the interesting skill set for them was the ability to listen to all of the discussions and deliberations that formed the backdrop to a recommendation, to develop a recommendation out of all that, and then to be able to translate that recommendation into a program.

Ghaffari: What was the FRCP experience like for you?

Guice: It was very interesting. First of all, it was getting to know the VA. The program had been moved from VHA, the Veteran's Health Administration, up into the office of the secretary, so I worked directly for Secretary Peake. That was important because the Federal Recovery Coordination Program is really a "one VA" program. The people who work for it are trained in both the health care aspects of what VA provides, as well as the benefit side and the DOD components.

The observation from the commission was that we transfer people between facilities an awful lot. While someone's in a facility or a particular catchment area, they have case managers to help them. But, when they leave to go to a new facility, all of the case management team has to get re-created. At that point, there are too many opportunities for things to get dropped or not completed or have expectations changed.

The recommendation from the commission was that—for the most severely wounded, ill, or injured—if you could have someone stay with that family and that individual throughout all the transitions as they went from one in-patient facility to another or in-patient to outpatient or from active duty military to veteran status, then that would provide the consistency they needed, as well as an ability to do long-range planning for these families and individuals to pull together everything that had to happen in a very smooth and cohesive way. That would provide significant improvements over the way things were being handled at that time.

The hypothesis was that a consistent care manager would be of great value to the service members and their families. The nice thing about this program is that it actually delivers on that promise. I wouldn't say 100 percent, because no program is 100 percent, but to a good percentage. We did the first-ever satisfaction survey for the program, and it came back with an 80 percent satisfied rating, which I think is good for a brand-new program.

We were really creating something that had not existed before. There was very intensive training provided to the staff and employees. It was a major challenge figuring out how to make a program work in a big bureaucracy that had several "stovepipes"—organizational or functional domains that were hard to penetrate. You had the VBA[4] over here, the VHA[5] over there, and the Department of Defense along with four services—Army, Navy, Air Force, Marines. We tried to balance the needs of the program, which really

---

[4] Veterans Benefits Administration

[5] Veterans Healthcare Administration

reflected the needs of the client, with all of these different programs and offices within the bureaucracy. That's what was so interesting.

When the program was set up, there were entry criteria that were fairly generous. But, the niche that the program best served was those service members with complex injuries or illnesses who required multiple engagements with health care providers and benefits to effect healing and recovery. They ranged from people who had devastating burns to those who had devastating PTSD[6]—physical as well as psychological injuries. But the problem these people faced was the same: during any transition, we need to make sure the information got through, that the benefits were aligned and delivered, and that they received follow-up and follow-through care. So much of what we did was simply to make sure that stuff got done in a way that made sense for the recovery of the individual and the needs of the family.

In my opinion—and I'm probably really biased—the program works really well.

It's a new concept, and a fairly unique program. People still have a hard time wrapping their heads around it. I couldn't understand how everyone couldn't see it as clearly as I could. After talking to a number of individuals, they value this additional resource so highly that some of them never wanted to give up their federal recovery coordinator, even though they didn't need the FRC anymore. They said, "This is just my safety line. I know that if I need something, this person will get it for me, or tell me how to get it, or help me get it." Essentially, we gave them the ability to reach out, understand all of the programs, and understand what things needed to be put together for their individual recovery plan.

Ghaffari: Do you see that there might be applicability of the program concept across all medical professions at the national level, not just veterans?

Guice: You're asking "Why wouldn't any medical program want to do that?" The answer depends on the payment stream. It's not that the private sector manages the transitional problems better than the military or the VA health system. It doesn't, but the real issue for the private sector is "who's going to pay for it?"

If you're a hospital person, you're going to be paid by the hospital, so you will only focus on services provided by that facility. You're not necessarily going to look at what happens if an individual is taken to another hospital or went to another hospital because they have Medicare or TRICARE.

---

[6] Post-traumatic stress disorder

The ability to provide better coordination of care within the federal health system has some unique aspects because the payer is the federal system. I think that concept would be very hard to replicate in the private sector—not that you couldn't do it, but the question is "who pays for that service?"

Ghaffari: Did you find that the program produced any significant cost savings?

Guice: We didn't measure cost savings, because we were trying to make sure, first, that we had enough individuals to cover project needs. We did just-in-time staffing where we would hire based on what our projected needs were. I'd do an analysis and conclude that we might need five more FTEs in the next six months based on our current referral pattern. Then, we had to pull together the educational part, make sure the program worked, get our IT solution together for documentation—all that was required to set up a program. Did we save money? That would be something to look at later. When you're just starting a new program, the priority is getting it functional.

Ghaffari: How did you get your current position as principal deputy assistant secretary for defense?

Guice: I was working in my office at the VA when one of the special assistants for the secretary of veterans affairs came over and said, "You've made the short list to be considered for the principal deputy assistant secretary for Health Affairs." And I said, "Oh. That sounds interesting. I didn't know I'd applied, but okay." And I'm still not sure exactly how that happened. He asked, "Do you want to be interviewed?" I remembered the philosophy of my dear friend, Marie Michnich—never ever refuse a job you've not been offered. My philosophy is you *always* learn something about yourself by interviewing for other jobs or exploring other employment opportunities. It makes you either grateful for what you have or it makes you think about how you want to reposition what you're currently doing. Sometimes you end up saying to yourself, "This is a job that I would leave now to go do that." So, I said, "Sure, I'd love to be interviewed."

That led to a series of interviews, each one of which, I must admit, I left feeling, "That's that. I won't be called back for another interview." Then I'd get called back for another interview, and it kept escalating to higher levels of people interviewing me. First was Dr. Jonathan Woodson,[7] then Dr.

---

[7] Assistant secretary of defense for Health Affairs and director of TRICARE Management Activity. See www.defense.gov/bios/biographydetail.aspx?biographyid=270

Clifford Stanley,[8] then Robert Rangel.[9] The next thing I knew, somebody said, "Well, congratulations—your paperwork is at the White House." And I went, "Oh. Okay."

I'm really glad I made the move. It was probably a good time for me to leave the FRCP to be sure the program wasn't functioning just because I was making it function, but rather because I had instilled some longevity in it. I certainly couldn't have asked for a better set of fun things to do than to take on this job.

Ghaffari: What do you do and why is it exciting for you?

Guice: That's exactly what my husband said when I told him I was going to be "the principal deputy assistant secretary for health." He said, "That's a very impressive long title, but what do you do?" After a bit of explanation, he then said, "Okay, I get it. You're the COO for the military health system." That's probably a reasonable way to describe it.

We have a lot of meetings on a variety of topics. Today, for instance, was a meeting on the integrated electronic health record and another meeting about BRAC[10] and how we're doing with all of our facilities moving through the BRAC process. The portfolio is quite diverse. There's never a dull moment. It runs the gamut of dealing with everyday things, such as hiring people, all the way to gathering information so that the secretary of defense can make a decision or at least be better informed. Every day is different, and frequently what I plan for the day is overcome by events, but that doesn't matter. It's fun, and I enjoy what I'm doing immensely.

Ghaffari: To whom do you report?

Guice: Dr. Jonathan Woodson, the assistant secretary of defense for Health. Part of what I do is help him get information to make decisions and give testimony. I also look at policy revisions. For example, what we need to look at in the area of graduate medical education. I'm heavily involved in trying to pull groups together, get consensus, get information, and manage information. The Pentagon is an interesting place where a lot of information transfer has to happen.

Ghaffari: How long do you see yourself in this position?

---

[8] Under-secretary of defense for Personnel and Readiness. See prhome.defense.gov/bios/cliffordStanley.aspx

[9] At that time, chief of staff to Secretary of Defense Robert Gates.

[10] The US Department of Defense Base Realignment and Closure

Guice: It *is* a political appointment—it rises and falls with elections. So it could be another year or it could be five more years. I have no idea. My basic promise to myself is always stay effective—if you stop being effective, that's when you know you need to go do something else. As long as I'm effective and can get things accomplished, that's my own internal benchmark for how long to stay in a job.

Ghaffari: Is your family also in DC now?

Guice: No, my husband is chief of surgery at the Children's Hospital of Wisconsin, so he's in Milwaukee. Our older son, Christian, is finishing his senior year at Davidson University in Charlotte, North Carolina. He's majoring in biology with a minor in Chinese. Our younger son, Brian, is a sophomore at Wake Forest in Winston-Salem, North Carolina, trying to figure out if he wants to major in biology or political science. What's fun is that the boys are actually just seventy miles apart in North Carolina, totally by accident. Keith and I are going to go down and visit them in a couple of weeks.

Ghaffari: Do you miss surgery—the medical practice?

Guice: I don't. When I was working on the Hill for Senator Jeffords, I got to know a couple of people working for the Congressional Research Service. One day, they said to me, "We just can't figure out why you're here doing this work because you actually take care of patients. I mean, you actually make somebody better, so why would you be here doing this kind of stuff?" And I said, "Well, because when I'm taking care of patients, I can affect one life at a time. When I'm here doing this kind of work, if I change an 'and' to an 'or,' the impact can be for thousands, if not millions, of lives." The impact is greater because of what I know and because I'm able to apply it in a different way. I feel like I'm helping more by where I am and what I do.

Ghaffari: Did you ever feel that you just wanted to throw up your hands at the Department of Defense and go away?

Guice: I've done that with every job that I've ever had. There are times when you're just frustrated that you can't get something done or you thought you had something locked up and somebody still tells you "no." There are periods of frustration with every single job, but I think the ability to step back and look at it and say, "Now, why didn't it work? How do I change it the next time? How do I get to 'yes'?" is something that everybody has to kind of grapple with, in any job. I remember times of great frustration as a practicing surgeon—frustration with the academic system, with a research experiment that failed time and again. Frustrations are inherent in any job, but I think part of personal growth is recognizing what's causing that frustration, then figuring out how to mitigate it and how to do it better next time.

Ghaffari: Of all the jobs or bosses that you've had, which one, if any, would you say had the biggest impact on you?

Guice: I would phrase that differently. I would say, "Which one would you go back to in a heartbeat?" I'd go back and work on the Hill again. I loved it. I had the best time. You know, there's nothing like it—it's a frenetic pace, but it was just the power of the office. When you work for the chairman of a committee, you have power. It wasn't me who was sitting behind the desk. It was that I was working for the senator, who was the chair. It was the ability to pick up the phone and say, "The senator wants this. Could you have it up here in an hour?" And it was there in an hour.

That means that you can get the Information you need to really influence things. It's a dynamic situation. It's the ability to sit with people, write legislation, put a bill together, and get support for it.

I had a really great boss. Senator Jeffords was just a delight to be around. We would be in meetings where somebody would ask a question, and he'd say, "Well, I don't know. She's the expert. Ask her." It was fun, interesting, challenging, and very rewarding all at the same time. Still, there were times I would get very frustrated with the inability to do something, but, as I said, that happens with every job you get.

Ghaffari: Have you had a lot of mentors in your life? How would you define a mentor?

Guice: A lot of people helped me, and I'm assuming that that equates to being a mentor. So when I worked at the American College of Surgeons, there was a senior woman surgeon, Olga Jonasson, who has since passed away, but she was a great supporter and a great friend. There are people who step into your lives in each of these jobs. They give you insight, support, and can help you grapple with your job at the time. There are many people like that in all my various jobs.

I would call Jim Peake a wonderful mentor when I was at VA. He forced me to do things where I thought he was nuts, but it turned out he was absolutely right. I learned a tremendous amount from that experience.

I've been blessed with wonderful friends. Marie Michnich, who was the executive director of the commission and now runs the Robert Wood Johnson Health Policy fellowship, is a wonderful mentor and friend. I can talk to Marie about anything because she has a very interesting way of looking at problems and thinking about problem solving in ways that I might not have considered.

Other people help you navigate or think differently. My husband is a mentor. It doesn't mean we don't disagree about things. He has a different perspective—I would call him much more pragmatic, while I'm probably more experimental. He kind of goes from A to B to C to D—very methodically. I go from A and then try to see if or how I might get to D without going through B and C.

We kind of balance each other off in a very good way. We give each other the benefit of our experience and problem-solving, not just with family issues but also with work issues. He'll ask me how I would handle a problem that he's got at work. And I will do the same. It's certainly been a partnership that's stood the test of time because I think we're coming up on thirty-one years of marriage now.

Chip Rice also has been in and out of my life. He started as a professor of surgery when I was an intern, and now he's the chancellor of USUHS, which is in our organizational structure under my reporting line. He's a good friend and supporter who gave me great advice. He came in and made me do something that I wouldn't have thought of doing, but it turned out to have tremendous value, both personally and professionally.

People come in and out of your life at interesting times, but throughout my career I've had good people to provide me with the support and advice and counsel all along the way.

Ghaffari: How would you describe your decision-making style?

Guice: I like data, so I'm sort of a data-driven person. I like to have data and information to influence decisions. Then, given the current job, there's always the political aspect, both in the building and in the administration. It was the same thing at the VA. There's always the political issue of how might this decision be aligned with a strategic plan or direction. But, if you have data and you can make your arguments based on clear evidence, then you will certainly have a better chance of winning. So, I always try to have the facts straight, the data in front of me, and make decisions that way.

Of course, it doesn't work that way all the time. Sometimes you've just got to go with your gut.

Ghaffari: Among all of the careers, what's your perception of your biggest achievement?

Guice: Staying married thirty-one years and having two children. Keith and I have two great kids.

Ghaffari: You say that as if you're surprised.

Guice: Well, you know, you always look back and say, "How did that happen?" They're good people—really good. That's one of those things you never know until it's over, whether you've done a good job or not.

Ghaffari: As you've come through this career path, were there a lot of other women alongside of you in the same fields?

Guice: When I was in medical school, I think there were seven women in my medical school class. When I went to my residency, there were three of us—three women out of probably forty residents. When I was in Galveston, there weren't any other women on the surgery faculty. There were women in other places, on other faculties. There were more women on the surgical faculty at Ann Arbor, but not by a lot, and I was the only woman on the faculty at Duke for a long time. So I would say that there have been other women, but not necessarily in the surgery field. More women would have been in internal medicine or dermatology or other areas. There certainly are more women in surgery now than when I was coming through the training program and was in my first several academic appointments.

Ghaffari: As you've been invited to talk to other young women in your fields—politics, academic, medicine—what is your key advice to them about their careers?

Guice: I tell them that they should be selfish. They should figure out what they need in order to make that next career move or wherever they see themselves next. Be really sure that when they take a new job or open the door to a new possibility, it's about where they want to be and what they need to get there. I advise them to be very introspective and think about it critically. I also remind them, based on my own observations, that they can change jobs. You don't have to stay in a bad one. You can move on. The interesting thing about bad jobs is that they often teach you more than good jobs.

Ghaffari: Do you think your advice is the same kind that you'd give to men?

Guice: Yes. I think it's applicable to anybody. You need to understand what makes you happy, what kind of work brings you joy, depending on where you are in life.

For what I'm doing now, my work habits are pretty nutty. But that's because I don't have family here—my husband has his job, and he loves what he's doing. My kids are in college, and they love what they're doing. I have different degrees of freedom now than when the kids told me we had discharged nine nannies. I have different degrees of freedom now than when I had my mother in our home, caring for her, post-stroke. Your life changes, and you have to be open to change and opportunities. Some of the best jobs I've had came to me because I simply opened a door, took the risk, and applied for it. There's nothing to be lost. Being able to look at opportunities and then take advantage of them when they come your way is advice that I'd give everybody. It's worked out extraordinarily well for me. I've had great fun and hopefully I've contributed along the way.

Sometimes, you need to make opportunity happen. Take the initiative. That was a lesson I learned from Jim Thompson, who was the chair at Galveston. He taught me to pursue grant money to do the things that interested me. Jim said, "Apply to as many granting institutions as you can because, you never know, somebody might come back with money."

It's the same philosophy about jobs. Try—you know, you can always say "no." If somebody accepts you for a program or a job, you can always say, "Well, upon reconsideration, I've decided not to do that" or "I'm not the best person for that." On occasion, I would be asked to go look at chairs of surgery departments. I would interview and talk to people and then I would take myself out of the running for whatever reason. But, I had the experience of going, thinking about it, and asking myself, "What would it take for me to do this job? Do I like it here? Does it feel as if I fit with this group of people?" If I had said, "No, I don't want to interview for the job," then I wouldn't have had that opportunity to both explore what I thought I might need as a person in order to learn, be productive, grow, and contribute.

Ghaffari: Where do you see yourself in the next five to ten years?

Guice: I don't know. I mean, seriously, truly, I don't know. I turn sixty this year. My husband and I talk about this about every weekend, "When are we going to retire? What are we going to do when we retire?" Since we can't ever seem to agree, we just keep working.

We're lucky to have the option of continuing to work. At some point, he's going to want to stop doing what he's doing. He may want continue to practice, but maybe be chief of surgery for only the next five years. Interests change, and maybe we'll want to be doing something else. We'll figure it out, I'm sure. But five to ten years from now, I'll probably still be working somewhere, doing something interesting.

I

Index